# Humana Festival 2003
## The Complete Plays

Humana Inc. is one of the nation's largest
managed health care companies
with approximately 6 million members in its health care plans.

The Humana Foundation was established in 1981
to support the educational, social, medical and cultural development
of communities in ways that reflect
Humana's commitment to social responsibility
and an improved quality of life.

# SMITH AND KRAUS PUBLISHERS
## Contemporary Playwrights / Collections

EST Marathon '94: The One-Act Plays
EST Marathon '95: The One-Act Plays
EST Marathon '96: The One-Act Plays
EST Marathon '97: The One-Act Plays
EST Marathon '98: The One-Act Plays

Humana Festival: 20 One-Acts Plays 1976–1996
Humana Festival '93: The Complete Plays
Humana Festival '94: The Complete Plays
Humana Festival '95: The Complete Plays
Humana Festival '96: The Complete Plays
Humana Festival '97: The Complete Plays
Humana Festival '98: The Complete Plays
Humana Festival '99: The Complete Plays
Humana Festival 2000: The Complete Plays
Humana Festival 2001: The Complete Plays
Humana Festival 2002: The Complete Plays

New Playwrights: The Best Plays of 1998
New Playwrights: The Best Plays of 1999
New Playwrights: The Best Plays of 2000
New Playwrights: The Best Plays of 2001
New Playwrights: The Best Plays of 2002
New Playwrights: The Best Plays of 2003

Women Playwrights: The Best Plays of 1992
Women Playwrights: The Best Plays of 1993
Women Playwrights: The Best Plays of 1994
Women Playwrights: The Best Plays of 1995
Women Playwrights: The Best Plays of 1996
Women Playwrights: The Best Plays of 1997
Women Playwrights: The Best Plays of 1998
Women Playwrights: The Best Plays of 1999
Women Playwrights: The Best Plays of 2000
Women Playwrights: The Best Plays of 2001
Women Playwrights: The Best Plays of 2002
Women Playwrights: The Best Plays of 2003

If you require pre-publication information about upcoming Smith and Kraus books, you may receive our semi-annual catalogue free of charge, by sending your name and address to *Smith and Kraus Catalogue, PO Box 127, Lyme NH 03768. Or call us at (603) 643-6431, fax (603) 643-1831. www.SmithKraus.com.*

# Humana Festival 2003
## The Complete Plays

Edited by
Tanya Palmer and Amy Wegener

*Contemporary Playwrights Series*

SK
A Smith and Kraus Book

A Smith and Kraus Book
Published by Smith and Kraus, Inc.
177 Lyme Road, Hanover, New Hampshire, 03755
www.SmithKraus.com

Manufactured in the United States of America

Cover and Text Design by Julia Hill Gignoux
Layout by Jennifer McMaster
Cover artwork © Mirko Ilic

First Edition: March 2004
10 9 8 7 6 5 4 3 2 1

Library of Congress Cataloguing-in-Publication Data
Contemporary Playwrights Series
ISSN 1067-9510
ISBN 1-57525-340-2

# Contents

# Acknowledgments

The editors wish to thank the following persons for their invaluable assistance in compiling this volume:

Claire Cox
Erin Detrick
Susannah Engstrom
Jen Grigg
Sarah Gubbins
Dan LeFranc
Marc Masterson
Jennifer McMaster
Steve Moulds
Mark Palmer
Karen Petruska
Jeff Rodgers
James Seacat
Kyle Shepherd
Wanda Snyder
Alexander Speer

Judy Boals
John Buzzetti
Val Day
Teresa Focarile
Susan Gurman
Mary Harden
Morgan Jenness
Joyce Ketay
George Lane
Sarah Jane Leigh
Carl Mulert
Bruce Ostler

# Foreword

Plays are written in privacy, developed in the shelter of rehearsal, and then launched into the most public of arenas through performance. Over 27 years, the Humana Festival of New American Plays has sent fleet after fleet of new plays into the world. Actors Theatre of Louisville believes in the value of embracing the playwright's personal vision—because we believe that part of our responsibility in premiering new work is to allow the writer to see the play that he or she imagined—fully realized.

During rehearsals, there is a strong sense of discovery and adventure that comes from the unmatched energy of having seven full-length and three short plays in development at once. Some of the finest theatre-makers from every discipline come together each year at the Humana Festival to dedicate themselves to the joy of building new plays. We thank them all for their talent and dedication in bringing these plays to life.

This year, we introduce a number of writers who are new to the Humana Festival. We relish the opportunity to include a diverse range of styles and worlds drawn from the most vital work being written in the American theatre today. We do so knowing that the work will find a great audience. The Humana Festival of New American Plays is a fantastic gathering of theatre lovers: passionate, intelligent, and ready to participate in the evolution of new work. Now, as we reach publication, we are happy to share this vital work with you.

*Marc Masterson*
*Artistic Director*
*Actors Theatre of Louisville*

# Editors' Note

Reading a script created for performance is an imaginative exercise like no other. Not only does dramatic literature invite the reader to envision a whole world in her mind's eye (and ear), but it assumes a live event that demands to be actualized in time and space. And to steal a potent metaphor from Kia Corthron's thoughtful interrogation of genetic engineering in this volume, it's as if the playwright has given the work a complete, evocative DNA makeup on the page, but its very nature is to transcend itself through nurture. This happens when the script and playwright collide with readers, collaborators and audiences, giving rise to new possibilities as the characters take on real voices, the images three dimensions, and the ideas a living, breathing response.

This creative collision occurs on a large scale each year at the Humana Festival of New American Plays, and it begins in a literary laboratory where we have the privilege of helping to select, from hundreds of scripts, a handful of plays and projects with some of the most intriguing theatrical DNA we've ever seen. Consider several of this year's discoveries. Where else but in the theatre could a live magic show become the central structure and metaphor of a love story, as it does in Rinne Groff's *Orange Lemon Egg Canary*? What forum is more ideally suited to the singing, pantomiming people of Quincy Long's delightfully silly, eunuch-enslaving society? Or to the passionate, political debate of *Omnium Gatherum*'s post-9/11 dinner party? What else but the stage could give rise to Russell Davis's abstractly beautiful representation of troubled psyche, or to Bridget Carpenter's hyper-real high school? Or to the *Rhythmicity* team's electrifying, multi-disciplinary performance poetry? All of these pieces, in completely distinct ways, make amazing use of the theatrical medium.

This wild diversity of sensibilities and voices is one of the defining traits of the Humana Festival, and this anthology documents and disseminates these plays in the form in which we first encountered them—for it all begins with the word and a playwright's individual vision. Though we can't re-create for you the intense, ephemeral flurry of activity that was the 27th Humana Festival—with its nearly a dozen productions, thirty-three writers, and energetic company of artists and staff—we hope that this volume gives a sense of its scope, quickly igniting our own vivid imaginings. The plays contained herein bear the imprint of their Humana Festival histories, but also point toward the future; for playscripts are the convergence, in the here and now, of past experience and uncharted possibility.

*Tanya Palmer and Amy Wegener*

# The Roads that Lead Here
## by Lee Blessing

# BIOGRAPHY

Lee Blessing's Humana Festival premieres have included *Oldtimers Game*, *Independence*, *War of the Roses* (retitled *Riches*), *Down the Road*, and a monologue in last year's *Snapshot*. Actors Theatre of Louisville also produced his play *Nice People Dancing to Good Country Music* as well as various short pieces. His play *A Walk in the Woods* was produced on Broadway, on London's West End and in Moscow. His Off-Broadway credits include *Thief River*, *Cobb*, *Down the Road*, *Chesapeake* and *Eleemosynary*. Mr. Blessing was the Playwright-in-Residence for the Signature Theatre's 1992-93 season, which included his plays *Fortinbras*, *Lake Street Extension*, *Two Rooms*, and the world premiere of *Patient A*. His plays have premiered regionally at Florida Stage, Contemporary American Theater Festival, and the Ensemble Theatre of Cincinnati, among others. Recent plays include *Whores*, *Flag Day*, *Black Sheep*, *The Winning Streak*, and *The Scottish Play*. Mr. Blessing's plays have received the American Theatre Critics Award, the L.A. Drama Critics Circle Award, the Great American Play Award, the Humanities Award, a Drama Desk Award, numerous Drama-Logue Awards, and the George and Elisabeth Marton Award.

## HUMANA FESTIVAL PRODUCTION

*The Roads that Lead Here* was produced at the Humana Festival of New American Plays in April 2003. It was directed by Joseph Haj with the following cast:

| | |
|---|---|
| Jason | Lea Coco |
| Marcus | Justin Tolley |
| Xander | Jason Kaminsky |

and the following production staff:

| | |
|---|---|
| Scenic Designer | Paul Owen |
| Costume Designers | John P. White |
| | Mike Floyd |
| Lighting Designer | Paul Werner |
| Sound Designer | Colbert S. Davis IV |
| Properties Designer | Doc Manning |
| Stage Manager | Leslie K. Oberhausen |
| Assistant Stage Managers | Michael Domue |
| | Andrew Scheer |
| Dramaturg | Steve Moulds |

## CHARACTERS

JASON, 29, oldest

MARCUS, 23, middle

XANDER, 20, youngest

## SETTING

Their father's house

## TIME

Here and now

Jason Kaminsky, Lea Coco, and Justin Tolley
in *The Roads that Lead Here*

27th Annual Humana Festival of New American Plays
Actors Theatre of Louisville, 2003
photo by Harlan Taylor

# The Roads that Lead Here

*It's bright and warm, the middle of the day. Marcus and Xander sit on a terrace, in white iron lawn chairs. They're huddled over a matching round table which is covered with folders, photos, notepads and various loose scraps of paper. Their speech is rapid, excited, a hint conspiratorial. They are both listening and not listening to each other as they rush excitedly on in their eagerness to share.*

MARCUS: *(Thrusting a photo at Xander.)* Look at this—

XANDER: *(Looking at it.)* Oh, *fantastic!* What is it?

MARCUS: Wolf Point, Montana.

XANDER: I *loved* Wolf Point! I was there last August—no, June. So cold; it actually snowed! *(Of the photo again.)* What *is* this?

MARCUS: Grass.

XANDER: *Grass!* It's so yellow.

MARCUS: *Dried* grass.

XANDER: Absolutely. *Dried.* That is so, it's just so… it's—

MARCUS: Wolf Point.

XANDER: Exactly! *(Thrusting a photo at Marcus.)* Look at *this.*

MARCUS: Great! What is that? Ice?

XANDER: Looks like ice, but it's water. Wave, close up. Pensacola. The sun was glinting—

MARCUS: I see! Spectacular! Jason'll love this. Where is Jason? Why isn't he out here?

XANDER: He's talking to the Eminent.

MARCUS: Still? He's *missing* all this!

XANDER: He'll catch up. We've got all night.

MARCUS: But there's so much. We haven't even seen his yet.

XANDER: Listen to this: *(Picking up a notebook and reading.)* "The dawn sky dipped down in red and white streaks over the endlessly repeating, cream-colored mounds of the empty badlands of west Texas—"

MARCUS: I know! I know!

XANDER: "Interstate 10 pulled me along, a parent tugging a child toward the bright front door of life, no promises, only an endless possibility."

MARCUS: *(Grabbing for a notebook of his own and reading.)* "The earth sinks, as if it were an enormous dish, as I approach Jamestown. Rolling over the far edge, I'm back on the endless table that is the rest of North Dakota—"

*(Xander turns to another section of his notebook and starts reading again. Marcus does the same. Both men read simultaneously with furious enthusiasm, almost as though they are "jamming.")*

XANDER:
The Columbia River gorge is the one cathedral not built by man. Its very existence is an act of praise. The Oregon side is pure emotion, green and steaming with life. The Washington side is hot, dry, blank— a desert staring at a jungle. Rivers and streams flow down from Mt. Hood like open hands—

MARCUS:
You could see the whole battlefield from Lookout Mountain. Along the ridge line to the south the monuments stood peeping out silently from under heavy summer trees. They whisper of long-dead regiments from Virginia, Ohio, Minnesota, Tennessee—men who lie here now part of the ridge itself, part of the mountain—

MARCUS: God, these are so *good!*

XANDER: I've got tons more!

MARCUS: Me, too!

XANDER: Where's *Jason!? (Starting to call out.)* Hey, Jace—!

MARCUS: *(Quickly shushing him.)* Don't! You know how the Eminent gets.

XANDER: But there's so much to go over. He's gotta see this. We should meet more than once a year.

MARCUS: No, once is best. We're more independent.

XANDER: Yeah, but if he misses stuff—

MARCUS: Calm down. It'll be fine. We all have to talk with the Eminent.

XANDER: Hey, listen!

*(Xander produces a small cassette tape player and plays it: urban noises— traffic, horns honking, skateboarders, a bus going by, dog barks, etc. Marcus listens intently under Xander's stare.)*

MARCUS: Denver?

XANDER: Nope.

MARCUS: Denver suburb—Aurora?

XANDER: I wasn't even in Denver this year.

MARCUS: Oh—*Phoenix!*

XANDER: You *bastard!*

MARCUS: *(Laughing at this small victory.)* Try this. *(Marcus produces his own cassette tape player and plays it: ocean surf, gulls screaming, wind, etc.)* Well?

XANDER: Shit. Shit. Lemme listen, lemme… um…

MARCUS: You have no hope.

XANDER: No, I'm close. It's… it's, um…

MARCUS: Time!

XANDER: Bethany Beach! Delaware coast!

MARCUS: *Bastard!!*

XANDER: Jace!

> *(Jason has appeared. Unlike his brothers, he seems subdued.)*

MARCUS: How'd it go?

XANDER: Yeah, how's the Eminent?

JASON: He had a present for me.

MARCUS: *(Surprised.)* A present?

JASON: He said since I'm turning thirty this year—

XANDER: Not for two more months—

JASON: And I won't be home for it—

MARCUS: Home? He knows we have to drive.

JASON: That he's going to give it to me now.

XANDER: What is it?

JASON: He wouldn't say. He had a look in his eye, though. I didn't like the look in his eye. *(To Marcus.)* He wants to see you next.

MARCUS: *(Starting to rise.)* Right now?

JASON: *(Shaking his head.)* He'll send word.

> *(A silence hangs over them as Jason sits down with them at the table.)*

XANDER: *(With renewed enthusiasm, trying to banish the uneasiness in the air.)* What'd you bring us, Jace? What've you got?

> *(Distracted, Jason pulls a small piece of darkish fur from his coat pocket. The others stare at it. Xander feels it.)*

XANDER: Wow! Feel this!

MARCUS: What is that? No, wait—make us guess!

> *(They ponder it carefully while Jason stares off in the direction from which he entered.)*

MARCUS: *(Stroking the mystery fur.)* It's not bear; it's too fine.

JASON: There was something different about him this year.

XANDER: Who?

JASON: The Eminent. Something's changed.

MARCUS: Of course things have changed. It's been a year. Things change every time. Wolf?

JASON: No. This was different. There's a look in his eye.

XANDER: Wolverine?

JASON: No.

MARCUS: Otter?

JASON: *(Absently.)* What kind?

MARCUS: Fresh water?

JASON: No.

XANDER: Salt water?

JASON: No.

MARCUS: Bastard! Beaver?

JASON: Getting colder. He said "thirty" in the strangest way. "You're going to be thirty, Jace. You deserve something very special this year." I said my life was already special—that all our lives were special. I mean, what other father would help make a project like ours possible?

MARCUS: Nobody.

XANDER: Dad is very special. Melanistic mountain lion?

JASON: *(At the absurd guess.)* Please. *(Returning to his subject.)* I said Mom would have been proud of him. So few fathers really listen to their sons. So few brothers stay intimately involved in each other's life through adulthood.

MARCUS: It's not raccoon... marten?

JASON: No.

MARCUS: Coatimundi? Were you in the Southwest?

JASON: I was all over, like always. No, not coatimundi. *(With a sigh.)* He didn't want to look at my pictures this year.

*(The other two look up, shocked.)*

XANDER: He *what?*

JASON: Said he expected they looked a lot like last year's.

MARCUS: They're different! There's always something different!

XANDER: This is a compendium! Encyclopedic!

JASON: I know. The whole point is accumulation—

MARCUS: From three different points of view. The gathering of experience.

XANDER: America as we see it.

MARCUS: With fresh eyes. Unjudged. The natural state.

XANDER: Images, writings, smells, tastes— *(Brandishing the fur.)* Feels!

JASON: The Eminent says we're not growing up.

*(The others are dumbfounded.)*

MARCUS: *We're* not growing up—?! *We're* not!!?

XANDER: How's he spend his day? How's he spend his... his... majorly grown-up day?! Screwing the public?!

MARCUS: Quiet! He'll hear you!

XANDER: I don't care! How can he say we're not grown up, just 'cause we don't want to go into the business?

JASON: Xander—

XANDER: He spends every waking minute advising mega-corporations how to get around federal law—

JASON: He helps business flow. He's like… like a plumber of money.

XANDER: *(Loudly.)* Up to his elbows in shit!

*(They all look towards where Jason entered. An anxious moment, but no sound is heard.)*

JASON: He was better when Mom was alive.

MARCUS: She always calmed him down.

XANDER: She never even blinked at our gasoline bills.

*(They fall into a reverie.)*

JASON: You think he got mad that we left again right after the funeral?

MARCUS: That was two years ago!

XANDER: We had to get back on the road.

JASON: I know, I know. Still… *(After another silence, as Marcus strokes the fur.)* Fisher.

MARCUS: What?

JASON: The fur. It's fisher.

MARCUS AND XANDER: *(With delight.)* Fisher! You *bastard!!*

XANDER: Great going.

MARCUS: Wonderful animal.

XANDER: Underrated.

*(They all ponder the fur.)*

JASON: Do you ever wonder if we shouldn't be doing more with our lives?

MARCUS: *More?*

XANDER: How could we be doing more? I drive 200,000 miles a year.

MARCUS: We all do. We have a project. We have a vision.

XANDER: America without the people.

MARCUS: How it survives, despite everything.

JASON: It's just that the Eminent said—

XANDER: Screw the Eminent. Hey, look! I've got some birds' eggs. *(Quickly producing them.)* Quick—Maine or California?

JASON: Xand—

XANDER: Maine or California?

MARCUS: Maine.

XANDER: Nope.

JASON: Guys—

MARCUS: California?

XANDER: Nope! I lied!

MARCUS: No fair!

JASON: *Quiet!! Both of you!! (As they look up, startled at his vehemence.)* The Eminent—*Dad*—said that he doesn't think our project is... helping us grow. *(Over their audible reactions.)* He thinks we should get married, for one thing—

MARCUS: Married? There's plenty of time for that!

XANDER: This is a calling!

MARCUS: These are our years before the mast!

XANDER: Our walkabout!

JASON: We're virgins.

MARCUS: And proud of it!

XANDER: Yeah!

MARCUS: How else are we going to have enough love for this country? It's immense!

XANDER: There's so *much* of it.

JASON: He wants grandkids.

MARCUS: I don't care! Women weaken resolve. When I wake up each morning, I give myself to that first look of the highway—the shadows of the trees crossing the asphalt like ties on a railroad—

XANDER: Or the sun holding the plains in his arms like a sleepy lover—

JASON: You've never *had* a lover! How would you know?!

MARCUS: You talk like you think he's right.

JASON: I'm not saying that, it's just…

MARCUS: Just what?

JASON: I miss him sometimes, when I'm on the road.

XANDER: You miss *him?*

JASON: I miss all of you. Don't you?

*(Marcus and Xander look at each other.)*

MARCUS: Sure, but… you know.

JASON: What?

MARCUS: America is a jealous mistress, Jace.

XANDER: Jealous.

MARCUS: We get lonely—lonely as hell. But when this project is finished, we'll have it all. You know? The whole country. A little touch of everything: pictures, words, plants, animals, objects, textures, soils, water from rivers, oceans, stones, feathers, fur, teeth, claws, thorns, seeds…

XANDER: Everything but the people. Everything they don't see, or feel or hear or smell or taste. Everything they forget about, every day—when they're only thinking about themselves or other people. We'll have something for every sense.

MARCUS: Something that *makes* sense.

XANDER: A record of love. A careful record of how much we love America.

MARCUS: Proof that it's still worthy of love. That no matter how many of us there are, no matter how badly we may behave, it's still here.

XANDER: Beautiful. Worthy. Waiting.

*(Marcus puts his hand straight out, palm down. Xander puts his hand on Marcus's. They look at Jason, who pauses. Finally he puts his hand on top of theirs. As they all smile quietly, a deafening explosion offstage. They stand stunned for a moment, then all rush downstage and look down into the audience as if over a balcony. They're shocked at what they see.)*

JASON: Oh, my *God*—!!

MARCUS: Jace—it's your car!

XANDER: It's the Eminent!!

MARCUS: He blew it up! He torched your car!

JASON: Oh, my *God!!!*

XANDER: *(To Marcus.)* Hey—! He's going for yours!

MARCUS: Dad—!! *Dad*—! **DAD**—!! *(Another explosion. The light of reflected flames dances across their faces. They stare dumbfounded for a long moment. A third explosion.)*

XANDER: Mine too?

JASON: He bought 'em…

MARCUS: And he blew 'em up.

XANDER: I had stuff in my car. From the project.

MARCUS: Me too.

JASON: Me too.

*(Another moment passes as they stare.)*

MARCUS: What's that sign he's holding up?

JASON: I can't read it. All the smoke—

XANDER: *(Struggling to make out the writing.)* It says… "You're grounded."

*(All three stare open-mouthed at the burning cars. The reflections of the flames very slowly become the only light. Then there is no light at all.)*

END OF PLAY

# The Faculty Room
## by Bridget Carpenter

# BIOGRAPHY

Bridget Carpenter is a 2002 Guggenheim Fellow as well as the NEA/TCG Playwright in Residence at Alaska's Perseverance Theatre. Her plays have been produced and developed at Berkeley Repertory Company, Center Stage, Trinity Repertory, the Public Theater's New Works Now! Festival, Shakespeare & Company and many other venues. Awards include a 1997 Princess Grace Playwriting Award, two Jerome Fellowships, a McKnight Advancement Grant and a 1999 NEA/TCG Playwriting Residency at the Guthrie Theater. Ms. Carpenter's play *Fall* is the recipient of the Susan Smith Blackburn Award and is currently under option for a New York production. Her play *Up (The Man In the Flying Lawn Chair)* premiered in the spring of 2003 at Perseverance Theatre. Ms Carpenter, a member of New Dramatists, lives in Los Angeles.

## HUMANA FESTIVAL PRODUCTION

*The Faculty Room* premiered at the Humana Festival of New American Plays in March 2003. It was directed by Susan Fenichell with the following cast:

| | |
|---|---|
| Carver | Greg McFadden |
| Zoe | Rebecca Wisocky |
| Adam | Michael Laurence |
| Principal Dennis | Colin McPhillamy |
| Bill | William McNulty |
| Student | John Catron |

and the following production staff:

| | |
|---|---|
| Scenic Designer | Paul Owen |
| Costume Designer | Lorraine Venberg |
| Lighting Designer | Mary Louise Geiger |
| Sound Designer/Original Music | Shane Rettig |
| Properties Designer | April Hartsook |
| Stage Manager | Leslie K. Oberhausen |
| Assistant Stage Manager | Andrew Scheer |
| Fight Director | Brent Langdon |
| Dramaturg | Amy Wegener |
| Assistant Dramaturg | Claire Cox |
| Casting | Jerry Beaver |
| Directing Assistant | Emily Wright |
| High School Anthem by | Chris Harrison |

# CHARACTERS

ZOE BARTHOLEMHEW, teaches Theater, about 30 years old
ADAM YOUNGER, teaches English, about 40 years old
CARVER DURAND, teaches World History (temporary regional
    certification), about 30 years old
BILL, teaches Ethics, somewhere between 40 and death
PRINCIPAL DENNIS, a voice on the P.A. System
A STUDENT

Zoe, Adam, and Carver are attractive; not particularly healthy-looking, though.
The Student is in 9th grade—boy or girl, doesn't matter.

# TIME
Now

# PLACE
An ugly small suburb in an ugly small town somewhere in the middle of the
United States of America. It feels like the middle of nowhere. It feels like the
center of exactly nothing. It feels like the moon.

# SETTING
A faculty lounge of a public school: Madison-Feurey High School.
The lights are fluorescent. The floor is linoleum. There are no windows.
The walls are some institutional color.
The coffee maker is always, always on.
The couches are drab vinyl.
There is a giant cardinal head from an old mascot costume perched atop a
    cupboard.
There are ashtrays everywhere, full to overflowing.
Lots of ancient inexplicable teacher shit is tucked in corners, scattered around
    the room.
It's a halfway place that smells like stale smoke and mimeograph ink.

Just like in casinos, in the faculty room, it's impossible to tell what time it is.

*NOTE—The Madison-Feurey School Anthem (Scene 2) has music composed by
Chris Harrison. For information and to obtain the music, please contact author's
agent.*

# ACTING NOTES
Talk fast, always. Jump cues.
Don't be afraid to be mean or make a joke at another character's expense.
Lean into confrontation.
When in doubt, be loud.

*The Faculty Room* was originally commissioned by Atlantic Theater Company.

Rebecca Wisocky, Michael Laurence, and Greg McFadden
in *The Faculty Room*

27th Annual Humana Festival of New American Plays
Actors Theatre of Louisville, 2003
photo by Harlan Taylor

# The Faculty Room

SCENE ONE
SEPTEMBER

*Carver grades papers at the table of the faculty room, a pile of books beside him. He appears somewhat ill at ease. Carver is clean-cut, organized, anxious, and full to bursting with big ideas.*

*Zoe enters, slamming the door. Zoe is disheveled in a sexy way that suggests she does it on purpose. Burnout well underway, Zoe's hard to fool, even though she's barely 30.*

*She doesn't acknowledge Carver. Instead she dumps her once-chic bag on the ground, rummaging through it with some urgency.*

*Carver looks at her. Now that she's entered, he seems even more awkward.*

CARVER: *(Clearing throat.)* Morning.
 *(Zoe keeps rummaging.)*
CARVER: Morning.
 *(Zoe looks up. She stares at him in silence for a longer-than-comfortable moment. She goes back to her bag. Carver, bewildered, returns to grading.)*
ZOE: *(Intense pleasure.)* Oh yes.
 *(She lights a cigarette, inhales, and leans back on the hard vinyl couch, holding in her smoke.)*
 *(Over the couch a handwritten sign has been taped to the wall. It reads NO SMOKING PLEASE!!!!)*
P.A. SYSTEM: *[Elephant trumpet.]*
 *(Click: P.A. System off. Click on again.)*
P.A. SYSTEM: Uh…midmorning announcements will begin in a few minutes. *[Elephant Trumpet.]*
 *(Click: P.A. System off.)*
 *(Adam barrels in, kicking the door open with his foot; it slams behind him. Handsome, unkempt, magnetic, and pushing 40, Adam has the energy of a pressure cooker. The potential to blow is always there. When he tells a long story, words come out of his mouth like water from a fire hose. His mood swings are extreme and instantaneous.)*

*(Adam holds three or four variously-sized handguns. He unceremoniously dumps them on the counter. )*

ADAM: *(A grand pronouncement.)* I Hate Morning Checkpoints!

*(Adam methodically checks each gun to see if it's loaded. After checking each one, he opens up a chute in the wall [not unlike a postal-box unit] and tosses the unloaded guns in. He sees Zoe smoking.)*

ADAM: Gimme, gimme you fucking *greedy* fucking cunt.

*(She hands Adam the cigarettes. He fires up with enormous pleasure, holding in smoke. They sit and smoke, paying no attention at all to Carver, who sneaks glances at them.)*

ADAM: *(Long drag. Exhale.)* Mother*fuck.*

*(Little pause.)*

ZOE: Yeah.

ADAM: Today at checkpoints I began talking with Janet Lundquist and Beth Fisher, both of whom are in my third period Lit class. They said they wanted to talk to me about a book they were both reading. Actually a *series* of books. I nearly fell over. My students, wanting to discuss books? I checked their pupils to see if they had been using. No. Then Janet explains: the books they're reading are about the Rapture. You've heard about the Rapture—it's when God calls all of the Christians home: one day they're walking around, shopping at Kmart, the next moment they're sucked up into the sky, inhaled by the breath of God, only he doesn't eat them, he deposits them gently in Heaven where they stay blissfully for eternity talking about whatever Christians talk about. But the books the girls are reading only mention the Rapture in passing. This series of books is about the people left behind. It's called "Sudden Awakening." Because you and me, Zoe, we're gonna be the infidels left here right smack in the middle of this grand country, all this flat blue sky and flat gray land around us like it is every morning we wake up, when the Rapture comes, it'll be just the same as it is every morning except for, you know, no Christians. More parking spaces. Suddenly awake, us.

And Janet and Beth, they're both near tears—not because they're afraid of the Rapture, no, they're both looking forward to the Rapture, as long as it happens *after* the Christmas formal—but they're weepy because they're worried that some of their less than holy friends might not make it up to Heaven, and then they're going to be up there, and their friends will be down here. And then what would happen?

ZOE: So you comforted them.

ADAM: I comforted them, I did, yes, I pointed out that perhaps there was a divine Guest List, a Guest List for the Rapture made out by none other than God himself, and that people who attend parties do not question why the host or hostess invited who he or she invited, that it was discretionary, and that Beth and Janet should perhaps consider that the number of people invited to the Rapture was in fact the will of God. And then I told them that I thought they could write about "Sudden Awakening" for English class, and they could speculate about who was called to the Rapture and why.

ZOE: Brilliant.

ADAM: You say that with an ironic edge, Zoe, but you know what? It *is* brilliant, it's brilliant because I am taking life information, basic life information and I am *crafting* it into an *assignment*: something easily digested, something accomplishable, something that provides a concrete product at its conclusion. Sooner or later Beth Fisher and Janet Lundquist and Josh Lathe and Daniel Herndon and Jin-He Tamako and Sterling Mills and Theresa Sorkin and Damon Fitzpatrick and Liza Corrado and Bernardo Lorne and Sandrine Chin and Theodore Malden and Ashley Richardson and Jesus Rodriguez and countless other students are going to have to realize that everything has an assignment embedded in it, life is just one assignment after the next, and I am doing them a favor by isolating each assignment and grading it appropriately and writing down the results.

ZOE: Beth Fisher wears a WWJD bracelet.

ADAM: WWJD.

ZOE: What Would Jesus Do.

*(Adam smokes thoughtfully.)*

ADAM: Jesus would take off the bracelet, to start, because bracelets are faggotty. Haven't seen much of you this week.

So where've you been.

ZOE: I don't know, Adam. Around.

ADAM: You got yourself somebody yet?

ZOE: Maybe I do and maybe I don't.

ADAM: Maybe I do, too.

ZOE: Whatever.

ADAM: How was your…the rest of your summer.

ZOE: It was decent.

ADAM: "Decent."

ZOE: I bought a raft at Kmart and every afternoon I drove to the St. Jude River and floated in the murky water and waited for September to come. Now it's here. That was my summer.

ADAM: I taught summer school. Driver's ed.

ZOE: You told me.

*(Silence.)*

ADAM: Fixed up your classroom?

ZOE: Got the girls to do it. They love making collages. Give 'em Exacto knives, it's like crack, they're in heaven.

*(Adam widens his eyes at Zoe.)*

ADAM: Hello!

*(He points to a sign on the wall that has a picture of an exacto knife with a red circle over it and the word, "NO!" underneath.)*

ADAM: Jay Pasolenski? Lost half an ear last year. Exacto casualty.

*(Zoe stares at Adam with some animosity.)*

ZOE: You're not wearing your Exacto-badge. Are you going to make a citizen's arrest?

ADAM: I'd just hate to see you get in trouble for breaking the rules, Zoe.

ZOE: Yeah I know how you love rules.

ADAM: Who are your little helpers?

ZOE: Last year's junior prom court. Marissa Dade, Polly Kamin, Annie-Kay Phillips, Cherry Duncan, Jessica Herbert.

*(Carver gets up to fix himself a cup of brackish coffee. He opens and shuts cupboards and drawers.)*

ADAM: What's he doing?

ZOE: I imagine looking for a spoon.

ADAM: Doesn't he know we don't believe in spoons here?

ZOE: Don't know what he believes.

ADAM: He's in for a disappointment when he understands the dearth of amenities.

ZOE: He'll have to learn to stir the non-dairy creamer with a Bic, like everyone else.

ADAM: Is he grading already? Did he give a quiz the *first week?*

CARVER: He *hears.*

*(Adam and Zoe look at him blankly for a moment, then continue talking as though there has been no interruption.)*

ADAM:

Have I mentioned that as of this month
I get up early before school to "work out."
It was either that, or gain forty
pounds like that tub of lard Coach
Salata who, incidentally, told me that
he'd like to take you out and quote
give you the time unquote.

*(Carver goes back to grading, irritated.)*

ZOE: You "work out."

ADAM: I joined Mega-Fitness.

ZOE: …Mega-shithole.

ADAM: Yeah, but it's a manly mega-shithole. Me and other mega-men are there, grunting, communicating without language, it's a mega-communication. We share a common understanding, we mega-bond. Shit I forgot to lock my car!

*(He runs out.)*

*(Carver puts his coffee down loudly.)*

CARVER: Can I ask you a question? How come you don't talk to me?

*(A beat.)*

ZOE: You spilled on your papers.

CARVER: Oh dammit…

*(He looks for something to wipe up with.)*

ZOE: *(Re: his search.)* Good *luck.* Here.

*(She uses one of her papers to wipe.)*

CARVER: Thank you.

But—that's a paper of your stu—

ZOE: I'll give her a B.

CARVER: Why don't you—why doesn't anyone talk to me? This is just, just bizarre. I mean, I, I meet the principal on the day before classes, he thanks me for accepting the position on such short notice, he shakes my hand, says he's sure I'll do fine, hands me a class schedule, I haven't seen him since. In a week. Every teacher drifts past me, nodding in my general direction but *no one* meets my eye and nobody stops moving. I'm the invisible man in the halls, and then once I get in front of the classroom, the kids stare at me like I'm from the planet Zeon.

*(Little pause.)*

ZOE: You're new.

CARVER: So?

CARVER:

—*Man.* Forget it.

ZOE: That's how it is.

CARVER: Weren't you a new teacher once upon a time?

ZOE: Yes.

CARVER: And?

ZOE: No one talked to me.

   …You get used to it.

CARVER: Where is Principal Dennis? He's disappeared.

ZOE: He doesn't like to leave the office. Don't talk about him in here, anyway—

CARVER: *(Scoffing.)* Why? It's bugged? I mean, this place is about a thousand miles from anything resembling a metropolitan area…

ZOE: Just don't. I'm trying to give you a tip.

   *(P.A. System clicks on.)*

P.A. SYSTEM: *[Trumpet flourish.]*

   *[Static.]*

   Good morning, everyone.

   This is Your Principal, Mr. Dennis.

   I'll just wait for everyone to get settled.

   I'm still waiting.

| | |
|---|---|
| Well. | CARVER: *(Overlapping.)* |
| I trust that you're all having a wonderful | I also don't get— |
| first week back at Madison-Feurey High. | |

*(Zoe shushes Carver.)*

*(She writes on the dry-erase board in large letters: HE CAN HEAR YOU.)*

P.A. SYSTEM:

| | |
|---|---|
| I see a number of familiar faces, | CARVER: |
| as well as faces that are new to me, | What are you talking |
| but that will soon become familiar… | about? |

*(Zoe puts her finger to her lips: SHHH.)*

*(She writes again: P.A. SYSTEM = MICROPHONE HE HEARS YOU!!)*

P.A. SYSTEM:

| | |
|---|---|
| That's what September is all about, | CARVER: *(Loud, overlapping.)* |
| recognizing the old, and welcoming | Come on, you're kidding. |
| the new… | Are you trying to tell me— |

*(On the P.A. System, the Principal stops for a moment.)*

P.A. SYSTEM: I'll just wait until everyone is listening attentively.

*(Zoe gestures: "Told you so.")*

P.A. SYSTEM: That's better.

Some of you may have been listening to announcements and wondering, What The Heck are all those noises? For example, the noise you heard a moment ago.

*[Trumpet flourish.]*

Well, Principal Dennis is here to tell you. On a recent sweltering afternoon in August, myself, the school board, and some dedicated members of the Madison-Feurey PTA decided in a Unanimous Vote to implement a change in format to our beloved P.A. System. This year, we will be using a variety of *new sounds* to denote the end of a class period. It's a new format, so we'll be giving lots of new noises a try! What an adventure! I'll be listening both to the new P.A. noises and to *your* noises…that, is, your *feedback*, ha ha. Let Principal Dennis know which sounds work for *you*. Remember, Madison-Feurey High is not just a place for *teaching*, but a place for *education*.

*[Trumpet flourish.]*

*[Drilling sound.]*

*[Lion roar.]*

*(P.A. System clicks off.)*

ZOE: Okay, now he's gone.

*(She glances at a book on Carver's pile.)*

ZOE: What is this? *365 Meditations for Teachers?*

You're gay aren't you.

CARVER: What kind of a person are—I mean, you haven't bothered to tell me your name, you talk around me like I'm some piece of furniture—

ZOE: I'm Zoe Bartholemhew. I teach theater. And speech.

CARVER: *(Grudging.)* Carver. Durand.

ZOE: Hi, Carver. Gay, right?

CARVER: Jesus Christ. Yes. You going to get me fired now? God. I really *need* this job, I moved here from the city to get it because there was nothing, nothing to be found—

ZOE: Last I checked, people didn't get *fired* for being gay.

*(Little pause.)*

CARVER: You don't read much, do you.

ZOE: That's funny! You *are* gay. Witty.

CARVER: That's offensive.

ZOE: Boo Hoo. Big deal. I said you were witty, I didn't call you an ass pirate.

CARVER: Unbelievable.

ZOE: …or, or a "fudgepacker." Or, what else. "Brother of the Butt."

CARVER: Thanks, Zoe. For not being insensitive like that.

ZOE: You're not from here.

CARVER: No.

And you, you're from…

ZOE: Here.

CARVER: Oh.

ZOE: I went here. For high school. This is my alma mater.

CARVER: Really.

ZOE: Adam went here too. And now we both teach here.

CARVER: Huh.

ZOE: "Huh." Surprised?

CARVER: Oh no it's just, uh—

ZOE: So small and ugly?

CARVER: No.

ZOE: A burnt-out strip mall with a few side streets?

CARVER: I'm sure it has its charms. Someplace. I don't know the area too well yet.

ZOE: Pretty much you drive past Beef Barn, Taco Towne, and the Used Tire Village, and you've seen the heart of town.

CARVER: Oh.

ZOE: You're from the city?

CARVER: Yes.

ZOE: I've never been.

CARVER: Oh. It's—

ZOE: Don't tell me. I like to imagine. I don't want you to ruin it.

CARVER: All right.

ZOE: Did Principal Dennis put you in charge of Spirit Days?

CARVER: Yes, How did you—

ZOE: He gives every wide-eyed wonder Spirit Days. Word to the wise: ignore it.

CARVER: Oh, I don't mind, I actually have some ideas for a kind of—

ZOE: And as for your sophomore advisees, make them *sign up* for office hours. If you do walk-ins, you'll never see any of them again and we're required by law to have them scheduled so keep records.

CARVER: I uh actually met one of my advisees already.

ZOE: Aren't you a champ.

CARVER: In fact I wanted to talk to somebody about uh...the meeting was well it was strange. She was strange. A strange girl.

ZOE: Of course she's strange, she's a sophomore.

CARVER: She was really strange.

ZOE: What's her name?

CARVER: Darby Weider.

ZOE: I don't know that name—oh wait does she not wear shoes?

CARVER: Yes.

ZOE: Sure, Darby. What's the problem?

CARVER: I don't know how to— First she *pointed* at me, she closed her eyes and pointed a finger at me until I said would you mind not doing that. Then she sat down and wanted to talk about, uh, prayer, actually she wanted to pray *with* me and I said I didn't think that was the best use of office hours, and then she wanted to hear my thoughts about the history of prayer, she was very articulate actually, but—

ZOE: ...strange. Yeah. What did you tell her?

CARVER: I said prayer was outside of my area of scholarship.

ZOE: Well you cleared that right up.

(*Adam enters jubilantly.*)

ADAM: I caught a freshman smoking *outside* of a designated smoking area and he had a FULL pack of Marlboros and Guess Who confiscated them! Oh LOOK—did Zoe make a new friend?

ZOE: That's Carver. He teaches—what are you, Biology?

CARVER: World History.

ZOE: Adam teaches English. Carver, Adam; Adam, Carver.

(*Adam fires up a Marlboro.*)

CARVER: I don't know why you haven't talked with me, our classrooms are right on the same hall.

ADAM: Well, see, I hate everybody who's on that hall.

ZOE: (*Clarifying.*) You hate everybody.

ADAM: I do. I do. —Well, I don't hate Zoe, I'm actually in love with her, pro-found, besotted love, but I also hate her because as it turns out she doesn't love me and perhaps never will. But I still carry the torch. So there's that.

ZOE: It is so boring when you go into that.

ADAM: Boring doesn't make it a lie, Sweetheart.

That's Zoe's worst insult, Carver. FYI. I've never seen her upset. The only way she registers irritation or frustration or impatience is to call something "a bore." Now I bet you're in charge of Spirit Days, huh?

*(Bill enters; Adam stops talking.)*

*(Bill is a teacher who wears a perpetually blank expression. He sets his brief-case down on the table, pours a cup of coffee, drinks it, rinses the cup, and places it in the sink. He opens the refrigerator, bends down, and stares inside with great intensity. He stays in this position a long time. The effect should be as though he has frozen there. Adam, Carver, and Zoe watch him avidly.)*

ADAM: HI, BILL!

*(Bill has no response, but Carver and Zoe jump at Adam's shout.)*

*(After an eternity, Bill straightens up, closes the refrigerator door, picks up his briefcase, and exits. Zoe and Adam smoke, unconcerned.)*

CARVER: Does he teach here?

ZOE: Oh, sure, Bill. Bill Dunn. He teaches Ethics.

ADAM: Never heard him utter a syllable, though.

CARVER: How long have *you* taught here?

ADAM: Forever, baby.

CARVER: I heard you went to school here.

ADAM: *(A quick glance at Zoe.)* You hear all kinds of things these days.

CARVER: *(To Zoe.)* How about you. How long have you been a teacher?

ZOE: Not as long as Adam. *(To Adam.)* Carver lived in the city.

ADAM: *(Registering Zoe's interest.)* And he came all the way out here to our little patch of paradise to teach with us. How senseless and fascinating. Where exactly were you teaching in the city?

CARVER: Oh uh a couple of places, here and there.

ADAM: Well go ahead and name one, my curiosity's piqued.

*(P.A. System clicks on.)*

P.A. SYSTEM: *[Organ chord.]*

Second period will begin in ten minutes. Thank you.

*[Horse gallop.]*

*(Click: P.A. System off.)*

ADAM: Where were we?

ZOE: Also Carver's sophomore advisee wants him to pray, but he doesn't believe in God.

ADAM: *(Overlapping each other.)*         CARVER:

Well that's too bad!                That's not true—

CARVER: …I should get to class. It was…nice…to talk to you both. See you later.

ADAM: Have you picked a girlfriend yet?

CARVER: Excuse me?

ADAM: Picked a girlfriend.

    *(Pause.)*

CARVER: I don't. Ah. That's not—I'm sure I'm misunderst—what, what do you mean.

ADAM: A Girlfriend. From Your Classes.

CARVER: Don't be silly that's a ridiculous statement you have to be kidding.

ADAM: Are you all right, Carver? You seem not all right.

CARVER: You're talking about "picking girlfriends"—that's not funny.

ADAM: Zoe's picked. Usually I haven't picked a girlfriend by this time—I tend to take my time—but Zoe *always* has her guy by the end of Freshman Orientation. She's got a good eye.

ZOE: Flatterer.

    *(Little pause.)*

CARVER: This is a kind of hazing ritual for new faculty, I assume. First you don't talk to me, then you ask me to tell you that I'm dating a *minor*.

    *(Little pause.)*

ADAM: You're sort of a drag, aren't you, Carver?

ZOE: He seems like it, but he's gay! —Funny!

ADAM: Ohhh.

    So have you picked a *boy*friend yet.

CARVER: Whatever it is you're implying, I don't get it, and I don't think it's funny.

ADAM: Which is it? Can't be both. If you don't get it, that's one thing, but if that's true, it's not logical that you don't think it's funny, because how can you decide it's *unfunny* if you don't get it?

CARVER: You pick.

ADAM: Carver, I'm sharing! I'm asking questions of a fellow teacher, I'm trying to tell you something personal, something about my life as a *longtime* faculty member at Madison-Feurey High.

ZOE: *(To Adam.)* And why is that.

ADAM: I just want to get to know our new friend.

    *(Carver goes along with the joke.)*

CARVER: Okay. Fine. So who's your boyfriend?

ZOE: Raphael Gilberto.

ADAM: Is that so!

ZOE: Yeah.

ADAM: You're sure.

ZOE: You bet I'm sure. Raphael.

ADAM: Well. *(To Carver.)* She goes for the sensitive types. Last year Raphael was voted "Still Waters Run Deep."

CARVER: *(Laughing.)* You guys are pretty funny.

ADAM: What's funny? How come you're not asking who my girlfriend's gonna be?

CARVER: I'm sure you'll tell me whether I ask or not.

ADAM: My girlfriend is going to be Jen Carlson.

ZOE: You're kidding.

ADAM: Have you seen her class picture yet? They just came back, and she gave me one.

ZOE: She takes a nice picture.

ADAM: Don't be jealous, Zoe, it's so unattractive on a woman your age. I don't know that you ever took quite so delectable a picture. Look at her. Look at that skin. That is the picture you see in the dictionary next to the entry "peaches and cream." —Jen was voted Best Complexion. I asked her what her favorite foods were, she said, pizza; rice cakes with peanut butter and honey; and Twix. I don't mind admitting it, I think I'm in love.

ZOE: That's too bad.

ADAM: Why's that.

ZOE: Polly told me this morning that Jen Carlson was in love with my Raphael.

ADAM: Bullshit.

ZOE: Adam, Polly Kamin is Jen's best friend. Polly *always* knows what's going on. You know that.

*(Adam looks grumpy. He does know that.)*

ZOE: Poor Jen.

Guess you'll have to find another girlfriend.

ADAM: I'm not finding another girlfriend, Zoe. You know the rules.

*(Zoe shrugs.)*

ADAM: Besides. This just makes things interesting.

ZOE: What's that supposed to mean?

ADAM: We'll have an interesting year.

—Look at him.

ZOE: Poor Carver.

ADAM: Thinks we're serious!

*(They laugh.)*

ZOE: Well, we are serious.

*(A moment.)*

CARVER: You two are very strange.

ADAM: You should have seen us when we were married.

## SCENE TWO
## OCTOBER

*Carver wears a Halloween costume. He's a ghost (so actually we can't tell it's Carver) and he wears a sheet with two holes cut out for eyes.*

*He stands in front of a portable keyboard which sits on the table, wearing headphones, picking at the keys, rocking out a little bit.*

*Zoe enters. She wears a witch costume. She carries a handgun and a rifle. As she speaks, she checks each gun to see if it's loaded (neither are) then dumps the guns down the chute.*

ZOE: That little Carrie Mulligan thinks she's such a smartass. I told her I'd check her purse, it's routine, and she insists it's too small to hold anything, it's all part of her costume (she says she's a hooker but I couldn't tell the difference between what she was wearing and what she usually wears) and lo and behold, when I open the purse, she's packing. It's ridiculous. They think just because it's Halloween I'm not going to *check*. Buddy Cummings came to school dressed as a cowboy, and he thinks he gets to carry a rifle around all day!? Think again.
*(Carver is still picking at the keyboard.)*
ZOE: Carver? Happy Halloween.
*(She takes off his headphones which he wears outside of the sheet.)*
ZOE: Boo!
*(Carver screams, recovers himself.)*
CARVER: Zoe, hi, I'm glad you're early, I need your help.
*(Adam enters in a priest's cassock, carrying a rosary. He makes the sign of the cross.)*
ADAM: *(Irish priest intonation.)* Hello my children. We are all of us sinners. Yet we can be redeemed if we confess. Come to me, confess your sins, and be freed of earthly troubles. Confess and make yourself eligible for the Rapture, God's Guest List, do not be left behind, allow yourself to awake, awake, awake.
CARVER: Adam, hi, good, I need you, too.
ADAM: All of us "need" each other, my son.
CARVER: I was digging around some old files in the storage room…
ADAM: Why?!

CARVER: No reason, anyway I found the Madison-Feurey school anthem! I bet you didn't even know we had an anthem. So last night I pulled out my Yamaha to fool around with the tune a little bit, and I made a new arrangement! So listen, you guys, I want you to help me out at assembly. We can teach it to everyone! I printed out the melody, it's very simple, you guys can look at the sheet music and follow along...

ZOE: Mrs. Lund is going to be mad.

CARVER: Why?

ZOE: She's the music teacher.

CARVER: All she cares about is the Spring Sing! She doesn't care about the anthem!

ZOE: It's your funeral.

CARVER: OK, I know everyone thinks they know the best way to do things, but indulge me and try this one idea.

ZOE: I have a soft spot for you because you're a fag stuck here, of all places. But suddenly—showtunes? For school? It's asking too much.

CARVER: It's not "The Rose." It's a school song!

ZOE: Are you trying to win some kind of McDonald's teaching award, Carver? Because we're not even on the radar. Your anthem is just a penny in a well. No one can read ABC, let alone music.

CARVER: Everybody can sing something. It's just for school spirit. Getting ready for Spirit Days!

ADAM: "Spirit Days." Vodoun.

The dead, resurrected from the earth.

ZOE: They *are* zombies.

ADAM: *(Singsong.)*

*Libera me, Domine, de morte aeterna...* [Free me Lord, from eternal death...]

*(Zoe and Adam smoke: no intention of singing Carver's song.)*

CARVER: Don't give up. You're giving up.

*(Adam makes the sign of the cross at him.)*

ADAM: *(Singsong.)*

*Requiem aeternam dona eis.* [Give me eternal peace.]

CARVER: You think that's pretty clever, huh.

*(Little pause; then, singing together as an answer:)*

ADAM/ZOE: *(A chant.)*

*Kyrie...eleison.* [Lord have mercy.]

CARVER: Goddammit. Goddammit. You're gone. You both gave up before I got here; before I knew anything about this godforsaken school, you had already begun and completed the process of total detachment. The thing that's scariest about you two, you don't look the part. You're employed, you bathe, you show up more or less on time, you carry on conversations—not normal conversations, but still—and you *maintain* the *illusion* that you participate. But you don't believe in anything, and you think it makes you safe—but it makes you small. YOUR WHOLE LIFE IS A SHRUG. THERE'S NOTHING THERE, NO STANDARDS, NO MORALS, NO BOUNDARIES! BECAUSE *YOU HAVE GIVEN UP!* QUITTERS! ZOMBIES! *THEY'RE* NOT THE DEAD ONES, YOU ARE! *YOU'RE* NOT A WITCH, AND *YOU'RE* NOT A PRIEST, YOU'RE BOTH *ZOMBIES! ZOMBIES!* ZOMBIES!

*(Little pause.)*

ADAM: Damn, Carver, I'll learn the song.

ZOE: I'll learn it, too, okay, calm down.

CARVER: I just want to teach you my version of the fucking school anthem!

ZOE: We said we'd learn it!

CARVER: Okay, great. *(To Zoe.)* Can you follow harmony?

ZOE: I guess.

*(They pick up the sheet music.)*

CARVER: I programmed the arrangement into my keyboard memory last night, so I just have to push a button. Okay, ready?

ADAM/ZOE: Yeah.

*(Carver pushes a button on the keyboard; the anthem begins, and the three of them sing together.)*

CARVER/ZOE /ADAM: *(Singing,)*

Oh:

Here's to the cardinal red and white
School colors brave and true

At Madison-Feurey High
Our colors won't change hue

Tradition and Loyalty are what we learn
Hearty education is the best return
Rallies, football, basketball, and Spirit Days
Those are the things for which we raise our song in praise.

We won't give up

We won't give in
We won't give out
We won't!

Soooo here's to the cardinal red and white
Not brown, or black, or blue

Oh Madison-Feurey High
We will remember you
Yes, we'll remember you

*(Pause. Adam wipes his eyes. Zoe clears her throat.)*

ADAM: That was really something.

CARVER: You have a good voice.

ADAM: No, I don't—do I?

CARVER: Yeah. You sounded good.

ADAM: That song did something to me. I feel…moved. Your song moved me.

CARVER; I just did the arrangement…the song was already there…

ADAM: I'm still moved.

CARVER: …Well, good.

ADAM: And you know what, you might have been right. About giving up. Zoe won't talk about it, but—

ZOE: Shut up.

ADAM: You shut up!

ZOE: No you shut up!

ADAM: I think you're jealous because I have the capacity to be emotionally moved by a song and you don't. You don't possess the capacity to be moved by, by what. Who knows. I mean go ahead, tell me what moves you!

ZOE: First of all, I'm emotionally moved by plenty of things, and secondly, you'd never know, because God knows it's never happened while you're in the room!

ADAM: Carver's right—you've given up!

ZOE: On *you.*

CARVER: Okay, this doesn't have to happen…

ADAM: Who asked you?

ZOE: Yeah, Carver, stay out of it!

CARVER: Jesus!

ADAM: *(To Zoe.)* You're angry because he created something that you have no idea how to respond to!

*(Adam slams out the door.)*

CARVER: Is this a…

I guess…maybe I should go get Adam?

*(Zoe doesn't answer.)*

CARVER: Yeah. I'm going to go find Adam.

*(Carver leaves.)*

*(Door opens. Bill enters. He doesn't wear a costume.)*

ZOE: Hi Bill.

*(Bill walks to a bowl of candy corn, picks one up, examines it, places it in his pocket, and exits.)*

ZOE: Costume kicks ass, Bill.

*(P.A. clicks on.)*

P.A. SYSTEM: …this thingy sets up and that red light goes on but I don't know where the *switch* is…

*(Whispering.)*

…feeds right into whatever room I want?

*(Whispering.)*

Okay great. I *got* it.

*(Different voice.)*

Ah, hello to the…teachers in the Faculty Room.

ZOE: Hello, Principal Dennis. It's just me here right now. Zoe Bartholemhew.

P.A. SYSTEM: Well hello Miss Bartholemhew! And Happy Halloween!

ZOE: Happy Halloween.

P.A. SYSTEM: How's the…debate team doing? Are we going to make it to the Nationals this year?

ZOE: We…don't have a debate team, Principal Dennis—

P.A. SYSTEM: oh.

ZOE: —remember you decided to redirect the funds to Wrestling. Who, by the way, are doing great this season, so: kudos.

*(Pause.)*

P.A. SYSTEM: Well, great, great.

How's the new P.A. System working out, in your opinion.

ZOE: Oh, it's—

P.A. SYSTEM: Now be honest Miss Bartholemhew!

ZOE: All right, it's—

P.A. SYSTEM: Because initially I wasn't sure about overhauling the current system, it seemed a touch expensive, and frankly *(Garbled, static.) waah zxjfl arphs ldofsm sdkjwe fakjl sadjkliuorto, mncxvasl*
*(His words continue at length, but are indecipherable.)*
*(Finally, he stops talking.)*
*(Little pause.)*

ZOE: Principal Dennis?

P.A. SYSTEM: Hmm?

ZOE: The new system's great.

P.A. SYSTEM: Fantastic! And Mr. Durand. How does he seem to be working out so far?

ZOE: He's fine.

P.A. SYSTEM: Well that's a relief.

*(Little pause.)*

P.A. SYSTEM: Just wanted to make sure he was transitioning. He had a rough time at his last school, but you teachers all bond, so I'm sure he's told you all about it…
*[Factory whistle.]*
Oooops!
…sorry about that…still some bugs in the system!
And I spy with my little eye Mrs. Egan standing at the door of my office, which means I am about to be late to a meeting, so I'm going to sign off right now!
Glad we had this little chat, Miss Bartholemhew.
*(Rooster crowing.)*
That's a good one.
*(P.A. clicks off.)*
*(Adam and Carver enter. Adam carries a tambourine and Carver carries a box of music, which he places on the table.)*

ADAM: It'll give it texture, it'll be uplifting!

CARVER: Just use it sparingly.

ADAM: *(To Zoe.)* When we sing the school anthem I'm going to play the tambourine.

CARVER: So long as it doesn't turn into a song *about* a tambourine.

ADAM: It won't. Hey, we just saw my girlfriend Jen Carlson in the parking lot and it looked like she was giving *Raphael* a ride somewhere.

ZOE: Feeling insecure?

ADAM: On the contrary. I was giving you a heads up in case you were worried about your guy…in case things weren't going A-OK. I mean, Jen dressed up as a nun this Halloween; that's not a coincidence. Anyway, while we're on the subject of, you know, boys and girls, we ran into Coach Salata in the halls and he brought you up again. Carver got *really* jealous.

CARVER: Fuck you.

ADAM: Coach Salata "likes" Zoe. You know once upon a time there were some football players—Coach Salata types—who wouldn't have fucked Zoe for *practice*. But *these* days, since his recent divorce from former cheerleader Kelli Keegan, Coach Salata "likes" Zoe, which is simply simply simply amazing.

ZOE: Lots of people like me, Adam.

ADAM: You know what, Sweetheart? I don't think that's true. Not even a little bit true. Nobody likes you. Coach Salata wants to fuck you, who can blame him, but he certainly doesn't like you. Principal Dennis doesn't like you—you freak him out. Every female teacher at Madison-Feurey loathes you. Come to think of it, I don't know anyone who likes you. Even you don't like you.

CARVER: I like her.

ADAM: No you don't, Carver, you just don't know what else to say. Come on, Zo, admit I'm right. You can't think of anyone who likes you. Anyone at all.

*(Zoe is pale.)*

*(Silence.)*

ADAM: I mean, really, who "likes" you.

Who likes you.

*(A beat.)*

ZOE: Raphael Gilberto likes me.

*(She exits. Adam and Carver sit in silence.)*

ADAM: Well he has to like you because he's your boyfriend.

*(Blackout.)*


SCENE THREE
NOVEMBER


*Zoe and Adam sit across from each other at the table. Zoe staples cutout paper leaves to a long swath of fabric. When she finishes with one swath, she drapes it over a chair.*

*We hear the KACHUNK of the stapler as Zoe works.*
*KACHUNK.*
*KACHUNK.*
*KACHUNK.*
*Adam grades papers, scrawling loudly on each one and then turning it over. The KACHUNKS and the SCRAWLS alternate.*

ADAM: What are you doing.
  *(KACHUNK.*
  *KACHUNK.)*
ZOE: Crafts.
ADAM: Want to know what I'm doing.
ZOE: No.
ADAM: I'm grading *Raphael Gilberto's* paper.
  *(KACHUNK.*
  *KACHUNK.)*
ADAM: I'm giving him a "D." "Minus."
  *(KACHUNK.)*
ADAM: Kidding, Zoe, he's getting a very respectable B plus, Zoe, you have to talk to me someday hello.
  *(Carver enters.)*
ZOE: Hey, did you get my message last night?
CARVER: I did, I fell asleep in front of the TV, sorry.
ZOE: That's okay, did you bring the paint?
CARVER: Oh, damn, I left it in the car, hold on. Morning, Adam.
ADAM: Morning!
  *(Carver exits again.)*
ADAM: Your good buddy Carver.
  *(KACHUNK.*
  *KACHUNK.)*
ADAM: Your dear, close pal Carver.
  I know what you're trying to do, and it's childish.
ZOE: Carver and I are friends, get over it.
ADAM: Has your chum Carver ever mentioned his old school?
ZOE: Don't get weird.
ADAM: I'll take that as a "no." No mention of the old school. That's interesting, you have to admit. I mean anytime we got a newbie before all we heard was "we did it *this* way at my old school, la la la." Funny.
ZOE: I don't think it's a big deal.

ADAM: Well I do, I think it's a great big deal, and who doesn't love a mystery.
*(KACHUNK.)*
*(Zoe finishes draping the leaves and surveys her work.)*

ZOE: That's going to have to do.

ADAM: What's a Fall Fling without fall foliage?

ZOE: Right.

ADAM: Polly Kamin told me what the thing is with Exacto knives.

ZOE: Polly Kamin is doing a scene from *Friends* for her semester project. I told everyone to choose a scene from contemporary drama. Polly taped an episode of *Friends*, transcribed it, and that is her semester project. Which I have to grade.

ADAM: Polly says that cutting is "in."
*(Little pause.)*

ADAM: Actually she showed me. One arm. It's the girls, mostly. They trace long red lines on their arms and legs. Not deep. Not life-threatening. Just enough to break the skin. Just enough to leave an elegant scar. Exactos are better than razors, Polly said, because the handles afford better control. Isn't it great that they can get as many Exactos as they need.

ZOE: Yeah, I believe Polly has a rosebud on her thigh. She's pretty good at it.
*(Adam watches her.)*

ADAM: She's not an artist, though. Like Raphael. She's no "Still Waters Run Deep."
*(Zoe meets his gaze.)*

ZOE: Exact-o.

ADAM: Don't you want to be friends again.

ZOE: We're friends.

ADAM: …Right, okay.
Hey! You should hear this. I got some papers back, and whose midterm turns out to be a fascinating read but Janet Lundquist! Of course she wrote all about the Rapture. Here we go.
*(Pause.)*

ADAM: I'm going to read out loud in a moment, I'm just trying to find a sentence that has both a subject *and* a verb. Hold on…still looking…
*(Almost offhand.)*
Someday you're going to marry me again, Zoe, you'll marry me for real and that's going to be the Rapture.
*(Zoe slaps Adam full across the face. Adam slaps Zoe back, same strength. Zoe slaps Adam. Adam slaps Zoe. Zoe slaps Adam. Adam slaps Zoe.)*

ZOE: Forget it!

You just asked me to marry you because I went to the Prom with Tony Wells.

ADAM: You know that is *bullshit!* Besides you said *yes.*

ZOE: And look what happened!

ADAM: Second marriages are always the happiest.

(*Zoe slaps Adam.*)

ZOE: What is the matter with you? Have you been buying pot from Glenn Moller again?

ADAM: One time, one time, and you smoked it with me!

ZOE: I didn't know you bought it from *Glenn!*

ADAM: You're hardly in a position to be judgmental.

ZOE: Yes I am! Glenn's weed is terrible. He ripped you off. If you're going to cop, the least you should get is a good deal. You paid too much *and* the drugs were substandard. That's embarrassing.

ADAM: What's the alternative!

ZOE: What do you mean.

ADAM: Who else deals.

ZOE: I'm not telling! I thought that was a one-time transgression, Adam, I was willing to let it lie, but if you're going to become a guy who scores pot off Glenn, I mean please, that's unbearably boring.

ADAM: Ahhh! There it is: "boring." My behavior is "boring."

ZOE: Don't start—

ADAM: Make no mistake, I admire it, I mean Zoe when you say something is boring, it's not just *dull,* I might as well crumple it up and throw it away. I might as well set it on fire. When you say something is boring, it becomes utterly worthless, the *idea* is worthless, *talking* about it is worthless, and that I even *entertained* such an idea for a minute makes *me* worthless…and I want to be worth something because I want to go to the Rapture.

ZOE: You want to go to the Rapture.

ADAM: Maybe. Maybe I do.

ZOE: Are you drunk?

ADAM: "Are you buying pot?" "Are you drunk?" What's with you and the—
Yeah I am a little drunk. Why do you ask.

(*Pause.*)

ZOE: No reason.

ADAM: You don't care.

ZOE: No, I don't.

ADAM: I hate Thanksgiving. I hate this month, it's so desolate, flat, brown. When I get up in the morning I look in the refrigerator and I stare at the corn bran, and then I stare at the milk, and then I stare at the orange juice and vodka and I pick.

ZOE: I guess you do.

ADAM: Don't act like we're so different, 'cause we're exactly the same.

ZOE: If it comforts you to imagine that, by all means go ahead.

ADAM: Zing! Good one! Dismissive, contemptuous, and pithy!

*(Little pause.)*

ZOE: Raphael told me that you promised an "A" for the *year* to anyone in English Comp who could make a convincing argument for "pre-tribulation."

ADAM: *Don't ever talk about me with Raphael.*

*(P.A. System clicks on.)*

P.A. SYSTEM: *(Big Charlie Chan Gong.)*

*(P.A. System clicks off.)*

ZOE; Well, time for class. We're working on scenes from Ibsen.

*(Zoe mimes shooting herself in the mouth and exits as Carver enters.)*

CARVER: How's it going.

*(Adam ignores him and takes a pull from a flask.)*

CARVER: *(Under his breath.)* Okay…

ADAM: *(Reading.)* Aww, listen to my girlfriend's essay. OK. "In a post-apocalyptic world, what can one expect"—*one*, that's so cute—"of those who are left behind, *suddenly awake* to the reality of the Rapture, and therefore *suddenly awake* to the reality of Jesus Christ?"

CARVER: Do you have Darby Weider in any of your classes?

ADAM: What year.

CARVER: Sophomore.

ADAM: Oh, sure. She's a kook. Got her paper in here somewhere. This is still Jen's…

*(Reading.)* "This novel tracks the actual events of the Book of Revelations in America."

CARVER: I had another conference with her yesterday and it was…it was very odd. Erratic.

ADAM: Why.

CARVER: She's always barefoot.

ADAM: Well she's a hippie.

CARVER: But it's thirty degrees outside! She could get frostbite! That's not being a hippie, it's being stupid!

ADAM: She's a stupid hippie.

CARVER: I don't think she was wearing underwear.

ADAM: Well, that's ironic.

I mean, it's wasted on you. Although, come to think of it, Darby *is* boyish looking…sort of the androgynous type…with some imagination…

CARVER: That's not funny.

ADAM: I'm not being funny, I'm being *helpful.* I don't want you to be alone.

*(Pause.)*

*(Adam indicates to Carver that he should continue.)*

CARVER: She was barefoot, and she had hacked off all her hair, and was wearing this awful tight white sweater dress that barely covered her…anything, and I just averted my eyes.

ADAM: Yeah, that's Darby.

CARVER: She speaks…inappropriately. She acts like she's…well yesterday she was in the back of the classroom and she, uh, spoke in tongues.

ADAM: *(Tries to speak in tongues.)*

Like that?

CARVER: No.

ADAM: Oh well. So what'd she say in the conference.

CARVER: She said that she wasn't a girl. She was a spirit. She was from somewhere else. Or something. That's why she cut her hair off…she said that I was a sign.

ADAM: You're a sign? Was she talking about the Rapture? Why are *you* a sign? Why aren't I a sign?

CARVER: I don't know.

ADAM: That seems unfair to me. Why you? Huh? Have you bothered to think about that?

CARVER: No, I haven't. I'm thinking about Darby!

ADAM: I don't expect you to listen to me—what do I know, I've only been teaching here since Hector was a pup—but here's my advice. *(Very serious.)*

*(Speaks in tongues, dissolves into giggles.)*

CARVER: Thanks for the help.

ADAM: No problem.

*(Adam reads. Laughs. He lights a marijuana pipe, tokes.)*

CARVER: Oh, Jesus!

ADAM: *(Reading.)* Yeah, he's the Man.

CARVER: Has it occurred to you that maybe you should try to curtail the drug use?

ADAM: No. God these kids are hacks.

CARVER: Why don't you teach them *not* to be?!

ADAM: Yeah, there it is…that tone. The dulcet tones that go bong bong bong—I'm judging you! Bong bong bong.

CARVER: Interesting word choice.

ADAM: I'm not listening I'm not listening I'm reading, I'm reading.

*(Carver: deep breath. Steels himself to tell the Truth in a tough-love kind of way.)*

CARVER: You really think you're the Big Man On Campus, huh? When I first got here I thought you were putting on a show. Now I think that you're really lost. *Gone. Nothing there.* Why don't you put this infantile bullshit behind you? I mean, *I'm* trying, *Zoe's* trying. What are *you* doing?

*(Adam closes a paper he's reading, narrows his eyes.)*

ADAM: *Zoe's* trying.

CARVER: Yeah, she is. We both are.

ADAM: Zoe and you. Remaking the system.

CARVER: Go ahead, say something snide.

ADAM: No, no; nothing snide to say.

CARVER: Yeah, right.

ADAM: I'm just—whoo. You took my breath away there for a sec. Zoe and you. Fighting the good fight. Isn't life a funny old thing.

I met someone who *knows* you.

You don't look surprised. Aren't you surprised? I mean, you're a long way from home. Let me tell you how it happened: I went to the SuperMart across the river and in the bargain liquor section I got into a friendly argument with this lady about the best way to make a vodka stinger (results TBA). Anyway she happened to be a *teacher!* And in fact she used to be a colleague of *yours!*

*(Pause.)*

ADAM: And you know it was funny, I had no idea *where* you taught. In the city. I don't believe you ever mentioned that. And this woman, oh shit what was her name, Mickey. No, Nicky. Micky. Volare, Volak—

CARVER: Nicky Vollansky.

ADAM: *Yes!* She used to teach in the city, so she told me and something clicked in the back of my mind and I went, hey, did you know a Carver Durand and she did!

CARVER: Huh.

ADAM: So I guess that means you knew her, right?

CARVER: Not well.

ADAM: Well that is fascinating, Carver, you're a fascinating guy. She was pretty closemouthed about you. It was almost weird. All she said was that you had missed her retirement party. And that they had all enjoyed working with you at Lincoln. And she was Very Sorry that you had left so *abruptly.*

Lincoln High. This was the school where there was some kind of, what was it, *arson?*

*(Little pause.)*

CARVER: You must be thinking about some other place.

ADAM: Must be.

She gave me her number. Becky.

CARVER: Nicky.

ADAM: Bicky. Invited me over for Thanksgiving dinner, actually, but I had to say no, 'cause I have other plans.

CARVER: And what are those.

ADAM: Well I'm going to my girlfriend's house. Duh. Jen Carlson's mother is going to roast the shit out of something that her father shot, and we're all going to eat it, and I'll talk about what a good student Jen is, and I imagine we'll close out the evening with some pie and chat about the Rapture.

I imagine Zoe is spending Thanksgiving with her boyfriend, she say anything to you about that?

CARVER: No, she hasn't.

ADAM: Well how about that, Carv, you want to talk about my Thanksgiving plans? Huh?

CARVER: Why waste the breath?

ADAM: *(Jovial.)* Why indeed, why indeed. That's a little piece of Euclidian logic, there, pal.

*(Adam reads, flipping through the papers.)*

ADAM: Oh look, here's an essay from your little androgynous hippie spirit flasher girlfriend.

CARVER: Darby's not my "girlfriend."

ADAM: Sure, sure. Lessee—did she do her dissertation on the Rapture, too?

*(He reads. Silence.)*

CARVER: Well?

*(Adam keeps reading.)*

CARVER: What'd she write?

ADAM: She didn't write about the Rapture. She wrote about Icarus.

*(Adam shows Carver the paper; Carver reads. After a moment:)*

CARVER: "Icarus was the son of an overbearing father, a man who could not bear for his child to be free. But Icarus understood what freedom was worth. Icarus placed the wings that his father had crafted on his shoulders, and he soared up towards the sun. He released himself from the boundaries of this world: he flew."

*(Carver is moved by the essay.)*

*(Adam stares at Carver intently.)*

ADAM: What the hell are you doing here, Carver.

*(The closet door opens, sort of suddenly. Bill steps out. Carver is quite startled. Bill's expression, as always, is blank. He sniffs deeply. He stands in the center of the room for a moment. Takes a comb out of his pocket. Combs his hair for a longer-than-normal period of time. Carver and Adam watch. Bill puts his comb away and exits.)*

CARVER: Do you think...was he...

ADAM: Yes.

CARVER: Do you know what I was going to ask?

ADAM: Who cares.

CARVER: ...What's in there?

ADAM: Narnia.

*(Carver opens the door and peers into the dark closet. He pokes around the coats. Goes in farther. Adam walks behind him, shuts the door, and locks it with a distinctive CLICK.)*

CARVER: *(Muffled.)* Hey! Hey!

Okay, ha ha ha.

*(Unhurriedly, Adam takes out a flask, sips, puts some stray papers in order, and departs.)*

CARVER: You got me: very funny!

Adam.

Adam.

Okay, enough's enough.

Adam. HEY.

Let me out.

LET ME OUT, YOU ASSHOLE!

*(P.A. System clicks on.)*

P.A. SYSTEM: *(Cow lowing.)*

Good afternoon, students and faculty, it's time for our after-lunch announcements. * Remember that during this Season of Thanks, we're still collecting food for those less fortunate than ourselves…

*CARVER: (Overlap; muffled yelling over the P.A.) HEY! HEY! SOMEONE COME IN HERE AND LET ME OUT!

Helllooo.

Let me out!

P.A. SYSTEM: I'll just wait until everyone is listening attentively.

CARVER: I'm in the closet! Hello! I'm in the closet!

P.A. SYSTEM: I'm still waiting.

(Blackout.)


SCENE FOUR
DECEMBER


*Something about the lights tells us it's nighttime.*

*Techno dance music can be heard faintly, coming from the gym—music from the Winter Semiformal.*

*Adam sits behind the couch. He wears a suit. He has a sock puppet with big googly eyes on each hand. Or maybe the puppets are realistic, like the ones that Mr. Rogers used to use. Adam uses the back of the couch as a stage. Voices.*

SOCK PUPPET #1: "I'm Holden Caulfield and I'm a disenchanted teenager!"

ADAM: Aw. Holden, what's the matter?

HOLDEN PUPPET: "I just got kicked out of school! But I don't care, cause every-one's a phony."

ADAM: Huh. Everyone?

HOLDEN PUPPET: "Yeah! Everyone! Except maybe this one girl…but she's probably a phony, too."

ADAM: She probably is.

HOLDEN PUPPET: "Why can't people just love each other?"

ADAM: You're kind of a whiny guy, aren't you Holden.

HOLDEN PUPPET: "Go to hell! You're a phony, too!"

ADAM: Maybe so. Maybe so. —But who's *this?*

*(His other hand joins them. A new puppet.)*

SOCK PUPPET #2: "I'm J.D. Salinger."

ADAM: The recluse!

J.D. SALINGER PUPPET: "Yes, and I created the character of Holden Caulfield, and I haven't granted you permission to portray that character."

ADAM: Oh yeah? What are you going to do about it?

J.D. SALINGER PUPPET: "This recluse is gonna kick your ass!"

*(J.D. picks up a [real] gun, which J.D. points at Adam and pretend-fires.)*

J.D. SALINGER PUPPET: "BLAM!"

ADAM: Ahhh!

*(He falls with a thud behind the couch, unseen. The puppets look down at him.)*

HOLDEN PUPPET: "That guy was an asshole."

*(The puppets disappear as Adam's arms drop limply to his sides. He's hidden.)*
*(Sound of running in the hall. The door bangs open and Carver and Zoe fall into the room, all giggles, like kids.)*
*(Zoe wears a beautiful closefitting shiny dress, and has long gloves that go to mid-bicep, like a princess.)*
*(Carver wears a sharp dark suit and tie.)*
*(When the door is opened, the techno music gets momentarily louder.)*
*(P.A. System clicks on.)*

P.A. SYSTEM: *(Harpsichord rendering of musical phrase "and a partridge in a pear tree.")*

Good evening, students and teachers of Madison-Feurey High School, Principal Dennis here to welcome you to the annual M-F Winter Semiformal. I'd like to wish you all an official "Happy Winter," and also to take a moment to identify Four Important Rules for tonight's Dance. I'll just wait until everyone is listening attentively.

*(As Principal Dennis enumerates the following rules, Carver and Zoe blatantly violate each one, stifling laughter.)*

One. Please Show Respect to your teachers and peers.

*(Zoe and Carver give each other the finger, then give the finger to the P.A. System.)*

Two. Please Show Responsibility. Any student under the influence of any intoxicant will be suspended, effective immediately. After a week's suspension, their records will be subject to review…and possibly expulsion.

*(Carver and Zoe drink copiously from a flask.)*

Three. Please Show Decorum. Any student wearing clothes which violate the Madison-Feurey Decency Code will be asked to leave the Dance.

*(Zoe yanks down her top so that her breasts are exposed.)*

And Four. Please Show Civility. No public displays of crude or inappropriate behavior. *(Musing.)* What does "inappropriate" mean? It means "*not* appropriate." Which means "not right; not right now." In short, just do your best.

*(Carver pulls down his pants; Zoe spanks Carver.)*

Thank you for your attention…I trust that you will behave like responsible members of your generation tonight. This is Principal Dennis saying Ho Ho Ho.

*[Reindeer bells jingling.]*

*(P.A. System clicks off.)*

ZOE: I want to find Bill. I need to dance with Bill.

*(Carver opens the closet door.)*

ZOE: What are you doing?

CARVER: Nothing.

ZOE: Ooh, I almost forgot, you need a boutonnière. I made you a craft boutonnière! Here…

*(From her purse, she extracts a big pink paper flower and pins it on Carver's lapel.)*

ZOE: I made it pink.

CARVER: Very thoughtful.

*(Music changes. It's "Sleepwalk." He and Zoe slow dance.)*

CARVER: Bring a date?

ZOE: No, I'm stag.

CARVER: *(Lame attempt at joking.)* Except for your boyfriend.

ZOE: Well of course. I'd never hurt Raphael's feelings like that.

*(Still dancing…)*

CARVER: *(Uncomfortable.)* Right. Raphael. Ha.

How was your Winter Semiformal here. Did you go?

ZOE: I had a dark green taffeta dress. Adam wore a bow tie the exact same shade of green. But he wasn't my date.

CARVER: Wow.

ZOE: Mr. Younger and I have been around a long time.

CARVER: And neither of you ever left.

ZOE: Neither of us left.

CARVER: That sounds…very romantic.

ZOE: Not really. You know some people for a long time.

CARVER: *(Pointedly.)* And then you get married.

ZOE: And then you get divorced.

CARVER: Why.

ZOE: Why *what*.

CARVER: Everything. Why'd you get married; why'd you get divorced; were you ever in love…

ZOE: Why does anybody do anything? Because you want the rush, you want something *more* than just your, your own mundane self, you want to be *awake*.

*(A little moment.)*

ZOE: And then you realize that a young marriage maybe isn't that.

CARVER: Adam…is, ah, unpredictable. At best.

ZOE: Diplomatic response. Boring.

You're afraid to say what you really think.

CARVER: Go ahead and tell me what I think. Save us some time.

ZOE: You think he's a bad influence on me.

CARVER: I think he's a bad influence on everybody.

ZOE: Adam's not *strong* enough to be really *bad*.

CARVER: Come on.

ZOE: He's a good teacher. As for the other stuff, he's all impulse.

CARVER: We should be doing things that matter. That's the problem with Adam: he's not doing anything that matters. It's irresponsible.

*(Zoe touches his cheek.)*

ZOE: Are we doing things that matter?

CARVER: I think so.

ZOE: Let's stop talking about Adam. Let's talk about you.

Tell me something scandalous about your past.

CARVER: I'm very dull.

ZOE: In an offbeat way.

CARVER: I teach. That's it.

ZOE: Do you have family in the city?

CARVER: My parents are dead.

ZOE: Huh. Brothers or sisters?

CARVER: No.

ZOE: No one to track down to find out who you really are, hm.

ADAM: *(Popping into sight.)* And don't you find that astonishingly coincidental?

ZOE: God! What are you doing there?!

ADAM: I'm sorry. Did I interrupt something?

ZOE: Don't be stupid. Are you spying on me?

ADAM: Not spying at all, sweetheart, *stalking*. And thank you for saying I was a good teacher—that warms my heart. You wanted to know something about Carver, right? As it turns out I know someone who knows Carver—*you* remember, Carver, Nicky Vollansky?—well she and I spent some quality time together recently and I found out a tidbit or two.

CARVER: Come on Zoe, we should get back and help serve the punch.

ADAM: No no no don't go! Not before I tell you about the little assignation, a li'l dark secret from Carver's past.

*(As a puppet.)*

"Zoe, you look beautiful!"

*(In his regular voice.)*

Big News: Our Buddy Carver was *fired from his last job because he had an affair with a student!*

*(Silence.)*

CARVER: That's not true.

ADAM: I should clarify: I don't know for certain whether they pink-slipped you because you had an *affair* or whether it was because your student *set himself on fire*.

I saw newspaper clippings! That Nicky Vollansky, she's a clipper. She clips everything that has to do with everything. Clip clip clip. A sixteen-year-old genius named Sam. He wrote love letters to you…lots of letters…pages and pages of letters…

CARVER: You don't have any fucking clue what you're talking about.

ADAM: …and then Sam set himself on fire because you broke it off! I knew I remembered hearing *something* about Lincoln…but it wasn't *arson*. Your student *immolated* himself. For love! Should have been a national story—can you imagine the coverage—but his parents had money. That's what Nicky Vollansky said. She's a very informed clipper, Nicky Vollansky.

You walk around here and you act so smug. You write anthems, and you act weepy about poor barefoot Darby boo hoo, and you plan Spirit Days, and in the meantime your ex-boyfriend from Lincoln High is a charcoal briquette. That, my friend, is something to consider.

CARVER: Don't listen to him, he's an asshole…

ADAM: Yeah, and who are you? You're a History teacher who *set a kid on fire!*

CARVER: *I never touched him!* He did it *himself* on the quad—

*(A moment.)*

CARVER: He—

It was after school.

I wasn't there.

He soaked his clothes in gasoline, and his hair. And lit a match.

And…

ADAM: Pffft.

They released only one letter…but he wrote hundreds…

CARVER: It wasn't a letter, it was an essay. About wanting to be a Phoenix. Rising from ashes.

ADAM: You've been holding out. And we tell you just about everything. Like for example did I mention that I'm starting a Book Club devoted solely to the Sudden Awakening Series?

ZOE: You feeling pretty good, Adam?

ADAM: I feel A-OK, yeah.

ZOE: This is a pathetic display.

ADAM: Yeah, you must be bored. That was some *boring* news. Don't worry, I've got something for you. Little while ago, I saw your boyfriend outside in a *heavy* making-out session with one of the Severine Twins. Wish I could say which, but I've never been able to tell them apart. Always give 'em both a B plus.

Zo? You hear me?

ZOE: I heard you.

ADAM: Good, good.

Well, what are you going to do? A Severine Twin is with Raphael! You gonna kick her ass, or do you feel you have an unfair advantage because of the age thing.

ZOE: Fuck off.

ADAM: Unlike your fickle Raphael, my girlfriend Jen Carlson falls more in love with me by the day.

CARVER: Adam, everyone knows that Jen is in love with Raphael.

ADAM: *(Jovially.)* Stay out of it, firestarter.

Raphael's got his hand on the tit of Severine number one. Jen'll get over him. But it looks like the beginning of a whole new world for Still Waters Run Deep.

*(Zoe starts to exit, fast.)*

CARVER: Zoe, wait—

*(Zoe looks at Carver. Then she's out the door.)*

ADAM: *(Singing.)* It's My Party And I'll Cry If I Want To…

You really think I have a decent voice? Can I still play the tambourine for Spirit Days?

CARVER: Fuck you.

ADAM: You're not the sign, pal. I don't care what Darby says.

CARVER: I don't know what you think you're doing, or what you want.

ADAM: Sure you do. You were dancing with it. I want the Rapture.

(Little pause.)

ADAM: Zoe doesn't get what you're up to. But I get it. You blow up your boyfriend, take off, try to make a break with the past. Shed your skin. Be somebody new. Maybe even get married, have a wife, a dog, an unsullied history. And who better to partner you on your new path than my Zo. You want the Rapture, too.

CARVER: You're not going to get it.

ADAM: Ooh, that looks like a gauntlet on the floor.

(Carver slams out the door.)

ADAM: (To sock puppet.) Well, I think we should get back to the dance.

(As sock puppet.) "Right on."

(As himself.) Right on.

(The puppet disposes of Adam's gun in the gun chute. Adam turns out the lights in the faculty room and exits. Eerie fluorescent light shines through the mottled glass panel on the door.)


(Sound of footsteps running down the hall.)

(Zoe re-enters the faculty room, but she does not turn on the lights.)

(She walks around the room unsteadily, shell-shocked, her arms wrapped around herself. She is becoming increasingly agitated.)

(Quite suddenly, she bursts into tears: heaving, ugly sobs that wrack her like cramps. She doubles over, keening. Her crying is a tidal wave, her face a grimace. She tears at her corsage and throws it across the room, she stumbles and crumples onto the couch, curling into a fetal position, weeping.)

ZOE: Aahhhhh—

(Zoe jumps up, opens a drawer so that the contents spill noisily onto the floor. She finds what she wants, slim and silver. It's an Exacto knife.)

(She takes off one of her long gloves and gently, deliberately draws the Exacto knife up one bare arm.)

(A single long line of blood appears.)

(Zoe sighs a deep breath of relief.)

(She has stopped weeping. She takes off her other glove.)

(Her face is tranquil, composed, at peace.)

(Blackout.)

## SCENE FIVE
## JANUARY

*The faculty room is empty.*

P.A. SYSTEM: *(Egg timer ticking for an inordinately long time to alarm brrrring.)* Good morning students and teachers, Principal Dennis here wishing you a Happy. New. Year. I know all of our Madison-Feurey teachers are eager to have you students back raring to go after a restful Christmas vacation.

And we're all looking forward to watching some exciting games when our very own Cardinals take flight on the court—first game of the semester, against Eastern High, is next week! Let's see you all there! Principal Dennis saying, that's all for now.

*(Sound of applause, cheering.)*

You're too kind.

*(Dog barking.)*

*(P.A. System clicks off.)*

*(Adam enters, hyper, singing the Madison-Feurey song.)*

*(Carver enters, bundled up and brushing snow off himself.)*

ADAM: Well! How was your Christmas vacation, buddy?

CARVER: That's none of your business.

ADAM: I prefer "beeswax." Seen Zoe yet?

CARVER: No.

ADAM: Really. Well she looks great. You're missing out.

Want to come to my Book Club meeting after school?

CARVER: Thanks but I'll pass.

ADAM: You should wake up, pal. Book Club is where it's at.

We have been having some kickass discussions about the Rapture. I'm very very well informed. Something big is going down. Everyone's involved. Bill's involved. But he doesn't know yet.

CARVER: You need help.

ADAM: I know!

My head needs to be clear because I need to erase all ambiguity. Forget Spirit Days; this is about the Prom.

CARVER: What are you talking about?

ADAM: Zoe might go to go to the Prom with Raphael.

CARVER: Right.

ADAM: I'm giving you information. Believe me or don't.

CARVER: I *don't* believe you! How about that! I wish you'd just allow everyone here to teach. TEACH. Get it? I want to talk about the Civil War, and Reconstruction, and the Industrial Age. I want to give a pop quiz and call it a day!

*(Zoe enters. She looks different. She wears baggy clothes, several long-sleeved t-shirts layered over one another, jeans that are too big. The effect should be both hip—she should look much younger—and strange, as though at first glance she could be a street kid.)*

*(Another thing: she also looks radiantly happy.)*

ADAM: *(To Zoe.)* I know what's going on. You hear me? I know what's going on.

ZOE: I'm sure.

ADAM: I'm *very clear* about what's going on. Very clear. You make my head hurt. My head hurts. Oh, damn damn damn.

ZOE: Get an aspirin from the nurse.

ADAM: I'm going to.

*(Pointing.)* I'm not done talking to you. Either of you.

*(Adam exits.)*

*(Awkward silence.)*

CARVER: *(Re: her clothes.)* Wassup Gee.

*(No response.)*

CARVER: That was a joke.

ZOE: "Ha."

CARVER: Ha.

Anyway.

How've you been.

ZOE: I don't know, Carver. Fine.

CARVER: Called you over vacation.

ZOE: I was pretty busy.

CARVER: How was your break?

ZOE: Fine.

*(She busies herself with papers.)*

CARVER: We should talk.

ZOE: If you want.

CARVER: I want to explain about some of the things that Adam said the night of the Christmas dance… I don't want you to have the wrong idea—

ZOE: *(Interrupting.)* The "wrong idea!" You—you know *rolled your eyes* every time I talked about *my* boyfriend!

CARVER: That's your thing with Adam! I don't want to get into that!

ZOE: "Get into that!" You're in! You and your old boyfriend from "out of town."

CARVER: He wasn't my boyfriend! Sam was my student. My student.

ZOE: Were *all* his teachers fired?

CARVER: He saw me as a, a mentor. When he…hurt himself, and the school found out *I* was gay, and I was his favorite teacher, that was a problem. The Problem.

*(Little pause.)*

ZOE: Right.

CARVER: That's what happened.

ZOE: How about the letters?

There were letters, right? Lots?

*(Little pause.)*

CARVER: Just because he wrote me letters and I'm not saying he did, doesn't mean that he was, that we were together.

ZOE: *(Losing interest.)* Well if that's what you say happened then that's what happened.

CARVER: Okay.

*(Zoe opens a note folded origami-style, reads it, giggles.)*

CARVER: What are you reading?

ZOE: It's personal.

CARVER: So…are we okay.

ZOE: Let's just move into the new semester, shall we.

*(Zoe puts headphones on and listens. She's really into the music—something up-to-the-minute contemporary. She takes out a Twinkie and plastic knife, cuts the top of the Twinkie off lengthwise, sprinkles some Fritos atop the cream, replaces the top, bites. She eats, drinks a Coke, ignores Carver.)*

*(Adam enters again.)*

ADAM: That doesn't look very healthy. Right, Carver?

CARVER: Not my business.

ADAM: Good boundary setting, pal. *(Loud.)* ZOE, ENJOYING YOUR MUSIC?

ZOE: YEAH.

ADAM: HOW'D YOU KNOW ABOUT *[He names the group she's listening to]*?

ZOE: I SAW A VIDEO.

ADAM: YOU DON'T HAVE A TV.

*(Zoe takes off the headphones.)*

ZOE: Yes I do.

ADAM: No you don't. You've never had a TV, you hate TV.

ZOE: Well I don't anymore.

ADAM: Carver, you know Zoe doesn't have a TV, right? You're her buddy, you know that: no TV. *(To Zoe.)* What are you eating?

ZOE: Slim Jim.

ADAM: You're a *vegan.*

ZOE: Obviously, not anymore.

ADAM: You're chewing on dried cow.

ZOE: People change.

ADAM: No more carrot sticks? No more celery strips? No Cliff Bars or raisins or apples.

*(Adam goes through Zoe's bag. He pulls out Twinkies, Ding Dongs, bags of chips, a Coke—lots of junk food.)*

ZOE: If you find anything you want, help yourself.

*(Adam becomes increasingly manic and upset by the food in her bag.)*

ADAM: All right. I get it. You want to play that way, fine. I'm taking this!

*(He slams out with a Ding Dong.)*

*(Zoe puts her music back on. Carver turns it off.)*

CARVER: Don't you think we should do something?

ZOE: About what?

CARVER: I don't think he should be around students.

ZOE: Who else would do English Comp? They'd never find anyone to come in mid-term. He can actually be a pretty incredible English teacher. He has this assignment where each student chooses a character from a Salinger story and a character from Greek mythology and then we'd write a conversation between the two—well anyway there's nobody in the district who'd take over a spot now so the point's moot.

Next week I have to have auditions for the spring play and I haven't decided what the play's going to be. Although *Darby* had a suggestion for me. Your hippie.

CARVER: I'm still concerned about her.

ZOE: Be concerned about her taste in *drama.* She gave me a proposal for this "play" which she called a "free adaptation" from one of these *Suddenly Awake* novels. Her writing skills aren't bad but the source material— pee-yew.

CARVER: Her behavior is still…

ZOE: Oh, she's one of the Rapture kids, big deal. Besides, she used to be a real loner and I've been seeing her around a lot of other students lately, so consider that a good sign. Except for the play. Yagh.

CARVER: Madison-Feurey must have a protocol for um, troubled students somewhere…

Zoe?

ZOE: Have you ever noticed Raphael's smell?

CARVER: His…smell.

ZOE: Raphael smells like fresh-baked bread. His skin smells like a scone. His hair smells like cinnamon. You cannot believe how good he smells. It's like smelling creation. It's Biblical. He smells like the beginning of the world. *(She sniffs, holds out her arm, smiling.)* Here—it's on my wrist. *(Little silence.)*

CARVER: I should get to class.

ZOE: Raphael beat me at PlayStation yesterday, but I'm getting better. I'm starting to give him a really good game. We play "Bomb Squad" to see who can defuse the bomb the fastest. I'm getting better every time.


SCENE SIX
FEBRUARY


*Carver sits eating his brown bag lunch: sandwich, apple, milk, carrot sticks, cookie.*


*Adam paces, hyper.*


ADAM: Sure you can call it a success but I got hounded all fucking night by a bunch of mothers who all wanted to talk about Oprah.

CARVER: I *told* you that was going to happen if you set up a booth for your Book Club.

ADAM: Parent-*Teacher* Meetings. The thing is, the problem is, we're here ostensibly to be *teaching* these kids something, we are being paid *money*— not a lot of money by any stretch of the imagination but money nonetheless—and by the time a single week goes by, it already feels too late, it feels like we're behind, it feels like we're never going to wake up, I mean catch up, catch up, and in any case the issues that we're addressing are so remedial when you get right down to it that to actually pay even cursory attention to the syllabus is laughable. Really it's absurd to think that parents care about the "syllabus" when they see us basically as free day care.

*(Adam is interrupted by a commotion in the hall outside.)*

ZOE: *(Loud; unseen; outside the door.)* I'm *not* making it a bigger deal! You just said you'd call last night, and then you didn't, and I'm mentioning it! That doesn't mean it's a big *deal!*

*(Mumbling younger voice.)*

ZOE: No I didn't!

*(Mumbling younger voice.)*

ZOE: What*ever!*

*(Mumbling younger voice.)*

*(Zoe enters, slamming door, wiping her eyes. She wears jeans and many, many T-shirts, even more layers than the last scene. Her hair is in a baseball cap, maybe.)*

*(Adam stares at her coldly and exits.)*

*(She sits and takes out her lunch, a pack of Sno-Balls.)*

CARVER: You missed some really great Parent-Teacher Conferences last night.

*(Zoe wipes her eyes, stuffs most of a Sno-Ball in her mouth.)*

ZOE: *(Mouth full.)* Sorry.

Can I have some of your milk?

*(She drinks.)*

CARVER: At my old school they stopped having ANY conferences because nobody came, there's way more PTC potential in this district.

ZOE: PTC potential?

CARVER: Parent-Teacher Conference potential. I was in charge of the Spirit Days Booth, I talked to a lot of parents, overall the feedback was really positive. Spirit Days are totally coming together. We're going to have the rally on the last day and then the Prom that night. Where were you?

ZOE: Making Valentines.

*(She takes out some construction paper and proceeds to industriously cut out hearts, gluing them to doilies, etc., for the remainder of the scene.)*

CARVER: …Right.

Have you heard that Loren Elliot is dealing E?

ZOE: I heard it was acid.

CARVER: It's E. I just sent Naomi Sanger home because this morning in class when I asked her about President Grover Cleveland she said that he was "a mad beautiful man, who had some fiercely awesome policies."

ZOE: She got it from Loren? He is such a supernerd.

CARVER: With E. Don't tell Adam.

ZOE: You finally meet your hippie's parents at the conferences?

CARVER: Darby's parents were there, yes.

ZOE: No kidding. Shoes?

CARVER: Shoes.

ZOE: How'd that go.

CARVER: I told them that I had concerns about Darby's uh general demeanor, about her frequent, uh prayer. But they just kept nodding, I don't think they totally got it because basically they stayed pretty cheerful. They said Darby told them I was responsible for everything that was happening for her this year. "She has *friends* now," her mother said.

ZOE: Have you noticed that Darby has buddied up with Jen Carlson? That is such a total crop circle. It's a safe bet that nobody talked to Darby for most of ninth grade. Because of the bare feet, the basic fashion decisions. But now she and Jen are as thick as thieves. Things change.

CARVER: It's fortuitous that you mention Jen Carlson, because I wanted to ask you if you've noticed anything unusual about her lately.

*(Silence.)*

CARVER: Like for example have you noticed that she weighs in the vicinity of say ninety pounds.

ZOE: Polly said that she took Jen to Psych Services.

CARVER: Once.

ZOE: So: progress.

CARVER: When she turns sideways she almost flickers out. She's still very fragile over... She's starving herself.

ZOE: No joke, I should fail her for her breath alone.

CARVER: You're *failing* her?!

ZOE: She's getting an F on her midterm acting project.

CARVER: You cannot do that.

ZOE: Hell I can't. She's constantly late, and for the midterm she read this half-assed monologue written by none other than Darby.

CARVER: What monologue.

ZOE: Oh you know, thunder, lightning, people growing wings, flights of angels, a hodgepodge of Greek mythology and the Bible and who knows what else. *Dawson's Creek.* All of it delivered in this monotone. "Then there shall be *fire*, then there shall be *rain*" —it's like the Book of Revelations as told to James Taylor.

CARVER: Jen's parents didn't show last night. I've left messages for Principal

Dennis but he hasn't responded. You can't just *fail* her, she's under a lot of stress.

ZOE: Hello! She's not doing the work and the other students are.

CARVER: *She has a broken heart!*

ZOE: Hey, that's what happens! You're sixteen, and your heart breaks, and then you're twenty-two, and your heart breaks, and then you're thirty, and guess what your heart breaks again! In the meantime you wipe your eyes and show up for your midterms!

CARVER: God, you are really...like *you* show up for Parent-Teacher Conferences!

ZOE: I told you I was *busy!*

CARVER: Making Valentines—for who!

ZOE: FOR THE CLASS.

CARVER: BULLSHIT.

I am getting so tired of trying to *work* when—*look* at you! Look at yourself!

ZOE: *(Lazily gives him the finger.)*

CARVER: You are ignoring students in *trouble.* You are fighting with students in the *hallway.*

ZOE: It was just a tiff!

CARVER: Right! As if everyone isn't aware of the rumors! That Raphael walked Andra Tilson home and he might invite her to the Prom!

ZOE: Andra Tilson is a *cow.* What's the matter, Carver, you jealous?! Haven't found a date for Spirit Days yet? Why don't you take another look at Darby because she's sure looking at you!

CARVER: *(Inarticulately furious.)* Fuck you! Fuck you! Fuck you fuck you fuck you.

*(Adam enters.)*

ADAM: I'm back.

CARVER: Fuck you!

*(He slams out. Zoe starts to rummage around in Carver's lunch bag. Adam does too. Carver enters and snatches his food.)*

CARVER: Fuck you!

*(Carver exits again.)*

*(Zoe calmly returns to her Valentine-making.)*

ADAM: What's with him.

ZOE: He's bent out of shape about the Parent-Teacher Conferences.

ADAM: Well we all missed you last night.

ZOE: You went?

ADAM: Sure I went.

ZOE: Mr. Younger goes to Parent-Teacher Conference night. That's a new development.

ADAM: I used to go all the time. Back in the day. Where I met *your* parents.

ZOE: *(Changing subject.)* Did you know that Loren Elliot's dealing E?

ADAM: No kidding.

ZOE: Loren got Naomi rolling in Carver's class today.

ADAM: Must have made for a lively history lesson.

Darby has been writing scene after scene of this Rapture play.

ZOE: I had to *hear* part of it. Before you say anything, we're doing *Camelot*, we're NOT producing a student-written play, don't try to change my mind.

ADAM: Fine, don't support student work. —Carver is a character, did you know that?

ZOE: What does that mean he's a character.

ADAM: He's a character in the play. The character's not *named* Carver but it most definitely is him.

ZOE: How do you know?

ADAM: I teach English Zoe, I can spot thinly veiled characters, it's in my job description.

ZOE: Have you read the whole thing?

ADAM: It's a work in progress but Darby and Jen are giving it to me scene by scene, yeah.

ZOE: Has Carver read it?

ADAM: No.

ZOE: *Should* he?

ADAM: He'll get to see it soon enough.

ZOE: What happens to his character?

ADAM: What do you think happens. He wakes up. Suddenly.

Making some Valentines there I see.

ZOE: Yup.

ADAM: That's one of the first memories I have about you. Have I ever told you that?

ZOE: *(Concentrating on her doily.)* Every Valentine's Day.

ADAM: I remember looking at you during study hall, and I walked over to you and I whispered, "What are you doing?" and you said, "Everyone deserves a Valentine."

ZOE: And you said, "Even Fred?"

ADAM: Fred Linter.

ZOE: Remember him?

ADAM: Please, who could forget. Poor guy was balding at seventeen. He looked like a monk with zits.

*(Zoe starts laughing really, really hard. So does Adam—a shared memory.)*

ADAM: He smelled, I don't know, like *baloney* all the time…which was bizarre since didn't he claim to be a vegetarian?…

*(Zoe laughs more.)*

ADAM: And everyone in class started calling him "Brother Linter."

ZOE: I know…OW!

*(Zoe has cut her thumb with an Exacto knife while making a heart. She laughs harder, then weirdly, instantaneously, begins to cry.)*

ADAM: Hey. Hey. You're okay. It's okay.

*(Zoe cries so hard it's difficult to understand her speech. Adam comforts her.)*

ZOE: I know

I just

ADAM: Shh. Valentines are a heavy responsibility.

*(She laughs a little but still cries. Adam strokes her hair. He is very gentle.)*

ZOE: I'm just

I feel so tired

ADAM: Shh.

I know.

Hey. Hey Zoe.

ZOE: Hey.

ADAM: It's me. You know me.

ZOE: I know.

*(Little silence. They are close together.)*

ADAM: Where've you been, huh?

ZOE: What do you mean.

ADAM: You've been gone a while, I've missed my Zoe, where are you…

ZOE: Not "your" Zoe.

ADAM: I need to ask you something serious.

ZOE: Don't.

ADAM: I have to.

ZOE: No you don't.

ADAM: Yes I do. For real.

Zoe. We didn't do this right before. Will you…

ZOE: Cut it out.

*(Adam gets down on one knee, takes out a box.)*

ADAM: Will you...

ZOE: Adam I'm not kidding, cut it out, I don't want to hear it—

ADAM: Will you go to the Prom with me?

*(He opens the box. It's a gardenia corsage.)*

ZOE: *Fuck!* No!

ADAM: Has somebody asked you yet?!

ZOE: You've *got* somebody.

ADAM: That doesn't answer my question!

ZOE: You have somebody and so do I. Those are the rules.

ADAM: *Fuck the rules!*

ZOE: No fuck *you!* We have an agreement.

| ADAM: | ZOE: *(Simultaneous.)* |
|---|---|
| We have a *history!* And history is more important than agreements! It can't continue to go on like it's been going on—I have too much in my heart, Zoe, I am too *full.* You haven't been invited to Prom yet so why are you telling me NO! | *Don't start with that— I am so tired of your talk about history because history is what is PAST. It's OVER. It's DEAD. I am not going to get into this with you again— —God we are not going to talk about the fucking PROM!* |

ZOE: YOU KNOW WHY!

ADAM: SAY IT! SAY IT! TELL ME!

ZOE: *(Overlap.)* I DON'T HAVE TO TELL YOU ANYTHING!

*(The phone begins to ring. They stop. Pause.)*

*(Zoe and Adam rush for the phone and struggle for it. Adam wins.)*

ADAM: —Faculty Room.

—Oh you *do.* Right. Just a minute.

*(Zoe grabs the phone and huddles in a corner to talk.)*

ZOE: —Yes.

—Hi.

—Fine.

—No, I am. Really.

*(She gets that gooey soft look girls get when they're making up after a fight.)*

ZOE: —I'm sorry too.

—No, I am. No, I am. No, I am.

—Baby...Really?!

*(Giggles.)*

—Yes. Yes. Uh huh. Uh huh.

—After seventh period.—

—You're a goofball. No you are. No you are. No you are.

*(Giggles.)*

—Love you too.

*(Little silence.)*

ZOE: I can't go to the Prom with you.

ADAM: Right. Fine.

ZOE: I'm *sorry*.

ADAM: How did he get the number to this room.

ZOE: Ch. It's posted in the front office.

ADAM: *(Coldly.)* It's called the faculty room for a reason. Student calls are inappropriate.

ZOE: Tss. I think I can recall a time when you weren't so strict about the rules of the faculty room.

ADAM: Things change.

ZOE: I said the exact same thing to Carver a little while ago.

*(She resumes making Valentines.)*

ADAM: *(Quiet.)* I miss you.

ZOE: I don't even know what that means.

ADAM: Well, things are gonna keep changing, Zoe, I can assure you of that. You and your boyfriend can't live in Shangri-la forever.

ZOE: That's what you think.

ADAM: Something's going to give.

*(Adam exits. Zoe makes Valentines.)*

*(P.A. System clicks on.)*

P.A. SYSTEM: *(Sound of coffee percolating.)*

*(Sound of someone drinking coffee, then saying "ahhh!")*

Study Hall will begin in five minutes.

ZOE: Principal Dennis?

P.A. SYSTEM: Hmm? Who's that?

ZOE: Zoe Bartholemhew in the Faculty Room, Principal Dennis.

P.A. SYSTEM: Well how the heck are you, Miss Bartholemhew.

ZOE: Pretty good.

I wanted to ask you a question—

You used to teach here, before you were principal…

P.A. SYSTEM: Oh, sure I did, absolutely…course that was, you know, before the *Civil War…(Laughter.)*

ZOE: *(Laughter.)*

P.A. SYSTEM: Ha, ha ha.

ZOE: Do you, um, remember me as a student?

P.A. SYSTEM: Sure I do, Sure I do.

*(Pause.)*

P.A. SYSTEM: Was there anything else, Miss Bartholemhew?

ZOE: I just wanted to know if teaching ever

Well did teaching ever—

Does teaching high school—and you know, Madison-Feurey's sort of off the main drag—

And, and kind of isolated—did teaching ever make you feel lonely?

*(Little pause.)*

ZOE: Because sometimes I think—I believe that people here, basically want to be lifted up, at least I know that I want to feel more, more—

And you need help to get there, it's not something you can do all by yourself—

Do you understand what I mean?

Principal Dennis?

Sir?

*(Silence.)*

*(Blackout.)*


SCENE SEVEN
MARCH

*A banner is up on the wall. It reads: SPIRIT DAYS ARE AROUND THE CORNER!*
*Zoe and Carver "act."*


ZOE: *It's about an abiding belief in God.*

CARVER: *That is what you say it's about. It might be something else entirely.*

ZOE: *Why don't you trust me?*

CARVER: *Because of your behavior.*

ZOE: *What have I done that you haven't done. Or wanted to do.*

CARVER: *Maybe I'm not strong enough. It's not just about—*

ZOE: *Belief. Faith. Love.*

CARVER: *I can't accept that.*

ZOE: *Craver, When the fire comes, you'll have a greater understanding of the Wrath of the Lamb. When the rain comes, you'll be closer to forgiveness.*

CARVER: *Am I awake?*

ZOE: *(Breaking.)* No—no—you skipped a part. Darby wrote a *huge* monologue for your character. It's her play. Respect it.

*(Carver returns to a previous moment.)*

CARVER: *Maybe I'm not strong enough. It's not just about belief. Faith. Love.*

*(She laughs. Carver stops.)*

CARVER: This is ridiculous. Forget it.

*(He tosses down the manuscript of the "play.")*

ZOE: It's pretty funny that your character's name is "Craver."

CARVER: It doesn't mean it's me.

ZOE: It's an anagram of your name, it's very clever. Carver, Craver.

CARVER: How long has she been writing this?

ZOE: I don't know, a few weeks, a month.

CARVER: You and Adam knew all this time. When were you going to tell me?

ZOE: I am telling you.

CARVER: This writing is incredibly disturbing.

ZOE: I told you as literature it stunk.

CARVER: I'm not talking about the style, it's the content…it gets very *violent* and frankly it feels like a documentary film…she writes about her parents stabbing each other with scissors and then praying…

ZOE: Along with all the smiting and smoting.

CARVER: *(Flipping through the pages.)* And the group of Believers seems so sad all the time.

They think they're going to *perform* this on the Spirit Days program!?

ZOE: Adam gave them permission.

CARVER: That is not his call! Spirit Days is mine!

ZOE: Well once a permission slip is signed, forget it. It's like a parking ticket. That play is happening. They're rehearsing it right now.

CARVER: God dammit. Everyone wants to sabotage my plans! First Mrs. Lund, now you!

ZOE: Hey, I don't want to sabotage anything, "Craver," I'm just showing you the script that's gonna be performed.

*(Carver gets on the phone.)*

CARVER: —Melanie, can you pull the class schedule for Darby Weider?
—Yeah.

—I want to know where she is right now.

ZOE: *(Simultaneously.)*
I told you they're rehearsing
on the quad.

—She has a free period?

—Where is she next period then.

—Okay. Thanks.

*(He hangs up.)*

*(Zoe's pager goes off. She looks at it, turns it upside down, gets it, smiles.)*

ZOE: Read it upside down—never mind.

*(Carver puts his head in his hands.)*

CARVER: I give up.

ZOE: What do you mean you give up?

CARVER: Clearly it's more relaxing on the other side. Wherever you are. The place you live, in the Land of Lost Judgment.

ZOE: I live in heaven.

CARVER: You are so...flip. I'm tired of feeling *outraged* all the time. Do you know how exhausting that is? There's more to me, only I've *forgotten* what it was. I used to play chess. I used to go antiquing. Lately all I can do is breathe. That's my hobby. I took this job for a reason, breathe in, I'm here for a reason, breathe out. Every day I wake up and I think, oh God, what has she done now? I think, the phone call's coming today. I should detach. But I can't. *(He breathes in, breathes out.)* I'm going to go and get Darby, and talk about her play, and I'm going to ask what's really going on once and for—*oh my God.*

*(...because Zoe has pushed up her sleeves to reveal her long scars; he's noticed them.)*

ZOE: —Don't be weird.

*(Carver holds her arm outstretched, examines it. He takes an audible deep breath.)*

CARVER: How long have you been doing this.

ZOE: A few months, I don't know.

*(Carver breathes in, breathes out. Thinks of something to say.)*

CARVER: Does it help?

ZOE: A little.

It provides a kind of, uh, sharp focus. You know I'm trying to do my best.

*(Adam bangs open the door. He's flying on Ecstasy.)*

ADAM: I feel like something wonderful is going to happen. I feel lighter than smoke. This cigarette tastes sublime. You should see how well the play rehearsal's going out there, my friends, it's going to put the "It" back into Spirit Days.

CARVER: Well the "play" wasn't approved for the program. Thanks a lot!

ADAM: I think Darby wanted to keep it a surprise. Come on, it's an utterly colorless day and the students are making Art. I say Bravo.

CARVER: You should have talked to me about this script earlier.

ADAM: Can I touch your hair?

*(Little pause.)*

ADAM: I don't *have* to touch your hair. It just looked soft in this glorious fluorescent light. It's cool. It's all cool cool cool. Coooool. May I tell you something personal?

CARVER: Okay…

ADAM: This is important. I'm concerned that you may not listen to me, and that's okay. I'd prefer that you did listen to me, but I'm also going to love you just the same if you don't. Here's the thing: Jen Carlson is not really my girlfriend. That is to say, I give Jen a ride home on some afternoons, and I have on occasion kept her after school doing various useless activities, and I do believe that her peaches-and-cream complexion is the eighth wonder of the world…but she is not…technically…my girlfriend. I have not known her *biblically*. I haven't kissed her, I haven't copped a feel, I haven't gotten a blowjob, I haven't even touched her skin. I may have placed a hand on her shoulder, but if it happened, it was inadvertent. It's a charade. But I've led Zoe to believe that Jen is my girlfriend. I've led Zoe to believe that I've had many Madison-Feurey High girlfriends, but none of it has been true.

*(Deep breath.)*

Something wonderful is going to happen, and soon. Have you ever felt that way? It's in the air. An early spring. You think that's possible?

ZOE: No.

CARVER: Adam. You seem…

ADAM: I'm wonderful.

I just wanted to tell you something personal. Something true.

*(He pats Carver's head.)*

ZOE: Liar.

ADAM: I was lying *before*, Zoe, don't miss the point of my revelation.

ZOE: Right. Whatever.

ADAM: Let's not talk about this anymore—I've told you what I wanted to tell you. And it makes me feel warmly towards you both. Not in a sexual way.

CARVER: Fine. I mean—

ZOE: Carver let it be.

ADAM: I scored some E from Loren Elliot. Loren gave me a really good deal—Zoe, you were right about Glenn, he *was* ripping me off. But Loren has fantastic goods, and he is a wonderful, wonderful kid. Just a very special person, you know?

CARVER: Come on.

ADAM: Loren and I took E together, and it was magnificent! It feels so good to be with both of you right now. Zoe, you're glowing, you know that? You're looking very healthy, very robust—actually you look fat.

CARVER: Adam—

ADAM: Shh it's okay, Carver, let's be honest, she looks *fat*—you look fat, but in a good way. Still pretty.

ZOE: Your girlfriend smells. Bad.

ADAM: I don't think you were listening: Jen Carlson is *not* my girlfriend—

ZOE: *(Tightly.)* Whoever she is, you should have a talk with her because she comes to class late and she smells *terrible* and the other kids are talking about her. She needs a bath.

ADAM: She smells because she's throwing up her breakfast and her lunch in the bathroom stalls and it's hard to lose that smell. She's trying to get very, very thin. She's trying to make herself disappear. You know why? Because she loves this boy in her class and *HE'S FUCKING HER TEACHER.* She thinks that if she gets thinner, maybe he'll love her again.

ZOE: Well someone should tell her that losing weight that way isn't an answer.

ADAM: Yeah, look at *you!* I mean, that's what Raphael likes, right? *Fat!*

CARVER: Both of you: *stop* going back and forth! Would you *listen* to yourselves!

ADAM: I am listening. I feel like something wonderful could happen, I really do. I can see the Rapture from here, and it is so beautiful.

ZOE: After you've talked for *years* about Beth Fisher, Chrissy Cornwall, Samantha Prado, Stephie Sommers, the "experiment" with Sterling Mills—you are full of shit, sweetheart.

I am inside of something so pure you can't even see it. I have waited my whole life to be loved like this. Raphael Gilberto is who I was made for. Every weekend all I do is eat. Pringles, Hershey's Kisses, Ben & Jerry's, Domino's double crust. All I do is watch movies where things explode. All I do is listen to music that splits my head wide open. All I do is touch his skin, the most perfect skin, unblemished, clean, with a smell like—like nothing else. He's not my boyfriend. He's *me.* We're soul mates. He is *why I exist.* Get it.

*(Bill enters holding a pistol from Morning Checkpoints. Adam grabs Bill by the shoulders.)*

ADAM: Bill! If I gave you a knife, would you cut my head open? Maybe not a knife, a machete. Not because I have a death wish, or a thing for violence, because I don't. But if my head were opened up, something wonderful could spring out. Something or someone glorious. A daughter. That's how Zeus had Athena. Goddess of wisdom. He had a headache, they sliced his head open, and out she flew. You think you could try something like that with me? Whadda you say.

*(Adam takes a marker and draws a dotted line across his forehead.)*

Right here.

*(Bill just stands there.)*

Blah, blah, blah, Bill, give someone else a word.

*(Adam grabs the pistol from Bill, opens chamber.)*

*Someone* was careless about ammo check! One left over!

*(He spins the chamber, places the barrel under his chin.)*

God, I feel *wonderful.*

*(He pulls the trigger. Click. He looks at the gun.)*

My only wish is that the Rapture would hurry the fuck up, because I'm not at all tired. I'm awake. I am as alert as a goddamn soldier.

*(Bell rings.)*

*(Everyone freezes, listening.)*


SCENE EIGHT
MARCH

*Warning bells. Distress signals.*

*A cacophony of noise outside the faculty room. Faraway gunfire, a mob of students running by, banging on lockers, breaking windows, throwing chairs. Whooping. Screaming. Voices through a megaphone in the distance. Sirens. Stray P.A. sound effects.*

*Another hoard runs by, hammering on lockers and the faculty room door, but the door doesn't open and they keep running until another door slams somewhere in the distance.*

*Adam and Carver are in the faculty room. They are both fairly wet.*

*The P.A. System clicks on. We can only hear something like every fifth word.*

P.A. SYSTEM: *(Static.)*

Everybody— ~~This is~~ Principal ~~Dennis speaking.~~

~~Please remain~~ calm. ~~The authorities have~~ surrounded ~~the buildings, and I know that no one wants to see anything~~ escalate. ~~I~~ know ~~we all~~ love ~~Madison~~-Feurey ~~High~~ and…

I'll ~~just~~ wait ~~until I have~~ everyone's attention.

*(Static.)*

*(P.A. System clicks off.)*

*(Carver stands close to the P.A. System and calls into it.)*

CARVER: Hello? Principal Dennis, HELLO!?

*(No answer. Carver tries to move furniture against the door as a barricade.)*

CARVER: Okay Adam HELP me!

ADAM: You think that's going to make a difference?

CARVER: YES. I DO. AND I NEED YOU TO HELP.

*(As they move furniture together:)*

ADAM: Carver. What if everybody is awake already?

CARVER: JUST FOCUS AND MOVE THE COUCH.

ADAM: What if the Rapture happened before we were born, before our parents or their parents were born?

*(Sound of shooting outside.)*

ADAM: Maybe it doesn't matter whether we're *awake*. Or *not*.

You just have to *do* Good. And the problem is: what's Good?

*(The barricade is complete.)*

CARVER: You— You do your best.

ADAM: But what if your "best" isn't *Good?* But it's still your best?

*(The phone rings. Carver runs for it.)*

CARVER: —Yes! Hello!

—Darby!

—Darby, this not a healthy way to achieve your goals!

*(Beat; to Adam.)*

She's speaking in tongues now.

*(He hangs up.)*

*(Footsteps running down the hall.)*

*(Banging on the door.)*

CARVER: YOU STAY OUT! GO AWAY! YOU HAVE NO BUSINESS HERE!

ZOE: *(Outside door.)* GODDAMMIT CARVER IT'S ME! OPEN THE DOOR!

*(Adam helps Carver move the couch somewhat away from the door. Zoe enters, climbing over/past the couch. Zoe is also wet.)*

ZOE: They are trying to arrest *every* kid out there! It's impossible to tell if anyone's in *charge.* It's fucking *mayhem* and the police are making it worse!

ADAM: Of course they are! Because something powerful is happening that they don't understand!

CARVER: What. Play rehearsal. Group prayer. *Lightning! Shooting!* Do *you* understand that?!

ADAM: Maybe.

ZOE: Darby wouldn't stop pointing. And praying.

CARVER: She just *called* here.

ZOE: They think she's armed.

CARVER: We confiscate every weapon, every day. There's a system.

ADAM: *(Pacing.)* They all kept rehearsing in the rain.

ZOE: *(Shaky.) Jen* had a gun, she—she fucking *aimed* it at me. Right at my face.

And then she started crying and she dropped it, and I ran. I just—ran.

CARVER: Oh my God.

ADAM: *(To Carver.)* Darby was pointing at you.

CARVER: FUCK YOU! AND FUCK YOUR BOOK GROUP!

ADAM: You know I thought everything we read would have prepared me for this. I thought I'd be ready.

CARVER: Those are police out there, not *angels.*

ADAM: But what if. *What if.*

*(The phone rings. Rings. Zoe picks it up.)*

ZOE: Hello who is this. *Hello.*

*(She taps the hang up button in frustration.)*

—Nobody there.

*(She hangs up.)*

CARVER: No one's going to help us.

*(Faraway gunfire.)*

ZOE: I never thought a student would point at—would *aim*—

*(Chanting/singing from far away.)*

*(Adam cracks open the door. They listen.)*

CARVER: They're singing my school anthem.

*(Adam shuts the door again.)*

*(Sound of GIANT thunder crack, rain.)*

*(The lights flicker; quite a few go out. Emergency lighting.)*

*(Little pause.)*

ADAM: This is like Campfire Girls.

CARVER: Shut *up!*

*(More rain.)*

ADAM: Zoe and I got married on a rainy Thursday afternoon just like this one. And the next day she still turned in her homework on time.

*(Little pause.)*

CARVER: What did you just say.

ADAM: I kept all her papers. Still have 'em.

*(Faraway gunfire.)*

CARVER: Tell me what you just said.

ADAM: I wanted to wait. I wanted to wait and I couldn't because, because, I don't know why. It was stupid—it was *idiotic* but it *wasn't* because I loved her.

ZOE: I knew.

CARVER: *(To Zoe.)* You were his student.

ADAM: One afternoon she walked into my homeroom and she said: "I know you love me."

ZOE: I was fifteen.

ADAM: My heart stopped. I couldn't breathe.

CARVER: *(To Adam.)* You were her teacher.

ZOE: When I looked at him I *knew.*

ADAM: In that moment, I believed in God, I was the infidel who became a believer.

*(Faraway gunfire.)*

ZOE: He *saw* me. He looked at me like birds were going to fly out of my hair. I'm supposed to say "no?" What would "no" get me? Nothing. I said: *yes.*

ADAM: What did I tell you.

ZOE: You said I was going to break your heart. You said that was how it worked.

ADAM: I said that. I'm pretty smart. I'm pretty stupid.

*(Gunfire, suddenly very close.)*

ZOE: *(To Adam.)* I don't love you anymore.

CARVER: I don't want to die. I don't want to die in here.

ADAM: *(To Zoe.)* I know.

ZOE: I'm sorry.

ADAM: I know.

Ah, fuck. My head feels so strange. There was this long burst of color and clarity and I understood everything and I liked everybody and I believed in God.

I want to be Awake. I want to do something Good.

*(Glass breaking in the distance; shouting.)*

ADAM: How come you're crying.

ZOE: I don't know where he is.

ADAM: I'll find him. I can do that. I'll find him for you.

It probably stopped raining.

*(Adam exits.)*

ZOE: I tried to stop loving him. Raphael. I did try.

I know you think I'm—sick.

CARVER: You don't know what I think.

*(More sounds of gunfire, voices through a megaphone.)*

ZOE: I should have told you before. About me and Adam.

ZOE: *(Cont'd.)* I just— it *upset* me when you wouldn't admit what had happened at your old school.

CARVER: *Nothing happened.*

*(Little pause.)*

ZOE: BULLSHIT. BULLSHIT, CARVER! DON'T YOU DARE GET FUCKING HOLIER THAN THOU. YOU WERE IN LOVE. WITH YOUR STUDENT. FUCK YOU FOR PRETENDING! EVEN NOW.

CARVER: *Love* him?! Love Sam?! He was an *annoyance.* He jeopardized my— everything. He fucked up my career.

I wanted to do good things, really good things. My first classroom. Then: the letters. The unceasing letters. Messages on chalkboards. All about me. I had to erase the board at the beginning of every class, every day. I called his parents. I filed a report with the district. The response? I should be able to *handle* a "crush."

So. I met with Sam. He brought me roses.

I told him that his behavior was inappropriate. I said he was in danger of being expelled. Sam said fine, great, perfect: then we could be together. He tried to kiss me. He said we were "soul mates." And something rose up in me.

And I said:

"Sam. This all has to stop.

I don't love you.

I don't *like* you.

You don't matter to me. You don't matter."

And Sam—backed away. He said "okay." He walked out and I breathed a sigh of relief. I did it! I would have my classroom back. I would have my life back. Later that night, he bought gasoline and...you know the rest.

I wasn't afraid to love him. I really didn't. Love him. I was his teacher, and I showed exactly how much I cared. Not at all.

*(Emergency lights flicker up—the regular lights return. The door begins to open.)*

ZOE: WHO IS THAT.

*(In walks Bill. He carries an umbrella. He is not wet. He shakes the water off the umbrella and closes it.)*

BILL: I believe you should know about the event I witnessed a moment ago. I was crouched down behind the statue of Dolly Madison. From my low vantage point, I saw our colleague Mr. Younger emerge atop the roof of the sciences building. The glare of the sun made it difficult to see. His arms were outstretched. He was empty-handed, quite still. There was some calling through a megaphone. I don't think he heard; at least he gave no indication that he did so. He seemed to be searching for something in the sky. Then there was a hailstorm of bullets; I ducked low again, and when I looked up, Mr. Younger was gone.

CARVER: He...fell.

BILL: No.

CARVER: What do you mean "no."

ZOE: He was shot.

BILL: No body. No sign of him anywhere. Not on the roof, not on the ground. One moment he was standing staring up at the sky; the next, he may as well have been absorbed into the sun.

CARVER: Adam...*disappeared?*

ZOE: People don't disappear, pfft.

BILL: I thought that, as well. Nonetheless. I saw what I saw. Excuse me.

*(Bill goes to the phone, dials.)*

BILL: Principal Dennis. Bill Dunn here.

—Because I don't *want* to use the P.A. System, Robert.

—I'm calling to tender my resignation.

—Effective immediately.

—Because I always said that I would do so when I saw a miracle.

—Yes, just now.

—You too, Robert. My best to Karen.

*(Bill hangs up; readies himself to exit.)*

ZOE: Bill. You...*talk.*

BILL: When I have something to say.

—There are a number of officers just outside holding a student at gunpoint. Apparently he'd been attempting to break into this building.

ZOE: Who.

BILL: Raphael Gilberto.

*(Gunfire in the distance. Zoe starts to race out.)*

BILL: Wait!

*(Bill gives her his umbrella.)*

BILL: Here.

*(She exits. Carver calls after her.)*

CARVER: Zoe—Zoe, don't—!

What is she *doing.*

BILL: We all do our best.

*(Bill opens his briefcase and tosses Carver another identical umbrella from his briefcase. Bill exits.)*

*(Carver looks at the umbrella, drops it, runs out the door.)*

*(Almost immediately: sound of gun shots, very close.)*

*(Several deliberate shots: BLAM. BLAM. BLAM. BLAM.)*

*(A moment of total quiet.)*

*(Then: an ambulance siren.)*


SCENE NINE
MARCH


*Carver sits at the table, pale. He holds an unlit cigarette.*

*The school is eerily silent. There is the abrupt sound of several people running down the hall...then it's quiet again.*

*A knock at the door. Slowly, it's pushed open. A Student stands in the door, unsure of what to do. Judging from the Student's size and demeanor, s/he's in ninth grade.*

STUDENT: Mr. Durand? Hey.

Wow. I've never been in here before. I always wondered what it looked like. "The Inner Sanctum." Ha ha.

*(Carver doesn't respond.)*

*(The Student wanders tentatively around, checking things out.)*

STUDENT : I mean…you know, the faculty room. "Oooh, don't go in there." Ha ha.

There are, um, you know, some people out there. Looking for you. You probably know that. I just thought I'd, ah, come in and tell you.

CARVER: Thank you. *(With some effort.)*

What grade are you in?

STUDENT: Uh, I'm a freshman.

*(A little awed.)*

There's camera crews out there and everything.

CARVER: Are you in my homeroom?

STUDENT: Uh no, I have Mrs. Lund.

*(Carver stares into space.)*

*(The Student looks around some more, spies the giant Cardinal head.)*

STUDENT: Oh my God, that *head* is still here…I remember that mascot from when my brother went to school here, and he graduated, like, a *long* time ago. Man. Why would you guys even keep that thing?

*(Realizing.)*

Wow, it is really, seriously ugly in here. I mean *ugly*.

CARVER: That's true. It is.

STUDENT: You guys need some light in here. It's ridiculous.

*(Carver has begun to cry. The Student notices.)*

STUDENT: Oh, oh, hey, I didn't mean to—I mean, it's ugly, but it can be fixed, probably. Don't worry, Mr. Durand. I mean, it's bad in here, but it isn't your fault. Right? I mean you can't have light with no windows. It's not your fault.

*(Carver keeps crying, his face in his hands. The Student approaches him.)*

STUDENT: It's okay, Mr. Durand.

*(Standing behind Carver, the Student places a hand on his shoulder as he cries.)*

STUDENT: Everything is going to be okay.

P.A. SYSTEM: *(Flapping of wings.)*

### END OF PLAY

# Slide Glide the Slippery Slope
## by Kia Corthron

# BIOGRAPHY

Kia Corthron's play *Slide Glide the Slippery Slope*, commissioned by The Mark Taper Forum, was produced by the Taper in June. In February 2003, Alabama Shakespeare Festival produced the world premiere of *The Venus de Milo Is Armed*. Other plays include *Breath, Boom*, produced by London's Royal Court Theatre, Playwrights Horizons, Yale Repertory and the Huntington Theatre, *Force Continuum* (Atlantic Theater Company), *Splash Hatch on the E Going Down* (New York Stage and Film, Center Stage, Yale Repertory, London's Donmar Warehouse), *Seeking the Genesis* (Goodman Theatre, Manhattan Theatre Club), *Digging Eleven* (Hartford Stage), and *Come Down Burning* (American Place, Long Wharf). She has been awarded the Daryl Roth Creative Spirit Award, the Taper's Fadiman Award, NEA/TCG, Kennedy Center Fund and the Callaway Award. Her play *Snapshot Silhouette* will premiere at the Children's Theatre Company in March, 2004, and *Light Raise the Roof* will premiere at New York Theatre Workshop in May, 2004. She is a member of New Dramatists.

# HUMANA FESTIVAL PRODUCTION

*Slide Glide the Slippery Slope* premiered at the Humana Festival of New American Plays in March 2003. It was directed by Valerie Curtis-Newton with the following cast:

| | |
|---|---|
| Erm | Tonye Patano |
| Elo | Cheryl Freeman |
| Retta | Shona Tucker |
| Sear | Dyron Holmes |
| Rosie | Bobbi Lynne Scott |
| Dell | Lizan Mitchell |

and the following production staff:

| | |
|---|---|
| Scenic Designer | Paul Owen |
| Costume Designer | Rondi Hillstrom Davis |
| Lighting Designer | Tony Penna |
| Sound Designer | Bray Poor |
| Properties Designer | Doc Manning |
| Stage Manager | Cat Domiano |
| Dramaturg | Tanya Palmer |
| Assistant Dramaturg | Susannah Engstrom |
| Casting | Orpheus Group Casting |

# CHARACTERS

ERM, rhymes with "term," a 36-year-old woman
ELO, rhymes with "mellow," Erm's identical twin
RETTA, Erm's adopted sister, 40
SEAR, Erm's son, 13
ROSIE, Elo's daughter, 10
DELL, 51
A NURSE, may double with DELL

All are black. Also, cameo appearances by The Sheep—white like Dolly—and a Stuffed Animal. Works best if The Sheep looks as real as possible.

The identical twin casting issue should neither be something to get too hung up on nor something to casually dismiss. I once saw an off-off-Broadway production (no budget) with identical twins as characters. In costume, the actresses looked identical. In life, nothing alike: one woman about four inches taller than the other.

# SETTING
The basic playing area is the living room of Erm's farmhouse—besides the couch, table, etc. are a computer and shelves jam-packed with all manner of books and magazines—with a few jaunts elsewhere that would best be represented simply, as by lighting.

# TIME
The present

*Slide Glide the Slippery Slope* was
Originally Commissioned by
Center Theatre Group/Mark Taper Forum
Gordon Davidson, Artistic Director
Los Angeles, CA

Lizan Mitchell, Tonye Patano, and Cheryl Freeman
in *Slide Glide the Slippery Slope*

27th Annual Humana Festival of New American Plays
Actors Theatre of Louisville, 2003
photo by John Fitzgerald

# Slide Glide the Slippery Slope

ACT ONE
SCENE ONE

> *Darkness. Now the light of a computer screen. Erm rapidly tapping the keys.*
> *Then, huge barnyard chatter: cow mooing, chickens clucking, pigs oinking,*
> *ducks quacking, sheep bleating. Lights up to a level indicating dawn. For just*
> *a moment, the faces of the complaining animals at the windows.*

ERM: SHUT IT!

> *(Instantly animals disappear; silence. Erm shuts off the computer.)*

ERM: Virgin birth!

> *(Erm moves to a light indicating the outside. She tosses feed to chickens; audi-*
> *ence doesn't see them but hears them cluck happily.)*

ERM: Ain't even daybreak and complaints, complaints. You'll get fed! I ever
missed a day? You know I gotta keep up, get the web updates latest on my
ol' friend Dolly. Poor friend Dolly.

> *(Another part of the stage: Erm collects eggs from a chicken coop. Chickens*
> *still clucking.)*

ERM: See these beauts? You laid 'em. And not a rooster in sight, otherwise my
scrambled eggs be some bloody mess. Virgin birth that's what she was ol'
Dolly Sheep. Dolly's cells froze from a sheep died 'fore Dolly conceived.
Her mama coulda been a slut but this *particular* birth: asexual. They enu-
cleate an egg—ain't really enucleated, disappearin' nucleus just a regular
stage a sex cell division YOU LISTENIN', RED? *(The clucking dies*
*down.)* Chromosomes just a swimmin', swimmin', everybody in that
nucleus just waitin' for spermy to wiggle by. *But!* Surprise, take that kary-
oplast, nucleus from somewhere else, stick it in the *(Fingers the quote*
*marks.)* "enucleated" egg. Like takin' the yoke outa a sunny side up and
stickin' in the yoke of a *better* sunny side up. Here's the clincher: give that
manipulated egg an electric shock, make it *think* it's fertilized… and it is!
Who knows? Some women prefer vibrator to the real thing. *(Guffaws.*
*Then serious, to a chicken.)* What? Filthy mouth? Maybe I am, I *do* read a
few things besides *Science* and *Nature* and *The New England Journal of*
*Medicine.*

> *(Another part of the stage: Cow is just off; audience only sees her udders. Erm*
> *goes to it.)*

ERM: You got Texas cousins made that way, prize cattle. *(Cow moos.)* But here's where *she* come from, my Dolly. Mammaries—well who you think they name her after? C'mon! Who got the winnin' ticket in booby traps? *(Chuckles.)* Clue: she sings. Country. Dang scientists! Ain't they a sensa humor? White male scientists ain't they sexist pigs? *(Distant roll of thunder. Looks up at the sky:)* Knew that heavy grey wouldn't be holdin' it too much longer.

*(Erm brings milk and eggs into the house. A Sheep looks at her. Erm puts food away.)*

ERM: Hey, didn't I tell you 'bout comin' inside, poopy sheep? *(The Sheep bleats.)* Sure, you always have a good excuse. Well, whatchu got to say for yourself? 'twas your species set the world in a tailspin few years back. And gone fast, ol' Dolly aged at an accelerated rate, arthritis at five and a half, finally the scientists took her before the lung cancer could, any thoughts on the matter? *(The Sheep bleats.)* Come on! Everyone say "stupid sheep" but I say you got somethin' on the brain, here's what's on mine: commonly ya hear discussion on the clone a Einstein clone a Hitler clone a Marilyn Monroe, but how come not much talk a bringin' back black people? Lemme do it! Blink and there he is, ten of him, fifty, glasses and pointed finger— *(Rips open her buttoned shirt.)* "Let's clone Malcolm X!"

*(Her T-shirt revealed: the famous picture of Malcolm X with pointed finger and the words "Let's Clone Malcolm X." Erm rolls on the floor laughing.)*

THE SHEEP: Cloning from embryos came easy but what would be the fun in cloning Malcolm X's embryo *before* he was Malcolm X when all we would have known about his embryo was that it was human? And how could we clone a whole Malcolm from an adult cell, or bone cell, or brain cell, or skin? G-nought hibernation! During mitosis cells go into it, becoming like early embryo cells, no specialization: ready for any calling, ready to recreate the entire being.

*(Beat. Then Erm grins.)*

ERM: *Some*body 'round here payin' attention.

*(Sound of car parking outside. Erm is startled. Footsteps to the door and a knock. The Sheep bleats and exits. Erm walks to the door, opens.)*

ELO: Erm?

*(Erm stares at her.)*

ELO: I'm Elo. *(Silence.)* I emailed you I was comin'. *(Silence.)* I'm your twin. *(Silence.)* Can I come in?

*(Erm steps back, lets Elo enter.)*

ELO: You knew I was comin', right? I emailed you I was comin'.

ERM: I delete junk email.

ELO: Oh.

ERM: 'f I don't recognize the source.

ELO: Oh. *(Beat.)* But you know about me. Right? You gotta know about me I known about you thirty-six years. Or thirty-five eleven months we got a celebration comin' up couple weeks, right? Whatchu thinka that? thirty-six. Fast glide to forty huh Sure smells like a farm 'round here.

ERM: *(Mutters.)* Dang sheep. *(Cleans up the poop.)*

ELO: We live here now. You know that, right? I grew up Chicago but our mother from here. Well, town. Thirty miles away. Now we back. You like my country cousin 'cept you my sister. *(Chuckles.)* You like it here? Middle a no place? Country people always sayin' the city so scary but tell ya what, some psycho with a hatchet come out these woods, scream your brains out no one to hear, like that thing: tree in the forest falls *(Silently mouths "no sound." Silence.)* You know the story, right? Our mother fifteen, couldn't handle no twins. Handle *one*, not two—

ERM: Why you here?

ELO: Meet my sister! ain't that reason? And our mother, here's the invitation, she like you come see her. *And* I have some very good news, very pleasant surprise I guarantee you be happy I strolled by.

ERM: How long you been livin' here?

ELO: Hmmmm. Well. Guess we came—

ERM: A year.

ELO: You know! For a second I's afraid you think I'm a crazy woman, but how couldja doubt me? Look at me you lookin' the mirror.

ERM: Took you a year find me?

ELO: You knew I was back! didn't see ya searchin' for me.

ERM: Had no intention searchin' for you.

ELO: Flesh and blood!

ERM: Might be my flesh and blood but ain't my family. My sister in town, said she heard you moved back, 'm I curious? "No! and don't you go snoopin' around neither." Don't tell me you moved two thousand miles lookin' for me but took a year to trek last thirty.

ELO: I ain't abandoned ya! Okay? if that's chippin' your shoulder I wa'n't nothin' but six months old, same as you when we split. F-Y-I she been beggin' me come with her for ages, move out here, year ago I finally say okay *Sister? (No answer.)* You mean that little girl, that sick little girl?

ERM: Whatta you know about it? Baby when you and her left.

ELO: I know that's why she took you in, our mother tell me, woman took you in got a sickle cell secret and fear to have any more her own. After her little girl spent alla her four years in and out the hospital. Well. Guess she ain't a little girl no more, we almost thirty-six, guess she forty. So our mother drag me back to her hometown, she know where you are but every time I ask "When you goin'?" she change the subject fast, a major feat since that's all the subject ever is, "Erma Erma Erma" her every other word but she don't know the definition. Today I find out the definition.

ERM: Erm.

ELO: I know, saw it on your mailbox. Didn't I address ya the diminutive when ya answered the door?

*(Beat.)*

ERM: So?

ELO: Definition? *(Erm nods. Elo shrugs, looks around.)* Keeps a neat house. Independent. Reads.

*(Erm waits for more. None comes.)*

ERM: Okay you found out whatchu need, you can go.

ELO: *(As if continuing her adjectival list:)* Rude.

ERM: How?

ELO: Ain't even offered me a cuppa coffee? jeez. And we city got the rep for unfriendly. And did I mention I got a surprise you be thrilled to unwrap?

ERM: You lucky I keep it for my sister otherwise be no coffee this house, I'm a milk drinker tolerate nobody's coffee. How you like your eggs?

ELO: Over easy, thank you.

ERM: Don't ask 'bout no bacon neither, this a vegetarian establishment. *(Starts toward kitchen.)*

ELO: "Found what I need" I ain't scratched the surface a that I need.

ERM: What, kidney transplant? *(Exits to kitchen.)*

ELO: What you been doin' last thirty-six, and I share the plenty I got to impart to you. Start at the beginnin', here's how our mother tell it, correct me you been informed different. Fifteen she was, couldn't handle no twins. Us cryin', her cryin', after she nicked her wrists to pieces cuz no one told her how to do it, not even enough blood her mother take her to the hospital the Nosy Neighbor step in. Took me years find out her real name, woman took you in, all our mother say "Nosy Neighbor." Musta spied our mother on the backyard swings with her bandaged wrists, or maybe our baby-hollerin' all the time I dunno, but here she come, talk 'bout "the authorities." "The authorities" a course is a terrifyin' word "Well you obviously too young take care a those twins." Our mother got a answer "Maybe you take one?" Probably just smartassin', didn't expect be took up on it. But guess Nosy Neighbor also too young for twins cuz she never ask complete her set.

*(Erm returns with coffee, eggs and toast for Elo; milk, eggs and toast for herself.)*

ERM: 'preciate you stop callin' her that.

ELO: Sorry. Then I grow up, school, learn to read, couldn't wait cuz now me and the library's best friends. You ever read up on 'em? identicals? Fascinatin'!

ERM: I know about twins.

ELO: You hearda the Jims a Ohio?

ERM: I know about twins.

ELO: These identical Jims, separated at babies, their wives had the same name, their kids. Uh... they didn't like baseball—

ERM: Jim Lewis and Jim Springer were identical twins, separated when they were a little more than a month old. They grew up eighty miles from each other in Ohio but never met 'til thirty-seven. At which point they discovered the following stuff and all of it happened before their meetin': they both drank Miller Lite, chain-smoked Salems, drove Chevies, loved sports particularly stock-car racing but didn't care for baseball. They each had once worked as a sheriff's deputy and each loved woodworking. They were romantic, each with a habit of leavin' love notes around the house for his wife. This was their second wife, they'd each married a Linda, divorced her and married a Betty. Each had a son named James Alan and a dog named Toy. I gotta finish my chores. *(Exits, leaving the front door open.)*

ELO: Amazin'! Separated as babies, meet as grown-ups and find out the eeriest commonness. Like the two Englishwomen who did this *(Wrinkles her upper lip to push up her nose.)* and each called it the same made-up word: "squidging." Like the Jew who grew up in Trinidad, moved to Israel, his twin raised a Nazi Hitler youth Germany, find out each would always flush the toilet *before* he used it! Like the American middle-aged women discover when they was both teenagers they had the same nightmare: bein' suffocated by their mouths with doorknobs, needles, fishhooks same body! Same mind! And I think about you, *my* weird sister, and wonder if you, *my* clone, might be thinkin' 'bout me.

*(Erm enters with a suitcase. Tied to it is a raggedy stuffed animal.)*

ERM: *Hey!*

ELO: I was passin' through! I ain't asked nothin' a you, I just wanted to meetcha *and* whatchu doin' snoopin' my car?

ERM: My property!

ELO: You didn't have no more chores! You just nosin' through my things!

ERM: Aintchu quick you musta inherited that from me.

*(Elo snatches the suitcase, holds it—the stuffed animal especially—close, protective.)*

ELO: *(Not looking at Erm.)* I had a great surprise I just stopped by to tell ya, meetcha.

ERM: I keep hearin' tell of this enormously fabulous surprise but no magician seem to snatch it out his hat yet.

*(Elo pulls out a check, hands it to Erm. Erm reads it, stunned.)*

ELO: Our father weren't anything more to me than he was to you, first time I see his face is the coffin. Prior to this, now and again she mutter somethin' about train conductor, every time I Amtrak I search faces for someone look like me, us: no one. Or everyone. But suddenly he's dead, chainsmoke like the Ohio Jims and now lung-cancer dead and insurance and pension all to us. Twenty-six thousand five hundred thirty-three and sixty-seven cents. Apiece.

ERM: When?

ELO: Eighteen months ago, two months after my baby die her phantom granddad follow. Paperwork though. It just come through your check bran spankin' fresh.

*(Beat. Sudden pouring rain outside.)*

ERM: Why the suitcase?

ELO: I dunno. This good excuse to come out, thought maybe we take a few days, get to know each other.

ERM: Sorry, my place kinda small. *(Elo looks around.)* I mean I got stuff all piled in the extra bedroom. Storage. *(Beat.)* You better hit it. Once in awhile cars get stuck in the risin' mud, out here it can flood up quick. *(Beat.)* Listen, come visit another day, you got my e-address, what's yours? so I make sure next time not to delete it.

*(Elo lifts her shirt to reveal severe bruises, old and fresh, all over her back. Pulls down her shirt.)*

ELO: Rather not go back to him.

ERM: Boyfriend?

ELO: *(Shrugs.)* Call it that.

ERM: Didn't you move back here with your mother? I thought you lived with your mother.

ELO: I'm almost thirty-six I don't live with my mother. Anymore.

ERM: Maybe you oughta go back to your mother's. For awhile. *(Beat.)* I grew up in a hick town and that was too crowded. Middle a nowhere I like my solitude, every other Thursday my sister come out spend the day. Love her visits, love my sister to bits. But I live alone.

*(Elo stares at Erm. Then silently turns to the door. When she opens it: a monsoon. Exits. Erm stares after her, then shuts the door, sits, sips her milk, stares at the check. Offstage sound of car ignition, then tires spinning in the mud.)*


SCENE TWO

*Hours later. A torrential storm outside. Elo sitting, sipping from a mug, completely engrossed in a book. Sound of Erm's stomping mud off her shoes just outside the door. Elo quickly hides the book.*

ERM: *(Enters.)* Squishin' now but I see a light, the distance. Bet it let up by evenin'.

ELO: Be back!

*(Elo quickly exits into the kitchen. Erm takes off her boots. Elo enters with a tray: another mug, two bowls and spoons.)*

ERM: Hot chocolate! With the baby marshamallows!

ELO: *(Off.)* Wisht I coulda done better 'n that package mess, little blond yodel girl. You should taste my homemade, still. Notice anything different? *(Erm stares at her, blank.)* Chocolatier?

ERM: *(Sips.)* Yeah!

ELO: Found a bar, melted it. *(Erm stares.)* Hope you wa'n't savin' that fifty-cent Hershey for no special occasion.

ERM: No. I mean, Sure, this is special. I found my twin. *(Not very successful mustering enthusiasm.)*

ELO: Well. For this I only used *some* a your veggies, 'case they already earmarked for some cotillion.

ERM: *(Tasting soup.)* Mmmm!

*(Elo smiles, pleased.)*

ERM: So guess you be hittin' it, first thing the A.M.

ELO: What they call you, Holly Hospitality?

ERM: I'm just calculatin' the game plan.

ELO: You think the monsoon's a good time to go house-huntin'?

ERM: I *said* I think it'll let up, I'm just a little steadfast 'bout my life schedule like ta keep a weekly planner my head.

ELO: I just got here today!

ERM: *Okay!*

>    (*They eat soup. Quiet.*)

ELO: I 'preciate your invite. I woulda been fine sleepin' the car, but surely warmer in here. Dryer.

ERM: By mornin' your car be A a boat or B a quicksand casualty.

ELO: Still. Not many be so kind. A stranger.

ERM: You're welcome.

>    (*Quiet.*)

ELO: You think it's gonna flood?

ERM: Pray not.

ELO: What we do?

ERM: Wait.

>    (*Quiet.*)

ELO: Not too many visitors out here huh.

ERM: Toldja every second Thursday my sister drop off her boy to school, spend the day with me.

ELO: *Boy?* Sickle cell you pass on he sick? sickles? (*Erm shakes her head no.*) Whew! Blessin'. (*Refers to a bookshelf.*) I saw that section: *Advances in the Pathophysiology, Diagnosis and Treatment of Sickle Cell Disease; The Molecular Basis of Mutant Hemoglobin Dysfunction; Sickle Cell Anemia and the Politics of Race and Health; Sickle Cell and Thal—Thal—*

ERM: Thalassaemia.

ELO: Your sister's daddy died young with it huh?

ERM: Twenty-five.

ELO: Before we were born? (*Erm nods.*) Your sister a baby? (*Erm nods.*) Sad. How old her boy now?

ERM: Thirteen.

ELO: Good age. I had a little girl, ten. (*Pause.*) Nice array a journals too. All the black stuff and *Ms.*, the gay pubs and *Mother Jones. Science, Nature, The New England Journal of Medicine.*

ERM: Gotta keep up.

ELO: You like women? Prefer 'em? (*Erm looks at her.*) Cuz I noticed those magazines.

ERM: You also noticed *NASA Bulletin*.

ELO: Just liketa know. Everything about you. Gay?

ERM: With who, the ewes?

ELO: I dunno. They say—

ERM: You start talkin' 'bout whatchu heard people do all alone the farm, nothin' but the animals you worn your welcome out.

*(Quiet.)*

ELO: You all well read but don't talk like it.

ERM: Talk any way I dang well please.

ELO: I like it! compliment! You could high-falute, but choose not ta. Down to earth. Sound like me.

ERM: Must be genetic.

ELO: I know that's a smartass *why*. You the one got a library on that subject too: *The Language of Genes, Nature's Thumbprint, Identical Twins Reared Apart. (No answer.)* I also noticed a fair amount a lit on fertility, you tryin' for a little guy?

ERM: Nope.

ELO: Ever been married?

ERM: Nope.

ELO: You born in town, what make you come out to this farm, all by your lonesome?

ERM: My lonesome. *(Pause.)* Growin' up I wanted to be a architect, writer, basketball player, astronomer, basketball player, astrologer, pianist, farmer, meteorologist, farmer. *(Beat.)* You?

ELO: What I do? or Am I married.

ERM: *(Shrugs.)* Pick.

ELO: Recipes. I got a knack. Look at a fridge, table full a seemingly unrelated items and build, arrange, somethin' new and luscious. Soup or casserole or three-course meal, but my special specialty is cakes. I got super creamers too many ingredients for any detective spy out, but if you think so many variances spoil the whole, guess you ain't among the forty-seven gimme fifty apiece for my cream dream Christmas quadruple layer. Sixty-eight on the wait list. *(Pause.)* Fourteen years. Married. 'til thirteen months ago. Not officially divorced but that's just cuz too much trouble. *(Pause.)* That's when I moved here, year ago. Movin' here pretty much sealed it, married no more. On the books we still wife and husband but for all intensive purposes...

*(Beat.)*

ERM: Intents *and* purposes. *(Beat.)* How come?

ELO: Huh?

ERM: Why you left him?

ELO: That's generous a ya. He left me. The house. After our little girl died. Mutual though, once we lost our child, ten years old. We was civil. For two people couldn't stand the sight a each other, least nobody hangin' on ta nobody's knees "Don't go! Don't go!" *(Pause.)* You ain't gonna ask me.

ERM: Respect your privacy.

ELO: How many times I gotta bring it up 'fore you stop respectin' my privacy?

ERM: How your little girl die?

*(Silence.)*

ERM: On the offchance it don't let up, seepin' under the door, get set to move: the important stuff, my books, computer, gotta go up to higher ground, second floor.

ELO: Miscarry miscarry miscarry, miscarry miscarry baby. So happy to get her, five miscarries then her weren't she a long-for. Miracle. We don't even risk the disappointment, try for a little brother sister, we got her all the blessin' we ever wanted. Black, black, thick long hair "How you born with all that hair?" Perfect perfect girl. We was spoilers, surprised? Every time she cry pick her up, "Rosie, Rosie" that's our grandmother's name, Rosemarie, her heart give out week before Rosie's born, "Rosie, you a little hungry?" "Rosie, you a little wet?" "Rosie, you just want Mama pick you up? Just want your daddy? You a little spoiled, yes you are, yes you are." So. Spoiled ten years bound to manifest itself a variety a ways: angel one second, the next little Satan, stomp, scream, the Tantrum Queen in action and here we lookin' at a six-hour drive to my favorite uncle's funeral. You'da liked Uncle Jack. Not forty minutes down the highway and Rosie already whinin', cryin', her dad snortin' and sighin' over the wheel. Now I know ten's big for my lap, but when her friends not around won't she ask, and somethin' always warm me that closeness. "Come on, Rosie." It ain't the safest, pull a kid over the seat at sixty but... Drivin' us all insane, figure get her to my lap quick save us all. *(Beat.)* Brakes screech. There she go, through the windshield. 'Course I... *we* broke the law and manslaughter ain't hardly a misdemeanor but judge, all chastisement and judgment and... mercy. He see we stopped eatin'. He 'preciate the hard, unselfishness a givin' in to the influence a that organ donation woman. He take into account miscarry miscarry miscarry before he pronounce us guilty a irresponsibility, stupidity *and* manslaughter and say our sentence already happened, buryin' a baby punishment plenty. *(Beat.)* Miscarry miscarry miscarry, miscarry miscarry baby, miscarry miscarry two more failures the year after judge say we free, two more fireworks turn out to be duds we figure we hate each other enough now, quits. *(Beat.)* You up on the readin'. Troubles carryin' to term, genetic? Or curable, don't answer.

*(Silence.)*

ERM: I had a baby.

ELO: *(Excitement.)* Boy or girl?!

ERM: Boy.

ELO: *(Seeing Erm's face.)* Oh. I know that face I'm the expert on that face. Sorry.

ERM: No, it—Not that. *(Beat.)* I dream about him —

ELO: Me too! Now all I dream nightmare of is Rosie naturally but before. All the little maybes, almost babies. *(Beat.)* I interrupted. You were talkin' 'bout your dreams.

*(Erm shrugs. Quiet. Then Elo takes out the hidden book.)*

ELO: I was readin'… This book —

ERM: Hey! *(Snatches it.)* Okay I don't mind you borrowin' 'em but please lemme know first cuz next thing, forget you have it, it accidentally packed with your stuff.

ELO: Sorry! *(Pause.)* Interestin'. Clonin'.

ERM: It got its pros and cons.

ELO: I'm clonin' Rosie.

*(Erm chuckles, then sees Elo is serious.)*

ERM: I *said* "pros and *cons.*"

ELO: I read about 'em.

ERM: In what, a hour?

ELO: Three and a half you been gone to be accurate, animals to the barn, sandbaggin' the fields when I finally seen ya return to the general vicinity I put on the soup and chocolate.

ERM: Three hours well there. You *are* the expert.

ELO: Rosie been gone less 'n two years, don't think all her organs already used up. I hope to God not *that* many ten-year-olds near dead in two years. Even if her heart gone, liver, must be at least a kidney left, somethin'. Just a sliver a cells enough.

ERM: There's risks. Look at Dolly. Old before her time, dead before her time—

ELO: I know about risks. Miscarry miscarry—

ERM: A few more. Dolly the only one made it only embryo come to fruition outa two hundred seventy-seven. Cloned fetuses ten times more likely die in the uterus than normal fetuses, cloned offspring three times more likely die soon after birth. Thirty percent a cloned animals have defects—

ELO: Well I don't have to bring her back this year. Give 'em a little time perfect the method—

ERM: You don't know when, *if* human clonin' be made legal.

ELO: I can wait. In the interim, I gotta call, tell 'em put a hold on those frozen body parts you mind I use your phone? I got a 10-10 code: nickel a minute.

ERM: In the *interim* you got these options: in vitro fertilization, intercytoplasmic sperm injection, fertility drugs—

ELO: That all sounds nice that ain't Rosie.

ERM: Ain't cheap.

ELO: Twenty-six thousand five thirty-three's a good start.

ERM: In vitro fertilization's fifty thousand a try and that try's no guarantee. Bet clonin' be more.

ELO: Then why you bring up in vitro? *(Beat: no answer.)* Well I bet people wants to volunteer in the experimental stage get a discount, I ain't worried, 'f I want it bad enough I have money enough what's it to you? Whatchu got against it, no sex unnatural? Well in vitro, all them things you push got nothin' to do with *(Gesturing with fingers:)* a little rod stick in a little hole neither scuze my colorfulness.

ERM: All them techniques employ the time-honored original meetin' a egg and sperm. Clonin' just a xerox a what already been.

ELO: Oooh guess you *ain't* gay after that little family values sermon I *want* a xerox I want Rosie!

ERM: Maybe won't be! Environmental influences, gene mutation as she grows—

ELO: One second you say the same, next second not, every book on the subject you got but when I suggest puttin' all your readin' to practice nothin' to do but fear a Goddin' me. *(Beat.)* Why I get the third degree? All I want is be a mother again.

*(Pause.)*

ERM: Just seein' you really wanna do it. Pretty fascinatin' to me. Maybe it'll work. Maybe it'll work. *(Pause.)* Was your mother… good to you?

ELO: She loved the bottle and the belt. Now, old age she found the Bible.

Sorry if this tick you off but, my opinion, you the twin got the best deal. *(Beat.)* I been tryin', tryin' the conventional, I toldju that, but all come to blood so. I assume it is. Heredity. I lose all my babies you lost your son.

ERM: My son weren't no miscarriage. I found out: Down's Syndrome. Couldn't deal with it, I made a decision. *(Beat.)* My dreams ain't nightmares, in my dreams I talk to my son. What he shoulda been smart. Strong—

ELO: *Abortion?*

*(Silence. Then water starts to seep under the door. Erm gasps. Starts unplugging the computer.)*

ERM: I got the computer, you start on the books.

*(Erm brings the computer upstairs. Elo stays put. Erm returns.)*

ERM: I have to do it by myself, all the books landin' on your bed, you sleepin' right where you sit, wet couch floatin' the livin' room pond.

*(Erm snatches a bunch of books, takes them upstairs. Elo doesn't budge.)*

## SCENE THREE

*Elo scrubbing the muddy living room floor. The stuffed animal on the couch.*

ELO: She probably thinks I planned this storm, stranded. I surely hate us stuck toppa each other just cuz the Lord and the Weatherman decide it. I offer to help with the animals but she say No thanks you just be in the way. I guess she think domestic chores more my line I ain't her wife! Godamighty I wouldn't be caught *dead* no farm middle a nowhere I didn't haveta, genes sure don't apply here do they. Nothin' remotely *similar* our personalities, let alone identical.

STUFFED ANIMAL: Many twins featured in Thomas Bouchard's Minnesota Twins Study showed no similarities. Others were slow in revealing, such as the California Japanese-American women, so unalike in interests and looks they had to blood-test them to prove they were identicals. Finally someone notices the same crack on same nail of same toe. Something will show, Elo, some little quirk. Your mother's egg cloned itself. You'd be surprised how similar two clones can be.

RETTA: *(Enters from the outside.)* Elo?

*(Elo looks up. Nods.)*

RETTA: Dontchu look like my sister! I'm Retta.

*(Retta holds out her hand to shake. Elo, muddy, hesitates but Retta grabs it anyway, firm.)*

RETTA: Need help? *(Retta helps, not waiting for an answer.)* Called first thing, once the phone lines restored, she tell me all about your surprise visit. Guess she out tendin' the animals. Glad you're here. Worry 'bout Erm way out in the nothin', no one talk to but the hogs and sometimes I worry she does. Only thing attract me to farm life is ham-'n'-potata breakfasts, who ever heard of a vegetarian farmer? Ever since ninth grade, that Hare Krishna kid transfer to her class… Call herself "chicken farmer" and keepin' a cow's normal, but the sheep? pigs? Well this be her dream, farmer woman, guess she got to go whole-hog, that ain't *just* a pun, if she'd been a writer she probably have to write history AND science fiction AND *How to Feng Shui Your Barn* AND *The Middle a Nowhere for Less than a Dollar a Day*, she'd been meterologist couldn'ta just smiled and got teleprompted, she be chasin' the twisters.

ELO: She meteorologist maybe she know about the flood beforehand, we not up to our knees in it.

RETTA: And what? Move the house? *(Beat.)* I guess that your car. Well, top half anyway look like the devil pulled the tires down under.

ELO: I called a tow truck. They gotta come out, take it in.

RETTA: That yours? *(Stuffed animal. Elo nods, embarrassed.)* Ain't it cute!

ELO: I just put it there keep it from gettin' wet aaaaaah!

RETTA: *What?*

ELO: Sorry. Crick in the neck.

RETTA: Her ol' guestroom bed I bet. Nobody but her dang boxes a who-knows-what ever had to sleep there before. Here.

*(Retta signals Elo over. Elo is hesitant, then moves. Retta starts massaging Elo's neck. Elo is tense, gradually relaxes.)*

RETTA: Don't this feel heaven? I went to some class once, some yoga thing, or tee chay I don't remember. When they said do this to your partner uh *uh!* I don't touchy touchy with no stranger sorry! But from the doorway I peek back, apply the skills I see to my own neck. In a emergency, Erm's too hard or soft mattress for example, it can be a soothe.

*(Pause.)*

ELO: Actually I slept on the steps.

*(Retta stops massaging.)*

RETTA: The what?

ELO: Me and Erm have a little disagreement... um... It was gettin' wetter down here, I just thought toppa the steps—

RETTA: Wait 'til she gets back—

ELO: Don't say nothin'! I gotta be here 'til my car ready please don't bite the hand can evict me!

*(Retta shakes her head, goes back to the massage.)*

RETTA: Better? Looser? *(Elo nods.)* You a sister one way, me a sister another. She tell ya anything about me?

ELO: You have a boy, drop him off school and visit every other Thursday. If you always drop him off, Erm never see him?

RETTA: Sure she see him. Summer, school's out, holidays, his birthday. Wouldn't think I have Thursdays off, wouldja. Government job. I been a good worker a long time, they gimme the flexibility, nice to have a week-day free, the bank. Other Monday to Friday only business.

ELO: Whatchu do?

RETTA: Secretary. Mayor's office. *(Looks around.)* She done alright by herself. Not many women could, middle a nowhere. Not many'd *want* to but... Property, independence. Yeah. She make me proud.

*(Erm enters with two pails of milk. Stares.)*

ERM: Thought I s'posed to be the gay gal.

*(Elo, startled, jumps up.)*

RETTA: My sister think she so funny.

ERM: *(Heading to the kitchen.)* I'll make the coffee.

RETTA: Your kitchen functional?

ERM: First thing I attended, I ain't starvin'.

ELO: *(Takes pails.)* I'll get it!

*(Elo exits into the kitchen, startling Erm.)*

RETTA: Definitely twins. *(Erm snorts.)* You don't like her.

ERM: She's fine I just wasn't expectin' guests obviously her mother didn't raise her to call before she show up somebody's doorstep.

RETTA: Thought you said she emailed.

ERM: And when I never answered she shoulda rang dang! I'm in the book.

RETTA: Seem nice enough. Got a husband? kids?

ERM: That question already come up over the phone, I repeat: Ask her your-self.

RETTA: Aw, Erm!

ERM: Divorced. Sorta. About forty-seven miscarriages and the one that lived died.

RETTA: Shame.

ERM: She wants to clone her little girl. *(Snickers.)*

RETTA: She come here with that idea or it a recent acquisition a ingenuity?

ERM: Snoopin' through my books she sure never asked me.

RETTA: Knew it! Your dang stuff, witchcraft!

ERM: Science? Witchcraft?

RETTA: Same! *(Erm rolls her eyes.)* I ain't never hearda no black person got such science fervor. Faith. Ever hear a little thing called Tuskegee? syphilus? Guinea piggin' black men? "As a little experiment, lessee which lives and which don't."

ERM: I know, Retta—

RETTA: Remember what the scientists, *doctors* done in Germany you wasn't hundred percent sane, their definition, Aryan whitey white?

ERM: That don't mean—

RETTA: We already won the war but don't they drop the atomic anyhow. On who? Not no white people coulda gone straight for Berlin but what target they choose? how many Germans in Hiroshima?

ERM: *Got it, Retta.*

RETTA: You just a little bit gullible little too easily swayed. First that Hare Krishna kid, now the scientists.

*(Erm sulks. Retta, peace offering, fishes through her purse. Pulls out a coloring picture.)*

RETTA: Looky! First time he stayed in the lines. *(Erm smiles.)* When I dropped him off school this mornin', his teacher say "Don't count on tomorrow, usually they don't retain it." But today: celebrate!

ERM: He's a good boy.

RETTA: You wannit?

ERM: *Here?* The *swamp?*

RETTA: Ya all cleaned up pretty good, down to a mud slide now.

ERM: You have any trouble? drive? *(Retta puts the drawing back in her purse, pulls out a talisman.)* That thing!

RETTA: "Our Lady a the Highway" saved me more 'n once, bad weather.

ERM: "Our Lady a the Dirt Roads" whatchu need. Like it do any good we ain't even Catholic!

RETTA: So what? Our Lady gonna put me in a collision? Who cares, Catholic I pray! I read the Bible!

ERM: Don't I know it. Listen. I gotta show you somethin'.

*(Erm takes the check out of her pocket, shows to Retta. Retta screams like she's witnessed an axe murder. Elo runs to look in.)*

ELO: *Okay?!*

ERM: Fine.

*(Elo is unsure but Erm stares her down. Elo back to the kitchen.)*

ERM: Her father left it to me.

RETTA: Whatchu gonna do?

ERM: I don't know. I was thinkin' —

*(Phone rings.)*

ERM: Hello? *(Puzzled.)* ELO! *(Hand over mouthpiece:)* She plannin' on movin' in? leavin' her number—?

RETTA: I come over here for the day, if I got somethin' important *I* leave your number.

ERM: *You* my sister.

ELO: *(Enters.)* Thanks.

*(Elo takes the phone into the kitchen.)*

ERM: Huh!

RETTA: Nosy!

ERM: Why not? Move into my place, now act like her business is nunna my.

RETTA: You gonna meet your mother?

ERM: She toldju?!

RETTA: Tol' me what?

ERM: That ol' bat. Thinkin' I wanna visit.

RETTA: You ever met her before?

ERM: You know dang well —

RETTA: Then how the heck you know she's a "ol' bat"?

ERM: I wanna know why *she (Points to kitchen.)* all behind my back, guess I show no interest in her mother she figure she appeal to my sister. Sneaky.

RETTA: She ain't said a thing about it, Erm, all I'm doin's thinkin' aloud, cheese 'n' rice. Just goin' with the common wisdom: Ain't most adoptees interested in their birth mother?

ERM: I dunno, you take a poll?

RETTA: I watch TV!

ERM: *My* mother died!

RETTA: I know!

ERM: Why people gotta put all that stock in blood? Even the in vitros look for donors look like the daddy *dumb!* *(Pause.)* But if we was blood, I'da given my mama some a my round blood cells, replace her sickles.

RETTA: I know.

ERM: Replace *your* sickles.

RETTA: I know. *(Beat.)* I mean, i'n't it interestin'? Someone look like you? Whenever the three of us walk down the street, people always remark how Mama just spit me out, then smile politely at you no comment.

ERM: And Mama always said, "I got two babies."

RETTA: But ain'tcha curious? See yourself in your mother's face.

ERM: I saw myself in my mother's face.

RETTA: Besides philosophical!

ERM: Suddenly you act like adopted, I ain't parta the family.

RETTA: I'm sayin' maybe you got a privilege you ain't honin'. Two families.

ERM: *(Raised voice:)* HOW LONG IT TAKE MAKE A CUPPA COFFEE?

RETTA: That how you treat a guest? Make her sleep on the steps now this? *(Erm about to explode.)* I dragged it outa her and she said please don't tell so leave her be.

ERM: I don't know how to treat guests Whole pointa me homesteadin' out here's so I wouldn't have to learn! Thought she weren't no guest anyhow thought she my blood. Ain't we related? Just look at our faces.

RETTA: You can cut the smartmouth any time.

ERM: Family ain't here *(Face.)*, it's here *(Heart.)*

RETTA: Oooh, bet your *next* statement be a *three*-Kleenex sentiment careful. Don't know you got enough toilet paper soak it all up.

ELO: *(Enters happy, returning phone.)* Thank you ever s' much for the use of your phone, that was a very important call, an exceptionally important call.

*(Elo exits back into the kitchen. Erm and Retta hear Elo's happy humming. Erm lets out an irritated bellow.)*

ERM: Sleepin' *my* house virtue kindness *my* heart and she come in all smug, *(Singsong:)* "I got a secret!" *(Starts mocking Elo's humming.)*

RETTA: All I know is look at her, look at you, yaw musta had some pretty mama.

ERM: Oh don't even try it, Retta.

RETTA: All I'm sayin's—

ERM: You my adopted! You the one s'posed to be worried my search for the biological take me away from you.

RETTA: A plane dropped a million dollars six miles down the road wouldn't be incentive enough take you away from here! When's the last time you stepped off this dang farm? the world's changed, Erm, little invention called a answerin' machine might make it less aggravatin' every time I call ring ring ring ring 'til the enda the world while you out pluckin' a chick or rollin' in the mud with the hogs.

ERM: Don't chastise *me* "technology," no email I get from you computer-phobic but I remember you first hired to the mayor's office, interview your way into a good job then I get the call *(Whisper:)* "Erm! How you work a fax machine?" I say "Retta, just dial the number." You "Oh no! gotta be more to it than *that.*" I say "Retta, you can dial a phone number you can do a fax," you: "Oh no!"

RETTA: Nothin' but clucks and moos and baa baa baa, no one talk to but the animals You gone crazy, started talkin' to the animals? Like what's-her-name? doctor? Eliza Doolittle, rain in Spain quack quack quack. *(Erm confused.)* I like to meet her. You my sister, closest thing to me in the world I like to know the vagina you snagged from!

ERM: Then *you* go with her! Maybe she have a drivin' companion she finally got reason to leave!

RETTA: Maybe I will!

ERM: And send me a postcard! So I can get all choked up *(Fake sobs:)* "That's my mama! Look just like me!"

RETTA: Maybe I will!

ERM: And don't forget—

*(Sudden enormous groan from Retta: severe stomach pain. Erm quickly to her.)*

ERM: Breathe.

*(Retta does. After considerable time the pain subsides.)*

ERM: Okay?

*(Retta nods. A few more quieter breaths. Eventually:)*

ERM: Retta. Sometimes… I get scared—

RETTA: It's okay, it's okay. *(Pause.)* Oh!

*(Retta gags, runs upstairs. Quiet a few moments, then Elo peeks in from the kitchen.)*

ELO: Retta leave?

ERM: Bathroom.

ELO: Good! I heard you all talkin', then it got quiet, 'fraid she left, I made coffee and… You still mad? Last night? I ain't no abortion doctor shooter, Erm, just like you to know you got no wacko livin' with ya I got no religion against abortion. Just… Sometimes hard. Thinkin' women who *can*… and my twin—

RETTA: *(Entering.)* How come you always gotta buy that cheap toilet paper? Bad enough on your behind but what if ya gotta blow your nose?

*(An oven buzzer off.)*

ELO: Oh!

*(Elo exits quickly to the kitchen.)*

ERM: Pain can't be gone. Once it starts... days—

RETTA: I'm okay.

ERM: *(Holds out the check to Retta.)* You take it. I wantchu find a good doctor, I don't want... *(Trails off.)*

RETTA: I got a good doctor. He gimme free sample medicine from his office. Government job, I got good insurance. *(Erm's arm still outstretched.)* Not many bad bouts like that recently don't worry. Ain't gonna be like Mama. *(Erm's arm still outstretched. Retta puts her own hand over Erm's hand clutching the check, and guides Erm's hand back into Erm's pocket, not letting Erm see. Elo enters with food.)*

RETTA: Omelettes?!

ERM: *Muffins?* How'dju—?

RETTA: Mmm! what's *in* this?

ELO: Not sayin'. But all from Erm's kitchen.

ERM: Didn't know all this food survived.

ELO: Ain't how much. 'S what you do with it.

RETTA: I see you know Erm choose milk over coffee. Guess you all gettin' to be friends mmm! Blackberries?

ELO: You gotta be creative. Most people go for the tried and true, or open a cookbook. The second a bit more adventurous but the *real* excitement is creatin' somethin' all new, scratch, never been before. Maybe it be perfect concoction, maybe not everything you hoped for but there's charm in the quirky too, point is the mystery, lottery cuz ain't the surprise, the unique amazin' in itself? *(Beat.)* I'm pregnant!

*(Erm and Retta stunned. After they recover from the shock:)*

ERM AND RETTA: *(Muttering:)* Congratulations.

*(Erm and Retta eat silently, eyes on food. Elo beams.)*

# SCENE FOUR

*Outside. Sear is dribbling a basketball, some fancy moves. Erm reading a science book.*

SEAR: Virgin birth!

ERM: Hardly. Baby have a daddy, don't she got the bruises to prove it?

SEAR: "Baby."

ERM: Maybe it'll take.

SEAR: Optimistic! She a fool?

ERM: Gotta have faith—

SEAR: Even if it does ha ha, hardly be perfect. *(Dunks the ball through the basket.)* I'm perfect.

ERM: Yeah yeah. Least it keep her mind off clonin'.

SEAR: You're dying for a clone!

ERM: Well. Pros and cons.

SEAR: Yeah, if it lean toward the cons, better her than you, Mama Scientist just sit back see how the experiment take.

ERM: Wanna whuppin'?

SEAR: Right.

ERM: Think thirteen too big put you cross my knee?

SEAR: Thirteen and a half.

ERM: You sure better be glad you's a dream, smartie, cuz lip like that don't always make it to fourteen.

SEAR: Why she wanna clone anyway? Nobody's perfect, not nobody with the eighty thousand times two genetic chances of egg and sperm. Problem with clonin' is you just repeating the original, repeating the mistakes.

ERM: Not a carbon copy! Ian Wilmut, man who cloned Dolly and who's wholly opposed to human clonin' by the way, same time as Dolly he also cloned Cedric, Cecil, Cyril and Tuppence—

SEAR: Sure from embryonic cells a kindergartener could clone from embryonic cells.

ERM: *Four rams cloned from the same embryonic cells* but quite varied in size, temperament. And environment, what a shocker, that has a little influence too.

SEAR: Remember that kook: "If cloning becomes legal, lesbians will reproduce themselves! If cloning becomes legal, unwed mothers get a free reign." *(Guffawing.)*

ERM: There's kooks both sides that argument.

SEAR: Lotsa more civilized reasons to be anti-clone. But genetic engineering: *there!* We go for perfection! You dumped me, Down's baby, but then afterthought, scooped out a little gene here, add a dash a gene there, voilá! Better me!

ERM: I didn't dump you!

SEAR: Changed me.

ERM: Just… fixed you. The gene, Down's Syndrome—

SEAR: Made me better!

ERM: No! Well…

SEAR: You *sorry?* I'm grateful!

ERM: Not sorry! Jus'… somethin' 'on't feel right, nag at me. All that control o'er a egg 'fore it's hatched.

SEAR: I'm grateful. Sure they make fun, what else eighth-graders do? "Sear, ain't he the genetically engineered kid?" Just jealous, i'n't that what you said?

ERM: Uh huh.

SEAR: My teacher all old school, one of the nay-says "*Oh* start with recombinant DNA next thing sliding down that slippery slope toward human cloning" "Oh start with oranges and grapes next thing your neighbors genetic engineering their daughter" great! I'm here! I'm here so enjoy the ride *I* am, smooth glide down the slippery slope.

ERM: I ain't somethin' awful! Not like I catalogue-ordered darker eyes, hair—

SEAR: Straight or nappy? I'n't *that* loaded!

ERM: You do your chores?

SEAR: Mom!

ERM: Think them hogs feed themself?

SEAR: Okay okay. But first lemme show you what I learned today.

*(As Erm speaks, Sear begins to play the piano expertly, outrageously sophisticated and difficult. He may be playing a box or table but the audience hears piano music.)*

ERM: Only next step anyhow, in vitro people already wantin' to know everything 'bout their sperm donor What he look like? Wa'n't a rapist, was he? Didn't pick his nose, did he?

SEAR: Eyes closed! *(Continues playing with eyes closed.)*

ERM: Amniocentesis, great invention, fortune teller: abort what ain't up to snuff. And China, one child per couple, suddenly newborn population lopsided toward males now wonder how that happen?

SEAR: Backside! *(Turns around in his seat, plays behind his back.)*

ERM: They been searchin' for a gay gene. They find it, better believe hetero parents be eliminatin' *that* sucker for posterity.

SEAR: Toes! *(Plays with his toes.)*

ERM: Same gene causes sickle cell codes for resistance to malaria, go on, play with nature. See what you get. *(Back to book.)*

SEAR: *(Playing normally.)* Dolly won all the sensation but Ian Wilmut considered his greatest creation Polly, year later. Cloned from cells genetically engineered with human Factor IX, a blood clotter—and she pass it on to the next generation! What a contribution to humanity! What a godsend to sound economics and wealthy hemophiliacs! Poll Dorset lamb with just an eensy beensy bit a human in her.

ERM: *(Slams book shut.)* All I wanted was you perfect!

*(Erm startled by her own outburst. Sear stops all activity, stands still and looks right at Erm.)*

SEAR: Yes. That would be somebody else.


## SCENE FIVE

*In the blackness, screams and cries of anguish, "NO! NO!" etc. Then lights up on the living room, middle of the night. Erm nervous. Elo's face is tear-stained: anger, bitterness.*

ERM: I think we oughta go to the hospital. *(No answer.)* I think, the toilet… too much blood I think—

ELO: *(Not looking at Erm.)* It's gone.

ERM: We'll get there quick, I can hot-foot the gas: emergency.

ELO: That *bitch.*

ERM: I think you need to see a doctor, blood—

ELO: Eight times b'lieve I know how to diagnose miscarriage.

ERM: I know, still you gotta be —

ELO: Bitch, that ugly… slut! Whore!

ERM: Elo—

ELO: I AIN'T GOIN' NO GODDAMN DOCTOR! *(Beat.)* She did it. Monster, can't lee me alone adult, haunt me Why I follow her? Hick town ain't nothin' gone right since I got here Can't build no customer base! Not with these stingies I hand out my card, the goin' rate they "*Oh,* that must be what they pay in She-cah-go not here" cheapskates! Hicks! Guess how many cakes I sold last Christmas? two!

ERM: I'd buy one, way you make soup, omelettes, bet dessert a real treat —

ELO: CUNT! *Lush* gimme the belt strap cuz *her* dirty dishes all over the place embarrass her fronta the fuckass she picked up, 3 AM I'm washin' scotch glasses dumpin' ashtrays *eight years old*. Then beat again cuz I oversleep next day's spellin' test. Fuckin' *bitch* hobble into my graduation whisky blind, smellin' HATE HER! She does it! Ain't a goddamn thing wrong with my ovaries bull*shit* you say there is! My *brain* can't have a baby! Her always on it, fear I do to them what she done…
*(Pause.)*

ERM: *(Quiet.)* You had a baby.

ELO: Yeah, how the hell that happen. *(Beat. Sudden horror:)* Maybe can't have any more… don't *deserve* any more cuz I do to them what I done to, what I done to —

ERM: It don't work that way.

ELO: She nothin'! nothin'! Crap mother, give one away and the other… my life… Fertile bitch! *twins?* What kinda God make that whore so fertile?

ERM: *(At a loss.)* God—

ELO: I was good! Good mama maybe… overprotective, spoiler that ain't worth punishment! Not *that* kind, not when that cunt smack me inch a my life she scot free CHRIST!

ERM: Don't make sense—

ELO: Hate this hick town! why I come? I got meetin' a the minds with nobody, country. All country all bluegrass, buckteeth—

ERM: 'Kay I know *no* one buckteeth—

ELO: *(Tears.)* She the one chance I had. Rosie, God gimme Rosie I blew it. Blew it. *(Sobs a little, then looks at Erm through her tears.)* I got another chance! I called the organ donor people. *(Smiles.)* Strangers on the street: "That sure is your baby" so alike: eyes. Nose. Know you think look alike means nothin' well there *is* one or two blood relations actually got love and in them cases look alike kinda nice. *(Sudden worry:)* I see movies. The clones walkin' around, no expression their voices, no expression their eyes. My nightmares.

ERM: That's zombies.

ELO: Clones!

ERM: That's Hollywood, they mix up zombies and clones. Clones just… kids. Babies. But won't they be scrutinized, come into the world with heck to live up to, when I was a kid the famousest person from our town was Mr. Winters. Mr. Winters played the major leagues. His only son Shannon miserable all his life: can't throw can't catch can't hit, but Mr. Winters' son so he get all the pressure to. But say he Mr. Winters' *clone*, you imagine? Ten times the pressure? expectation, *hundred?* Clones cloned for some purpose, somethin' in the original somebody wanted back, or wanted a spare of, how they ever live up, be what they was somebody's brainstorm to be? All the responsibility but in the end clone ain't nothin' but a kid, just a kid.

ELO: Where your baby come from?

(Pause.)

ERM: I was a nerd. *A*s all my papers but if twenty percent a the grade was class participation *B* minus I get at best, so quiet. Guess all those years takin' care a my mama, I didn't... Retta was oldest, biggest responsibility fall on her, but I grew up cleanin' bedpans, cleanin' vomit, luckily I had no friends so no worry 'bout the embarrassment a bringin' 'em home. 'Ere I was, sweet twenty-two and never been nothin', so imagine my surprise when Ernie take a likin'. Mama dead six months and suddenly he at our house all the time, get on Retta's nerves, every second she look up he's on the couch "Why 'on't you stay home with your brother sometime?" he share the trailer house with his brother. Still, least I'm talkin' a bit now, she like that. Hand in hand down the street every afternoon, one day we peekin' at the engagement rings in Zaylor's window, I say Guess this a time say what I gotta say. He listen. Smile. Don't worry, I gonna be a good daddy. I can't believe it, good guy! So I call next day. His brother "He ain't here." Day after same, day after same, six days a ringin' and no answer, finally I knock knock knock, nobody come knock knock knock knock knock his brother whip the door open "He don't live here no more!" slam! (Pause.) Well. I been through worse no big... But the baby I let go of, and next day I see a ad for a farm, cheap. No neighbors so lucky people never was one a my favorite things.

ELO: You don't know! How it feels, you can have all the babies you want. You don't gotta go through it! Midnight terrors the toilet!

(Pause.)

ERM: You know what? This is the problem. This is the problem I been givin' you all conventional medicine advice heck there's more 'n one way to skin a infertile cat. (Goes to her books.) Lessee Chinese medicine... Ooooh acupuncture... Looky here, here's a whole shelf a holistic—

ELO: Bumpkin.

  *(Elo exits to the upstairs. The phone rings.)*

ERM: Hello? *(Pause.)* Well she… she can't come to the phone right now wait it's 3:30 AM who *is* this?

  *(Erm gets her answer: a lengthy pause. She fights tears, can't speak, silently nods. Finally gathers herself enough to call:)*

ERM: Elo?

  *(No answer. Erm puts the receiver down, goes closer to the stairs.)*

ERM: Elo? It's your mother. *(No answer.)* It's your mother she said you called her a few minutes ago she wants to know if you're okay. *(No answer.)* Elo—?

ELO: *(Off, from upstairs:)* IT'S *YOUR* MOTHER.

  *(Erm, afraid, stares at the receiver off the hook. Then exits up the stairs.)*


END OF ACT ONE



## ACT TWO
## SCENE ONE


*Elo is sick in a child's bed, a bad cold. Rosie enters with a sheet of paper, shy.*

ELO: Come in, sugar, Mommy just has a little cold. *(Rosie takes a step in.)* You wonder why Mommy's in your bed? *(Rosie nods. Elo puzzled.)* I dunno. You wanna hop in bed with Mommy? *(Rosie nods.)* Come on.

  *(Rosie happily jumps in with Elo, snuggling. Elo puts her arm around Rosie.)*

ELO: Ring around my Rosie, pocket full a posey. *(Elo tickles, Rosie giggles.)* Let's see whatcha got. Oooh, family tree. This for school? *(Rosie nods.)* Okay you got me and your daddy… Someday you'll meet him, baby, I swear. Just takin' him a little time to come around. And lessee. Grammaw, okay her name has *two* Ls, and Granpaw—

ROSIE: FUCK!

  *(Beat.)*

ELO: What?

ROSIE: *FUCK!* I forgot that bee-atch, *(fingers the quote marks:)* "first" Rosie.

ELO: Don't say that word!

ROSIE: What word I'm s'posed to say—*original* Rosie?

ELO: That's not the word I mean you know the word I mean.

ROSIE: "Fuck" or "bee-atch"?

ELO: Both! Neither!

*(Beat.)*

ROSIE: You sure ain't like the first Rosie what was she, a goddamn nun?

ELO: You sure ain't like the first Rosie.

ELO: You could be good! You know she was good you just tryin'… *(Beat.)*

ROSIE: Have my own personality?

ELO: That's not what I—

ROSIE: You want me be more like Rosie?

ELO: You *are* Rosie, you're your own Rosie.

ROSIE: Want me be more like *the* Rosie?

ELO: You *are the* Rosie and no, I don't want you to be more like your sister.

ROSIE: *(Half muttering.)* My sister, good thing she didn't live or wouldn't that be confusing. "C'mere, Rosie! No not you, *Rosie.*" *(Exits.)*

ELO: *(Calling:)* This is a very good family tree. Aunt Erm. Oh, this is cute, Aunt Retta. But you know Retta ain't your real aunt she's Aunt Erm's AAAAAH!

*(Rosie had entered with ketchup blood all over her face. Now she has only one arm.)*

ROSIE: Now I'm like Rosie. Rosie through the windshield.

ELO: Wash that off.

ROSIE: *(Being a zombie.)* Look: "Fifth Grade Clones from Outer Space."

ELO: Wash that off!

ROSIE: Where do I put Rosie on my family tree? cuz she's not my sister for damn sure, her daddy didn't conception me.

ELO: 'Course he did. Her cloned cells from his genes, my genes—

ROSIE: Hey! Maybe Rosie's my mother! Come from *her*, right?

ELO: No.

ROSIE: And that would make more sense, our names. Like I'm Rosie Junior.

ELO: WASH THAT DAMN KETCHUP OFF YOUR FACE!

*(Silence.)*

ROSIE: I screwed it up and it's the final draft. I had one before but I messed that up too.

ELO: *(Clenched teeth:)* Rosie. If you don't wash—

ROSIE: Okay okay!

ELO: And stop playin' like you lost an arm it's not funny!

*(Rosie looks at her. Tears.)*

ELO: What?

ROSIE: I can't help it my arm got messed up, birth.

ELO: Oh come on, Rosie, you didn't have that before— *(Elo sees real tears.)* Aw. Aw I'm sorry, baby. Mommy's sorry, Mommy didn't notice.

*(Rosie exits rubbing her eyes. Elo begins banging her back against the pillow.)*

ELO: Wake *up*, Elo, damn psycho dream, wake *up*, wake—

*(Elo is puzzled. Reaches under her pillow, finds a file folder. Leafs through it. Rosie returns. She now limps as if one leg is shorter than the other.)*

ROSIE: Lemme show you the first draft.

ELO: What're you doin' with your sister's medical records?

*(Silence.)*

ELO: Rosie!

ROSIE: I just wanna know what's gonna happen to me! And *when*, that a crime?

ELO: You shouldn't worry—

ROSIE: I *ain't* worried I *like* knowin'! 'Cept not the chicken pox! 'Cept not the early acne 'cept not show my thing to Mark Wilder while he show me his! *(Elo, confused, searches the file for this information.)* Skimmed her diary too.

ELO: Hey!

ROSIE: No way I'm stayin' past ten years four months seventeen days that was the end a her, after that I wouldn't know what's comin'! Too much mystery. *(Shows her paper.)* This was my first draft family tree, all the Rosie embryos they tried before me but even though I made 'em small, I only got seventy-two and ran outa paper. Then I did the next draft and forgot Rosie altogether. 'Cept me.

ELO: Don't blame ya, mad at me. People compare siblings ain't right. And I act like she's the angel uh uh. I spoiled her too she could be a little smart-ass too. *(Smiles affectionate.)* You just like her.

ROSIE: Is that a compliment?

*(Elo still smiling, then suddenly unsure.)*

ELO: Yes. *(Beat.)* No.

ROSIE: Is that a compliment?

*(They stare at each other.)*

## SCENE TWO

*Sear's bedroom. Sear playing a board game by himself, rolling the dice and moving the pieces.*

ERM: Hi.

SEAR: *(Doesn't look up.)* Hi.

  *(Pause: Sear rolls, moves.)*

ERM: Wouldn't that be more fun with someone?

SEAR: *Who?*

ERM: I dunno, kid from school?

SEAR: You mean a *"friend"*? You ever heard me mention I have anything like a *"friend"*?

ERM: Kids makin' fun again, that it? "Light bulb"? *(Sear rolls, moves.)* I'ma go down there, talk to that principal.

SEAR: Don't.

ERM: Try not take it s' hard, just jealous. Just cuz they got no brains, come up with the ideas theyself.

SEAR: They don't call me "light bulb" cuza my ideas, "light bulb" cuz I'm G.E.: genetically engineered.

ERM: Oh.

  *(Sear rolls, moves.)*

ERM: You goin' out for track? *(Sear rolls, moves.)* You been settin' the alarm 5 AM, takin' out your Christmas stopwatch, I see you whippin' 'cross the meadow—

SEAR: How I go out for track? When you G.E.'d me you forgot speed. Enough for basketball but when track season comes I don't even make third string.

ERM: *(Vaguely amused.)* Too bad when the decisions happened you wa'n't 'round to consult.

SEAR: *Yeah. (They stare at each other. Then Sear back to his game.)* 3 o'clock I'm their tutor. 4 they're released to the field, I watch 'em through the fence. I wish my legs fly the hundred meter like Andrew Laird's, wish my body soar up clear six feet like Malcolm Emery's.

ERM: Careful whatchu wish for.

SEAR: What's that mean?

ERM: *(Puzzled.)* I dunno. Some ol' timey sayin'.

SEAR: We can tear down every tree in the rainforest, kill off all the animals cuz no such thing as endangered species we can always make new ones, better ones. No breast cancer—if it's in her genome we just preemptive strike chop 'em off when she's twenty. No more cystic fibrosis, no more Alzheimers, last year aging became a curable disease "Be careful whatchu wish for"? What's left to wish for?

ERM: Agin', not dyin'. *(Sear stares at her.)* Curable. *(Sear rolls his eyes and the dice, moves.)* You know what? Who needs those kids, *brats* no they *ain't* G.E.'d just look at their report card. I got along fine without 'em, had my sister and my mama. You got me.

SEAR: You're not my friend you're my mother.

ERM: Monopoly not my forté but how 'bout I get the deck? Five hundred, Dirty Hearts ain't we brung the sun up with 'em? You and me: Double Solitaire?

SEAR: You're not my *friend* you're my *mother*.

ERM: *Best friend! (Beat.)* Well. Guess you at that age, needin' to see who care for you outside a love unconditional. Guess I was *never* that age s' hard for me to understand it. Mama's girl, I don't *get* bein' ashamed a family, anyone ask me *my* best friend I pipe up "My mother,—"

SEAR: *Which* doesn't shame you? Your mama or your mother.

*(Pause, staring at each other. Then Sear turns back to the game. Suddenly an earthquake. It roars and shakes. Erm grabs the table, trying to maintain her balance, but falls on her butt. Sear keeps playing, completely oblivious. Finally, it is over.)*

ERM: You feel that? *(Sear rolls, moves.)* If the Richter tops at twelve that was at *least* fourteen! *(Sear rolls, moves.)* Must be *some* game. *(Erm looks at the board.)* Hey, ain't Monopoly. What *is* that?

SEAR: "America." Object is to accumulate all the stuff you can. Clothes and money. Big house and money. Mercedes, swimming pool, Prozac and money. This is the latest edition. Roll doubles three times in a row and you can design a baby destined for Harvard.

ERM: Never heard of a board game you play solo.

SEAR: Works *best* playing against yourself. Think it's easy? wrong. Never ends! I keep getting the cash the *stuff,* keep thinking I'm ahead, I want everything in the world and get it. But it never yields a perfect score. Have it all have it all but no matter how many times I play, I still always need just one thing to win: More.

## SCENE THREE

*Dell, a cross around her neck, smoothes her dress, touches the flowers, checks the hors d'oeuvres (potato chips in a bowl), nervously makes sure everything is right. A Bible on the table. Knock at the door. Dell answers.*

DELL: Erma? *(Erm nods.)* C'mon in, c'mon in 'fore the rain start, look like some downpour comin'. And after that 'quake last night, you feel it? *(Erm and Elo enter.)* Oooh I'm seein' double, been waitin' thirty-six years to see double. Siddown. My aintchu pretty, aintchu both s' pretty. *(They all sit. Erm a bit tense, Elo sulky.)*

DELL: Erma Erma Erma. Well you can call me Dell. Or... *(Trails off.)*

ELO: *(Completing the thought.)* Mom! *(Guffaws.)*

DELL: *(Nervous.)* Yaw have a nice drive? *(Erm nods.)* Pretty drive. Well where you live, Erma, country, awful pretty. Orchards.

ELO: How *you* know?

DELL: I know this place! grew up here. So nice to be back, I still had a few friends left, Maureen, dirty little white girl I used to swing trees with now got a dirty house her own, brought forth a whole brood and presently raisin' three a *theirs*. I don't remember no tremors as a kid, nothin' like last night. Didn't suffer no damage didja?

ELO: She slept through it.

DELL: *That?* *(Erm nods, embarrassed.)* Eat! Or dontchu like barbecue. I got plain, the kitchen.

ERM: *(Takes a chip.)* These are good, thank you.

DELL: Whatchaw want to drink? Coke?

ERM: Please.

DELL: Manners! Coke, Elo? *(Elo glowers at Dell.)* I go get 'em. *(Dell exits to kitchen. Off, she sings "Just a Closer Walk with Thee." After awhile, Elo slides her finger across the table.)*

ELO: Looks like she dusted for ya. *(Her reflection:)* Oooh, looky me! *(Picks food she sees in her teeth.)* Vacuumed. Sure ain't the pigsty I grew up in oh ain't she been all God Housekeepin' since she found the Gospel.

ERM: *(Looking around.)* I think it's nice. *(Flowers and chips table arrangement:)* I think this is nice.

ELO: Say "I think she's nice" and I slug you.

DELL: *(Enters with tray.)* Here we go. Now I brought three glasses cuz I know Elo love a col' Coke but she probably won't drink, seem like she mad at me.

ELO: "Seem like she mad at me."

DELL: *(To Erm:)* I'ma ignore that. Where she pick *up* that I don't know, talk to her elders, mama like *that*. Not from me and polite as you is, Erma, not from you neither.

ELO: Erm. *(Dell stares at Elo.)* She don't like Erma, Erm.

ERMA: It's okay.

DELL: No! wanna call you whatchu comf't'ble with, whatchu... whatchu used to.

ERM: Erma's fine.

ELO: That's not whatchu told me.

ERM: Well right now I'm not talkin' to you.

ELO: *Hah!*

DELL: You wanna sandwich? little chipped ham?

ERM: No thank you.

ELO: Not unless it's vegetarian chipped ham.

DELL: Vegetarian? *(Beat.)* Oh I didn't... I didn't know—

ERM: It's okay.

DELL: *Knew* I shoulda perused the salad bar. *(Notices Erm glancing at photos in frames.)* That's Elo, first grade. Ain't she cute? *(Erm mesmerized.)* Bet she look like you, same age. Bet you think it's yourself.

ERM: My first grade... Even the dress. So close.

DELL: Oooh I wisht I'da thought ask ya bring pitchers a you growin' up. *(Elo files her nails.)*

ERM: Don't have that many.

DELL: Still. You don't know how it hurt... Missin' it. You. All them years *Stop that! (Elo startled.)* 'Round the food. *(Elo, sulky, puts file away.)*

ERM: Is that Rosie?

DELL: Yeah my granbaby, poor little granbaby. Her on this earth too short. *(Beat.)*

ERM: Any a... your husband?

DELL: Who? *(Beat.)* Oh, your *father.* Mmmm, just this. *(Goes to a drawer, pulls out a newpaper clipping.)* Obituary.

ERM: Musta been important. Picture in the paper.

DELL: From what I hear was important to half the women the Midwest one time or 'nother. We was married brief. Few months. Me fifteen, him grown man, twenty-five. Mess from the start, we didn't particularly care for each other with the lights on. But you all born at that time, you all had a limited but, turns out, lastin' impression kinda relationship with him since you two got the inheritance 'steada all the pups he surely littered Nebraska to Ohio. *(Beat.)* You go to church? *(Erm shakes her head no.)* How come? *(Erm shrugs.)* Ever been? *(Erm nods.)* They took you? little?

ELO: They who? *(No answer.)* Oh, you mean Nosy— *(Melodramatically puts hand over her mouth.)* Oh! Better not say *that*, she don't 'preciate *that*.

DELL: *Well.* I didn't find God 'til late in life.

ELO: Better not touch her *family* she real close to her *family*.

DELL: *I was lucky!* Survived a lotta heartache, bad times— *(Elo looking at Dell.)* Yeah, most I put on myself, wrong men. Didn't always do right by my baby. Babies. But lived through it and now. *(Touches the Bible.)* You own one, right?

ERM: Somewhere.

DELL: Dust it off. They say you don't know the hour Christ'll come maybe your lifetime. Maybe next five minutes. And whatchu got to say to God it all suddenly end? Get struck, lightnin'. Fall down your stairs. You coulda crashed your car way over here—

*(Elo makes a sudden groan and exits quickly.)*

DELL: Sensitive. Can't even mention a car crash without… I wanna know about you! Everything: kids? husband? I pump Elo for info but that a dry well.

ERM: I live on a farm. Alone. No kids, no husband. That's what I wanted, that's what I got.

DELL: 'til your siblin' move in.

ERM: *Visitin'!* *(Surprised and embarrassed by her outburst.)* She just stayin' awhile—

DELL: I hope… I don't expect ya understand but I 'pologize, Erm, I… Just a kid myself, I couldn'ta took care a two. Sounds like them people was good to ya, better 'n… Sorry.

ERM: 'S okay.

DELL: Never even drew up no papers, just a… understandin'. Ain't nobody contestin' nothin' we all… And *please* don't think I picked Elo over you! so happened you's the one *she* picked, I think she come in and Elo hollerin', hangin' on to me, she just picked the one at the moment felt less attached, her, that woman raised you—

ERM: Mary Clayton. That was her name.

DELL: She was good to ya?

ERM: She was *very* good to me.

DELL: Relief! *(Beat.)* Well. What it like? suddenly a grown sister.

ERM: I got one.

DELL: Blood sister, real sister.

ERM: *Is* my real—

DELL: Twin!

ERM: *(Beat.)* It's nice. *(Beat.)* She's nice.

DELL: I know you real close to them took you in—

ERM: My family.

DELL: Yeah but don't it… This is somethin' different Sure they nice people but… We got somethin'… shared. You and me. Elo.

ERM: Genes.

DELL: Genes! I mean… don't that make some kinda connection? special? If we passed on the street strangers, I feel like we… You know? *(Erm stares at her.)* And you and Elo, Lord! See your reflection yourself 'cross the sidewalk. *(Beat.)* My fault. Somethin' we had, inside, but never got to hone. Blood. Bond. *(Beat.)* So happy you come see me! I been waitin', waitin' so long.

ERM: How come you never come see me?

ELO: *(Entering.)* She don't b'lieve in drunk drivin'.

DELL: I ain't drank in ages, Elo, don't make out like I do.

ERM: Not in thirty-six years not in the last year thirty miles away.

DELL: Erm… *(Pause.)* Didn't know if you wanted it. Scared. *(Beat.)* You wanted it?

*(Beat.)*

ERM: I dunno.

ELO: I'm clonin' Rosie. *(Beat.)* I got that father money I'm bringin' her back. Takin' pieces of her thigh bone turnin' 'em into a whole her.

*(Pause.)*

DELL: Well. Eve come from Adam's rib. Lemme get the cake!

*(Dell quickly exits into the kitchen. Elo and Erm look at each other, startled.)*

ELO: Did you hear me? *(No answer.)* DID YOU HEAR ME?

*(Dell returns with a birthday cake.)*

DELL: *(Sings:)* "Happy bir—" I feel like it's *my* birthday, both my girls here. Both my beauties thirty-six-year-old angels. *(Sings:)* "Happy" see? *(Reads the cake:)* "Happy Birthday Erma and Eloise."

ELO: Why she first? *(They stare at Elo.)* I'm not sayin' favorites, just… I was first.

DELL: Naw, Erma. Erm. *(Points to Erm:)* Six o' seven AM. *(Points to Elo:)* Six: nineteen AM.

*(Beat.)*

ELO: You told me—

DELL: Who knows what I told you, Elo, you always needin'. I wanted you feel good, that make me a monster?

ELO: You make me feel good puttin' all those welts my legs? back?

DELL: *(Shaking her head.)* She remember history whole lot different 'n me, hard to fathom we's same house.

ELO: And why you bring up car accident? Rub it in my face—

DELL: Aw, Elo, I wa'n't even talkin' about—

ELO: *(To Erm:)* You heard her! You heard her!

DELL: This bakery dee-vine. Next to Elo, she ever bake for ya? Elo got *talent*, people know it, stand in line, her treats. You Birthday girl, you the first piece.

ELO: Grew up fixin' for myself, peanut butter sandwiches breakfast, lunch, dinner *days* 'til you show your face, I didn't even know you was goin' no note. Just I come home from school, house empty. Again.

DELL: Cuz that birthday girl I guess don't want her piece. You like chocolate, right?

ELO: Bread all hard and moldy but I eat it, hungry and no money left for me.

DELL: Elo sure got a 'magination. Elo oughta write for the paperbacks.

ELO: DON'T SAY IN MY HEAD!

DELL: *(A bite.)* Uh! Melt in your mouth!

ELO: Sick, vomitin' but you don't hold me, comfort me like the other mamas. *(Dell, content, cutting pieces of cake, humming "What a Friend We Have in Jesus.")* Lucky Uncle Jack happen by, snot, throwup all over me, some of it old, crusty. Take me to the doctor *strep*. Fever, they consider puttin' me in the hospital but say Let's see how the antibiotics work, they got a warped idea I better off home taken care by my mama. Lucky Uncle Jack... I coulda died! I coulda died!
*(Dell continues humming a few more notes, then stops. Looks at Elo.)*

DELL: Oh you finished? Too bad Jack ain't around, convenient your sole witness to this so-called outa the picture dead.

ELO: Convenient for *you!*

DELL: Answer me this. I all that kinda witch, why you move out here with me? Your never-speak-to-you-agains never last more 'n three days why you here now?

ELO: I don't know. I don't know!

DELL: You gotta eat your cake, Erm, now don't tell me calories. *(Silence.)* What. Believe Elo?

*(Beat.)*

ERM: I—

ELO: You don't *know?*

DELL: Well guess you would.

ELO: Believe *her? I* toldju—

DELL: Guess you would twins. They got special relationships. I hear 'bout twins got their own languages, secret—

ELO: You gotta be raised together for that you gotta have a mother responsible enough keep both her babies for that.

DELL: Oh! forgot somethin'! *(Exits quickly.)*

ELO: You like her, dontchu. *(No answer.)* You believe her. Believe me! She done it!

DELL: *(Off:)* Erm, I know Elo tryin' to fill your head with the anti-truth. Don't believe it.

ELO: Everyone likes her. Uncle Jack, favorite uncle, 'f he hadn't been there I coulda died. I love Uncle Jack why didn't he take me? Him and Aunt Lottie, she lemme help with the homemade ginger snaps when I visit, Uncle Jack teach me shoot pool. Or report her. Child welfare, least I be raised by someone better, couldn't be worse. Why didn't he call child welfare? Why didn't he pick up a goddamn phone? Blood! Can't do that to blood his baby sister, bitch, never do that his stupid, ugly baby sister bastard *hate* him!

DELL: *(Enters, a belt playfully dangling from her hand.)* Elo! Bring back memories? *(Elo and Erm horrified.)* Aw, kiddin'! Just self-fulfill prophecyin' her tales for her.

ELO: *(Tears.)* Not funny.

DELL: You tellin' me.

ELO: God God if there's God how come you all healthy?

DELL: *(Shaking her head.)* Elo, Elo.

ELO: How come you ain't reaped your sins?

DELL: Oh I have. Guess I never get another granbaby, one daughter some dyke on the farm, other all she issue turn to blood, down the toilet or through the windshield.

*(Silence. Then Elo runs out of the room.)*

DELL: *(Trembling, near tears.)* I didn't mean that! Aw hope you don't think I meant that, Erm, I got a evil streak! I got a nasty side when I'm hurtin' aw

I miss my granbaby so bad! *(Wipes her tears, recovers.)* I admit it. I was a better grammama than mama who ain't. Sweet little thing, spoiled thing. *(Beat.)* Clonin'. Hmm well, might be okay. Her bone. Be us. Blood.

ERM: Don't think it's playin' God?

DELL: You challengin' me cuz I turn Christian? Everyone always wanna litmus the Christian for hypocrisy.

ERM: No. Just wonder 'bout the answer myself, askin' for your insight.

DELL: *(Beat.)* Genesis. God said man have dominion.

ERM: Over the creatures a the earth God never said man create man.

DELL: Well. He might need a little help. Get rid a the crazies. Rapists, gays, drug addicts.

ERM: That's genetic engineering.

DELL: Yeah.

ERM: That's not clonin' that's genetic engineering.

DELL: Whatever.

*(Beat.)*

ERM: Get rid a the drunks?

DELL: *(Gets Erm's meaning.)* Yeah, probably woulda been for the best.

*(Golf balls on the roof, startling them both. Dell runs to the window.)*

DELL: *Hail? (Erm comes to the window.)* There's God. Cocky as we wanna be, thinkin' humans toppa the species triangle. Maybe, maybe not but so what if we are: there's things bigger.

*(Dell studies Erm's face, then goes to a drawer, pulls out a personal letter-sized envelope. It looks old.)*

DELL: *(Smiles.)* Happy birthday. *(Erm stares at it.)* Do me this I never ask nothin' else.

*(Erm opens the envelope. A photograph. Surprised. Affected. Looks at Dell.)*

DELL: Yours. *(Erm looks back at the picture.)* Two little doll faces, four months ol'. You the left.

ERM: We look happy. *(Dell beams.)* We were happy babies?

DELL: Sure were that day. Oh I's too young but I tried, loved yaw to pieces and I think feelin' was mutual. This week my mama was away, she had her moments too, some man she found workin' the Holiday Inn who knows. So don't hear from her a few days, I grab my chance: girl again! Boy come in with the fair, I follow him next town we have ourself a little torrid. Back four days and Mama just come home day before herself, "Why you lee them babies alone!" But yaw smelt s' bad by then *she* wouldn't touch ya, so I go down to the basement, nice bed I set up for ya there, 'f I'd left ya upstairs Nosy Neighbor surely'd heard the hollerin' night and day. I clean ya up, lotion your little butt sores, feed ya *so* glad see your mama! That evenin' took a picture see? Yaw don't look underfed to me. That was the sweetest memory, when I first come home, little angels my babies so sweet asleep I didn't care 'bout the damn smell that pretty picture. She "They ain't 'sleep! they passed out the hunger" naw. I know what I see: trust, love. Yaw knew your mama always come back.

## SCENE FOUR

*Retta in a hospital bed. She has had a stroke. Something in her face may be vaguely contorted, such as one side of her mouth in a strange, frozen half-smile. Erm sits in a chair next to Retta, reading from the Bible.*

ERM: "And God said, Let us make man in our image, after our likeness: and let them have dominion over the fish of the sea, and over the fowl of the air, and over the cattle, and over all the earth, and over every creeping thing that creepeth upon the earth" this is borin'. *(Flips pages.)* Ooooh good 'n'. "And they said, Go to, let us build a city and a tower, whose top may reach unto heaven; And the Lord said, Behold, the people is one, and they have all one language; and this they begin to do; and now nothing will be restrained from them, which they have imagined to do. Go to, let us go down, and there confound their language, that they may not understand one another's speech" tryin' to get higher, higher, see God, be God, *their* tower turn to Babel, my scientist people: aneuploid, endoplasmic reticulum, zona pellucida. Well. Babel to the lay crowd, to my scientist people regular small talk. Chit chat.

RETTA: *(A sudden panic:)* Air ear?

ERM: Downstairs in the playroom don't worry. I told the woman watch out for him. You know, 'til kinda recent, they didn't call science "science," called it "natural philosophy." Biologists were philosophers, this is what their job was way they saw it and everyone else: *observe* God's creations. Enlighten others, *God's* creations.

*(Retta puts her hand on the Bible, scraping it as if clutching the words, a signal for Erm to continue.)*

ERM: Okay. *(Erm flips pages. Reads:)* "Know ye that—" *(Retta drools. Erm wipes it up.)* "Know ye that the Lord he is God: it is he that hath made us, and not we ourselves; we are his people and the sheep of his pasture."

RETTA: *(A sudden panic:)* Air ear?

ERM: Downstairs in the playroom.

ELO: *(Enters in a rush.)* I didn't know where you went! Middle a the night, wake up, house empty. I don't like that, no note.

ERM: *(Reading:)* "And the angel took the censer, and filled it with fire of the altar, and cast it into the earth: and there were voices, and thunderings, and lightnings, and an earthquake."

ELO: Erm—

RETTA: *(A sudden panic:)* Air ear?

ELO: Wha she say?

ERM: "Where Sear." Downstairs in the *playroom.*
   *(As Elo speaks, Retta will start sucking her tongue as if her mouth is dry.)*

ELO: Didn't know where you were, grabbed your phone hit "redial." Her neighbor answers, says "Didn't Erm tell ya? Ambulance. Hospital."

ERM: Thirsty? *(Pours Retta water from the pitcher—not enough to fill the cup.)*

ELO: Her neighbor says "I didn't know Retta had another sister." I say, "I don't have a ride." So she come out get me. Thirty miles. Nice lady.

ERM: Drink, Retta.
   *(Erm holds the cup for Retta. Retta takes a couple of sips, then moves her mouth away, finished.)*

RETTA: Oo aa oo ay im.

ELO: Wha she say?

ERM: *(Reading:)* "Therefore will not we fear, though the earth be removed and though the mountains be carried into the midst of the sea—"

RETTA: Oo aa oo ay im!

ERM: *(Picks up pitcher, to Elo:)* You mind bringin' this to the nurse? Ask her to fill it.

ELO: Sure.
   *(Elo takes the pitcher, goes to the doorway, looks down the hall, turns around.)*

ELO: One at the desk?

ERM: *(Eyes on Retta.)* Yep.

ELO: She's not there.

ERM: She be back. Go wait for her.

ELO: I can see the desk from here. I can wait here 'til she gets back. 'Case you need me. Help Retta to the bathroom, somethin'.

RETTA: Er.

ERM: Hmm?

RETTA: Oo aa oo ay im.

ERM: I know.

ELO: Wha she say?

ERM: I hope you're not sick a the Psalms I'm kinda partial to 'em.

ELO: I didn't know sickle cell caused strokes.

ERM: "Though the waters thereof roar and be troubled, though the mountains shake with the swelling thereof."

ELO: Is that how your mother—?

ERM: *Family business! (Silence.)* Keep your nose out.

(*Elo exits.*)

ERM: Retta. I don't know what to do about her she don't seem to be leavin'. Every week call from the garage: The ignition's fixed but now the breaks. The breaks fixed but now the engine. The engine's fixed but now the windshield wipers she never seem too disappointed every time she report the latest ailment of her car, keep her stranded my guest room. I let it go awhile but now she startin' to get all in our business. *(Shrugs.)* She got no family her own, no real family. Lord, ya oughta meet her *mother*.

RETTA: Er! Oo aa oo ay im!

ERM: I know I have to take him. *(Beat.)* It's time.

ELO: *(Returns with bottled water and pitcher.)* I caught her midstream. Runnin' to some bedpan emergency, she gimme the bottle, asked I mind fillin' the pitcher. 'Course! Least I can do for my sister's sister. *(Pouring.)*

SEAR: *(Enters.)* Retta!

(*Sear has Down's Syndrome. His speech distorted, his movements awkward. He goes to Retta, puts his arms around her. A nurse stands in the doorway.*)

RETTA: Ear.

NURSE: *(Kind:)* You tol' me he start cryin' for Retta, bring him up. Right?

(*Erm nods. Nurse exits.*)

SEAR: Retta sick! Retta sick!

ERM: She be okay, Sear.

(*Sear only now seems to notice Erm. Goes to her.*)

SEAR: Mama!

(*Sear hugs Erm tight. Elo stares at Erm. Erm looks at Elo.*)

ERM: You're the one said "abortion." All I said was Down's, I give him up.

SEAR: Retta! Retta!

(*Sear goes to her, hugs her.*)

RETTA: Ear.

*(Sear pulls out a deck of cards.)*

SEAR: Retta, look. Heart. Spade. Diamond. Spade. Spade. Heart. Club.

*(Sear continues pulling a card off the deck and naming its suit. Eventually:)*

ERM: Hard. Spend so much a my life carin' for my poor mama I couldn't… *(Pause.)* And Retta! Retta the stronger for it, stronger sister. Retta dyin' for a baby but terrified she pass the gene on, I tell her the daddy gotta have the trait too but she 'on't listen she… *(Beat.)* 'Case you wonder. I wholly offer him call her "Mama," she earned it. Retta's the one say Naw, keep things straight, no confusion.

SEAR: Club. Diamond, no heart. Heart. Club. *(Continues.)*

ERM: I had the high hopes. Nine months huge, starin' out a window, how I tell my sick sister I'm so relieved we don't share genes. My poor sickle cell family but happy my child never get it, my perfect perfect child. Then my water broke.

RETTA: *(Scraping the Bible.)* Er! Er!

ERM: Wish I coulda shared it, Ret! Why you gotta go through all the pain? me none not fair! You the good one! good sister!

SEAR: Mama!

*(Sear runs to Erm, puts his arms around her. Now notices Elo. Stares at her, curious. Then suddenly runs to Elo, puts his arms around her.)*

ERM: *(Surprised.)* He looks like you.

ELO: *(Shakes her head.)* You just see yourself in me. He looks like *you*. *(Tears in Erm's eyes.)*

SEAR: *(To Elo:)* You play cards?

ERM: Sear.

*(A lengthy pause: Sear and Elo stare at Erm.)*

ERM: This is Aunt Elo.

SEAR: *(Trying out the word:)* Elo? *(Laughs and laughs.)* You play cards… Elo? *(Laughs and laughs.)*

ELO: Sure.

SEAR: *(Laying out the cards.)* Club. Diamond. Spade. Club. Spade. Heart. *(He waits; no response from Elo.)* Your hand!

ELO: Oh! *(Picks up her cards.)*

ERM: Tell you what, Retta. If genetic engineering coulda made things different, I be first to sign up. If they said this knock out the damn sickle cell, if I coulda had a sister healthy, healthy—

RETTA: Aa oo ee umbaa el.

ELO: Wha she say?

ERM: I dunno.

SEAR: I know! She say, "That would be somebody else."


## SCENE FIVE

*Erm and Elo sit in a meadow.*

ELO: System 1: Retta in my bed, Sear on the couch, me and you share your double. *(Erm shakes her head no.)* Figured that. System 2: Me in my bed, Sear on the couch, you and Retta share your double.

ERM: Sear scared, downstairs by himself.

ELO: We gotta have a plan, Erm, Retta comin' tomorrow.

ERM: *(Smile to herself.)* Retta comin' tomorrow.

ELO: Preliminary scheme, us prepared for a recoverin' stroke patient, right? Need ta keep Retta upstairs, right? Same floor's the bathroom.
*(Erm nods. Sear enters from one side of the stage, laughs, fully self-entertained (chasing a butterfly?), runs across and off the other side.)*

ELO: You know she won't be the same. I mean, lot better than in the hospital but…
*(Elo trails off. The Sheep enters, bleats.)*

ERM: Over the phone we converse now, I understand her she understand me. Come a long way so far, and miracles happen every day. No harm in prayin' for one.

ELO: That's the second time I heard you mention prayer, ain't prayer against your religion? science?

ERM: More I learn a one, more I do a the other.
*(Sear enters, running and giggling again. Sees The Sheep. Curious, he stops in front of it, looking it over, looking it in the face.)*

ELO: Sear found a friend.

ERM: Maybe she found him. Guess she feel neglected, was a time animals my only buddies, now so many people my alone-farm start to feel like Gran Central rush.

THE SHEEP: *(Only Sear hears:)* The phenomenon of genomic imprinting stipulates that mothers add proteins to DNA in certain ways and fathers in others: clone or no, embryos must have DNA from both a mother *and* a father to develop. *(Sear giggles.)*

ELO: Privacy you gonna miss. How long 'fore you kick us all out? You ain't used to it: bumpin' into people, every time you look up face in your face.

ERM: I'm adaptable.

*(Elo looks at Erm. Erm looks at Elo. They both break out laughing. Meanwhile:)*

THE SHEEP: In '71 Janet Mertz caused an uproar when she recombined DNA from various sources, starting us down the slippery slope to genetic engineering. *(Sear giggles.)*

ERM: Anyhow, the house use a little expansion. Maybe a nice room and toilet first floor so Retta get outside, never gotta fool with the steps. And Sear gettin' older, house full a women he gonna need walls sometime. And a few improvements I been meanin' get to awhile, leaky roof, new chicken wire. Plus, cookin' business, aintchu require extra stove? sink? Develop the kitchen 'cordin to your specs I got twenty-six thousand expendable.

ELO: Me too.

SEAR: Mama, blow.

*(Sear holds a dandelion in front of Erm's face. Erm rubs her nose with her finger, then blows. Sear giggles. Elo misses this, her eyes on The Sheep.)*

ELO: That kinda breed. Like Dolly?

ERM: Finn-Dorset, the same.

ELO: Some sheep, huh. *(The Sheep bleats, exits.)*

SEAR: Elo, blow.

*(Elo rubs her nose with her finger, then blows the dandelion Sear holds in front of her face. Sear giggles.)*

ERM: Hey!

ELO: What!

ERM: You always do this? *(Rubs her nose.)* Rub your nose before you blow a dandelion?

ELO: *(Confused.)* I don't...

ERM: Give her a dandelion, Sear.

*(Sear holds another in front of Elo's face.)*

SEAR: Elo, blow.

*(Elo makes a few attempts at blowing without rubbing her nose but it feels strange; she can't. Finally quickly rubs her nose and blows.)*

ERM: Me too! Twins.

*(Erm and Elo laugh.)*

SEAR: Now I'm gonna pick uuuuuum... *(He thinks.)* Now I'm gonna pick uuuuuum... *(He thinks.)*

ELO: Blue, blue, not a cloud.

ERM: The honeysuckle. *(Erm and Elo both take deep, luxurious breaths.)*

SEAR: Clovers! *(Sear runs off.)*

ERM: *(Calling, pointing:)* You stay outa that patch there, Sear! You hear me? Poison oak! Itch!

ELO: What a place. Unfettered. *(Laughs, waves to Sear in the distance:)* I see you!

ERM: I read about Yup'ik Indians, Canada. Still live off the land, pure land, but feel it encroachin': us. From far, far away us take from them what we need and they just better get used to it. They call us "the people who change nature," their astonishment only thing outweigh their dread. *(Beat.)* We in a field a clones. *(Chuckles.)* Grass and dandelions, clovers for some things, asexual reproducin's all nature.

ELO: If you was worried 'bout him bein' a little different, you was right. All the healthy kids, perfect kids in the world and the lottery, instead, give you Sear. Jackpot.

SEAR: *(Enters, running.)* Look, Mama! Four-leaf. *(Giggles.)*
*(Sear holds out the clover to Erm. Erm gazes at the clover, then up at Sear.)*

END OF PLAY

# The Second Death of Priscilla
## by Russell Davis

# BIOGRAPHY

Russell Davis' plays have been produced at various theatres, including People's Light & Theatre, Long Wharf, Center Stage, and St. Louis Repertory. They have also been presented at Mark Taper Forum's New Work Festival, New Harmony Project, Sundance Playwrights Lab and National Playwrights Conference. He was resident playwright at People's Light & Theatre for the Theatre Residency Program of the National Endowment for the Arts/Theatre Communications Group. He received two earlier fellowships from the National Endowment for the Arts and grants from the McKnight Foundation, Tennessee Arts Commission, New York Foundation for the Arts and New York Council on the Arts. He is a past member of New Dramatists. He has also worked and performed as a juggler.

# HUMANA FESTIVAL PRODUCTION

*The Second Death of Priscilla* premiered at the Humana Festival of New American Plays in March, 2003. It was directed by Marc Masterson with the following cast:

| | |
|---|---|
| Priscilla | Barbara Gulan |
| Peter | Will Bond |
| Second Peter | Jon Held |
| Jacqueline | Graham Smith |
| Aramanda | Jen Grigg |
| Second Priscilla | Jenna Close |
| Coquelicot | Katherine Hiler |

and the following production staff:

| | |
|---|---|
| Scenic Designer | Paul Owen |
| Costume Designer | Lorraine Venberg |
| Lighting Designer | Tony Penna |
| Sound Designer | Vincent Olivieri |
| Properties Designer | Doc Manning |
| Stage Manager | Nancy Pittelman |
| Assistant Stage Manager | Andrew J. Paul |
| Videographer | Valerie Sullivan Fuchs |
| Video Engineer | James Tittle |
| Dramaturg | Sarah Gubbins |
| Assistant Dramaturg | Susannah Engstrom |
| Directing Assistant | Joseph Haj |

# CHARACTERS

PRISCILLA, a person upstairs in her room

PETER, her friend

JACQUELINE, a fabulous person from a neighboring land

ARAMANDA, who lives in her body

COQUELICOT, who lives in her head

SECOND PETER and SECOND PRISCILLA, two jugglers/dancers

# SETTING

Priscilla's bedroom, the big, blue sky outside, and a forest

# TIME

The present

Barbara Gulan and Graham Smith
in *The Second Death of Priscilla*

27th Annual Humana Festival of New American Plays
Actors Theatre of Louisville, 2003
photo by Harlan Taylor

# The Second Death of Priscilla

## ACT ONE
### SCENE ONE

*A large, empty, blue space.*
*A window frame with pale curtains hangs down from above.*
*Priscilla sits in a chair. Nearby is a second chair.*
*Enter Peter. He carries a large, black suitcase, or trunk.*
*He sets the suitcase down.*
*He looks at Priscilla.*

PETER: That's very beautiful, Priscilla.
*(No response.)*
I like your dress. I like it very much.
*(Pause.)*
I like the birds flying. All those birds in the air. On your dress.
*(Pause.)*
May I join you? Can I sit?
*(Peter sits in the second chair.)*
Your grandmother told me you were sitting up here. She tells me you call your bedroom the big, blue space. You like to sit all alone. In this big, blue space.
*(Pause.)*
I like your grandmother. How she repeats the things you say. They seem important to her.
*(Peter gets up. He goes to the window. He looks out.)*
Nice, huh? I love this window. What you can see out there. I've always liked how you can see the woods. How they're perched up here with the house. On a cliff above the sea. A bluff. I like the rocks down below too. The sandy land. Sense of wilderness. I like it especially when there's wind. When a wind comes from other lands, like the big, bad breath of another planet, and those trees, the whole forest outside this house, bends.
I like days like this too. I like all the sky. Nothing but big, blue sky.
*(Pause.)*
Your grandmother says when you're not in here, you wander outside. Sometimes at night. She's had to go out and find you in the night.
*(He goes back to his chair.)*

PETER: Or she hears talking. You talk in here. Call out. Speak of things she's not heard before.

*(Pause.)*

She gave me a piece of paper. She found this paper one night. Outside your room. With words on it, or names.

*(He takes out a piece of paper. He opens it.)*

Aramanda. That's a word. Or name. Sounds like a boat. A ship from Palestine. Or Spain. Maybe a language. Sounds like a language we spoke. Aramanda.

I want to ask you about all these words.

In particular, this one, Crackle. When I saw Crackle on this paper right away I knew what it was. It's the word we used when we couldn't talk anymore. We'd say, Crackle. Which meant we'd have to stop again, talking. And the other person was meant to understand.

So you want to tell me about Crackle? Why it's here on this paper?

Or how about Peter? You have my name here too. You want to tell me how come my name's down here? Close to Crackle?

Uh huh. How about Coquelicot? Is this a name, Coquelicot? Some flower?

Or Jacqueline. Who's Jacqueline?

*(No response.*

*Peter folds up the paper. He puts it in his pocket.*

*He goes to the suitcase. He opens it.)*

I brought some things, Priscilla. A few things we used to do together. For example, this. Remember these?

*(Peter takes a number of small, white balls from inside the suitcase. He places them on the ground. He rolls them one after the other past Priscilla.)*

You remember? You remember any of these?

*(Priscilla pays no attention.*

*Peter walks past her. He collects the balls.)*

You don't remember how we worked? All the work we did. How much we had to practice?

*(No response.*

*Peter puts the balls back in the suitcase.)*

Well, there're the balls. Some hats in there too. Juggling rings. Juggling clubs. There's lots we used to do in here.

*(He takes out a juggling club. He spins it. He drops it down to his foot. He kicks it back up into his hand. He puts it back in the suitcase.)*

PETER: I may just have to practice, Priscilla. That's all. Right here. It's what I do anyway. I could practice in front of you. Get to do my practice today. Maybe you'll get to remember. Want to practice too.

*(Pause.)*

There were things you do, lots of them, what you used to practice, I could never do some of the things you do. To this day. You could dance too. Play the violin. I remember you playing a violin. And that's one thing I loved, Priscilla, about you. How much you always wanted to practice. You wanted to every day.

*(Pause.)*

Anyway. It's all in there. My suitcase. Whenever you want to again. I got more too. Lots more outside in the car.

*(Peter goes back to his chair. He regards Priscilla.)*

I guess, Priscilla. All the stuff I do with my body, all my practice, the tricks, I guess I've begun to wonder, deep down, if it doesn't seem arbitrary. This body. To have hands. Or a face. Five fingers. Certain limbs which work. Because there's something I'm not comfortable with anymore. About this body. A longing now I can't express. I don't know how. The most I can express is a cage. I'm in a cage which I long to get out. And all the tricks, these hard earned skills, are no longer enough. They're like I'm banging now. Banging at the edge of this cage.

*(Pause.)*

I think of my body sometimes as a horse. I ride this horse to get places. But there are certain places I can't take the horse. I have to tie it to a tree. Walk on up ahead. Just myself. No horse.

And that's how I guess I think of you. Sometimes that's the only way to approach you. Get to really talk. If I have no horse.

*(Pause.)*

It's thoughts like this I learned from you. You're the thinker. I think I taught you tricks and skills. You taught me thoughts. A way to perceive. Like I was a creature, once upon a time, responding only to what I could see. What was visible. And I haven't seen you in some years, but this way you taught to perceive, it's entered me, finally.

Made me come back.

Because I always felt there was a journey. A most amazing journey you had to take. So I think I've come to see if this is it. The journey. And if it is, I've come to wait. I'll be waiting, I guess, for when you come back. Sitting right here, reading. Or practicing. And if I do anything silly, like take your hand, or talk to myself, that's fine. I'm fine. I'm just waiting back here, that's all, at your point of departure. This place you last left.

*(Peter goes to the suitcase again. He takes out some juggling rings. He turns away from Priscilla.*

*Music.*

*Second Peter appears upstage with a number of juggling rings. He juggles them.)*

PRISCILLA: Peter?

*(Music stops. Second Peter exits. Peter turns.)*

PETER: Yes?

*(Pause.)*

PRISCILLA: I'm glad you're here, Peter.

PETER: Yes, I'm Peter.

PRISCILLA: Good.

PETER: Thank you. I'm glad too.

*(Peter puts the rings back in the suitcase.)*

PRISCILLA: You okay?

PETER: What?

PRISCILLA: How are you? Are you well?

PETER: I'm fine. Thank you.

PRISCILLA: I'm fine too.

PETER: Good.

*(Pause.)*

PRISCILLA: What is it, Peter?

PETER: What's what?

PRISCILLA: You look like you have something to say. To tell me.

PETER: You have a very beautiful dress, Priscilla.

PRISCILLA: Hm?

PETER: Your dress. I like it.

PRISCILLA: Yes?

PETER: All the birds, yes. Flying into the air on your dress. I like that.

PRISCILLA: Oh. I hadn't noticed.

PETER: It's nice.

PRISCILLA: Thank you.

PETER: You're very welcome.

*(Pause.)*

PRISCILLA: It's lovely, Peter. Some of the things you say.

PETER: What things?

PRISCILLA: Well, about the horse. I loved you talking like that. About a horse.

PETER: You heard me?

PRISCILLA: Oh, yes.

PETER: What else did you hear?

PRISCILLA: Just the horse.

PETER: Nothing else?

PRISCILLA: Well, no, you said a journey. Something about a journey. But I didn't hear. I was still thinking about the horse. How you leave it sometimes. To get on ahead.

    *(Pause.)*

PRISCILLA: What are you looking at?

PETER: Nothing. Your room.

    I haven't seen it in a while. This room.

PRISCILLA: Yes. It's still here.

PETER: Yeah, I can see. Can see all the brick wallpaper still here. From when you lived at home.

PRISCILLA: I took it down.

PETER: What?

PRISCILLA: I took some of the brick down over there.

PETER: That's right. You did.

PRISCILLA: I scraped it off. It was peeling.

PETER: Right.

PRISCILLA: Maybe it should be different wallpaper in here.

PETER: You think so?

PRISCILLA: I don't know. It's been up so long.

PETER: I guess.

PRISCILLA: Yes, I'd like to take it all down. Sweep it away. It's not doing anything, this wallpaper.

PETER: What would you put up instead?

PRISCILLA: I'm going to paint a gate. A picture of a gate.

PETER: On your wall?

PRISCILLA: Yes, there should be some kind of gate. Which I could go through. When I want to think about what it could be like outside. But also for when I come back. I want a gate. Something I can close behind.

PETER: What's the matter with the door downstairs?

PRISCILLA: Hm?

PETER: For going outside.

PRISCILLA: I'd rather have a gate, that's all. In my room.

PETER: Okay.

PRISCILLA: You don't think my own gate would look nice?

PETER: Sure, of course, it could. You could paint a beautiful gate, I know, on these walls.

PRISCILLA: Well, that's all, Peter. I'd just like something like that. Something I can shut. So I can sit safe in here.

PETER: You don't feel it's so safe here?

PRISCILLA: I guess so. I guess I can be safe.

PETER: Good.

PRISCILLA: But I'd still like to do that, wouldn't you? We could do that together, Peter. Get out some paints. And put a gate right there in the corner.

PETER: Okay, sure.

PRISCILLA: Yes, where the brick was peeling.

PETER: Sure, Priscilla. We can do that. We can paint a gate for you in here.

PRISCILLA: Good. Thank you, Peter.

*(Peter goes back to his chair.)*

PRISCILLA: I've been writing a speech, Peter.

PETER: You have?

PRISCILLA: Yes. I'm almost done with it.

PETER: What's the speech?

PRISCILLA: I can't tell. You'll laugh.

PETER: No, I won't.

PRISCILLA: Yes, you'll think it's funny. You'll tease me.

PETER: You like to be teased.

PRISCILLA: Not this time, no.

PETER: Fine. I didn't think your gate was silly.

PRISCILLA: What gate?

PETER: The one you wanted. Right here in the wall.

PRISCILLA: Oh.

PETER: So tell it to me. I want to hear your speech.

PRISCILLA: No, it's not finished.

PETER: Then say the beginning.

PRISCILLA: I can't.

PETER: Come on, we've said silly, unfinished things to each other before. It's why we like each other.

PRISCILLA: It's spoken by a wolf.

PETER: What?

PRISCILLA: It's a wolf speaking. In my speech.

PETER: What wolf?

PRISCILLA: Well, the wolf, you know. Who wanted to eat the three pigs.

PETER: Oh, really? That wolf?

PRISCILLA: You think that's silly?

PETER: Well, no, I didn't hear it yet.

PRISCILLA: I'm sorry it's so silly.

PETER: Hey, no, I make up crazy things to say. All the time.

PRISCILLA: Like what?

PETER: You just heard a whole speech. About my body. I called it a cage. I said my body was a horse. I had to leave this horse. When I come to visit with you.

PRISCILLA: That wasn't silly.

PETER: Well, sure sounded it to me. Sounds like the same old silly Peter. In your presence. All over again. So I think you should tell me right now. About this silly wolf. Get it off your chest, you know. I want to hear the speech. The beginning of a whole speech you're working on. To be spoken by a wolf.

*(Priscilla gets up. She goes to the suitcase.)*

PRISCILLA: Is this your suitcase?

PETER: What?

PRISCILLA: You brought a suitcase to me?

PETER: Yes. Yes, I brought a whole suitcase.

PRISCILLA: Can I look inside?

PETER: Of course, sure. Take a look.

*(Priscilla looks inside.)*

PRISCILLA: Peter?

PETER: Yes?

PRISCILLA: I can't see in here.

PETER: What? What can't you see?

PRISCILLA: I can't see what you've brought.

PETER: Come on. Of course you can see.

PRISCILLA: No, Peter. There's nothing here.

PETER: What?

PRISCILLA: Sssh.

PETER: What for?

PRISCILLA: *(Afraid.)* I can't talk anymore.

PETER: You can't?

PRISCILLA: No, I'm sorry. I can't.

PETER: But we just got started.

PRISCILLA: I've got to go, Peter.

PETER: No, we're talking.

PRISCILLA: I have to, I'm sorry.

PETER: Where? Where are you going?

PRISCILLA: Crackle.

PETER: What?

PRISCILLA: *(Distracted.)* Crackle's coming.

PETER: No, wait. Priscilla, wait!

*(Priscilla goes quickly back to her chair. She sits. She withdraws.*
*The sound of a creature walking across the wet sand.*
*Peter hears it. He looks out the window.*
*A shadow, or cloud, passes across the stage. Peter sees it.*
*He looks at Priscilla.)*

PETER: Priscilla?

*(BLACKOUT.*
*The sound of a galloping horse.)*


SCENE TWO

*The empty, blue space.*
*The two chairs and suitcase are gone.*
*A huge window frame, about twelve feet high, and seven across, has replaced*
*the small window which hung down from above. This frame stands upright*
*on the ground. Pale curtains billow in it.*
*Enter Jacqueline through the window curtains. She has a full head of white*
*hair, like a grandmother, or frumpy godmother, except her face seems younger,*
*and masculine. She wears an ill fitting dress or nightgown.*
*She comes downstage.*

JACQUELINE: *(To audience:)* Nice, this curtain, don't you think?

This billowing one. In the large window here.

It makes me very happy. Makes me think so many things, a curtain like
that. It's like a veil. A wifty thing. A shadow perhaps between us. Because
I live the other side. In a land of endless, empty expanse. And you live
here. In a place of tiny, particular things. We're like neighbors. This curtain is our fence. We have a tiny, flimsy fence between us. Through

which we can catch a glimpse of each other. Take a peek. Maybe even get to speak. Like now. Because I find it hard, yes, for us to be neighbors. We have such differences. Hardly ever see each other. In fact, most of what I do is invisible to you. Unsuspected. And what seems so visible to you makes little sense to me.

*(Pause.)*

You can call me Jacqueline. If you should find yourself close again sometime to our fence, our little window here, call out Jacqueline, Jacq, and I will answer. From a land you cannot go to. A place you could never ride to, no, not on a horse.

*(Pause.)*

I'm trying to remember the first time I saw Priscilla. The first glimpse she caught of me.

*(Pause.)*

I think a physical perception of life, this world you see out here, is like a straw house. Or a house of sticks. Something you built. And I think that's when Priscilla first caught a glimpse of me. When she could see how flimsy these things were, what we build, what we believe we can see.

*(Pause.)*

I think sometimes of what's out here as surface. Little sand castles. And the other side where I live are invisible depths, and waves, beneath. The real influence. And I think of children. How they see monsters. Until it's explained we don't see monsters. We're civilized.

And so these monsters become no longer seen. Though we're all sure they're still there. Right beneath the eyes. Huge ones, yes, as big as you can make or suppress them in your mind. I know. I've seen them. How they can walk right through under everything you say. And I think of myself as what might be like a lion tamer to you. I am here perhaps to show your monsters. To parade them before your eyes. Make them do their tricks for you.

*(Sound of someone, or thing, walking across wet sand.)*

For example, we have a wolf. Which is not like any wolf you could ever see this side of our window. This wolf has no sense of physical limitation, no understanding of how a wall, or the door to a house, is meant to keep him separate from getting to us. This wolf walks on ceilings at night. Likes to stare down at you. He can come from nowhere, like the wind. The big, bad breath of another planet. All things blow aside in his path.

And where this wolf lives a day is like a thousand years, and there's no brick on earth, what can withstand a day or two like that.

And this wolf has words for you. He can speak. Whole speeches. He can tell you what you see out here, as a wolf, is the bare tip of what a wolf can really be.

*(A shadow, or cloud, passes across the stage.)*

Priscilla hears this wolf. She has. All his nimble words. Prowling outside her room. Waiting for her to fall asleep.

*(The sound of a galloping horse.)*

But I think there's nothing to be so afraid of. Really. In this land I speak from. This place I tell. We're neighbors, I said. We have the same fence, the same dark forest, our backyards are next to each other under the same big, blue sky. And I think I should come over more often. I should beckon to you. Pull aside this veil sometime. Let you know who I am.

*(Jacqueline reaches to pull aside a curtain. Her dress parts slightly. It reveals the hind leg of a Wolf.)*

*(To audience:)* I just love this curtain, don't you? This window here where Priscilla sits. Through which I can come out to you.

*(The curtains continue to billow.*
*BLACKOUT.)*


SCENE THREE

*The big, blue space. There are streaks of yellow.*
*The huge window frame is gone. Instead, a small window hangs down again from above. The window is closed.*
*A young girl, Aramanda, sits in the chair where Priscilla sat. Aramanda has short cropped hair and wears an eyepatch. Her face is dirty and scarred. She wears the same dress Priscilla wore.*
*Peter sits in the other chair. He is asleep, holding an open folder in his lap. Nearby is his suitcase.*
*There is a silhouette of a large horse grazing upstage.*
*Aramanda watches the horse.*

ARAMANDA: *(Whispering to Peter.)* Is that your horse?
*(No response.)*
Is that your horse out there? In the big, blue space?

*(Peter remains asleep.)*

*(Aramanda gets up and goes to Peter. She takes the folder from his lap. She looks at it. She closes it and puts it back. She reaches into one of his pockets. She takes out a folded piece of paper. She crumples it and puts the paper in her own pocket.*

*She goes back to her chair. She sits.)*

ARAMANDA: *(To Peter.)* I asked you, Is that your horse? Did you come here on that horse?

*(The silhouette of the horse moves upstage.*

*It comes to a stop. It grazes again.*

*Aramanda watches the horse.*

*Peter wakes up. He sees Aramanda.)*

PETER: Priscilla?

*(No response.*

*Aramanda continues to watch the horse.)*

Priscilla, I'm sorry. I fell asleep.

*(He looks down at his lap.)*

I fell asleep looking through this folder. I found it open. Right here in the room. I wondered if you left it open for me. You have stories in here, Priscilla. I never knew you were thinking about these stories. All these thoughts.

*(Pause.)*

Would you rather I didn't then? Look at any thoughts you have, Priscilla? In this folder?

*(No response.)*

I can tell you, actually, what I saw in here. It's not much. Cause what I saw started me thinking. All my own thoughts about you. And somewhere I got tired. Real tired from driving here. Made myself fall asleep.

But I'd like it, I would, if you'd read sometime from this folder. Some of the things in here.

*(No response.)*

I guess not.

*(Peter puts aside the folder.)*

ARAMANDA: Is that your horse?

PETER: Hm?

ARAMANDA: The horse. Did you come here on the horse over there?

PETER: There's a horse?

ARAMANDA: Yes. It keeps moving. You really should tie it up better. What if it decides to come wander over here? You shouldn't ride up, you know, so closely on a horse.

*(Peter goes to the window. He looks out.)*

PETER: I don't see a horse. Any horse out there.

ARAMANDA: You don't see that horse?

PETER: No, what horse? I see the shore below, that's all. And the woods. The woods right here at the top of the cliff. The bluff. There's no horse.

ARAMANDA: You really shouldn't tease, you know.

PETER: What?

ARAMANDA: Or pretend like this.

PETER: I'm not teasing.

ARAMANDA: Then why are you saying you can't see a horse?

PETER: Because I can't.

ARAMANDA: I never met anyone before who couldn't see their own horse.

PETER: I don't have a horse.

ARAMANDA: Then how did you get here?

PETER: What?

ARAMANDA: I don't know how you could have gotten here. Except on a horse. Because if that's not your horse over there, then there has to be another one. Another horse to get here. And if that's true, there's another, then that means someone else is here. And I need to worry. Someone else too rode up on a horse.

*(The horse upstage moves. It stops.*
*Aramanda watches.)*

PETER: Priscilla, come on. Don't be in a strange mood with me, okay? I just woke up.

ARAMANDA: You're strange yourself.

PETER: What?

ARAMANDA: Calling me Priscilla.

PETER: You don't want that?

ARAMANDA: No. There is no Priscilla anywhere around.

PETER: No? Where is she?

ARAMANDA: How should I know?

PETER: I don't know. You sure look like her.

ARAMANDA: I do not.

PETER: You don't look like Priscilla?

ARAMANDA: No.

PETER: Then who do you think you look like?

ARAMANDA: I don't know who you think Priscilla should look like. But it's not me. I don't look at all like how you think a Priscilla should look like.

*(Peter sits in his chair. He regards Aramanda.)*

PETER: *(Gently.)* Sure, you do. You look exactly like I think Priscilla should look. The same long, lovely, fair hair. Just like Priscilla. And the same pretty, pale face. Like you always had. Almost transparent. Like if I looked too hard I could see to the other side of you. And you have the same dress. This lovely, blue dress with birds on it. I just love how you sit in that dress, Priscilla. How you perch. Like you could fly away. Any moment. And your forehead too. I love that line down your forehead when you're thinking. Did you know that? Did I ever tell you? Your face gets all distant when you think like this. You make me feel like I'm out here, watching. In a world faraway from you. A whole different place. There seems so little of you left when you're in there thinking. You get so thin and frail. Like you could vanish, your whole body. Like if I tried to touch you, my hand would go right through. And all that's left is what's in your eyes. These same, big, wondering eyes. Full of things to think about. And when I take a look too, down your eyes, I swear I can see some other, even deeper person. Some other person you are, Priscilla, down there in your eyes.

*(Aramanda stands. She slaps Peter.*

*Pause.)*

ARAMANDA: My eyes aren't big. Nor do they wonder. My eyes are small. And one is missing. I have an eyepatch. An eyepatch, yes, because it's not there anymore for me to see out of. There's nothing to see down here in my eyes. So don't lie to me, ever again, about my eyes. And don't tell me either I have long, lovely hair. My hair is short and crooked. And my face is not pretty pale. It is dark and ugly.

PETER: Your face is never ugly.

ARAMANDA: Oh, don't be so stupid. Of course it's ugly. It has four big scars right here across it.

PETER: What scars?

ARAMANDA: You can't see scars?

PETER: No. I do not see any of your scars.

ARAMANDA: You are such a liar.

PETER: No, I'm not lying. I do not see these scars on your face. I see no eye-patch. I can see none of this stuff you tell me now you can see.

*(Pause.)*

ARAMANDA: How can you look at me and tell such a lie? How can you not see these scars right here on my face?

*(Aramanda goes to the window. She looks out.*
*Pause.*
*Peter looks through his pockets.)*

PETER: Priscilla? I had a piece of paper, Priscilla. Where is it? Your grandmother gave me this paper.

Did you take away my paper? All the words I had, the names you wrote?
*(No response.)*

Come on, Priscilla. There were words on that paper. Like Aramanda. Jacqueline. Like Crackle. You wrote down Crackle on this paper. Where is the paper, Priscilla?
*(No response.)*

Fine.

*(Peter goes to his suitcase. He opens it. He takes out three juggling clubs.*
*The sound of a violin.*
*Peter turns upstage away from Aramanda. He juggles the clubs.*
*The sound of juggling clubs landing in Peter's hands.*
*Aramanda watches.)*

ARAMANDA: What is it you're doing?

*(Peter doesn't respond.)*

It sounds lovely, what you're doing.

*(The big, blue space darkens. Then shifts to yellow.*
*The sound of the violin and sound of Peter continue.*
*Aramanda goes to Peter. She stands next to him, watching.*
*The horse upstage moves away. It comes to a stop.*
*Aramanda reaches out her hand. She takes one of the clubs.*
*Peter turns to her, holding the others.)*

ARAMANDA: Did you see? Just now?

PETER: What?

ARAMANDA: The horse.

PETER: What about it?

ARAMANDA: It moved. It's moved all the way over there. Away from us.

PETER: Okay.

ARAMANDA: It may leave us soon. For good.

PETER: Okay, good.

*(Peter reaches to take back the third club. Aramanda holds onto it.)*

*(Music. The sound of a violin continues.)*

ARAMANDA: I know you don't think it's yours. The horse. You think it's mine. Whatever I see. And I don't want to argue. About some horse. But I think I better tell you. I should say how I appreciate, I do, you came here. You stopped by. Made this journey. All to find me. But it doesn't belong to you, no. A journey like this. To come so faraway. From any world you know. Any place you could ever live.

And so if that could be your horse, if there's any chance, you should go over now and get it. Ride away, I know, from here. Because once the horse is gone, once it leaves, or something comes to take it away, there's no way left, you see. To escape from here. No way you could get out fast enough on foot.

*(Pause.)*

Just a warning, that's all. I'm like a gatekeeper, you know. To the land ahead.

*(Peter takes Aramanda's hand.)*

PETER: *(Softly.)* Come, Priscilla.

ARAMANDA: Hm?

PETER: I want you to do this with me.

ARAMANDA: What? What will we do?

*(Peter holds two clubs in his free hand.)*

PETER: Let's do this together, Priscilla. Come on. What we used to do.

ARAMANDA: It sounds so pretty when you call me that.

PETER: Priscilla, come.

ARAMANDA: So very pretty.

PETER: Come. Just throw the club.

ARAMANDA: Hm?

PETER: Throw it to me, yes. Toss it.

*(Still holding her hand, Peter tosses a club to Aramanda with his other hand. She tosses one back to him. They juggle together, each using one hand.*
*The sound of a violin continues.*
*Upstage, the horse is gone.*
*Lights dim.*
*Two figures, Second Peter and Second Priscilla appear upstage. They dance together, passing clubs between them.*
*The sound of a chorus.*
*Sound of an orchestra. The violin continues.*
*BLACKOUT.)*

# SCENE FOUR

*The big, blue space.*
*Priscilla is asleep in the chair by the hanging window. A violin rests in her lap.*
*The other chair is empty. Peter's suitcase is nearby. Three juggling clubs are lying on the ground.*
*Jacqueline stands outside the closed window. She walks back and forth. She comes back to the window. She regards Priscilla through the window.*
*Priscilla wakes up. She sees Jacqueline.*

JACQUELINE: *(Tapping on the window pane.)* May I come in?
*(No response.)*
I thought it would be good. If I came in.
*(Pause.)*
I've been waiting out here for quite some time. I thought I could see you asleep. I thought if you awoke, I'd like to ask if I could come in. Make myself at home. Right in there where you are.
*(Pause.)*
I know you've seen me before. It's not good to pretend like this. Not to speak to me.
*(Pause.)*
I'm the one who told you there was a wolf. A wolf is coming. You wouldn't want me to get caught out here, would you? When the wolf comes?
*(No response.)*
You know, I've always wondered about that. The words huff and puff. Why would a wolf ever say that? I will huff and puff. All your house down. Sounds demeaning to me. A wolf actually speaking like that. Besides, how could a wolf do that anyway? Blow a house down. That's simply not what a wolf does, how he frightens. And so I think if a wolf could speak, I mean, if we live in a land now all around where the wolf speaks, then why, I would like to know, would the wolf say something like huff and puff your house down? That's not what any wolf would speak to me. I mean, not if I was meant to be frightened. By the words of such a wolf.
You know what the wolf would speak? If it came to me? I mean, if I happened to be passing through some patch of land, a wilderness maybe, where if a wolf looked at me I could hear it speak? All its words?

JACQUELINE: I think what the wolf would speak would be the word bluff. That word. Not huff or puff. But bluff. And he wouldn't mean a person who bluffs or misleads. No, not at all. He'd mean like a cliff. A bluff, yes. A high, steep and precipitous place. Where he would tell me I have built my house. Overlooking a large body of water. Like the sea. And he would want to know, naturally, why I built my house in a place like that. On a sandy bluff above the sea. Did I not know that there could be a wind sometime? Winds will blow? Rains will descend, floods come? And beat upon this house?

Did I not know that?

Hadn't I been told?

And if I expected my house to survive perched like this in the path of wind, rain, and all the flood, and if I didn't expect the fall of my house to be very, very great indeed, ruinous, in fact, then I should have built it, my house, yes, on rock. Given it a good firm brick footing. A foundation to count on.

*(Pause.)*

Yes, I think those are words I could hear a wolf speak. If it spoke to me.

And I think I can hear it further say to me that he'll be waiting. That's all. Outside my house. For all this wind and rain and flood to come up. He'll just be prowling out there. Like a wolf. Prevent my leaving. Make me stay in this house. This place I have built myself. On a bluff like this. Above the sea.

*(Pause.)*

That's how I think. Yes. How a wolf would speak. At least to me.

*(Priscilla stands. She goes to Peter's suitcase. She places her violin on top of the suitcase.*

*Jacqueline follows her from a distance.)*

It's amazing. Amazes me how a few small details can get bollixed. Then add to the original bollix a couple of millennia and a whole story is distorted. Used as something to soothe our children. Because I think this little child's tale, with words like huff and puff, and the wolf who comes down the chimney, which a wolf cannot do, it's wind what comes down a chimney, not a wolf, and how can you boil wind in a pot of water, all of which proves my point that this story is a red herring. Something charming, yes, to distract us. From what really may have happened. Because I do believe there was indeed a wind. Lots of rain and flood too. And I believe there was a house which fell. And a wolf too. Just waiting outside, I know.

JACQUELINE: And I have to ask myself, I do, who was it, then, who changed this story? Bollixed the details. I mean, we assume it has a happy end. We assume history belongs to us. The victors. But what if somebody came along in the calmness after, after all the wind and rain and all the flood, and tampered with our story? Twisted it just a little. Made it slightly silly. So we wouldn't know, really, what happened. Take it too seriously. And so for the rest of our life here on earth, we'd tell this slightly skewed story to our children. Each one, as they grew up.

And when I think about this story in this light. That it's been tampered with, then I have to question its ending too. About the inhabitant in the brick house. I have to wonder is there really such an inhabitant around? Some moral like that which really, effectively exists?

Or is it actually the wolf? The wolf is still around. Telling these stories? So we won't know where he is. We can't see him. All the things he's up to.

*(Priscilla goes back to her chair. She sits.*

*Jacqueline regards the violin on top of Peter's suitcase. She regards the juggling clubs.)*

You have a friend. A visitor, I see. He's come by. I can see his suitcase. All his stuff. I imagine he'll be back soon enough. Be nice to have him here, wouldn't it, for when the wolf comes?

I should like to meet him myself, I would. Stand right there in that room with you and meet your friend. Yes. I imagine I'll do that sometime. Be in that room and meet your friend. But I must be off now, I'm afraid. You wouldn't want me to get caught out here, would you? When the wolf comes?

*(Jacqueline goes to the window. She taps on it.)*

By the way, will I find him here, your friend? The visitor? If I come back, will he be visiting you here, in your wonderful brick house? Or will he stop by where Aramanda once did live? Or Coquelicot. Will I find him in the forest with Coquelicot? In the house where she did live?

It'd be an awful shame if your friend had to witness that. What the wolf did to them. How the wolf tore up the face of Aramanda. Took her eye out. And poor Coquelicot. What he did to her. How he broke her wing. How they fled, both of them, back to their houses. And now they're all ready, yes, to be finished off. Never had a choice, did they, living like they did?

*(No response.*

*Jacqueline taps on the window again.)*

JACQUELINE: But that's what I like about you. You're smarter how you live. I can't imagine any connection. Can't imagine what happened to them happening to you. Nah. Because then I'd have to imagine I could be all that's left. To be here, you know, in that room. Right there where you sit. When the time is come, yes, to meet your friend.
(*Jacqueline taps on the window again.*
*A pane of glass cracks.*
*A large crack appears across the big, blue space behind.*
*Jacqueline regards the window.*)
Oooo, look. Look right there. It's a crack. Imagine that. A crack in your window. I'm sorry. It's a shame no matter where you live there's always got to be a window. Always some spot to look through. See what's coming. No matter what you do.
(*BLACKOUT.*)


SCENE FIVE

*A forest. The forest has a large crack crossing indiscriminately through it.*
*The window hangs as before. A pane of glass is cracked.*
*Coquelicot sits in the chair. She has wings, one of which is clearly broken. She wears the same dress Priscilla wore. She holds the violin in her lap.*
*Nearby are the other chair, Peter's suitcase, and some juggling clubs.*
*Enter Peter.*

PETER: Hi.
(*Coquelicot smiles.*)
You okay?
(*No response.*)
Listen, I'm sorry. I had to get out of here. Go for a walk. You should do that too, I think. Get out and walk. It's obsessive, Priscilla, how you want to stay in here. You won't budge. Like you're some little girl again, you can't leave this room. There's terror down the hall. Some idiotic thing you can't get past. And if you could talk to me sensibly about it, I would understand, I could help. But I don't get it, Priscilla. I can't help when everything you say seems so damn elliptical. It's obsessive in here. I mean, at first, it's exciting, wow, to come back to you again, everything has extra added meaning, extra air, some other perspective to each thing, each word

we speak, like it's all an allegory, a parable, all pointing to some great, big depth below. Like we're these icebergs. This body of mine is the tip of an iceberg, and you and I bump, we slide past each other in all kinds of ways we can't possibly see from here. The tip of an iceberg. But then after a while, Priscilla, no, this is not fun anymore. At all. This is just plain, damn complex, it's always been between us, and I don't know how I decided to forget all that, all what is complex, just so I could remember this other free spirited thing, this dolphin you are, bouncing up and down in the sea, slipping away under the surface, coming back again from nowhere, like you speak to me from other worlds. And much that I love you, Priscilla, I do, I will always love you, I have to mention this is not what I love about you. It's what I forgot. This maddening obsessiveness you have sometimes. This ridiculous extreme the other side of you, and this is not anything I can like, or ever did like it, when you get stuck like this on one damn, stupid issue. When you circle like a moth around some tiny flame. Some worthless campfire, which you should just kick to pieces, and get the hell out of here.

*(Pause.)*

I'm better now. I went for a walk.

*(Pause.)*

COQUELICOT: Come.

PETER: Hm?

COQUELICOT: I want to sit by you. Right here.

*(Coquelicot goes to a chair. She sits.)*

I'm sorry. I won't do it again. Be obsessive. Like you say.

PETER: You can't help it, no, I'm sure.

COQUELICOT: No, it will never happen again. To be obsessive. See? All gone.

PETER: *(Smiling.)* Right.

COQUELICOT: I want you only to have all good memories of me.

PETER: They are good.

COQUELICOT: No, no frowning allowed when you think of me. No mothballs in the campfire. Only magic moments, okay? Only magic forever.

PETER: Okay.

COQUELICOT: Good. And I will think the same of you. Only magic. It's nothing now but magic. Each thought I think of you.

PETER: Fine.

*(Peter sits.)*

COQUELICOT: Good. So what can we talk about now? That will be magic. That will enchant again. All your memories of me. How can I be again for you like the dolphin?

*(Coquelicot takes Peter's hand.)*

Was I talking again? About the wolf?

PETER: It's okay.

COQUELICOT: Oh, I hate it. I'm sorry. It's not me when I talk like that about a wolf.

PETER: I know.

COQUELICOT: You must just shoot me, that's all, next time. Take a shot. Put away my misery. Because I am nothing again if I am obsessive. I am become again like a horse, that's all, with a broken leg.

PETER: Oh, come on.

COQUELICOT: No, it's becoming now serious, I think. What can we do, do you think, to stop all this talk of a wolf?

PETER: I don't know.

*(Coquelicot strokes Peter's cheek.)*

COQUELICOT: Do you tell me, Hush?

PETER: Yes. Yes, I do.

COQUELICOT: You smile and say, Sssh, all the wolf is gone?

PETER: Yes, I smile.

COQUELICOT: Good. I'm glad you smile. I'm glad you say hush for me. No more wolf.

PETER: Uh huh. I shout too.

COQUELICOT: No, you don't.

PETER: Yes. I really yell.

COQUELICOT: No. Why should I remember that? Your face when you yell? Please, never yell. Promise to just say, Sssh, tell me the wolf is gone. And I will listen.

PETER: No, come on.

COQUELICOT: Yes, it is only you and me, that's all. Together again. Sssh. Who cares now about a wolf? He is nowhere to be seen.

*(The sound of a gentle breeze in the woods.)*

Magic, yes?

PETER: Hm?

COQUELICOT: It feels like magic. To sit together like this. When there is no wolf. I like to hold your hand. I like to smile. Faraway from all this talk of a wolf.

PETER: Right.

*(Peter leans his head on Coquelicot's shoulder. He closes his eyes.)*

COQUELICOT: You know, when I talk about a wolf, I have only your word for it. How I talk. And I trust it, of course, your word. Everything you say. But it is like if I should snore, in my sleep, and you should tell me I kept you up all the night, I was snoring. And I can only say, I'm sorry, that's not me, to do such a thing to you, to snore, and keep you awake all the night.

When I talk about the wolf, it's like that. I can't remember. I remember nothing when we are together like this. It is only magic to me. Every word I speak, I want to be magic for you. And every word you speak, I hear magic too. I can see no danger all around. There is nothing near, nothing faraway, to cause us trouble.

*(Pause.)*

You know, when you tell me, when you come back like this with stories of a wolf, I think two things.

I have thought perhaps you heard yourself. You who talked like that. It is you who snored, and you wake yourself up, and think it was me, who snored.

Just kidding. You could never snore. You are way too perfect for me.

And what else I think is you will rescue me anyway. From this wolf. If he is real, somewhere faraway I cannot see, you will find where he lives. You will capture him. And if he is just a dream, you will also track him down and stop all our talking of him.

Because if he is real, or just a dream, he is still only a wolf. Who wants to take you away from me.

*(Pause.)*

PETER: Would you do something for me?

COQUELICOT: Of course.

PETER: While you're in this mood.

COQUELICOT: Of course. What mood?

PETER: Read to me.

COQUELICOT: Read? Yes, what should I read?

PETER: Read to me, please. One of your stories.

COQUELICOT: What stories?

PETER: Come. I'll get the folder.

*(Peter stands. He gets the folder lying on top of the suitcase. He brings it to Coquelicot.)*

PETER: Here. Read from this.

COQUELICOT: What's in here I should read?

PETER: I don't care. Just anything. Read.

(*Coquelicot looks down at the folder.*)

PETER: You going to read?

COQUELICOT: Yes. Yes, I will read.

PETER: What's the matter, then?

COQUELICOT: Nothing, no.

PETER: No, you look troubled.

COQUELICOT: No, I'm just hoping, that's all. You will like if I read.

PETER: Of course I'll like it.

COQUELICOT: Okay.

PETER: I've always liked it. Just read.

COQUELICOT: Okay.

(*Coquelicot adjusts herself. She smiles to Peter. She opens the folder. Pause.*)

PETER: What's the matter?

COQUELICOT: Hm?

PETER: I said, What's the matter?

COQUELICOT: I don't understand.

PETER: What?

COQUELICOT: What I am reading.

PETER: What's there to understand, come on, you wrote it.

COQUELICOT: I wrote it?

PETER: What?

COQUELICOT: This was written, yes, by me?

PETER: Yes. It's your handwriting.

COQUELICOT: Good. I'm glad I can be so clever sometimes.

PETER: You don't remember writing this?

COQUELICOT: No, I never remember when I am clever. I am not clever, in fact, at all.

PETER: Who wrote this, then? It's all your handwriting.

COQUELICOT: I don't know. You tell me. You are clever. You decide, please.

(*Pause.

Peter takes the folder.*)

PETER: I'm sorry. We should do something else, Priscilla.

COQUELICOT: Hm?

PETER: For magic, I think.

COQUELICOT: Yes?

PETER: I think so, yes. Let's find something else for now. What would you like?

COQUELICOT: I'm happy, I told you. Just to sit here.

PETER: Fine, then, I'm sorry. Really. Let's do that, okay? Let's sit.

COQUELICOT: Good. I'm glad.

PETER: Okay, good.

> *(They sit together.*
>
> *Peter reaches over. He takes Coquelicot's hand.*
>
> *The sound of a gentle breeze in the woods.)*

COQUELICOT: Magic, yes?

PETER: Hm?

COQUELICOT: It feels to me like magic. When we sit like this. I like when you take my hand again. When you take me faraway. From all this talk of a wolf.

> *(Coquelicot smiles.*
>
> *Sound of a breeze getting stronger.*
>
> *BLACKOUT.)*


SCENE SIX

> *The big, blue space.*
>
> *The crack across it is wider now. There are dark streaks of yellow.*
>
> *The window hangs as before. A pane is cracked.*
>
> *The sound of a strong wind.*
>
> *Aramanda sits in a chair. She wears Priscilla's dress. The scars on her face are wider, and she seems blind in her other eye. She has lost a leg.*
>
> *Piled to one side, as if against a door, are the other chair, Peter's suitcase, the violin, and juggling clubs.*
>
> *Jacqueline stands outside the window. She walks back and forth. She lifts her face. She breathes in the wind.*
>
> *She regards Aramanda. She comes back to the window.*

JACQUELINE: *(To Aramanda:)* It's amazing, this wind, isn't it?

> *(No response.)*

The first time I heard this wind, I thought, amazing. You'd think nobody could hear a bleeding thing in a wind like this. I mean, what's normal is a wind strong like this would blow all my words clear away from you. You'd have this gesticulating figure, yes, that's all, outside your window, with a mouth running wild, but no words you could hear. Perfectly natural that, not to hear someone speaking outside your window in a wind strong like this.

*(Pause.)*

But my words can be heard, can't they?

*(No response.)*

Yes, I think so. Each one. Like a bell.

I think what must be happening in a wind strong like this is my words are getting carried, yes. Each one right there to sit where you sit. All my words is ringing, I bet, each one in your very ears. Like thoughts. You can hear your own thoughts. There's no wind what could blow away any of these thoughts.

*(The wind continues.)*

What's your name, dear? We might as well talk since we can hear each other so clear.

ARAMANDA: Aramanda.

JACQUELINE: Ah, Aramanda. It's nice, that name. Very nice, hmm. Aramanda.

*(Jacqueline taps on the window.)*

Aramanda, then. If you could divide yourself into three parts, one part body, one part what's in the mind, and the last part is all the soul, what part, then, do you think will last the shortest? What part is the least of all these parts? Might be just the body. Right? What lasts the shortest. It's like straw. The barest whiff of wind can blow it away. Like it was never there.

*(The wind continues.)*

Hmm. Nice this wind. Must be picking up, I believe.

*(She regards Aramanda.)*

Oh, I'm sorry. Aramanda, then. I believe we were talking. And here I am saying everything again all to myself.

Pah.

What is it, then, you'd like to talk about, what last words, Aramanda, could be in store for you? What possible conversation?

ARAMANDA: Aramanda.

*(Pause.)*

JACQUELINE: That's all? That's all you can tell me? Just your name? Aramanda?

*(No response.)*

JACQUELINE: Hmm. Aramanda.

> You know, Aramanda, then. I believe the world's going to melt away someday. Yes. Vanish from our sight. Like it was never there. Just like what the Bible says. Mountains and hills will melt like wax. Drop, they will, and tumble to the sea, and the sea itself will be no more. Like what the Bible says.
>
> Do you read that book? What the Bible says?

ARAMANDA: Aramanda.

JACQUELINE: Yes, I can't either. Myself. Can't find my bleeding name anywhere in that book. Must be the wrong book, I think. To be looking, I mean, for my name. But I do like what it has to say. How all this world and all its elements will melt. Tear, it will, right down the middle. Fold up and go away. Like it never was. Never did happen. And if this in the end never did happen, all my words, all your body, all mountains and seas, the teeth of lions, the heavens too which shall pass away, what is it, then, that did happen? What's left, do you think, after all this that didn't happen?

ARAMANDA: Aramanda.

JACQUELINE: Yes. It's like a thousand years out there, Aramanda, then. One day is a thousand years, like a watch in the night, and it doesn't take but a few such days like that, right, Aramanda? To cancel all we thought has happened?

> (No response.)
>
> Looks like a wolf or something's been eating you, Aramanda, then. Chunks are missing, I can see, of flesh.
>
> Won't be feeling that body, I suspect, much longer. It's being taken away from you. Like it never was.

> (The wind is stronger.
>
> The window sways back and forth.
>
> Jacqueline holds onto her white hair.)

JACQUELINE: It's looking somewhat flimsy, Aramanda. Your wall here.

ARAMANDA: Crackle.

JACQUELINE: What was that?

ARAMANDA: Crackle.

JACQUELINE: I can't hear you anymore, I'm afraid, sorry, Aramanda. Must be the wind.

ARAMANDA: Crackle.

JACQUELINE: It's picked up, you see, the wind. I'm not even sure how long your wall here can hold up in a wind getting stronger like this.

ARAMANDA: Crackle.

JACQUELINE: Looks like rain too. Hmm. All sorts of flooding, I can see, coming this way.

*(The window falls to the ground.*
*A white wig blows off the head of Jacqueline, revealing dark hair and a face which is utterly male.*
*Aramanda stands up on one leg.*
*Jacqueline approaches her.*
*The sound of a creature walking across wet sand.)*

ARAMANDA: Crackle?

*(Jacqueline continues his approach.*
*BLACKOUT.)*


## SCENE SEVEN

*The big, blue space. A large crack passes indiscriminately through it.*
*The window hangs from above. Every pane is broken.*
*Priscilla is unconscious in one of the chairs.*
*The other chair has been overturned. Peter's suitcase has been opened and its contents of balls, rings, clubs, and props strewn all across the floor. Papers from Priscilla's folder are scattered on the floor.*
*Priscilla's violin lies to one side, its neck broken.*
*Enter Peter. He carries a heavy shopping bag.*
*He sees the room.*

PETER: Priscilla?

*(Peter puts the shopping bag down. He approaches Priscilla. He kneels beside her.)*

Priscilla?

*(No response.*
*He inspects her.)*

Come on, Priscilla. Don't do this to me. Wake up.

*(Priscilla stirs. Peter straightens her up in the chair.)*

Come on, Priscilla. What are you doing like this in your chair? Let's get up, okay. Come on, Priscilla.

*(Priscilla remains in the chair, unconscious.)*
PETER: Priscilla?

Priscilla, please, what happened here? In your room?

*(No response.*

*Peter stands. He regards the room, seeing the broken window for the first time. He picks up the second chair. He places it next to Priscilla and sits. He takes Priscilla's head and places it against his shoulder. He strokes her hair.)*

*(Softly.)* Priscilla, I bought some paint. I bought us paint and brushes too. So we could paint your gate. You wanted a gate right there in your wall, Priscilla. Remember where the wallpaper came down? You wanted a gate?

*(No response.*

*Peter sees the broken violin lying to one side.)*

*(Quietly)* Oh, my God.

*(Peter gently straightens Priscilla again in her chair. He stands and crosses to the violin. He sits down on the ground beside it. He holds its broken neck. He looks out front.*

*The sound of a violin.*

*A figure, Second Peter, appears alone upstage. He juggles three balls.*

*The sound of a chorus. Sounds of an orchestra.*

*The violin continues.*

BLACKOUT.)*


END OF ACT ONE


# ACT TWO
## SCENE ONE

*The big, blue space. The large crack has shifted to one side.*
*The window hangs from above. All the panes have been replaced.*
*The chairs stand side by side.*
*Peter's props have been returned to the suitcase. Priscilla's papers have been put back into the folder.*
*A gate hangs also now from above. Peter and Priscilla are painting it. On the ground between them is a can of paint.*
*The violin lies to one side, its neck still broken.*


*(Pause.)*

PRISCILLA: Peter?

PETER: Hm?

PRISCILLA: Peter, I can't feel it again.

PETER: What, Priscilla? What don't you feel?

PRISCILLA: My body. It's gone.

PETER: Oh.

> (Pause.)

PETER: Would you like to stop, then?

PRISCILLA: I'm sorry?

PETER: Painting?

PRISCILLA: No.

PETER: You want to keep painting?

PRISCILLA: Yes.

PETER: Okay.

PRISCILLA: Yes. I want to paint.

PETER: Well, let's just rest, then. Okay, Priscilla?

PRISCILLA: Yes?

PETER: Uh huh. We'll rest right here. Till you can feel it better again. Your body.

> (Peter takes Priscilla's paint brush. He puts the brushes in the can.
> Pause.)

PETER: It's awfully pretty, Priscilla. Your body. I mean, for something you can't even feel sometimes.

PRISCILLA: (Quietly.) It doesn't belong to me.

PETER: What?

PRISCILLA: It doesn't belong. Like it never was.

PETER: What doesn't belong? What never was? Your body?

PRISCILLA: I don't know.

PETER: It's not yours, that body? You just imagine it? That's why it's here?

PRISCILLA: I don't know.

PETER: Yeah? Well, you imagine something awful pretty, Priscilla.

PRISCILLA: It's not pretty.

PETER: It is to me. Always has been.

PRISCILLA: (Abruptly.) I don't care, Peter, if it's pretty.

> (Priscilla goes to a chair. She sits.
> She looks out at the crack in the big, blue space.)

PETER: What's the matter, Priscilla? If I say it's pretty.

> (No response.)

PETER: What's the matter? Can't I clown anymore?

Really, Priscilla. Can't I tease?

I mean, I understand we have to stop once in a while, for whatever reason, and wait for you, or your body, whatever, to catch up again. I understand there's some kind of mental slope going on here, and you need to take these rests. No matter what simple thing we do. But frankly, Priscilla, it would help, I'm sure, just to smile a little. Give a little nod. Come on, Priscilla, nod for me. Break out into a grin. Beam. I want to see you beam for me.

*(Priscilla gives a smile.)*

That's better, yeah. I like it, I do, Priscilla. When you break out. You beam a little for me.

*(Pause.)*

You feel it again?

It's come back to you? Your body?

*(Priscilla gives a nod.)*

I'm going to paint, okay? Paint a little more of this gate. You come and join me. When you're ready.

*(Peter takes a brush out of the can. He paints.*
*Priscilla watches.)*

You know, I think of you as a scout, I do. Whatever mental slope this is you're climbing, I feel I'm going to have to do it too, yes, someday. I'm going to have to stop looking around like this in a body, looking to this world we live to keep me happy.

In fact, I think of you as a scout for all the rest of us. Everybody back here in the world. Because, frankly, there's got to be some kind of mental slope out of here. Out of this place we got left somehow to die.

And I can imagine, yes. A scout must get astounded sometimes. Scared. All alone up there. Seeing what the rest of us have yet to see. What we will have to see too. When we finally have no choice left, no more excuses. But to catch up to you.

*(Priscilla stands. She goes to Peter. She takes the paint brush from him.)*

PRISCILLA: Peter. I know it seems, to you, I'm sort of some scout. I see what's up ahead. A whole kingdom, I suppose, within. A place we have to get to, right, without our bodies?

And I'm sorry. To give such an impression.

Because, Peter, I watch you sometimes. I do. And I don't feel ahead. No. I'm left behind. I can't believe how far you've gone on. How grand you

look to me. How safe. How sound. And when you take my hand sometimes I feel I could open a door. There's a door, right there, in front of me.
Within my grasp. Where I can come in. From all the rain and all the flood
out there. And I feel windows too. Places to look out. A view. Where I can
see the world from how you can see. I can see a man. And a woman too. I
can see everything that should have been there up ahead for us.

*(Pause.)*

You shouldn't come back like this. I shouldn't keep calling you back
like this.

PETER: You're not calling me back, Priscilla. At all.

*(Peter reaches for Priscilla's hand which holds the paint brush. He takes her
hand and guides the brush along the gate.)*

You know, Priscilla. I've reached out and touched several people. In this
life of mine. Reached all the way over there and touched what I could see
of them. Brought them as close as I could.

But never, I guess, have I ever felt as close as I felt when close to you. And
all I did was take your hand. That's how close we were, Priscilla. Taking
hands.

*(Peter lets go of Priscilla's hand. She continues to paint the gate.*
*The sound of a violin.*
*LIGHTS DIM.*
*A figure, Second Priscilla, appears beyond the gate. She is juggling rings.*
*The sound of a chorus. Sounds of an orchestra.*
*BLACKOUT.)*


SCENE TWO

*A forest. The forest seems darker. There is a second crack now.*
*The window and a partially painted gate hang from above.*
*Coquelicot sits in a chair. She is wearing Priscilla's dress. She has lost an arm*
*and one wing is still broken. The other wing lies in her lap.*
*Nearby are the other chair, Peter's suitcase, and a broken violin.*
*Jacqueline stands outside the window. He walks back and forth. He straight-*
*ens his wig.*
*He goes to the gate. He regards it. He regards Coquelicot through the gate.*


JACQUELINE: *(To Coquelicot:)* Did you do this? Is this your gate?

*(No response.)*

JACQUELINE: Seems a strange thing to do to me. Paint this gate on a wall.
Whoever heard of painting a gate on a wall? Walls is for wallpaper. Or
pictures. Pretty little pictures of houses and family, all sorts of pets, pictures, yes, of nature, that's what should be going on here on a wall.
Not somebody painting like this a gate.

*(Jacqueline turns sideways. He measures himself, and his large dress, against
the gate.)*

Seems awful narrow to me, this gate. Much too narrow, I bet, way too
straight, to be of any use at all, yes, in this wall.

*(Jacqueline steps away from the gate. He regards Coquelicot.)*

I hate to have to do this, but would you mind, once again, telling me
what it is your name?

COQUELICOT: Coquelicot.

JACQUELINE: Ah, yes. That's it, of course. Coquelicot, then. It's very nice, I
think, that. For a name.

*(The sound of a breeze in the woods.*

*He lifts his face. He breathes the air.*

*The stage darkens.)*

Awful nice in here, Coquelicot, then. What a lovely forest. All this forest
you have. In your head.

*(Pause.)*

It's dark, though, isn't it? Having a forest like this can get dark. Amazing
how dark sometimes. It can get in a forest.

What's amazing also to me is how clear I must appear to you. How distinct you look to me. How the eyes adjust. What they get used to. I
mean, you'd think what's normal in a darkness like this is I would be all
blurred. Just some dark shadow, that's all, lapping at your window.

*(Pause.)*

I've been wondering Coquelicot, then. Did you happen to hear what happened to Aramanda?

*(No response.)*

Or are you not aware? Of our little Aramanda, then? What used to live in
the first house. On my way to here.

*(Jacqueline taps on the window.)*

Coquelicot, then. Tell me. If you could divide yourself into three parts,
one part body, one the mind, and the last part all the soul, what part,
then, do you think will last the middle? What part is the second part of all

these parts? Might be the mind. Right? What lasts the middle. It's like sticks, I think. Yes. A good firm gust of wind could blow them sticks all away. Like they was never there.

*(Jacqueline continues to regard Coquelicot through the window.)*

Pah. It's horrible these days.

How I find myself all alone like this. Talking to myself.

*(Sound of a breeze getting stronger.)*

I bet, however, I know one thing we could talk about. Yes, in this forest. I bet we could talk about your friend. What he wanted you to read for him. In that folder. What I see right there. Lying on a trunk.

Would you like that, Coquelicot, then?

If I tell what's in that folder? If I speak to you all the handwriting in there?

COQUELICOT: Coquelicot.

JACQUELINE: I thought so, yes. I knew it could please you no end, yes, to tell our friend what's in our folder. All our harmless stories.

So why don't you pass it to me, then? That folder. What's lying there on the trunk. Pass it to me right now through this window. So I can read to you.

COQUELICOT: Coquelicot.

JACQUELINE: That's right, good Coquelicot, then.

*(Coquelicot stands. She picks up the folder on Peter's trunk. She goes to the window. She hands the folder to Jacqueline through the window.*
*Jacqueline opens the folder.)*

JACQUELINE: Hmm. Lovely. It looks so lovely to me. All these words in here. All this handwriting.

*(Jacqueline turns a page.)*

Ah, yes. It's about a wolf.

Did you know that?

COQUELICOT: Coquelicot?

JACQUELINE: Yes, Coquelicot, then. All about a wolf in here. What he says. How he thinks. And this wolf, it claims in here, is not what we all believe got boiled in a pot of water at the foot of a chimney and all the pigs went dancing.

No, that's not what's here. No wolf like that.

No, the wolf in here is much more, I think, than can meet the eye. What could boil in water. What could be contained in a simple story like that about what is good and what is evil. All taking place in some literal world. Some fantastic land where people believe what they can see.

JACQUELINE: What kind of land is that?

Where all the wolves is out there? Where we can see.

(*Jacqueline turns a page.*)

Hmm. It's talking here about what are internal wolves. What's in our midst. A wolf in here more relative. It's saying we should always look to who the author is. Who is it telling. And not just the story. It says here what could look to the naked eye like a pig living nice and peaceful in a lovely brick house could actually be the wolf. Heh. It's a wolf in there living nice and peaceful in a lovely brick house. He's telling a story, yes, to all our children.

(*Jacqueline turns a page.*
*The sound of wind. A wolf howls.*)

JACQUELINE: Hmm. It's very stirring, don't you think? What's in this folder.

I mean, the implications of this are immense. That a story, where we killed the wolf, is actually being told to us by the wolf that was killed. Now, I mean, either the wolf is killed and that's the story, and we should-n't be building any house of straw and sticks. We have a place of bricks to go to. Or else the wolf isn't killed. And we have no house at all of bricks to go. Because if the wolf isn't killed, then who can be telling this story he was killed, except a wolf who wants us to think he's killed. A wolf who is bluffing. Who came to our door and we let him in. And once he's in, there's really no wall left, is there, between us and any story he could please himself to tell.

It's like the fox wearing the livery of a hen. The devil aping God. I mean, this is elementary. It's easy breaking into houses. Yes. When you get your-self invited in. And if the wolf's already invited in, I can see no sense either running off to that brick house we were told.

(*Jacqueline closes the folder. He hands it back through the window.*
*Coquelicot reaches for it. Jacqueline takes Coquelicot's wrist as she grasps the folder.*)

JACQUELINE: (*Holding Coquelicot's wrist.*) Quiet. You seem awful quiet to me.

What is it, then? Making you so quiet?

(*The stage darkens.*)

Listening, are you, then? That's it. For some still voice? Some angel of the air? To lead you out of here?

(*No response.*)

I can't stand like this when a person doesn't answer to me.

*(Jacqueline twists Coquelicot's wrist. The sound of a bone snapping.*
*Coquelicot cries out as Jacqueline forces her to the ground.*
*The wind is stronger. A wolf howls again.*
*The window sways as Jacqueline leans through it.)*

JACQUELINE: It all comes back in the end, Coquelicot, then. To the house which was built, you know, on rock. And the other, what was built on sand.

Because I do believe, long ago, in the days when they thought this world was flat, some millennia ago, I believe there was indeed, once upon a time, a house you could build on rock. A very kingdom, yes, within. Separate from all this world without.

But that rock, whatever it is, that kingdom got covered long ago by what is all around us now. By all this vast expanse we have, all this world, yes, of sand.

*(The window and Jacqueline's wig blow to the ground.)*

COQUELICOT: Crackle?

*(Jacqueline drags Coquelicot across the stage.*
*The sound of a creature walking across wet sand.*
*BLACKOUT.)*


SCENE THREE

*The big, blue space. The cracks are gone.*
*The window and gate hang down from above.*
*Jacqueline sits in a chair. His wig is gone. He wears Priscilla's dress.*
*Nearby are the other chair, Peter's suitcase, and a broken violin.*
*Enter Peter.*

PETER: Hi.

*(Jacqueline smiles.)*

You okay?

*(No response.)*

You know, something came back to me. Outside. Something you said one time. Probably you don't even remember, but I remember. Because what you could say was so frustrating to me. So ludicrous. How you would have these thoughts sometimes, an idea, the very moment when all I wanted ever to do was just to kiss you.

*(Pause.)*

PETER: You were like a child. Questions bubbled up in you. Asking, like a child, if this is a dream? Some kind of sleep, that's all, the world we live? These things we're saying, right now, in the end if they never were. Never did happen.

Until I didn't know myself anymore. How to respond. Except to get out of the way. Decide, finally, to take off. Let you ask yourself this stuff without me trying all the time to stop you.

(Pause.)

What came to me outside just now was how you told me one time you could feel, deep down, how this body, yours, was nothing but a veil. That's right. A covering. And I said, Come on, your body isn't a veil. It covers what? And you said this thing, you said, Your view of God. And I said, Oh, yeah? Your view of God? You'd see God, would you, if you had no body, no veil like this, if you were invisible, that's what you'd see? God? And you said, Yes. That's what you could decide to see.

Whereas I said, I'm not so sure what I might decide to see. Beyond this body. In a big, blue yonder. What's invisible. I might see, finally, what's opposed to God. What lurks behind the bushes. The adversary.

(Pause.)

That's what came back to me. That conversation. What I said to you. Right before I left.

(Peter sits in the other chair.)

JACQUELINE: Surprised to see me, aren't you?

PETER: Hm?

JACQUELINE: Thought I was still outside.

PETER: No. I thought you were here.

JACQUELINE: What?

PETER: In here.

JACQUELINE: Oh, funny. Yes. And I thought I was outside, heh, heh. Imagine.

(Pause.)

PETER: I didn't know you were outside. You should have told me.

(Pause.)

Where have you been, then? Outside.

(Pause.)

JACQUELINE: What are you looking at?

PETER: Hm?

JACQUELINE: You seem to be looking at something.

PETER: I'm sorry. I was thinking.

JACQUELINE: Ah.

PETER: That's all.

JACQUELINE: I'm thinking too, it's good, I think, to be thinking. Would you like to know what it is, then? That I'm thinking?

PETER: Yes?

JACQUELINE: Good. Because I'm thinking if you were to describe your friend Priscilla to someone, say what's important to you about her, all her qualities, what might it be, then, you think you'd say?

Eh? About Priscilla?

*(Pause.)*

PETER: I'd say her honesty.

JACQUELINE: What?

PETER: That's right. Your honesty.

JACQUELINE: What honesty?

PETER: How you're willing, that's all, to look within yourself. That's what I'd say. This inner vision you have. This constant need. To see behind what you assume.

*(Pause.)*

You seem surprised.

JACQUELINE: Hm?

PETER: To hear honesty.

JACQUELINE: Yes. Yes, that quite surprises me.

PETER: Why? What would you have said?

JACQUELINE: About Priscilla?

PETER: Yes. How would you describe yourself? To a friend?

*(Pause.)*

JACQUELINE: I'd describe her as hard to capture, myself.

PETER: Hard to capture?

JACQUELINE: Yes. It's no easy matter, no, capturing the likes of Priscilla.

*(Pause.)*

PETER: I agree.

JACQUELINE: Do you really?

PETER: Yes, she's hard to capture. Hard to describe. Hard to ever know what to assume about Priscilla. I mean I once assumed, for example, all your beliefs were foolish.

JACQUELINE: What beliefs?

PETER: Well, that we shouldn't get to know each other. Physically, I mean. That sort of belief.

JACQUELINE: Really?

PETER: Yes, that's what you believed.

JACQUELINE: Amazing.

PETER: Hm?

JACQUELINE: It's amazing what a belief can do.

PETER: Yes, you thought we better be married.  I mean, to get to know each other like that.

JACQUELINE: *(To himself.)* Oh, my dear.

PETER: And so I thought, great, this is what has to be. I'll get married. Be like that for her, man and wife.

JACQUELINE: Oh, my, my.

PETER: But I shouldn't have assumed that, it seems.

JACQUELINE: Assumed what?

PETER: Well, that you wanted, that's all, to get married.

JACQUELINE: Ah, yes.

Well, it's hard, as I say. To capture Priscilla.

*(Pause.)*

PETER: Yes. Capture. I think that's a good word. You seem terribly afraid sometimes. Of capture. Something about you could be captured. Some spirit in the body. And one way to look at this is to think this is crazy. This woman is crazy. Who is it that has traumatized her in such a way that she thinks she could be captured by her own body?

It's ludicrous.

But then I watch you. The things you used to do. How you used to practice all the time. You played that violin. How you could perform, and I would see, yes, she's right. I can see what's spirit there. What's innocent. Wants to break out free. I see how lovely. How you long for all of an open space out there. How you reach out all the way to the end of where your body will go, out there beyond any grasp. And I see myself following you. See these glimpses, watching you, of what a body could never express. I hear words. Some sort of singing in words. And I hear myself singing. I sing words when I watch you. Hear words in my mouth I could never express.

*(Peter suddenly stands. He goes to the window. He looks out.*

*He looks back at Jacqueline.)*

It doesn't surprise me sometimes, Priscilla. To see you under such an assault.

JACQUELINE: An assault?

PETER: Yes, there's some crisis. Obviously. Some battle to get you.
And I get nervous. Sometimes I'm nervous just speaking each word I
speak to you.

*(Peter steps away from the window.)*

JACQUELINE: Well, that's rather silly. Getting nervous like that. Speaking
words to me. Because, frankly, there's nothing at all for you to be nervous. Nothing to see.

*(A crack appears in the big, blue space. In the crack can be seen Priscilla's
dark outline.)*

Hmm. Looks like it's about to break apart again. Out there.

*(Jacqueline stands. He goes to the window. He looks out.
He looks back at Peter.)*

Speaking of glimpses. Tell me. Do you think within each one of us is a
wolf?

PETER: A wolf?

JACQUELINE: Yes, tell me.

PETER: What sort of wolf?

JACQUELINE: Just a wolf, that's all. Any sort.

PETER: I don't know.

JACQUELINE: You've never looked a person in the eye and thought, that's a
wolf I see in there?

PETER: I don't know.

JACQUELINE: Oh, come on.

PETER: Sure, I suppose I've seen such a wolf.

JACQUELINE: Yes?

PETER: On occasion, sure.

*(Pause.)*

JACQUELINE: How about now?

PETER: Hm?

JACQUELINE: Can you see what's a wolf in me?

PETER: No. I could never see a wolf in you.

JACQUELINE: Why ever not?

PETER: It's not anything I could imagine. A wolf in you.

JACQUELINE: How about when I'm really silent? Dark, let's say, and brooding.
Any such glimpses then, you think, of a wolf in me?

PETER: No. No such glimpse I can remember.

*(Pause.)*

JACQUELINE: Hmm. I think there's wolves in all of us. Even you.

PETER: You think I got a wolf in me?

JACQUELINE: Oh, yes. Something wolfish, I bet.

PETER: What would that be?

JACQUELINE: You don't know yourself?

PETER: I'm just asking what you've noticed.

JACQUELINE: About the wolf in you?

PETER: Yes.

JACQUELINE: Ah. Well, it seems to me that your wolf is not just a regular wolf.

PETER: No?

JACQUELINE: Yes, we're both quite the dandies, aren't we?

PETER: Dandies?

JACQUELINE: Yes, I mean, all this primping and prancing. In what is sheep's clothing. All this honesty you claim. Inner vision. This need to look behind what we assume. That's just a cover-up we have. It's clothing. All this layer of stuff on top, hiding from view, how ravenous we have always been. Rapacious. I mean, for what could be between us. This force, I feel, pressure all the time. Like gravitation. Keeping us gravitated to each other on this earth.

*(Pause.)*

Well, don't look so startled. I've given some thought to this. I told you I've been thinking. And what I think is I come from a long line of wolf. I mean, what's a wolf inside. A long line of that. From mother to son, son to his daughter, and on and on like that could last forever. What I feel for you could last us here forever.

*(Pause.)*

If I were to describe Priscilla to someone, I'd have to mention, I'm afraid, her desire to kill the wolf in her. Stop all this long line. Keep it at bay. Can you imagine? Kill what is natural in her. I mean, most people, they accept a little wolf in their life. A little wolf is what can bring people together. Give us picnics and boating parties, all because of a little wolf, what got them started.

That's what amazes me about Priscilla. Trying to chase away like this her natural wolf. Which makes me think what's a little wolf to all of us, what's a nice excitement, is something big and bad to her. Quite grievous. What may have mauled her once. Come upon her as a child. Pulled the wings off a young woman. What's a little wolf to us, what keeps us happy, she saw take apart her body. She got a peek, a glimpse, of all the big, bad land, what's lurking there, behind our very body.

JACQUELINE: But I do think, still, it's no use fighting like this any wolf. A wolf's not so big when you don't fight. He can be just a tiny part, that's all, in your life, a slight hunger, what's in the background, yes, what's hardly even noticed, if you do not fight it. Keep a wolf like this at bay.

*(Pause.)*

PETER: Why are you talking like this?

JACQUELINE: Like what?

PETER: Like you're speaking for Priscilla.

JACQUELINE: Who else can speak for Priscilla?

PETER: No, you keep using the third person.

JACQUELINE: What person?

PETER: As if you're separate from Priscilla.

JACQUELINE: But that's my point. My point all along. I do not have to be separate at all from Priscilla.

PETER: No, why are you talking as if Priscilla isn't here?

JACQUELINE: Because she isn't here.

PETER: No? Then why are you here?

JACQUELINE: Because I've come here. For Priscilla.

PETER: What, if you're Priscilla and Priscilla isn't here?

*(Pause.)*

JACQUELINE: I can see you understand nothing. You understand nothing to do with Priscilla.

*(Jacqueline takes a crumpled piece of paper out of his pocket.)*

I believe this paper's yours. What's crumpled here in my pocket.

*(Jacqueline flicks the paper over to Peter.)*

All the names, what's on that list, it's all mine. It's all come to me. Each little name in there is what I've met along my path.

Including your name.

I've seen it, yes, your name. Right there. On that list.

*(Peter picks up the paper.)*

My name is Jacqueline. You can call me Jacq.

*(A second crack appears in the big, blue space.)*

Now can you see the wolf in me? What's been lurking all the time?

*(No response.*

*Jacqueline picks up the broken violin.*

*The sound of a gentle breeze.)*

Do you like these birds? All the birds you see flying in the air? On this dress I wear?

*(No response.*

*The stage darkens.)*

JACQUELINE: Can you see Priscilla now?

How she's standing here. Right before your eyes. In this lovely dress? All the birds upon this dress. Beckoning.

*(Sound of a breeze getting stronger.)*

And below all the birds is these shoes. Priscilla's feet. What's in these shoes. What you see walk like dancing. Seen tapping when she plays the violin here.

*(The sound of wind.)*

But it's her eyes, isn't it? Above all the birds in this world is her eyes. How they look to you. How she calls. And all this world between can vanish. Yes, if you just reach out, right now, your hands, and take this moment.

*(The wind is stronger. A wolf howls.*

*The dark outline of Priscilla in the first crack stirs.)*

Come. Fill your hands right here.

PRISCILLA'S VOICE: Peter?

JACQUELINE: Feel a wind rise, strong and furious in you.

PRISCILLA'S VOICE: No, Peter?

JACQUELINE: What's been held back in you all these years. The heart and soul of what you really want.

*(The wind is furious.*

*Pricilla steps out of the crack. She comes downstage.*

*A wolf screams at her.)*

PRISCILLA: No, Peter.

JACQUELINE: *(Continuing to Peter.)* …Feel it break out and rain in you. Feel the flood rise up…

PRISCILLA: Peter, no. Listen.

JACQUELINE: …all the fury grip you like a vast current, carry you faraway from any land, until you are free and wild again…

PETER: *(Seeing Priscilla.)* Priscilla?

JACQUELINE: …like the beast you are to bite and devour!…

PRISCILLA: Yes, Peter.

*(The big, blue space cracks open once again, throwing Peter into darkness.*

*Jacqueline turns on Priscilla. The window falls to the ground.*

*The sound of a wolf tearing at something.*

*Jacqueline grabs Priscilla by the neck. He forces her to the ground and stands over her.*

*The wind begins to abate.)*

JACQUELINE: I found my way, didn't I, my dear? Into your brick house. I just followed the names right there. On that list. Till I got to the name of your friend there. That's what let me in. Your friend. All that you feel for your friend.

(Pause.)

Hmm. Gone quiet again, I see.

It's amazing how quiet it gets in here.

I can't stand it like this when you're quiet. What did I tell you about going quiet like this on me?

(No response.)

Listening, are you, then? That's it. For some still voice? Some angel of the air? To lead you out of here? Some sign of a kingdom within? Some other house you might live?

Is that what's making it all so quiet here?

Heh heh.

(No response.)

Hmm. I can see no kingdom within. No other house. Here we are, you and I, this very moment, in a land beyond all lands of body, and I can hear no little voice of spirit. There's nothing pure and simple God has made. No kingdom within to conquer all this big, bad world without.

It's just you and me, that's all, my dear. Yes. In this within.

(Jacqueline twists Priscilla's neck. The sound of something snapping.)

It all goes back to the tempter, I think. What took Christ to the wilderness mountain. And showed him all the kingdoms of this world in a moment of time.

And it's very nice, isn't it, how Christ refused this world, because this world wasn't his world to be king of. He had another world, didn't he? Our little kingdom within. A house built on rock.

Very nice, yes.

And it's amazing to me, it is, to watch all these Christians go out themselves to conquer now all this world he refused. Into every land, every nook and cranny, all the little Christians have sent their warriors, all their merchants, what they teach, all of it still out there trying to conquer what's left to conquer in this world.

All their lands out there of body.

Heh.

Sounds like that rock turned into bread. The bread of this world. Sounds like we tossed ourselves off the pinnacle, didn't we?

*(Jacqueline twists Priscilla's neck. The sound of something snapping.)*

JACQUELINE: It's like I said. There's no pig in any brick house. It's a wolf himself in there.

So what's the sense left to all this quiet? This listening, then. For some way to lift up yourself out of here. Beyond my grasp.

You should be howling right now. Loud and clear, yes, as I approach. Make my advance on what's left of you. Come, Priscilla. Howl with me. Let us howl together in the huge dark of night. In this chaos we can howl together. There's no need anymore to be separate like this.

*(The sound of wind is gone.*

*Jacqueline regards Priscilla.)*

Hm. What is it makes it so quiet here? I can't stand it quiet like this. I've told you.

*(Pause.)*

Thoughts can be disturbing in a quiet such as this is quiet.

*(Pause.)*

JACQUELINE: Listening, then? For some still voice? Some angel of the air? To lead you out of here? Some sign of a kingdom within? Some other home you might live?

*(Pause.*

*Priscilla stands.)*

PRISCILLA: You repeat yourself.

JACQUELINE: Hm?

PRISCILLA: I've never heard that before. How you repeat yourself.

JACQUELINE: I repeat myself? Is there something wrong, then? To repeat myself.

PRISCILLA: *(Realizing.)* This is not home.

JACQUELINE: Heh?

PRISCILLA: You are not my home.

JACQUELINE: What's not, my dear, your home?

PRISCILLA: Any place you could enter. That's not my home.

*(Priscilla steps out of the room.)*

JACQUELINE: *(Unaware.)* Oh, really? Not your home? What I could enter? Well, that's quite remarkable indeed. Because I can see no other home, no other house left anywhere all around, except this one right here. Where I have indeed entered. That's what I see. It's all that I see.

*(Priscilla continues to walk outside the room.*

*Jacqueline prowls, unseeing, inside the room.)*

JACQUELINE: Is there something else, then? That you see?

(*No response.*)

And where is it, then? This something else. What you see.

(*No response.*)

You're not going to tell me? Not going to show proof, then? Of what you see? Some little glimpse, maybe, of proof?

Or are you just going to afflict me? With this quiet. Because you are afraid I may mock it. Your proof. Huff and puff it down. All over again. Each proof.

Pah!

This is what makes you so quiet. That's it, then. Some notion. The paltry thought. I'm not your home. Where you live.

(*A silhouette of a large horse has appeared upstage.*
*Jacqueline sees the horse.*)

JACQUELINE: What's that? What's that horse over there? Is that your horse?

(*The silhouette of the horse upstage moves. It comes to a stop.*)

I asked you, Is that your horse? Are you leaving here on that horse?

(*Priscilla remains quiet.*)

You better tell me about this horse. What is it you'll do. On that horse.

(*Pause.*)

PRISCILLA: You never touched him. My friend.

JACQUELINE: What?

PRISCILLA: That's my friend's horse. You never got close.

JACQUELINE: Oh, yes, I am. Very close. I felt him listen. With all his heart. To what you feel for him. Like gravitation.

PRISCILLA: But you don't speak for me.

JACQUELINE: What?

PRISCILLA: You never did.

JACQUELINE: Of course I speak for you. All the time. I hear it loud and clear. What you know is true. Makes sense. What you've seen, oh, yes, with your own very eyes. What you have witnessed. From the day you were born. All the wolf you have seen. In a house built on rock. All the cracks right here. You see across the sky.

PRISCILLA: It's not your business. What I see.

JACQUELINE: Not my business?

PRISCILLA: Nor do you speak for me.

JACQUELINE: Is this what you have to say? After all this time? It's not my business?

JACQUELINE: Is this what you hope, then? Your last words to me?

It's not my business?

(*Pause.*

*The silhouette of the horse upstage moves again. It stops.*)

I don't like it like this, I don't.

When I find myself fumble. For words. What made us so close, so dear. Our thoughts.

(*Pause.*)

What is it you do, when you get quiet like this?

I'd like to know in this quiet is there something I could hear? Would you tell? Some little word. What might really speak? Some land you might dwell?

(*The cracks in the big, blue space have begun to fade.*

*Priscilla watches them.*)

PRISCILLA: (*Softly.*) Crackle. The cracks are going.

(*She regards Jacqueline.*)

It's hard to believe it now. How afraid you made me.

All this time.

How much sense you made. How your words could sound. Like my very own thoughts. What I want.

Or fear.

(*Pause.*)

I no longer fear what you could make me do. All your actions. How you lurk in the background. Your huge past. All your heredity. How hard you were to understand.

Because I can see you now. All of you. Out here in the open. I can hear you too. Each thing you want. All that you could have ever done to me.

I see how far you've traveled, how desperate, to follow each step I take out of this world.

(*The horse moves again. It stops.*)

I'm going back now to see my friend. He's waiting for me.

(*Pause.*

*Priscilla picks up the violin.*)

I know I will see you again. Hear you many times still.

But you are no longer in front of me. You are what's behind.

(*The sound of a violin.*)

You could not possibly dwell, ever, in any land where I will go.

(*BLACKOUT.*

*The violin continues.*)

## SCENE FOUR

*The soft sound of a violin still playing.*
*A large, empty blue space.*
*The window frame with pale curtains hangs down from above.*
*There are two empty chairs.*
*Priscilla appears. She comes to the window. She pauses. She goes to one of the chairs. She sits.*
*Enter Peter. He carries a large, black suitcase, or trunk. He sets the suitcase down.*
*He looks at Priscilla.*

PETER: That's very beautiful, Priscilla.
*(No response.)*
That dress. I like it very much.
*(Pause.)*
I still can't get over the birds flying. All those birds in the air. On your dress.
*(Priscilla smiles.)*
PRISCILLA: Peter?
PETER: Yes, Priscilla?
PRISCILLA: I'm glad you're back.
PETER: Good.
*(Priscilla stands.)*
PRISCILLA: It's lovely, Peter. The things you say.
*(Priscilla goes to Peter.)*
I feel I could wait sometimes forever, Peter. Go through a second death, even. Just to come back and hear the things you say.
*(Priscilla takes Peter by the hand. She holds his hand.*
*Lights dim.*
*Two figures, Second Peter and Second Priscilla, appear upstage. They dance together, passing clubs between them.*
*The sound of a chorus. Sounds of an orchestra.*
*The violin continues.*
*BLACKOUT.)*

## END OF PLAY

# Trash Anthem
## by Dan Dietz

# BIOGRAPHY

Dan Dietz's plays include *Tilt Angel, tempOdyssey, Dirigible* and *Blind Horses,* and have been seen in New York, Los Angeles, Seattle, Austin and elsewhere. Recent honors include a James A. Michener Playwriting Fellowship, the Austin Critics Table Award for Best New Play and nominations for the George Oppenheimer Award and the Roy Crane Award in the Arts. He was a finalist for the 2001 and 2002 Princess Grace Awards. Mr. Dietz has developed his work at HotHouse, PlayLabs, the New South for the New Century Festival and the Millay Colony for the Arts. He received his M.F.A. in Playwriting from the University of Texas at Austin in 1999 and is currently the Artistic Director of Austin Script Works, a playwright services organization. Dietz is a Resident Company Member of Salvage Vanguard Theater.

# HUMANA FESTIVAL PRODUCTION

*Trash Anthem* premiered at the Humana Festival of New American Plays in April 2003. It was directed by Jennifer Hubbard with the following cast:

Woman . . . . . . . . . . . . . . . . . . . . . . . . . . . . . . . . . . Rebecca Wisocky
Boots . . . . . . . . . . . . . . . . . . . . . . . . . . . . . . . . . . . Michael Laurence

and the following production staff:

Scenic Designer . . . . . . . . . . . . . . . . . . . . . . . . . . . . . Paul Owen
Costume Designers . . . . . . . . . . . . . . . . . . . . . . . . . . John P. White
Mike Floyd
Lighting Designer. . . . . . . . . . . . . . . . . . . . . . . . . . . . Paul Werner
Sound Designer. . . . . . . . . . . . . . . . . . . . . . . . . Colbert S. Davis IV
Properties Designer . . . . . . . . . . . . . . . . . . . . . . . . . Doc Manning
Stage Manager . . . . . . . . . . . . . . . . . . . . . . . . . Leslie K. Oberhausen
Assistant Stage Managers . . . . . . . . . . . . . . . . . . . . Michael Domue
Andrew Scheer
Dramaturg . . . . . . . . . . . . . . . . . . . . . . . . . . . . . . . Steve Moulds

# CHARACTERS
WOMAN
BOOTS


# SETTING
Little house, Big South

Rebecca Wisocky
in *Trash Anthem*

27th Annual Humana Festival of New American Plays
Actors Theatre of Louisville, 2003
photo by Harlan Taylor

# Trash Anthem

*Little house. Big South. A pair of men's cowboy boots. Woman stands dressed in cheap but professional clothing. She holds a shovel. Her body is streaked with dirt. She stomps the shovel to the floor three times, then turns to the boots and approaches them in a slow march, stomping a rhythm with the shovel.*

WOMAN: *(Sings under her breath.)*
    *I am earthy*
    *I am raw*
    *My man's in pieces*
    *Down in the soggy soggy*
    *(She stands next to the boots in silence. Drops the shovel. Raises her hands above her head, screams, and thrusts her hands into the boots. Woman pulls out her hands—they are covered in rich black soil. She's got fistfuls of it.)*

*(New start. A pair of men's cowboy boots. Woman slowly approaches them. She stops, considers them for a moment, then shifts the boots so the left boot is on the right side and the right boot on the left. She smiles to herself, walks off. Pause. The boots talk to the audience.)*

BOOTS: Ow. Goddammit. Hey. Scuse me. Y'all in the seats there. Yeah, could one of you, uh, come down here and move these back? Please? I'm serious, this hurts. Come on. One of you men take pity on me. I'm twisted up genital-wise. Please?

*(New start. Woman stands by Boots.)*

WOMAN: My man ain't a cowboy. 'Cept at his feet. Cowboy feet, leather-wrapped and stinky. My man ain't a cowboy.

My man ain't a talker. 'Cept with his hands. Talking hands, reach out and touch someone, long distance cellular kinda hands, still feel 'em back of my neck, gripping in a man way, slipping in that same man way, you know, down. Ain't a talker, nope.

So I fell in love with his hands and his feet. We'd go dancing, and I'd spend the whole time looking down at his boots. Felt like as long as I kept my eyes locked on them, we could dance across the Gulf of Mexico and never fall in. I loved them hard, those feet, those hands. Listened hard to the heartbeats at the tips of his fingers and toes. Tried to decipher. Unravel the code in bloodflow. Find the secret that binds forever.

WOMAN: Failed.

*(Woman raises her hands, screams, thrusts them into the boots, pulls out fist-fuls of earth. The boots scream back. The Woman smiles.)*

BOOTS: What do you want from me?

WOMAN: Talk.

BOOTS: I don't talk, you know that.

WOMAN: I know. You use your hands. Crack open peanuts when I'm talking to you. Stare at the wall.

BOOTS: I communicate through peanuts, like all men do. I pop the little bug-gers out of their shells like mussels, like mollusks, like deep-sea snails. I dip them behind my lips, shake the half-shell, rattle 'em into my mouth. And then I crunch. And this combination of pop, rattle, crunch is a lan-guage. Sweeter'n English.

WOMAN: You ain't gonna be popping peanuts no more.

BOOTS: Nope. Got myself popped instead.

WOMAN: Your own fault.

BOOTS: Hardly deserving of an execution.

WOMAN: I was pissed off.

BOOTS: Oh. Well. In that case fire away.

WOMAN: I did! *(Pause.)* I hope it didn't hurt.

BOOTS: Course it hurt! Jesus.

WOMAN: Sorry.

BOOTS: Me too.

WOMAN: But you deserved it.

Wish to god this story was more original, folks, but it ain't. I swore when I started paralegal classes I wasn't gonna live the stereotype no more. But here I am, stuck back in that same old same old white trash anthem: Woman finds her man with his dick inside the neighbor. Woman grabs the rifle off the rack. Blah-de-blah-de-blah. It ain't fair. I drive a Jetta.

BOOTS: Well, there is a twist.

WOMAN: Ain't no twist.

BOOTS: Oh, there's a twist all right.

WOMAN: Shut up.

BOOTS: See, folks, what Genevieve ain't saying…

WOMAN: Don't you say another word!

BOOTS: What Genevieve ain't exactly being forthcoming about is the fact that…

WOMAN: I said, shut it!

*(She grips the boots at the top, squeezes them shut. Boots continues talking, muffled and incomprehensible.)*

WOMAN: *(Sings.)*
> I am earthy
> I am raw
> My man's in pieces
> Down in the soggy soggy
> *(Boots is silent.)*

WOMAN: Hey. You gonna behave? *(No answer.)* You ain't gonna make me regret this are you? *(No answer.)* Okay.
> *(Woman releases Boots.)*

BOOTS: The neighbor was a man.

WOMAN: GODDAMMIT!

BOOTS: Sorry, babe, they got a right to know. It was a man, folks. The dick she is referring to was deep inside a—

WOMAN: PLEASE! Shit.

BOOTS: Jesus, you can be so stone age. Twenty-first century, Jenny. Wake up and smell the tolerance.

WOMAN: I just don't get it. You were so butch.
> *(Pause.)*

BOOTS: Did you get Jeff, too?

WOMAN: Nope. He's fast.

BOOTS: More ways'n one.

WOMAN: You mighta got away too, if you hadn't had your boots on. Stuck in the sheets like a drowning man. Boots in bed. Walking on water.

BOOTS: He's got the police headed your way right now.

WOMAN: Probably. How long you been like this?

BOOTS: I don't know. How old are my veins?

WOMAN: I loved you. I gave you a home. We danced. You ever dance with Jeff?

BOOTS: In this town? We'd get our asses kicked.

WOMAN: I'd pay money to see that.

BOOTS: Look. You shot me, okay? You buried me in the backyard, you win. What more do you want?

WOMAN: I don't know.

BOOTS: Well then, woman, LET ME IN PEACE.
> *(Woman screams at Boots. Boots screams back. Silence.)*

WOMAN: How many?

BOOTS: Besides Jeff?

WOMAN: How many *times? (Pause.)* I never cheated on you.

BOOTS: Okay. Thanks.

WOMAN: *(Stomps the toe of a boot.)* FUCK YOU.

BOOTS: Ow! Goddamn, Jenny, these are my dancing boots. *(Pause.)* You gonna turn yourself in?

WOMAN: Nope.

BOOTS: They're gonna find out.

WOMAN: Maybe.

BOOTS: No maybe about it. You're going down. They're gonna slice your eyes open with them flashing blue lights. Till you tell 'em all your secrets.

WOMAN: Wish I could work that kinda magic on you. Man flows to your doorstep. You let him in. Man flows over the house, his smell washes everything in your home, a weird kinda clean. Saltwater clean. Let him in. Makes life a mystery. Confusion. The bed a place of foreign noises. Muffled sounds. And you can't for the life of you get the water outta your ears.

BOOTS: I didn't mean to get everything in a snarl.

WOMAN: Two years, you and me. When was Jeff?

BOOTS: June. Four months.

WOMAN: He's got a sunken chest.

BOOTS: Nothing makes sense, you know that.

WOMAN: More peanut talk.

*(Sirens in the distance, getting closer.)*

BOOTS: They're coming.

WOMAN: Yep. Listen. I turned my pockets inside out for you. I turned my self inside out. Can't you give me something? Something real, something I can hold in my hands for just a second?

BOOTS: Like what?

WOMAN: When you said you loved me, what did that mean?

BOOTS: There's a mole on your back, the one shaped like the Statue of Liberty.

WOMAN: Bullshit.

BOOTS: Well, like the torch part anyway. I loved that mole.

WOMAN: Not good enough.

*(Sirens are getting closer.)*

BOOTS: There was a way you dug your fingers into me when we made love. Like you were gonna leave your prints on my bones. Like some kinda fossil.

WOMAN: You loved that?

BOOTS: Scared me.

WOMAN: Not good enough.

BOOTS: Baby, I used you, I'm sorry, you're here, I'm not, you're up on the ground and walking around, I'm dead and bleeding and sinking into the soggy soil right beneath your feet! NOW WHAT THE HELL I GOT YOU WANT?

*(Woman screams. Boots scream. Sirens outside scream. Woman thrusts her hands into the boots, still screaming. Suddenly, Woman and Boots aren't screaming—they're singing. As they sing, the Woman dances on all fours, her hands in the boots.)*

BOOTS:

*Sea-water body*
*These boots can't hold me*
*Salt-fingers touching to your lips*
*Still we danced*

*Always you drink me*
*Always you thirsty*
*Can't get the water past your lips*
*Still we danced*

WOMAN:

*I am earthy*
*I am raw*
*My man's in pieces*
*Down in the soggy soggy*

*I am earthy*
*I am raw*
*My man's in pieces*
*Still we danced*

*(Blue lights flow around the room. It looks like they're surrounded by an ocean of water. Sound of waves crashing. Then pounding on the door. The blue lights speed up—police lights. Woman rises, removes her hands from the boots. She picks up the shovel. Pounding on the door. Woman stares defiantly out to the audience and stomps the shovel to the floor. Blackout.)*

## END OF PLAY

# Orange Lemon Egg Canary
## by Rinne Groff

# BIOGRAPHY

Rinne Groff is a playwright and performer. Her plays, including *Jimmy Carter Was a Democrat, Orange Lemon Egg Canary, Inky, The Five Hysterical Girls Theorem, House of Wonder, Three Short Plays about Flying* and *The Ruby Sunrise* have been produced by P.S. 122, Target Margin Theater, Clubbed Thumb, HERE, Soho Repertory, New Georges and Andy's Summer Playhouse, among others. Ms. Groff is a founding member of Elevator Repair Service Theater Company and has been a part of the writing, staging and performing of their shows (both in the U.S. and on European tour) since the company's inception in 1991. Ms. Groff is an instructor at N.Y.U. Tisch School of the Arts and a member of the Dramatists Guild. She is a graduate of Yale University (1991) and New York University (1999).

# HUMANA FESTIVAL PRODUCTION

*Orange Lemon Egg Canary: A Trick in Four Acts* premiered at the Humana Festival of New American Plays in March 2003. It was directed by Michael Sexton with the following cast:

Great . . . . . . . . . . . . . . . . . . . . . . . . . . . . . . . . . . . René Millán
Henrietta . . . . . . . . . . . . . . . . . . . . . . . . . . . . . Wendy Stetson
Trilby . . . . . . . . . . . . . . . . . . . . . . . . . . . . . . . . . . . Nell Mooney
Egypt . . . . . . . . . . . . . . . . . . . . . . . . . . . . . . . . . . . . . Roz Davis
Magician's Assistants . . . . . . . . . . . . . . . . . . . . . Richard Furlong
Brian Nemiroff

and the following production staff:

Scenic Designer . . . . . . . . . . . . . . . . . . . . . . . . . . . . . Paul Owen
Costume Designer . . . . . . . . . . . . . . . . . . . . . . . . . Suttirat Larlarb
Lighting Designer . . . . . . . . . . . . . . . . . . . . . . . . . . Tony Penna
Sound Designer . . . . . . . . . . . . . . . . . . . . . . . . . . . Shane Rettig
Properties Designer . . . . . . . . . . . . . . . . . . . . . . . . Mark Walston
Production Stage Manager . . . . . . . . . . . . . . . . . Paul Mills Holmes
Production Assistant . . . . . . . . . . . . . . . . . . . . . . Andrea J. Berkey
Script Consultant . . . . . . . . . . . . . . . . . . . . . . . . . . . Steve Cuiffo
Magic Coach . . . . . . . . . . . . . . . . . . . . . . . . . . . . Dr. Bob Escher
Sleight of Hand Consultant/Coach . . . . . . . . . . . . . . . Paul Gertner
Illusion Consultant/Coach. . . . . . . . . . . . . . . . . William Schmeelk
Dramaturg . . . . . . . . . . . . . . . . . . . . . . . . . . . . . . . Tanya Palmer
Assistant Dramaturg . . . . . . . . . . . . . . . . . . . . . . . . . . Claire Cox
Casting. . . . . . . . . . . . . . . . . . . . . . . . . . . . Liebhart/Alberg Casting
Directing Assistant . . . . . . . . . . . . . . . . . . . . . . . . . . West Hyler

# CHARACTERS

GREAT

HENRIETTA

TRILBY

EGYPT

TWO MAGIC ASSISTANTS (non-speaking)


# SETTING

a lot of RED VELVET (like a Magic Show!)

a couple of apartment CHAIRS and a TABLE

a large FOOTLOCKER

and the following magic trick set-ups (each covered at the start by a red velvet cloth):

a BIRDCAGE, the PENETRATING KNIVES ACT, i.e. a painted wooden box with knives sticking through it (this illusion is for show only and does not have to function) and the apparatus for IMPALED (a large metallic spike sticking up from a frame).

At the top of the play, some jeans and other clothes are scattered about the stage.

# TIME

The late twentieth century

Nell Mooney and René Millán
in *Orange Lemon Egg Canary*

27th Annual Humana Festival of New American Plays
Actors Theatre of Louisville, 2003
photo by Harlan Taylor

# Orange Lemon Egg Canary

PROLOGUE

*As the audience enters the theater and takes seats, there is a man wearing a dark suit, waiting at the foot of the stage. His name is Great. He carries a deck of cards. Great approaches various members of the audience and does impressive card tricks, complete with charming patter, one-on-one or for small groups. He is a fantastic magician. By the time the audience is seated and the theater doors are shut, Great has made his way back to the foot of the stage. He performs one final card trick…*

GREAT: Hi, folks; my name is Great. Thanks for coming tonight. You had to come. Or, if you hadn't, I don't know what I would've done because without you… I couldn't bear the weight alone. You do most of the work, you see. That's my trick; that's the trick. You guard the line and you know when to cross it. The line. The line that separates what you actually see, feel, think from what you believe you see, think, feel.

*(He holds up the deck and does the following Morphing Card Trick as he continues speaking.)*

GREAT: You see, here in my hand, here we have the Two of Clubs. Obviously, you can see it's the Two. It's real. It's tangible: I'm the only one touching it, but believe me, I'm touching it. And you, you're guarding the line. Watch it. Protect it. It's such a gorgeous line. Because as soon as the Two crosses the line, over into illusion—the line that you made, mind you—your imagination takes over, your heart beats faster and you start seeing more vibrant colors, and the Two begins to look very much like the Queen of Hearts.

*(The Two 'becomes' the Queen in Great's hands as he passes it over this imagined line.)*

GREAT: But remember, that's just because of the line. When the Queen crosses back again, it's, of course, still the Two. Because that's what it is: a lowly Two.

*(The card is a Two of Clubs again.)*

GREAT: It's not what you think it is. It's different than you think.

*(Great pours himself a shot of whiskey. He drinks it down in one gulp.)*

GREAT: *(Confidentially.)* Look, I can explain. How it works… You've got the line; of course, you do, it's your line, each of your lines. And the line, as lines are wont to be, is infinite. It divides the entire world, the universe into two parts, two halves of the whole: Drunken-ness and Sobriety. But seriously, Truth and Lies. Magic and Reality. Or, if you prefer, Illusion and… No Illusion Whatsoever. Now you see, the Two can get very close to the line, see, and as you bring it closer… *(He does so.)* …but it's still the Two, right? And you bring it closer, closer, but it's always either here or it's… *(As the card becomes a Queen.)* … over here. That's where it becomes the Queen. See what I mean? The Queen of your mind, the Queen of the best parts of you. What's wrong with that? Let it stay there, let it keep: regal, your Queen. It's your queen.

*(Great holds out the Queen for all to see.)*

GREAT : Because for me, it'll always be the Two of Clubs.

*(And the card transforms back into the Two of Clubs right in front of the audience's eyes.)*

GREAT: But maybe that's just me.

*(By this time, Henrietta has entered. She wears an old-fashioned magician's assistant outfit: sparkly and sexy. She is a sassy 1930s broad. She has been watching Great finish his act.)*

*(Great puts the deck of cards away and makes his way onto the stage proper. He doesn't hear Henrietta speak.)*

HENRIETTA: Everybody loves Magic. Everybody loves to be fooled. Everybody loves to be tricked. Everybody loves to be caught with their pants down. Everybody loves to be cheated and misled. Everybody loves it when someone lies to them. Especially when they watch that certain someone very closely and they're trying to catch him in his lie, but he's quick with the sleight of hand, too quick; and a girl is left feeling both stupid and angry, and third of all, empty. People love that.

*(As Henrietta talks, Great takes off his tie, his suit jacket, his shoes and socks. He takes a seat at the table.)*


# ACT ONE: ORANGE
SCENE ONE

*In Great's apartment. Trilby enters, wearing nothing but a black cape.*

TRILBY: I found this.
GREAT: Take that off.

TRILBY: I'm naked.

(*Henrietta fades from sight.*)

GREAT: Where are your clothes?

TRILBY: I thought you might know.

(*Great looks around and finds Trilby's jeans. He tosses them to her.*)

TRILBY: Panties?

GREAT: Where did you leave them?

TRILBY: You don't remember removing my underwear?

(*Great looks around and finds her underwear.*)

GREAT: They're pretty.

(*He holds them out to her.*)

TRILBY: Too late. (*Because she's already got her jeans on.*)

(*Trilby takes off the cape. Underneath she wears a tee-shirt.*)

GREAT: Thought you said naked.

TRILBY: You said, "they're pretty;" who's the bigger bullshit artist?

GREAT: They're nice underwear.

TRILBY: Keep 'em.

GREAT: Thanks.

TRILBY: Can I keep the cape?

GREAT: No.

TRILBY: Why do you have a cape?

GREAT: Why do you have panties?

TRILBY: I wear them.

GREAT: Not right now.

TRILBY: But sometimes you wear a cape?

GREAT: No.

TRILBY: Why can't I have it then?

GREAT: You're going to wear it a lot?

TRILBY: If I told you I would wear it every day, would you give it to me?

GREAT: Trilby.

TRILBY: You remember my name.

GREAT: Yeah.

TRILBY: 'Cause it's a hard name. I thought for sure I'd get Trudy, Tessie... Or avoidance tactics. But I suppose you're not the type who says honey. Maybe babe.

GREAT: What's my name?

TRILBY: I don't recall what you told me.

GREAT: It's...

TRILBY: Hush, I know your name.

GREAT: You do?

TRILBY: Are you quizzing me?

GREAT: I'm asking you a question.

TRILBY: You think I don't know.

GREAT: I'm asking if you know.

TRILBY: You're challenging me.

GREAT: I really don't care.

TRILBY: I like a challenge.

GREAT: It's not like I'd be hurt.

TRILBY: You're not sensitive?

GREAT: Completely insensitive.

TRILBY: It's Great.

GREAT: What?

TRILBY: Your name is Great.

GREAT: Who told you that?

TRILBY: You did.

GREAT: I didn't.

TRILBY: Throes of passion.

GREAT: I didn't.

TRILBY: You don't even remember sliding my underwear down my thighs—
and it was a long slow slide; it was perfect and tender; it was perfect—and
now you're gonna claim full cognizance of every word that was spoken
between us last night?

    *(Pause.)*

GREAT: I remember removing your underwear.

    *(Pause.)*

TRILBY: You must have a hang-over.

GREAT: No worse than you.

TRILBY: I don't get hang-overs. Can I make you coffee?

GREAT: No.

TRILBY: You want me to leave?

GREAT: There just isn't any.

TRILBY: I may be new in town, but I know a magical place where lovely
women bring you toast with so much butter, and there's always coffee.

GREAT: I think I've heard of this place.

TRILBY: I work there Wednes. through Sat.

GREAT: No wonder you look so familiar.

TRILBY: Wanna go? On the house.

GREAT: I'm not hungry.

*(Trilby goes to the Penetrating Knives Trick. She removes the cloth covering.)*

TRILBY: What's this?

GREAT: A box.

*(She pulls a knife from the box.)*

TRILBY: What's this?

GREAT: A knife.

TRILBY: Why do you keep knives around?

GREAT: I'm scared of intruders.

*(She is about to remove the covering from the birdcage.)*

GREAT: Stop.

*(She does.)*

TRILBY: You're a magician.

GREAT: You think that's funny?

TRILBY: I slept with a magician.

GREAT: Congratulations.

TRILBY: Can you teach me?

GREAT: Teach?

TRILBY: As in those who can't do. But you can do, can't you?

GREAT: You don't teach magic.

TRILBY: You didn't learn magic?

GREAT: You don't teach you.

TRILBY: It could be fun; you know: Sorcerer's Apprentice like in *Fantasia*. I could play Mickey.

GREAT: You're going to fill my apartment with water?

TRILBY: Could you make it right again if I did? Put that army of brooms back together?

GREAT: No, I got nothing to stay the flood.

TRILBY: But your master might.

GREAT: Master?

TRILBY: Who taught you magic. Who did teach you magic?

GREAT: How did you wind up here?

TRILBY: I asked you first.

GREAT: My grandfather taught me.

TRILBY: Maybe I could get him to show me a thing or two.

GREAT: He's dead.

TRILBY: I'm sorry.

GREAT: Me, too.

TRILBY: You miss him?

GREAT: He was my grandfather.

TRILBY: He was a magician, too?

GREAT: Not a very good one. And he gave it up.

TRILBY: What makes a magician good?

GREAT: What are you asking me?

TRILBY: How you became really good, really Great.

GREAT: Did China send you here?

TRILBY: China? This keeps getting better and better.

GREAT: How did she find me?

TRILBY: China is a woman?

GREAT: Don't play dumb.

TRILBY: Look, Great, I moved here two weeks ago; I don't know from China.

GREAT: How do you know my name?

TRILBY: It's written in your cape.

*(Great picks up the cape and looks inside the lining.)*

GREAT: It's not my cape.

TRILBY: It's his?

GREAT: Was his.

TRILBY: What else did you inherit? Besides a name?

GREAT: It's not my name.

*(Trilby moves to the footlocker.)*

TRILBY: Besides this.

GREAT: Leave that alone.

TRILBY: What's inside?

GREAT: Nothing.

TRILBY: But you keep it locked.

GREAT: It came that way.

TRILBY: From where?

GREAT: They sent it when they cleaned out my grandfather's house.

TRILBY: You think it's haunted? Oh my god, you should see your face. You do.

GREAT: No.

TRILBY: You think it's touched by his ghost.

GREAT: You believe in ghosts?

TRILBY: Sure. Don't you?

GREAT: I don't know one way or the other.

TRILBY: So you lock it up and make sure you'll never find out. What are you so afraid of?

GREAT: Listen, I'll call you.

TRILBY: Wow.

GREAT: What?

TRILBY: Cut straight to "I'll call you."

*(Great doesn't respond. Trilby puts on her shoes.)*

TRILBY: You have skills. Skills with your hands.

GREAT: What makes you say that?

TRILBY: Last night.

GREAT: What about it?

TRILBY: Skills with your hands.

GREAT: Making people believe things that aren't true.

TRILBY: Wow.

*(Trilby exits.)*

HENRIETTA: It's easy to get stuck. I got stuck the same way it happens to any other person: by accident. I was studying to be a nurse… hey, I could have been a nurse. One day after classes, my friend, my fiancé, if you're a stickler for details, took me to see a magic show. Boy oh boy, this magician. He did the usual tricks, the usual stuff—billiard balls, cards, ummmnn, cigarettes, the classics—but it was my first time. I had never seen, I, I, I, had never even heard of a profession like that. I was knocked, completely. I was sitting like this…

*(She makes a slight open-mouthed expression.)*

HENRIETTA: That's probably why he chose me, called me to the stage. The stage! Plus he liked to call on girls in the audience who had their boyfriends in tow. Their fiancés. Stickler. He said pick a card, any card. *(Whispering.)* The Queen of Hearts. I held it close to my breast. *(Full-voice again.)* He told me to sit on it. Excuse me? He provided the chair. "Wait," he said, "Face up," and he reached his hand under my thigh. He pulled the card, without looking at it, naturally, flipped it, and slid it back under. Then he asked me to part my lips. Okey-dokey. "Open your mouth wider." Yeah, sure. My fiancé's watching this. He took a small telescope and slipped it inside my open mouth, just a bit, just enough to give me the taste of metal. When I laughed, my teeth came down on it. "Careful," he said. "Be careful." I looked into his eyes. He gazed down my throat, saw straight through every part of my insides, and he guessed my card. He knew my card all right.

And that's what I mean by "stuck."

## SCENE TWO

*In the restaurant. Trilby enters with a waitress apron on. She sees Great at the table and, after a beat, approaches.*

TRILBY: Can I get you something?

GREAT: I'll take a coffee. Can I buy you one?

TRILBY: You wanna buy me a coffee?

GREAT: Yeah.

TRILBY: Why don't you put an extra buck on my tip instead?
What are you staring at?

GREAT: Am I staring?

TRILBY: Are.

GREAT: You have really amazing hands.

TRILBY: Flattery?

GREAT: I'm sorry about the other night, the other morning.

TRILBY: Apology.

*(Trilby sits at the table.)*

GREAT: Are you going to get in trouble?

TRILBY: And concern. You're on your best behavior. Feeling lonely?

GREAT: Aren't you going to get in trouble?

TRILBY: I could possibly get fired; is that what you mean?

*(Trilby lights up a cigarette.)*

GREAT: You can't smoke in here.

TRILBY: You wanna be the waitress? You seem to know all the lines.

GREAT: What should my lines be?

TRILBY: Do I have to tell you everything?

GREAT: Can we start again?

TRILBY: The question everyone's dying to know the answer to.

GREAT: You have really amazing hands.

TRILBY: They're cold all the time.

GREAT: It's smoking.

TRILBY: What is?

GREAT: Smoking wrecks your hands.

TRILBY: I thought, your heart.

GREAT: My heart?

TRILBY: One's heart. Among other things.

GREAT: Among other organs?

TRILBY: Among other things that wreck one's heart.

(*Pause.*)

GREAT: I brought you something.

TRILBY: The cape?

GREAT: You can't have the cape.

TRILBY: What can I have?

(*He takes her panties out of his pocket and holds them out to her.*)

(*Pause.*)

TRILBY: Maybe I left them with you for a reason.

GREAT: What's that?

TRILBY: Voodoo.

GREAT: You believe in black magic?

TRILBY: It worked. Lured you here.

GREAT: What are going to do with me now?

(*Pause.*)

TRILBY: Anyway, I don't want the cape. I want the stuff.

GREAT: What stuff?

TRILBY: The stuff in the locker.

GREAT: There's nothing there, Trilby, no mysteries to unveil. There's a notebook, some notebooks and out-dated magic texts, that's all.

TRILBY: And you're not gonna share them with me.

GREAT: Magicians don't share.

TRILBY: Waitresses don't sit, but look at me now.

GREAT: I am looking at you.

(*She grabs his hand.*)

TRILBY: Want me to read your palm?

GREAT: No.

TRILBY: I can do it. You think you're the only one with powers.

(*She looks at his hand.*)

TRILBY: This is the life line. Good long life.

GREAT: Runs in the family.

TRILBY: I see here some fear.

GREAT: How interesting.

TRILBY: Yes, a lot of fear. You've been hurt before.

GREAT: My line must look a lot like a lot of people's. What else is in my palm?

TRILBY: You drink too much and you treat women like shit.

(*Pause.*)

GREAT: Maybe we can put that in the past tense.

TRILBY: You're trying to escape from your past?

GREAT: Evidently I'm trying to escape from my hand.

TRILBY: *(Refocusing on his palm.)* But it's not all bad. This right here... a very particular sign... very interesting.

GREAT: Oh yeah?

TRILBY: You wanna know what it means?

GREAT: You're pretty good at this.

TRILBY: You wanna know what it means?

GREAT: Maybe I know what it means; it's my sign.

TRILBY: Why don't you tell me what it means?

*(He takes his hand away from her.)*

GREAT: I want to see you again, Trilby.

TRILBY: I love the way you say my name; it's like you know me.

*(She gets up. She hands him the cigarette.)*

TRILBY: You can't smoke in here.

*(Trilby walks away from the table and off-stage.)*

*(Great makes the cigarette Vanish.)*

HENRIETTA: I never saw my fiancé again. I never saw my mother again. She was sore I abandoned the medical profession. Sore I disappeared. Disappeared. Ha ha. But the magician makes the void, and the assistant rushes in. No news flash: you've seen it a million times. And I knew it even then—it doesn't take a genius—I knew that one day he'd be sorry for taking my innocence. And I don't mean innocence like that, not like how you think. Although he did that, too. No, his crime was teaching me how illusion is manufactured. That's the saddest loss of innocence of all: eyes forever open too wide. Such is the lot some of us get in this life.

Deception depends on stillness. A stillness that hides activity. A still hand. With your other hand, the one that's doing nothing, you wave like a drunkard. Be flamboyant! The assistant, a.k.a. the Victim, she's like the hand that doesn't move. Or rather the gams that don't. You gotta got good gams. Watch her when she's being still. In her tranquil time. Look deep. Watch her.

# SCENE THREE

*In Great's apartment. It is dark. Trilby, wearing a tee-shirt and underwear, is snooping. She goes to the birdcage and removes the cloth covering. She screams. Great rushes in, also in underwear.*

GREAT: What the hell?

TRILBY: It's dead.

*(Great turns on a light.)*

GREAT: What time is it?

TRILBY: The bird is dead.

GREAT: What are you doing?

*(Great approaches the cage. He sees that Trilby is looking at a canary lying on the bottom of the cage.)*

GREAT : Shit.

TRILBY: That's all you have to say? It's a bird.

GREAT: It's a prop.

TRILBY: It's real.

GREAT: It's not.

TRILBY: Now it's dead. Like a rat.

GREAT: Rats are real.

TRILBY: You don't even care.

GREAT: Should I throw it in the garbage? I care.

TRILBY: Could have fooled me.

GREAT: Her name was Elsie.

TRILBY: And you throw Elsie in the garbage?

GREAT: What do you want me to do?

TRILBY: Mourn.

*(Great takes the bird out of the cage.)*

GREAT: Here, you want it? You can mourn.

*(He tries to stick it in her hand.)*

TRILBY: Keep that away from me. It's got disease.

GREAT: Take it, Trilby.

*(He grabs her hand and shoves the bird into it. Trilby squirms, but then stops.)*

TRILBY: It's plastic.

GREAT: I know.

TRILBY: I'm not clever.

*(Great tosses the plastic bird back into the cage.)*

TRILBY: What do you do with Elsie?

GREAT: Let's go back to bed.

TRILBY: It's not like I'm asking you to reveal secrets.

GREAT: But you are.

TRILBY: Was your grandfather famous?

GREAT : Had a popular show for a while. A husband-wife act.

TRILBY: Act?

GREAT: They were never married, I don't think.

TRILBY: Why not?

GREAT: I don't know; she died and he married someone else.

TRILBY: She died. How did she die?

GREAT: I don't know.

TRILBY: Then how do you know she died? Is it in the notebooks?

GREAT: I've barely read the notebooks.

TRILBY: Then how do you know they pretended to be married?

GREAT: All the telepathy stunts back then were matrimonial teams.

TRILBY: They could read each other's minds?

GREAT: The magician would cast a spell on his wife…

TRILBY: His not-wife.

GREAT: On Henrietta. Next they would kiss. And at the moment when their lips touched, all her senses would be transferred to him; she would give her body over, trust him with it completely, as the magic would have it; and once it was in his possession, everything that she experienced, he would feel as well.

TRILBY: Big responsibility.

GREAT: Henrietta would blindfold him…

TRILBY: Oooh.

GREAT: …and then walk into the audience and solicit stuff from people. She would hold an object in her hand, and Great, unable to see a thing, thirty feet away, could say what it was.

TRILBY: Because he could feel it? He could feel what she felt?

*(Great touches his forehead as if in deep concentration.)*

GREAT: A brown leather wallet with seven dollars inside. A gold-*plated* watch—cheapskate!—purchased from a street vendor on the Bowery, and you're running six minutes slow. You got that derby from your brother, sir. Size seven and a half is too small for you; buy a new one or you'll never find a sweetheart.

TRILBY: Amazing.

GREAT: It's mediocre magic, but it was very popular.

TRILBY: And that's love?

GREAT: What?

TRILBY: When two people become one like that.

GREAT: I'm not sure what you're asking.

TRILBY: Do you love me?

GREAT: I don't know; am I supposed to know already?

TRILBY: Do I love you?

GREAT: I don't know; yes, yes, you do. Is that what I'm supposed to say?

TRILBY: Maybe I should go.

GREAT: What? Wait a second; because I don't love you?

TRILBY: You don't love me?

(Pause.)

TRILBY: Not even a little bit?

(Longer pause.)

TRILBY: I'm kidding. Jesus; we hardly know each other.

(Great says nothing.)

TRILBY: What was the spell?

GREAT: What spell?

TRILBY: The spell that made them like one.

GREAT: You look so beautiful in the moonlight.

TRILBY: Don't try to distract me; I want to know and I won't ask anything else.

GREAT: No, that was his spell: You look so beautiful in the moonlight.

TRILBY: That was his spell?

GREAT: That was one of his spells.

TRILBY: Great...

GREAT: I hate it when you call me that; I shouldn't have talked magic with you.

TRILBY: Honey?

GREAT: What?

TRILBY: Say it again.

GREAT: What?

TRILBY: You know, the spell.

GREAT: Trilby.

TRILBY: Please.

GREAT: You look so beautiful in the moonlight.

(She rushes to him and kisses him passionately. A moment passes. She looks in his eyes.)

TRILBY: It worked. You feel me.

GREAT: Trilby, it was an act; they had a code.

TRILBY: Sure. Let's go back to bed.

*(Trilby drags him to the bedroom.)*

HENRIETTA: She's going to get pregnant tonight. *(Less committed.)* Or some other night. How do I know? Because there are places where magic still exists. You don't believe me? Locations in this universe where the world is a world of astonishment.

It wasn't a code. Code, shmode. We lived in magic. We danced there. Great ran away, but I stayed. I decided to move in. I'm still here. I can never leave. Not until Great lifts me up. If only he could lift me up... A world of astonishment. Sometimes it's not as sweet as it sounds.


SCENE FOUR

*In the restaurant. Trilby and Great sit at the table with two empty water glasses in front of them. Egypt enters.*

EGYPT: *(Loudly.)* Oh my god, I thought you were dead.

*(Great looks up.)*

GREAT: *(Seeing Egypt.)* China.

EGYPT: Wishful thinking.

*(Egypt approaches.)*

GREAT: China, what are you doing here?

EGYPT: My name is Egypt.

GREAT: Excuse me?

EGYPT: Your assistant's name was China. My name is Egypt.

GREAT: Egypt.

EGYPT: Birthplace of civilization.

TRILBY: Hi, I'm Trilby.

EGYPT: You're the new one?

TRILBY: One what?

EGYPT: Assistant.

GREAT: She's not...

EGYPT: Let me see your legs.

*(Trilby begins to rise.)*

GREAT: Sit down.

TRILBY: What about my legs?

EGYPT: Nice.

TRILBY: I'm not his assistant. *(To Great.)* I thought you didn't work with an assistant.

EGYPT: Is that what he told you? He works with them all right.

GREAT: I no longer work with assistants.

EGYPT: Then I've accomplished something of value in my life.

TRILBY: It's because of you?

GREAT: What are you doing here… Egypt?

EGYPT: I came six hundred and fifty-nine miles for a really good breakfast. I hear the toast is out of this world.

TRILBY: If you like it buttery.

EGYPT : So we both wind up here.

I still have the scars, you know.

TRILBY: Scars?

EGYPT: From our triumphant finale: the Hypnotic Balance.

*(Egypt turns around and pulls up her shirt, exposing the small of her back. There is an ugly, red sore spot right on her spine.)*

TRILBY: What did you do to her?

EGYPT: And here.

*(Egypt shows her thighs to Trilby. They also have scars.)*

EGYPT: Wounds that never heal.

GREAT: Those were trick knives.

EGYPT: They sure felt real to me. It all felt very real.

TRILBY: She has scars.

EGYPT: But he never felt guilty about it. No guilt. Special set of rules for a special man. Screw around with any dumb awestruck bitch in the audience, but you should be glad he comes home at all. And maybe he'll have a little taste of regret and apology when he finally makes it through the door, stone drunk. You've been pulling your hair out, contemplating suicide since three a.m.

TRILBY: He's trying to escape from his hand.

EGYPT: Excuse me?

TRILBY: People can change.

EGYPT: He's already drawn you in.

TRILBY: He's not drawing me in.

EGYPT: That's how he does it: draws you in so deep, you think you're drawing him in.

GREAT: What are you doing here?

EGYPT: Making a name for myself in the big city.

GREAT: A new name.

EGYPT: What are you doing, Great?

TRILBY: He doesn't like to be called that off-stage.

GREAT: There's lots of reasons to move to a city.

EGYPT: Running away from shame is as good as any.

TRILBY: What shame?

EGYPT: It seems that Great here was on stage one night and a little bird—maybe it was Elsie?—had tipped off his biggest fans as to how he did that tired old "Line That Separates Magic and Reality" trick.

GREAT: Do we really have to re-hash…?

EGYPT: And that was just for starters. Illusion after illusion: revealed, exposed, destroyed. You should have seen your face.

TRILBY: It sounds awful.

EGYPT: It wasn't pretty, but it was deserved.

You're not still doing the "Two Becomes a Queen" routine, are you?

GREAT: Is that a threat?

EGYPT: Because I'd love to see your show. Your new girlfriend and I could go together.

TRILBY: He doesn't let me come to his shows.

GREAT: Trilby.

EGYPT: I wonder why that is?

TRILBY: Yeah, why is that?

GREAT: Trilby, please.

EGYPT: Have I inspired a fight?

GREAT: No.

TRILBY: So you're a magician, too?

EGYPT: Planning a big show for September. Mind control.

GREAT: Really?

EGYPT: I learned from the biggest mind-fuck of them all.

TRILBY: You read minds?

EGYPT: Control them. Inanimate objects, too.

GREAT: Diverse talents.

TRILBY: I need some water.

EGYPT: Sit; I'll get it.

TRILBY: I work here.

EGYPT: Are you working now?

TRILBY: No.

EGYPT: Then we're equals.

*(Egypt goes to get a pitcher of water.)*

TRILBY: I need a cigarette.

*(She takes one from her pack.)*

GREAT: You can't smoke in here.

TRILBY: Give me a break, Great.

GREAT: Don't call me that.

*(As Trilby looks for her matches, Egypt returns with the pitcher. She takes Trilby's glass off the table and starts to fill it with water. Egypt sees Trilby searching for a light. She lets go of the glass in order to pull a lighter from her pocket. But the glass remains there, suspended in the air! Egypt lights Trilby's cigarette. The glass continues to float. Trilby stares at the Airborn Glass. Egypt continues pouring. Once the glass is full, Egypt hands it to Trilby who is amazed.)*

TRILBY: Thanks…

GREAT: I didn't know you smoked. China didn't smoke.

EGYPT: You don't know how I do it.

GREAT: Of course I do.

EGYPT: It's not what you think.

GREAT: I thought you controlled what I think.

EGYPT: How did I do it?

GREAT: Magic.

EGYPT: Can I give you some advice—what did you say: Tessie? Trudy?

TRILBY: You can call me babe.

EGYPT: He's a magician. A drunk, a liar, a cheat. Illusion is his trade.

TRILBY: I could say the same about you; is that right?

*(Egypt once again shows the mark on the small of her back.)*

EGYPT: I'm just saying.

*(Egypt exits.)*

*(Trilby smokes and drinks water. Great is silent. Finally…)*

TRILBY: Amicable break-up?

GREAT: She's crazy.

TRILBY: No big wonder: you used to stick her on a spike.

She gave away your secrets?

GREAT: The ones she knew. I didn't tell her everything.

TRILBY: You kept some tricks hidden from her?

GREAT: Need-to-know basis.

TRILBY: And you spiked her because she betrayed you?

GREAT: It was an act. There's no because.

TRILBY: The act: a magician, a drunk, a cheat.

GREAT: China's crazy; I told you.

TRILBY: Her name is Egypt.

GREAT: She's crazy.

TRILBY: But is she true?

GREAT: No. What do you mean, true?

TRILBY: I mean, are you the one that made her crazy?

*(Henrietta picks up the glass that was airborn moments ago.)*

HENRIETTA: Wires? Is that what you're thinking? Or magnets. Or mirrors. But where would the mirrors be, sharp guy, and why didn't she crash through them when she came in? How could she perform the wire rigging so quickly and impromptu? In the middle of a restaurant? How in BeJesus's name do you think magnets could help the situation? Give over. Give over. Trust me: you might as well give over.

*(She takes a sip of water from the glass.)*

HENRIETTA: I've got a mark on my back, too, more horribler than hers, believe me, but I was raised in such a way… call me old fashioned, but it's not polite to strip. I may have worked the theaters, but I was never a roundheel and I won't be displaying any telling marks on my torso any time soon.

Picture it: the Hypnotic Balance. A scantily clad girl—and this was between the World Wars, mind you, when deshabillé, that's what they call it in France, still meant something—perfectly balanced and serene on a sturdy, protruding, spikey shaft. Great spins me around, chanting spells in my ear. It still gives me goosebumps. Commitment, faith, trust—why not?—love. There I said it. Don't move, don't even blink or the spike just might thrust right on up through you. Don't you want to see that? Don't you want it? Love.

*(Henrietta jerks the glass towards the audience as if to throw water on them, but it's only Magic Fairy Dust that floats through the air.)*

## SCENE FIVE

*Great walks into his apartment wearing his suit. It is dark.*

TRILBY: Welcome home.

GREAT: What the hell?

*(Great turns on the light.)*

GREAT : Shit, you scared me. How did you get in here?

TRILBY: Picked the lock.

GREAT: You what?

TRILBY: Bribed the super.

GREAT: Trilby.

TRILBY: He recognized me as your girlfriend and let me in. Is that so nuts?

GREAT: What are you doing here?

TRILBY: You're not happy to see me?

GREAT: Of course. How did you get in really?

TRILBY: Magic. I appeared here. Speaking of magic, did you have a good show?

GREAT: Fine.

*(Great comes over to kiss her; she pushes him away.)*

TRILBY: You smell like lemons.

GREAT: What?

TRILBY: You stink. Have you been drinking?

GREAT: I had a couple drinks.

TRILBY: A couple drinks.

GREAT: I was performing.

TRILBY: What tricks did you pull?

GREAT: What do you mean?

TRILBY: What'd you perform tonight?

GREAT: The usual stuff.

*(Trilby picks up a deck of cards.)*

TRILBY: Pick a card, any card?

GREAT: Sort of.

*(Trilby mocks Great's act using the card deck.)*

TRILBY: Here's the Queen. But it's not the Queen, it's just a bunch of bullshit. See, it crosses the line that you made up in your head, and it all turns to shit. I'm smarter than you, I'm better than you. *(Throwing the deck at him.)* I hate you.

GREAT: You saw my show.

TRILBY: Yeah, I saw your show all right. I waited outside her door for two hours.

GREAT: It's not what you think it is. It's different than you think.

TRILBY: Oh excuse me, were you on the other side of the line? Stay away from me. You probably have herpes. I wish you had herpes. I bet you picked up herpes from one of those girls you screw after your shows.

GREAT: I'm sorry that you had to see that.

TRILBY: Sorry that I saw or sorry that you did?

GREAT: I'm sorry. But we never said…

TRILBY: …that we wouldn't hurt and humiliate each other?

GREAT: It meant nothing. I thought of you.

TRILBY: Gross. Gross.

GREAT: Trilby.

TRILBY: Egypt warned me. I should have listened. I'm a moron.

GREAT: Don't say that.

TRILBY: A moron, an idiot, a retard. I'm a retard. Why should you feel bad about lying to a retard?

GREAT: Please stop.

TRILBY: I wish I'd never walked through this door.

GREAT: Wait, stop, wait. I love you.

*(Pause.)*

TRILBY: How many times have you lied straight to my face?

GREAT: I don't want you to leave.

TRILBY: How could you do it? I couldn't even do it. My body couldn't. And don't give me the it's-the-act-you-don't-ask-why bullshit. There's a why. You do this to someone you love, you say you love.

GREAT: I love.

TRILBY: You learn it from your grandfather? Long line of magicians hurting women.

GREAT: It's got nothing to do with that.

TRILBY: It does: your upbringing, your models.

GREAT: My father wasn't a magician. He sold appliances.

TRILBY: Same difference. You're cursed.

GREAT: Nobody's cursed.

TRILBY: Cursed to repeat the same old tricks.

GREAT: It won't happen again.

TRILBY: How can I believe you if you don't even ask why?

GREAT: You don't want to hear why.

TRILBY: Don't tell me what I want.

Pathetic as I am, I think I cared more about the fact that that stupid perky imbecile gets to watch your shows whenever she wants, and me, I have to sneak in. She knows more about your magic than I do.

GREAT: All she knows is an act.

TRILBY: Your act. You.

GREAT: No.

TRILBY: You make her more important than me.

GREAT: Nothing's more important than you.

TRILBY: Another lie.

GREAT: What can I do to make you believe me?

TRILBY: Do you love me?

*(Pause.)*

TRILBY: You said, I love you.

Do you love me?

HENRIETTA: It's always a kick when you hear people describe an illusion back to you. You do the magic for them, and you know what you did, but to hear them tell it, boy oh boy, it's a whole different ball of wax. And they saw it, they saw it; don't you try to tell them. They'll testify in court that you never put the hat down for a moment when truth be told, between you and me, it sat on the table for seven seconds. They'll tell you how there were three coins at the start, no doubt about it; how the scarf was completely white end to end; how the girl wiggled her torso. They saw it all. With their own eyes. And they'll swear. Because we want lies. Our hearts are too old and too wise for lies, and lies are all we want.

# ACT TWO: LEMON
## SCENE ONE

*Great and Trilby in his apartment. A lesson is beginning.*

GREAT: Say you could do magic. What would you do with your powers? Feed the poor?

TRILBY: Sure.

GREAT: Trick your boss? Catch the bus?

TRILBY: Get someone to fall in love with you.

GREAT: You wouldn't though.

TRILBY: What, love's not important?

GREAT: Anything that you care enough to want, you wouldn't want from magic.

TRILBY: You're saying magic's no good?

GREAT: That's not what I'm saying.

TRILBY: What are you saying?

GREAT: I wanted a chocolate chip cookie, but my mother told me to wait 'til dinner: no snacking. None of my temper tantrums changed her mind. She sends me off to bother my grandfather. I find him and tell him my sorrows, but I'm pretty surprised when he agrees to help. "Yes, my boy, we'll finesse it. But we need a plan." So this is the plan: I go to the kitchen and ask my mom if I can have a piece of fruit. "Okay, sweetie, take an orange from the basket," and she turns back to the stove. I quickly sneak the cookie, hide it under the orange and take off.

TRILBY: Is the magic that he got you to eat an orange instead of a cookie?

GREAT: I go out to Grandpa. He takes the fruit. "Kudos, my boy." But before I can get the cookie in my mouth, he's already peeling. "Oh my, what's this?" There's no fruit underneath the rind. Well, another fruit: a lemon.

TRILBY: Under the orange?

GREAT: Under the peel. "Why, how terrible; I wanted something sweet." But he starts to peel the lemon anyway. When he gets the rind off, there's an egg underneath. Grandpa cracks it right over the carpet.

TRILBY: No yoke?

GREAT: And a canary flies out.

*(Trilby moves to the bird cage and removes the plastic bird.)*

TRILBY: Like Elsie?

GREAT: Like Elsie, but more vibrant.

*(Great tosses the plastic bird back in the cage.)*

TRILBY: You picked this orange from the fruit basket?

GREAT: And that's magic. Why?

TRILBY: Because of the canary. Because of all of it.

GREAT: Because I didn't want a cookie anymore. To this day, I don't know what happened to that cookie. I magically stopped thinking about cookies which is exactly what he wanted me to do. Asking for cookies was the wrong question. He got me asking the right question.

TRILBY: What's the right question?

GREAT: The one the magician wants you to ask, and no others. How do you get a bird inside a lemon?

TRILBY: How do you?

GREAT: That's advanced.

TRILBY: Begin me.

*(Great takes a quarter out of his pocket.)*

TRILBY : You're gonna teach me to make it disappear?

GREAT: You're going to teach you to catch it.

*(He tosses it to her. She catches it.)*

TRILBY: There. Learned.

GREAT: Toss it up and catch it.

*(She does.)*

TRILBY: I'm a natural.

GREAT: Five hundred times.

TRILBY: Are you kidding?

GREAT: Practice makes genius, as the original Great said. When you can do it five hundred times without dropping it, I'll give you another task.

TRILBY: You're trying to dissuade me.

GREAT: You said you wanted this. I'm being honest.

TRILBY: A bitter fruit.

*(Trilby begins tossing the coin and catching it.)*

HENRIETTA: Most tricks have a simple structure: the performer does something that seems impossible! Et voilà. That's what they call it in France. For some folks, that's enough: "I wonder how he did that!"

But when you make Real Magic, the structure is more complex. The audience is made to believe in forces beyond what they know, beyond what they think of as possible: Clairvoyance, for example. Or the Mutability of Solid Forms. Or that Love is Something You Can Count On. It takes a complex set-up to get us to believe in that.

Ask yourself before you get swept away, what is the magical structure that this trick puts forth? One) who is being involved here? The Personalities. Two) what is being exhibited? The Phenomenon. Three) why is the routine performed? The Purpose. And) how is it achieved? The Proof.

Ask yourself about the Proof.

## SCENE TWO

*The restaurant. Egypt sits at the table. Trilby wears her waitress apron.*

TRILBY: Hi.

EGYPT: Hi.

TRILBY: You came by here?

EGYPT: Why not?

TRILBY: Great stops by sometimes when I'm working.

EGYPT: There's no law against me coming in here.

TRILBY: I'm not worried about Law.

EGYPT: What are you worried about?

TRILBY: It seems stupid, that's all.

EGYPT: How's it going?

TRILBY: Fine.

EGYPT: Show me.

*(Trilby takes a quarter out of her apron. She tosses it in the air and catches it.)*

EGYPT : That's it?

*(Trilby puts the coin on the table. She covers it with a napkin.)*

TRILBY: You look so beautiful in the moonlight.

*(She lifts up the napkin and the quarter has Vanished.)*

EGYPT: That's it?

*(Trilby pulls the quarter from Egypt's bra. Egypt grabs her hand.)*

TRILBY: You've gotta start somewhere.

EGYPT: We're running out of time.

TRILBY: I'm doing the best I can.

EGYPT: The show is coming up.

TRILBY: I'm trying to find out.

EGYPT: Have you tried asking?

TRILBY: How?

EGYPT: "Teach me your half of the procedure for the Hypnotic Balance." Form those words with your lips.

TRILBY: How am I even supposed to remember the name of that routine?

EGYPT: Point to the spike and ask about it.

TRILBY: But I don't know anything about magic. I'm Trilby.

EGYPT: Does he trust you?

TRILBY: And I don't want to blow it.

EGYPT: Not that he's capable of real trust. "I no longer work with assistants." What an asshole.

TRILBY: An asshole, a liar, the devil, the evil that must be ripped from the world; I know, Egypt.

EGYPT: He'll never change. Part of his m.o. is that he tempts you to change him by being such a creep. But you'll never change him. Not even love will change him.

TRILBY: I know. You don't have to worry.

*(Egypt reaches her hand into Trilby's bra. They kiss. Egypt removes a quarter.)*

EGYPT: I do worry: I've thrown you in the viper's den.

TRILBY: I'm not easily seduced by snakes.


## SCENE THREE

*Henrietta stands by the footlocker. She opens the lock and lifts the lid.*

HENRIETTA: Would you like to shoot a bullet at me? I can catch it between my teeth. Bring a dead bird back to life? I re-animate it with my perfume breath.

*(She picks up a bunch of books out of the locker and brings them to the table.)*

HENRIETTA: It's all in here. The secrets. Canary in the Lightbulb, the Spirit Cabinet, Piercing a Woman, the Floating Ball.

*(She looks at a particular book.)*

HENRIETTA: Hypnosis. I'm an expert at hypnosis. I mean at being hypnotized. To have it done to you is the toughest part; don't kid yourself. Anyone can control. But only special people can fully allow themselves to be controlled. Great called them women.

*(She picks a notebook up out of the locker. She opens the notebook and looks inside.)*

HENRIETTA: *(Reading.)* I got stuck the same way it happens to any other person: by accident. I was studying to be a nurse. I could have been a nurse. *(Flipping through the notebook.)* Ah look, here's an entry from June, 1937. We were in Philadelphia.

*(Henrietta hears someone coming. She places the notebook on top of the pile of books on the table.)*

*(Trilby enters. Trilby can't see Henrietta, but she senses a presence.)*

TRILBY: Hello? Hello? Honey? Are you home? Who's there?

*(Trilby notices the notebook on the table.)*
TRILBY: Anybody home?
*(She picks up the notebook.)*


## SCENE FOUR

*Great's apartment. Trilby sits at the table, studying a book from the pile in front of her. Great enters. Trilby closes the book in front of her and repeats from memory.*

TRILBY: Production, Vanish, Transposition, Transformation, Penetration, Restoration, Animation, Anti-Gravity, Attraction, Sympathetic Reaction, Invulnerability, Physical Anomaly, Spectator Failure, Control, Identification, Thought Reading, Thought Transmission, Prediction, Extra-Sensory Perception.
GREAT: Impressive.
TRILBY: Every magic trick known to man can be classified in one of these categories.
   And you think I can't learn.
GREAT: That's not what I think. Why would I show you my library?
TRILBY: But all you teach me is coin tricks. Let's talk about Penetration.
GREAT: All right, let's.
TRILBY: I'm serious.
   Isn't there some trick, some illusion, some something in your repertoire that goes beyond all that?
GREAT: Nothing comes to mind.
TRILBY: Tell me about when you used to perform with Egypt.
GREAT: Her name was China.
TRILBY: You think I'll be jealous?
GREAT: Yes.
TRILBY: Why should I be? She was hypnotized out of feeling anything.
GREAT: Who told you that?
   *(Trilby holds a book out to him. He opens it.)*
GREAT: Where did, where did you get that?
TRILBY: You gave it to me.
GREAT: That's a dangerous book. You don't need to learn hypnosis.
   *(Great starts to look through the books on the table.)*

GREAT: These aren't the books I pulled for you. You went into the locker. How'd you get in there?

TRILBY: I didn't. The books were on the table. I thought you left them out for me.

*(He sees the notebook. He grabs it.)*

GREAT: What are you doing with these?

TRILBY: I told you: they were here. It was all here.

GREAT: These are my grandfather's notebooks. You can't…

TRILBY: What, what can't I?

GREAT: This is a mistake.

*(Great gathers all the books together.)*

TRILBY: It's not.

GREAT: A big mistake.

TRILBY: Give that back.

*(They struggle over the books.)*

GREAT: We don't need to be doing this.

TRILBY: Doing what?

GREAT: Doing magic.

TRILBY: We do.

*(Great pushes Trilby off of him.)*

GREAT: No.

*(He puts all the books back in the locker and slams it closed.)*

*(Trilby goes to the Penetrating Knives Act box. She takes a trick knife in her hands.)*

TRILBY: But I want magic.

*(She stabs it into her leg.)*

TRILBY: Owww.

*(Her leg bleeds.)*

GREAT: Why did you do that? How did you do that? *(Looking at her wound.)* Oh shit, Trilby, it's deep.

*(Great runs off-stage.)*

TRILBY: I lied to you. You didn't pick me up at the restaurant.

*(He returns with bandages and starts to fix her up.)*

GREAT: We should get you to a hospital.

TRILBY: I'm not gonna lie to you anymore.

GREAT: What are you talking about?

TRILBY: *(Pushing him off her leg.)* Stop it.

GREAT: You're bleeding.

TRILBY: I know. I was born in Pittsburgh.

GREAT: What?

TRILBY: I saw you perform at Jonathan Gilbert's bar mitzvah.

(Great stops bandaging.)

GREAT: Jonathan Gilbert.

TRILBY: You must've been thirteen, too. I watched you on the party circuit for years, but when you moved away… it wasn't until you were gone that I realized… I've been searching for you. I tracked you down. And when I found you, when I saw you perform again… I need to get in. Your magic is as real and amazing as…

GREAT: But it's not real. It's tricks. Lies.

TRILBY: You're wrong. I wanna be a magician. Teach me the Hypnotic Balance.

GREAT: The Hypnotic Balance.

(Trilby limps over to the Impaled apparatus and pulls the red cloth off it, revealing the gleaming metal spike.)

TRILBY: Please. I'm telling the truth now. I swear. I love you.


SCENE FIVE

Flashback to a magic act. Egypt and Great perform for the audience.

GREAT: Good evening, folks. My name is Great and this is China. My lovely assistant China.

(Pause for applause.)

GREAT: Love is strange. It makes you see things that aren't there.

EGYPT: And fail to see things that are.

GREAT: Thank you, China. My lovely assistant China, ladies and gentlemen.

(The first illusion they perform is Paper Balls over the Head, which requires a volunteer from the audience.)

GREAT: Who knows why you fall in love? Or how? Or why? Love is blind.

EGYPT: Yes, love blinds you.

GREAT: To prove our thesis, can we have a volunteer from the audience? Male or female, it doesn't matter.

(Egypt selects a volunteering audience member. Great addresses her choice.)

GREAT: Whoever you are, I tell you you're about to fall in love with China. It's nothing to fear, and regardless, fear won't help. The love is inevitable; she's too powerful. China, why don't you bring your new squeeze up here?

*(The volunteer is brought on-stage.)*

GREAT: Now that you're in love—are you in love? It doesn't matter what you say; you're also blind—now that you're in love, your friends will start to get critical. They'll sense why it can't possibly work out. They see it so clearly. "He's no good for you." "She's a twisty tramp." But it won't help because…*(Turning to the volunteer.)* …you're in love. You see only what China wants you to see.

EGYPT: Is that so terrible?

GREAT: Terrible? It's divine. Give him or her a kiss.

*(Egypt kisses the volunteer.)*

GREAT: All right, enough. Take a seat.

*(The volunteer sits in a chair center stage.)*

*(Great gets a roll of toilet paper. He holds it up to the audience.)*

GREAT: You see this? This is love.

*(He brings the roll over to the volunteer and places it in his or her hands. He tears off a big wad.)*

GREAT: *(Displaying the wad.)* And this, this is a wad of love. You see it? Come closer. It's right here. You see it? It's right here.

*(Great makes it disappear, right under the volunteer's nose.)*

GREAT: Oops. Gone. A wad of love. Gone.

*(Great takes another wad of paper.)*

GREAT: You want it back? Love. Here it is again. Take a good look. Blow on it. Believe in it.

*(Great makes the second wad disappear. Great continues presenting wads of toilet paper and making them disappear right in front of the volunteer's face.)*

GREAT: Want to try again? Here we go. Concentrate on it. Don't let it go. For god's sake, don't let it go.

*(Great takes an even bigger wad of toilet paper, finishing the roll.)*

GREAT: Sometimes love is so big that you think it could never disappear, so big that it will be here forever. I mean, look at this. I couldn't possibly hide this up my sleeve. I couldn't possibly make this disappear. Right? It's gotta still be there. Did you see it go? Did you see it leave? Of course, you didn't because it's still there.

*(He shows that the wad is still there.)*

GREAT: But blow on it. Come closer. Concentrate hard. Because even with a big big love…

*(He shows that the big wad, just like all the others, is now gone. He shrugs.)*

GREAT: So it goes, way of the world.

*(Paper Balls over the Head is a trick wherein the volunteer is "watching" the paper disappear in thin air, and the audience is observing his amazement, but at the same time the audience can see the wads of paper flying over the volunteer's head. It is a master trick of sleight of hand, and pretty mean-spirited as the volunteer looks foolish on two counts: his credibility about what's happening in front of them and his inability to see what's happening around them.)*

GREAT: And that's it. Love is gone. China, get rid of this one. But let's give him or her a consolation prize.

*(Great hands the spent toilet paper roll to the volunteer.)*

GREAT: Better to have loved and lost?

*(Egypt helps the volunteer back to a seat. She gives him or her another kiss, longer than the first, while Great isn't looking.)*

GREAT: Where was I?

EGYPT: Love is strange.

GREAT: Sad and strange. More than strange. My grandfather used to say, go into a crowded room and shoot two arrows and whomever...

EGYPT: He was an old guy; he said "whomever."

GREAT: Thank you, China. My lovely assistant China, ladies and gentlemen. Whomever the arrows hit, those two must be lovers, must fall in love and make it work. It's no crazier than any other system. As long as you can imbue, yes, he was the type of guy who'd say "imbue."

EGYPT: An old guy.

GREAT: Imbue those two individuals with belief, with faith, then they can do it; they can feel love. And who doesn't want to feel love?

EGYPT: Everyone wants to feel love.

GREAT: But this old guy, my grandfather, had more than a theory; he had a praxis.

EGYPT: Like a practice.

GREAT: Yes, and I, his sole living magical heir, am the beneficiary of this practice.

EGYPT: He means he stole it.

GREAT: Yes, I stole it. But I only steal from the best.

The Hypnotic Balance.

China, are you ready?

EGYPT: You bet.

GREAT: Are you eager?

EGYPT: Don't get greedy.

*(Egypt faces downstage. She rolls her eyes back in their sockets. Slowly, while keeping her eyes gazing upwards, she begins to lower her eyelids.)*

GREAT: Lights, please.

*(A change effects the stage: lovely, mysterious light. Two male magic assistants enter and wait.)*

GREAT: You look so beautiful in the moonlight.

*(Great places his hands over Egypt's eyes.)*

GREAT : Did you hear me?

EGYPT: I look so beautiful in the moonlight. Are you going to kiss me?

GREAT: That would be dangerous.

*(He removes his hand from her face. Her eyes are closed.)*

GREAT: *(To the audience.)* I must ask you to maintain absolute silence. She is in a very delicate state.

*(To Egypt.)* You can hear me? China?

EGYPT: Yes.

GREAT: I'm going to count backwards from ten. Are you asleep?

EGYPT: No.

GREAT: Ten, nine, eight. You're still conscious?

EGYPT: Yes, Great, I am.

*(He places his hand on her cheek.)*

GREAT: Seven, six. Can you feel my hand? Five, four.

EGYPT: Yes.

*(He slaps her. She slaps him back.)*

EGYPT: I said, yes.

GREAT: Right. Sorry, folks. Three. China, when I reach the number one, you will feel no sensations of pain.

EGYPT: Yes, Great.

GREAT: Two.

*(Pause.)*

GREAT: One.

*(He slaps her hard.)*

GREAT: Did you feel that?

EGYPT: Did you kiss me?

GREAT: Did it feel like a kiss?

EGYPT: It felt like you wanted to kiss me.

GREAT: We're going to continue. Are you under?

EGYPT: I'm under your control.

*(The two magic assistants picks Egypt up and carry her to the spike which Trilby unveiled in the previous scene.)*

GREAT: Are you eager now?

EGYPT: Oh, baby.

*(They line her up on the spike, placing the small of her back on its sharp point.)*

GREAT: Do you feel any pain?

EGYPT: No, my love.

*(They let go of her body. She is balanced there. It is beautiful.)*

GREAT: China, can you do a little something for me?

EGYPT: Anything.

*(As the assistants exit, Great begins to wave his hands around Egypt's torso in a magic wand kind of way. He whispers to her gently, seductively.)*

GREAT: I love you. I love you. I love you. You're amazing. You're perfection. Everyone pales in comparison to you.

*(Egypt's legs and arms begin to move. She writhes.)*

GREAT: There are so few things in my life that I've ever pursued. I've always waited and seen what fell into my lap. But you I pursued. I wanted you. And I made the right choice. It paid off. In spades. I love you so much. I love you.

*(Great pushes Egypt's legs away from him. Slowly at first, her body begins to rotate around the point of the spike.)*

GREAT: Those other women, they mean nothing to me. Please, they're a joke. They can't compare to you. You're the only one. You're China. Everybody knows that you're China. You're the only one I ever wanted really, the only one I love.

*(As Egypt's body completes the first rotation, Great pushes on her legs again, spinning her faster this time.)*

GREAT: What we have is special. And this place on you, where your thigh meets your body. Every part of you is the right combination of hard and soft. I can't believe how soft you are, how good you smell, how perfect you are. It's the truth. You're perfect.

*(He is spinning her faster and faster, her body flying round in circles.)*

GREAT: From the moment I laid eyes on you. I can remember it exactly, and I thought, no way, no way I'll ever be able to get a woman that desirable, but she agreed. I've got her now. You agreed. Oh, China, let's run away together. Some place new. I want to make a baby with you. Soon. Now. Oh my god, you smell so good.

*(Great is no longer pushing on her. Egypt's body is just spinning and spinning from its own momentum.)*

GREAT: You look so beautiful in the moonlight.

*(She continues to spin as the curtain falls.)*

# ACT THREE: EGG
## SCENE ONE

*The stage is restored to how it was at the beginning of the show: all the illusions covered with their red velvet cloths. Great and Trilby are on stage.*

TRILBY: Owww.

*(As the curtain rises, Great is bandaging Trilby's leg for a repeat and continuation of their last scene.)*

GREAT: Jonathan Gilbert.

TRILBY: You must've been thirteen, too. I watched you on the party circuit for years, but when you moved away... it wasn't until you were gone that I realized... I've been searching for you. I need to get in. Your magic is as real and amazing as...

GREAT: But it's not real. It's tricks. Lies.

TRILBY: You're wrong. I wanna be a magician. Teach me the Hypnotic Balance.

*(Great gets up. He walks away from her.)*

GREAT: The Hypnotic Balance.

*(Trilby limps over to the Impaled apparatus and pulls off the red cloth, revealing the gleaming metal spike.)*

TRILBY: Please. I'm telling the truth now. I swear. I love you. I'm not gonna betray you like Egypt did.

GREAT: Honey, you're bleeding.

TRILBY: Don't feel sorry for me. I'll heal.

GREAT: How did you cut yourself with a trick knife? How do you women do that?

TRILBY: If you deserve something enough, it cuts.

GREAT: Why would you deserve that?

TRILBY: Because I lied.

GREAT: But the lying is behind us now.

TRILBY: Because I'm so confused.

GREAT: What do you want?

TRILBY: I want things to be good between us.

GREAT: Things are good now.

TRILBY: Things are half.

GREAT: A good half.

TRILBY: If you can't give me the Hypnotic Balance, you're giving me nothing.

GREAT: It caused her harm. I knew that. It scarred her—you saw the scars— and I kept doing it.

TRILBY: This isn't about her; this is about us. You telling me your past, your secrets, that's for you and me together. I want it all with you. I do.

*(Great kneels before Trilby. He looks at her bleeding leg.)*

GREAT: Just promise me you'll never do something like this again.

TRILBY: Give me the Illusion.

*(Henrietta crosses to the trunk.)*

HENRIETTA: If you witness the trick close-up, repeatedly, time after time, you begin to catch it. Catch the moment where the magician reloads the gun. You notice when he picks up the fresh deck of cards. You sit there and watch him make eye contact with the woman from Philadelphia who has a front row seat every night for a month, and astonishment, well, it tarnishes.

*(As she continues speaking, she unclasps a necklace from around her neck and drops it into the trunk before closing it.)*

HENRIETTA: You're on the inside now, seeing the smoke for smoke and the reflective quality of mirrors. And it's time for the honeymoon to end.


SCENE TWO

*Egypt's apartment. Trilby sits in a chair. Egypt hovers over her.*

EGYPT: Come on; try it again.

TRILBY: I'm tired, honey.

EGYPT: Great's been keeping you up at night?

TRILBY: Don't.

EGYPT: It's not as if I don't know.

TRILBY: Know what?

EGYPT: I saw you.

TRILBY: Saw what?

EGYPT: Through the window.

TRILBY: You were spying on me?

EGYPT: Making sure you're okay.

TRILBY: How long were you watching? What did you see?

EGYPT: That you seemed okay.

TRILBY: You're the one made this plan.

EGYPT: I'm glad if it's fun for you.

TRILBY: Yeah, it's a blast. We do magic all day and screw all the night.

EGYPT: I'm crazy to be jealous? He has his hands on you.

TRILBY: I wish you wouldn't torture yourself.

EGYPT: I'd rather torture him, but that's coming.

TRILBY: I'm sorry you had to see that.

EGYPT: It's not like I couldn't imagine it. I've been with him, too, remember.

TRILBY: But to see it.

All this will be over soon.

EGYPT: What do you mean? Did you find out?

TRILBY: Wouldn't I tell you if I found out?

EGYPT: So what do you mean?

TRILBY: Sweetheart, your show is in less than a month.

EGYPT: Our show.

TRILBY: And I can't even do *my* part yet.

EGYPT: You're getting better. You're getting good. We just need to know Great's angle.

TRILBY: Even if I get him to teach me how he straightened you out, do you really think you're gonna master…

EGYPT: Don't worry about my mastery.

TRILBY: All right, fine. I'm ready.

EGYPT: Roll your eyes back.

*(Trilby's eyes roll back in their sockets.)*

EGYPT: Now slowly, lower your lids.

*(Trilby's eyelids descend over her upturned eyes.)*

EGYPT: Slowly.

TRILBY: Okay.

EGYPT: I'll count back from ten.

*(Trilby tries again. She rolls her eyes back and slowly, to Egypt's count, lowers her lids.)*

EGYPT: Ten. Nine. Eight. Seven… You're going too fast.

*(Trilby's eyes open.)*

TRILBY: I'm tired.

EGYPT: You don't want this? Because I thought we wanted this.

TRILBY: Of course, we want this. Egypt.

EGYPT: What?

TRILBY: Why do we want this?

EGYPT: What?

TRILBY: Why this? You're amazing. You could do anything.

EGYPT: The Hypnotic Balance is mine.

TRILBY: But it's not. It's his.

EGYPT: I deserve it.

Haven't I taught you anything? Break it down. The Personalities, the Phenomenon, the Purpose, and the Proof.

The Personalities: the magician and the girl who loves him.

TRILBY: Or her.

EGYPT: Or her. The Phenomenon: a girl is quite content to be spun around as long as the magician keeps talking trash to her.

TRILBY: Maybe the Phenomenon being demonstrated is that with love anything is possible.

EGYPT: No. There are some men who can make you believe anything, and belief is a powerful thing.

TRILBY: Or women.

EGYPT: Or women who can make you believe anything.

TRILBY: Maybe there's another way to look at the trick, and if you look at the trick another way, it's not so brutal. And it could be a new trick that way, a trick about two people doing something together, instead of now you want to do to me what you think he did to you.

EGYPT: Then you clearly don't understand the trick. You don't understand. The Purpose…

TRILBY: Because there is no Purpose. The magician just sticks her on a spike.

EGYPT: She wants it. She wants to be up there. She likes it.

TRILBY: How do you know? Maybe she's helpless. Maybe she was young.

EGYPT: That's the assistant's job: to convince an audience that it had to happen. Otherwise it's a Purpose-less illusion.

TRILBY: The Proof?

EGYPT: There she is, balanced on a razor's point.

TRILBY: And that's a good thing?

EGYPT: It's good while it lasts.

*(Trilby stands up.)*

EGYPT: Where are you going?

TRILBY: I need a glass of water.

(Trilby takes a step but stumbles.)

EGYPT: What happened to you?

TRILBY: I hurt my leg.

EGYPT: You hurt your leg?

TRILBY: I cut it.

EGYPT: You cut your leg? Let me see.

TRILBY: It's fine.

(Beat.)

EGYPT: We can take a break if you want, Trilby; start in the morning.

TRILBY: I'm so confused.

EGYPT: What?

TRILBY: What if I can't do it? Ever.

EGYPT: Do what?

TRILBY: What if I can never learn my part?

EGYPT: Don't say that; you will.

TRILBY: You never have doubts?

EGYPT: Doubts?

TRILBY: Doubts that we make a good team. Maybe you'd be better off with a different assistant. Someone more…

EGYPT: More what?

TRILBY: I don't want to let you down. I'm afraid of letting you down.

EGYPT: So don't.

TRILBY: It's just… I need some water.

(Trilby exits.)


## SCENE THREE

*The restaurant. Great, wearing an apron, clears off a table. Egypt enters.*

EGYPT: So it's come to this?

GREAT: You again.

EGYPT: Scrubbing tables.

GREAT: Making an honest living.

EGYPT: Taking over your girlfriend's shift, no less. I feel I can finally gloat.

GREAT: How did you know this is her shift?

EGYPT: Are you fixing me a drink?

GREAT: What'll you have?

EGYPT: Oh, Great, don't bother pretending you don't know.

GREAT: Call me Michael.

EGYPT: Really?

GREAT: Can I call you Ellen?

EGYPT: No, and don't you dare tell anybody.

GREAT: Who would I tell?

(Great fixes a drink for Egypt.)

EGYPT: You're not going to join me?

GREAT: I'm working.

EGYPT: Never stopped you before.

GREAT: People can change.

EGYPT: False.

GREAT: You should try it.

EGYPT: Change?

GREAT: I feel good.

EGYPT: Not Great?

GREAT: Good has its advantages.

EGYPT: And you're a waitress now?

GREAT: Covering a shift for a friend.

EGYPT: What's she doing that's so important?

GREAT: She's reading.

EGYPT: Reading?

GREAT: She's obsessed with my grandfather's notebooks.

EGYPT: And you're mopping up beer spill so she can do this?

GREAT: She couldn't get anyone else to cover.

EGYPT: It's not all because of me, is it?

GREAT: What?

EGYPT: That you're giving up on magic?

GREAT: I'm not giving up; I'm taking some time off. How did you know that?

EGYPT: Maybe I can smell it. Is it because of me?

GREAT: You're so vain.

EGYPT: I'm a magician.

GREAT: Exactly why I need a break.

EGYPT: Please, you taught the course in Vain.

GREAT: I know I hurt you a lot. I was an asshole. I was a liar.

EGYPT: Oh my god, stop. Am I supposed to say that I was an asshole?

GREAT: Not for my sake.

EGYPT: I think I might have been an asshole once or twice. I wrecked your show that night. I revealed a fellow magician, and that was wrong. But you never treated me like a magician. I was always the assistant.

GREAT: We didn't bring out the best in each other.

EGYPT: Are you saying you forgive me?

GREAT: We were kids.

EGYPT: Because I don't forgive you.

GREAT: Your prerogative.

EGYPT: This is all very strange.

GREAT: Why?

EGYPT: Did you love me?

GREAT: I think I loved you more than you loved me.

EGYPT: Bullshit.

GREAT: Why?

EGYPT: You named me for the teeming communist horde.

GREAT: I named you China for something mysterious. You were unfathomable to me then.

EGYPT: All I wanted was to please you.

GREAT: You wanted to be a magician. And you got that.

EGYPT: You think all I cared about was the magic.

GREAT: Not all. But yes.

EGYPT: And what about Trilby? What does she want?

GREAT: You remember her name?

EGYPT: She seemed nice. Pretty.

GREAT: She is.

*(Great pulls Henrietta's necklace (the one she placed in the trunk a few minutes ago) out of his pocket. He shows it to Egypt.)*

GREAT: You like it?

EGYPT: It's incredible.

GREAT: I found it in my grandfather's stuff. I never noticed it before.

EGYPT: You're going to give it to her?

GREAT: You think it's good?

EGYPT: I think it'll look nice around her neck.

*(Egypt hands the necklace back to him. He puts it in his pocket.)*

GREAT: Do you ever think about the Hypnotic Balance?

EGYPT: What?

GREAT: Our finale. The Hyp…

EGYPT: I know what it's called. What are you asking me?

GREAT: I guess I'm asking if you want it.

EGYPT: Want?

GREAT: I've been thinking about it, lately, about you... Egypt.

EGYPT: Call me Ellen.

GREAT: The parts you didn't have. And that doesn't seem exactly fair. I've been teaching it to Trilby, but I figure, well, don't you deserve it? You probably don't even want it.

EGYPT: You've been teaching it to Trilby?

GREAT: I wouldn't sweat it, competition-wise. She's no magician.

EGYPT: No?

GREAT: I mean she can vanish a coin, but...

EGYPT: You don't say.

GREAT: Brilliantly actually.

EGYPT: When did you start teaching her the Balance?

GREAT: I don't know maybe a week, a couple weeks. You'll catch up quick. You already know half of it.

EGYPT: Yeah, half.

GREAT: You should come by the apartment. Since Trilby's moved in, it's even nice.

EGYPT: I'll stop by tomorrow. Fifth floor?

GREAT: You know where I live?

(Pause.)

GREAT: How do you know where I live, Ellen?

EGYPT: I think maybe you should go ahead and have that drink.


# ACT FOUR: CANARY
## SCENE ONE

*Great's apartment. Trilby has a stack of notebooks to her right. She is reading one, finishing the last pages as Henrietta hovers over her.*

HENRIETTA: People thought my death was an accident. My death: a tragic accident, the inevitable consequence of life lived the way we lived it. Play with knives and spikes, play with pain, and can you be surprised when someone gets hurt? It was dark on the stage. Show over. Great was in his dressing room, transforming himself back into Frank. Yes, his name was Frank. I was lingering, staring at the spike as it caught what glimpses of

Philadelphia moonlight there were. I remember thinking, how fancy. It was the jewel in our crown. Our crown. And I thought about how sharp the point was: how sharp, how dangerous, how fancy. I knew that in a moment Frank would come up from the bowels of the theater on his way to meet this week's floozy. I didn't want him to do that. I wanted that to stop. If he knew how bad it hurt me, if he *saw* how bad… I was a magician. I could make spikes real. I could make them cut.

*(The two male magician assistants enter. They are dressed in old fashioned costumes that match Henrietta's.)*

HENRIETTA: Just a little late night practice, boys. You don't mind helping out, do you? It's just one more go before I call it quits.

*(Trilby closes the notebook and places it on the stack.)*

TRILBY: Henrietta.

*(Trilby goes to the spike.)*

HENRIETTA: Yes?

*(She touches its sharp point and shudders.)*

TRILBY: *(Trying to connect to Henrietta, not seeing her.)* I know you're here. I know you left the notebooks out for me to read.

HENRIETTA: And you said you weren't clever.

TRILBY: *(Sensing her.)* But what do you want from us?

HENRIETTA: A second go-round, a second chance.

TRILBY: What am I supposed to do?

HENRIETTA: Just act natural. And remember what you've learned. You'll do fine.

TRILBY: I'm scared.

HENRIETTA: You're right to be scared.

*(Great storms into the space. He is drunk.)*

GREAT: Do you have something you want to tell me?

TRILBY: *(Thrown.)* Yes.

GREAT: Well, hello; I'm home. I've returned to our sunny home, no illusion whatsoever.

TRILBY: You're drunk.

GREAT: Is that what you have to tell me?

TRILBY: What?

GREAT: Don't you have something you want to tell me?

TRILBY: I do. It's about Henrietta. I know how she died.

GREAT: I have something to tell you, too. I just screwed Ellen. It was fabulous. But you would know all about that.

TRILBY: Who's Ellen?

GREAT: Ellen. Come on, you know Ellen. Poor Trilby; she doesn't even know Ellen.

TRILBY: I don't know what this is.

GREAT: Have you been working your act?

TRILBY: I've been reading the notebooks. Henrietta needs something. I don't know what, but she's here. She's in the room, Michael.

GREAT: Call me Great.

TRILBY: Why didn't you tell me that your grandfather did the Hypnotic Balance? That you got the trick from him.

GREAT: So I'm a thief, too. Hardly the worst of all my crimes. But I'm not a traitor. I'm not a lying whore who told me she loved me, but the whole time was laughing behind my back with my ex-girlfriend while they tried to steal my best illusion.

TRILBY: Oh.

*(Beat.)*

TRILBY: It's not what you think it is. It's different...

GREAT: Jesus Christ, Trilby, that's my line. I taught you that line.

TRILBY: You have a right to be angry.

GREAT: Do I? Do I have rights?

You look so beautiful in the moonlight.

TRILBY: What?

GREAT: I'm going to count backwards from ten.

*(He places his hands over Trilby's eyes. She pushes him away.)*

TRILBY: Listen to me. Henrietta is haunting us. This is for real.

GREAT: There's no such thing as real. It's all tricks and practice. But we got good, huh? You and me. Rehearsed our hearts out.

TRILBY: Henrietta died on the spike. She killed herself. On the spike.

*(Great grabs her and spins her around towards him.)*

GREAT: Ladies and gentlemen.

*(He wrestles her to the ground.)*

TRILBY: Michael, no.

*(He covers her mouth.)*

GREAT: I must ask you to maintain absolute silence. She is in a very delicate state. You can hear me? China?

TRILBY: *(Struggling.)* What are you doing?

*(He holds her down and covers her eyes.)*

GREAT: Are you asleep? Ten.

TRILBY: Don't do this. Please.

GREAT: Nine, eight. You're still conscious? Seven. Can you feel my hand? Six.

(*Trilby tries to break free, but he overpowers her.*)

GREAT: Five. When I get to one, you will be under my control, but you will feel everything. Every slap, every spike.

TRILBY: No.

GREAT: Four. Yes. Three.

TRILBY: Don't.

GREAT: When I reach the number one, you will experience every sensation of pain. Two. One.

(*Trilby no longer struggles against him. He slaps her.*)

GREAT: Did you feel that?

TRILBY: Yes.

(*He hits her again; she winces but doesn't fight back.*)

GREAT: Are you under?

TRILBY: I'm under your control.

(*The two assistants move into place.*)

TRILBY: I see two men.

GREAT: And I thought I was drunk.

TRILBY: Who are these men?

GREAT: You're hypnotized.

TRILBY: There's magic happening here, Michael. Be careful.

GREAT: Ladies and gentlemen, my lovely assistant China will now attempt something very dangerous.

(*The two assistants grab Trilby and lift her up. Great behaves as if he is the one doing the lifting, but they are doing all the work. Great apparently does not see the assistants.*)

GREAT: You had something you wanted to tell me?

TRILBY: I met a woman named Egypt. We became lovers. I promised that if I could get to you, I would give her your secrets.

(*The two assistants carry Trilby to the spike.*)

TRILBY: But I didn't; I haven't. Michael, please, I love you. I've loved you since you were thirteen and I saw you at Jonathan Gilbert's bar mitzvah.

GREAT: All you are is lies.

TRILBY: No, I'm also truth.

(*The assistants lower Trilby onto the spike. She cries out in pain.*)

GREAT: Can you do a little something for me?

TRILBY: Anything.

GREAT: I love you. I love you. See, I can say it, too. It's a spell. Nothing more. Any third rate magician can learn it. But I don't mean it.

*(Great begins to wave his hands over Trilby's torso.)*

GREAT: I wanted to have you, and I got you. That's all. I like the bodies of strangers.

*(Trilby's legs and upper body begin to move. Every slight movement is incredibly painful for her.)*

GREAT: And why shouldn't I have everything? Every woman is a new opportunity. For pleasure, for risk. Or just one night in a different bed. Why should I deny myself that? Don't I deserve some kind of treat to make up for the fact that life is boring and painful?

TRILBY: Michael, please.

*(Trilby's body evenutally stiffens. It is perfectly straight, perfectly balanced on the point of the spike. Her expression is pained.)*

GREAT: I want to change something in my life—I'm tired of life—and I use sleeping with you as the blunt instrument to make it happen. And you, you're nothing but a stupid something to make me feel better about myself.

*(Great pushes Trilby's legs away from him, rotating her on the spike.)*

GREAT: I want the confirmation of strangers, the yes, the yes of your yes. It makes me feel good. It makes me stronger.

*(He spins her faster and faster.)*

GREAT: And basically I like your eyes. That's it: you have nice eyes and that's all it is. I like your ass, your name, your hands, whatever. I like the chance to get in some strange girl's pants.

TRILBY: It hurts.

*(Trilby begins to black out from the pain and the spinning.)*

GREAT: I told you you didn't want to know. To know me.

*(Trilby's body is spinning now from its own momentum, but he keeps pushing on her.)*

*(Egypt bursts through the door.)*

GREAT: But I'm glad it hurts. If nothing else, I hope it hurts you.

EGYPT: Michael, what are you doing?

TRILBY: *(Delirious.)* Egypt?

GREAT: What do you care? She betrayed you, too.

EGYPT: You're going to kill her.

GREAT: She betrayed us both.

TRILBY: *(Very clearly.)* It hurts, but I wanted to know.

*(Suddenly Trilby falls a half a foot with a violent jerk. The spike comes shooting up through her torso. Trilby screams in anguish.)*

TRILBY: Henrietta, no!

EGYPT: Oh shit.

*(Trilby loses consciousness.)*

*(Suddenly, we flashback to the Past. Great magically (with the help of the two assistants) transforms into his grandfather (i.e. Frank). He wears a top hat and a cape. Egypt and the two assistants disappear from the stage. Great/Frank slowly approaches Trilby's body, confused at first by what he sees.)*

GREAT: Henrietta?

*(He touches the point of the spike sticking up through Trilby's body. Touching the spike, he finally panics.)*

GREAT: Help. Help me.

*(He turns to run off-stage.)*

GREAT: Henrietta's been hurt. There's been an accident.

*(Henrietta goes to Trilby. She cradles her head in her hands.)*

HENRIETTA: *(Softly.)* Frank.

*(He stops.)*

GREAT: Yes, it's me, it's Frank, I'm here.

HENRIETTA: Don't say accident.

GREAT: What happened? What happened to you?

*(Great goes to Trilby's body. Even though Henrietta is talking, Great reacts as if the voice comes from within Trilby.)*

HENRIETTA: Imagine that we had a kid.

GREAT: Darling, we will, I want us to, I'm ready.

HENRIETTA: That's not what I'm saying, Frank; would you shut up? I felt certain that here, like this, you would finally listen to a word I had to say. Was I wrong?

Imagine our child. Now this kid of ours is clever, 'course, very clever. And he's ours, so right away we're teaching him about illusion. And he gets it. He doesn't look at a bird and say, "Bird." He points and says, "That is probably a bird."

GREAT: Are you in very much pain?

HENRIETTA: We've gotta teach him the next question: "Is it also really a bird?"

GREAT: The next question?

HENRIETTA: Yes, it is. It is also really a bird. It is also really a cage.

*(Trilby's body swoons. Her head falls back.)*

GREAT: Henri.

HENRIETTA: It's really a spike. It's really pain.

GREAT: I know.

HENRIETTA: You don't know. You didn't even tell me that I look beautiful in the moonlight.

GREAT: You do. Of course, you do. You're my jewel. My jewel.

*(Great takes the necklace out of his pocket. He places Henrietta's necklace around Trilby's neck.)*

HENRIETTA: It's not enough. You have to experience what it's like to be me. Why don't you kiss me? Cast your spell and kiss me. That's the only way for you to feel what I feel.

GREAT: I'm going to get help.

*(He turns to go.)*

HENRIETTA: Coward.

*(He stops.)*

HENRIETTA: Coward. Killer. Look at me. You did this to me. I went against my family to be with you. I lost my fiancé. I could have been a nurse. And this is how you repay me. This is how you make me feel. I'm a ghost. No one sees me anymore. I'm lurking and lost. A ghost. There is a special circle of hell for people who hurt the ones they love. You're gonna rot there. You are rotting there, I promise you. You kill me.

*(Great exits.)*

HENRIETTA: Come back and kiss me. Frank.

*(Beat.)*

HENRIETTA: Frank, I was pregnant.

*(Henrietta slowly backs away from Trilby's body. )*

*(Trilby comes back to consciousness on the Spike and cries out in pain as Egypt and Great (back to being the Great we know; i.e. Michael) run on stage.)*

EGYPT: Oh shit.

*(Trilby raises her head and sees the spike coming through her body.)*

TRILBY: Oh Christ.

*(Great and Egypt rush closer to her.)*

GREAT: Trilby.

EGYPT: Are you okay?

TRILBY: I know what she needs from us. I know it all now.

GREAT: Trilby?

TRILBY: I'm sorry, Michael. I did fall in love with you. I'm sorry, Egypt; I fell in love.

EGYPT: My name is Ellen.

TRILBY: Oh, so you're Ellen. Have you guys met Henrietta?

GREAT: Call an ambulance.

TRILBY: This is Henrietta. She would have been your grandmother, if Frank hadn't been such a wimp.

EGYPT: What is she talking about?

GREAT: Trilby, you're delirious.

TRILBY: You're the one delirious. Do you see any blood anywhere? What's an ambulance gonna do for me?

EGYPT: You have a spike sticking up through your body.

TRILBY: You're an old softie at heart. But you know what? You've gotta go now.

EGYPT: What?

TRILBY: Go pull a rabbit out of a hat.

EGYPT: Excuse me?

TRILBY: I don't hate you for what you've done. But you need to understand it. Michael's grandfather blew it. He didn't get to live with the woman he loved.

EGYPT: I don't know what the hell you're talking about, but I'm going to get you off that thing.

TRILBY: You can't. You've been damaged, Egypt/Ellen.

EGYPT: *I've* been damaged?

TRILBY: But you've gotta get over it now. If you would quit picking at that sore in the small of your back, you could be a great magician.

EGYPT: I am a great magician.

TRILBY: You're haunted. Fall in love, maybe that'll help.

EGYPT: I fell in love with you.

TRILBY: You fell in love with my ability to cause your ex pain. That kind of love is never gonna give back.

EGYPT: You're crazy.

TRILBY: That's what everyone says about their ex-es.

EGYPT: Ex-es? You're impaled on a spike and you're dumping me?

TRILBY: If I live through this, we're gonna be great friends one day. Good-bye, Egypt.

EGYPT: It's Ellen.

TRILBY: And my real name's Theresa.

GREAT: Theresa?

TRILBY: I'm joking. Michael, show Ellen out. We've got work to do.

*(Great walks Egypt off-stage.)*

TRILBY: Henrietta, am I going to die here on your spike?

HENRIETTA: I did. But I did lots of things.

TRILBY: But if Michael can save me, won't that make a difference? For you, too.

HENRIETTA: You think he's gonna save you?

TRILBY: Maybe he and I can save each other.

HENRIETTA: "Maybe" doesn't even get you a cup a coffee.

TRILBY: You orchestrated this whole thing and now you're Miss Forget-About-It?

HENRIETTA: Frank didn't lift me up. You go back to the past, but that's the trouble with the past, it's always the same old thing. I was dumb enough to think that this time would be different.

TRILBY: This time hasn't happened yet. This time is now.

*(Great returns.)*

TRILBY: We're so lucky, Michael, because so few people get a second chance and we could give a second chance to so many people, including ourselves.

GREAT: I have no idea what you're talking about.

TRILBY: All we have to do is get me off this spike.

GREAT: Are you in a lot of pain?

TRILBY: Soon you'll know how much. Say the spell.

GREAT: You look so beautiful in the moonlight?

TRILBY: Like a spell.

GREAT: You look so beautiful in the moonlight.

TRILBY: Come here and kiss me.

GREAT: Trilby.

TRILBY: Do it. Feel what I feel. Don't be afraid.

GREAT: I'm not afraid. I'm afraid for you.

TRILBY: That's sweet. But naive.

*(He leans over and kisses her.)*

GREAT: Oh my fucking god: the spell!

*(Great writhes to the floor in pain.)*

TRILBY: Now you know what it's like to be up here.

GREAT: Jesus Fucking Christ.

TRILBY: I know. Believe me, I know.

GREAT: But fuck. Fuck.

TRILBY: Get up.

GREAT: It hurts.

TRILBY: I've been telling you.

> (*Great stands with some difficulty.*)

TRILBY: Now do it.

GREAT: What?

TRILBY: The next illusion.

> (*Great begins to wave his hands over her body.*)

TRILBY: You think I'm perfect?

GREAT: Fuck.

TRILBY: Concentrate.

GREAT: (*Still waving his hands.*) You're—shit shit fuck—perfect.

TRILBY: I'm not.

GREAT: You are.

TRILBY: No, I'm not the most amazing woman in the world. I'm the woman that you love. Love is what makes the lie of "she's perfect" possible. And what a fantastic lie.

GREAT: You're not perfect.

> (*Trilby's body begins to straighten.*)

TRILBY: No.

GREAT: You hurt me.

TRILBY: We hurt each other and lied.

GREAT: We can forgive each other.

TRILBY: We can know each other.

GREAT: We can love each other.

TRILBY: You're a magician.

GREAT: You're a magician.

TRILBY: And there are places on this earth where magic still exists.

> (*Trilby is perfectly straight. Great (with Henrietta's help) lifts her off the spike. They are both still shaken from the pain. They collapse to the floor.*)
> (*Long silence.*)

TRILBY: Oh, Michael.

GREAT: I know. Baby, I know.

TRIBLY: Wow.

GREAT: Cut straight to "wow."

TRILBY: It's so sad.

GREAT: Sad?

TRILBY: That it's not going to work.

GREAT: It is working. What are you talking about? It worked.

TRILBY: Yeah, you got me off the spike, but…

GREAT: Wasn't that the whole idea?

TRILBY: It's there forever now. I can feel it. It's different when you feel it.

GREAT: Feel what?

TRILBY: *(Gently touching her own back.)* The sore red mark on the small of my back.

GREAT: It will heal.

TRILBY: How can it?

GREAT: Magic.

TRILBY: But the wound is the magic.

GREAT: Then, we'll live with the wound. I've got one, too, now.

*(He lifts his shirt and shows her: a horrible wound on the small of his back.)*

HENRIETTA: Ewww. His is worse than mine.

*(Trilby looks at Henrietta whom Great still can't see.)*

TRILBY: You stuck around.

HENRIETTA: Pretty impressive magic.

TRILBY: You don't need to keep haunting. Do you know that? You can go now.

HENRIETTA: Go?

GREAT: You want *me* to go?

TRILBY: You've got what you need now.

HENRIETTA: How do you know?

TRILBY: Were you just watching this? It happened. On my body.

GREAT: Trilby?

HENRIETTA: I wanted him to lift me up.

TRILBY: He did now.

HENRIETTA: I wanted to have my baby.

TRILBY: You can have a baby in heaven?

HENRIETTA: Who said anything about heaven?

GREAT: Trilby, what are you talking about?

TRILBY: Walk through the door and you'll be free.

HENRIETTA: I've been stuck in this place for so long now. I'm scared.

TRILBY: You're right to be scared.

GREAT: Who are you talking to?

TRILBY: Henrietta.

GREAT: Henrietta talks to you?

TRILBY: Yes. But she's leaving now. She's not haunted anymore.

GREAT: Henrietta is here?

*(Henrietta exits.)*

TRILBY: She was here.

*(Beat.)*

TRILBY: And it's time for me to go, too.

GREAT: No.

TRILBY: I told you it was sad; let's not make it worse.

GREAT: But you're wrong. You and me. Together. We did real magic.

TRILBY: Too late. It was too late for them: too much pain, too much history. She's lucky she got free from having to haunt your grandfather's trunk night and day, but that's all she gets. She doesn't get the guy.

GREAT: Stop talking about them; we're talking about us.

TRILBY: Maybe we'll do better the next time around.

GREAT: I don't want another time around. I've had so many arounds.

TRILBY: Around and around.

GREAT: I won't lose you. I can't.

TRILBY: Sometimes you can find lost things.

*(She touches the necklace at her throat.)*

TRILBY: Thank you for the necklace. It means a lot. Thank you for teaching me how to be a magician.

GREAT: I could say the same to you.

*(Trilby heads towards the exit.)*

GREAT: Wait. Don't go. Can't we start again?

*(Pause. She looks at him.)*

TRILBY: The question everyone's dying to know the answer to.

*(Trilby disappears from the stage.)*


EPILOGUE

*Great addresses the audience. He holds an orange in his hand.*

GREAT: Hi, folks, thanks for coming. You had to come. Or, if you hadn't… I can't bear the weight alone.

*(Despondent, he drops the orange.)*

GREAT: Hi, folks, thanks for coming. My name is…

*(He paces a bit.)*

GREAT: Hello. Hello. I'm going to try something new here. I'm not sure if this will work. But I saw a guy do this once.

*(Great puts on his suit jacket. He picks up the orange. He takes a breath. He*

*waves his hands over it in a magic wand kind of way and then begins to peel it. Sure enough, underneath the rind is a lemon. Great seems almost surprised.)*

GREAT: Great. Thanks for coming tonight.

*(He begins to peel the lemon.)*

*(Henrietta enters the stage behind Great. She is in her assistant's costume, but now she is pregnant. She watches Great.)*

*(Underneath the lemon rind is an egg. Great displays it to the audience.)*

GREAT: You do all the work, you see. You straddle the line. This side, that side, this side, that. Sometimes you're in both at once. Don't be afraid. It's a fuzzy, hazy line that separates illusion and…

*(Great cracks the egg with bravado. A runny yoke drips down his fingers. No canary; just a plain old egg.)*

GREAT: No Illusion Whatsoever.

*(Great, disappointed, wipes the egg off his hand. He turns and sees Henrietta who stands near the covered birdcage. He is seeing her for the first time.)*

GREAT: Henrietta?

HENRIETTA: C'est moi.

*(Henrietta removes the red velvet cloth covering from the cage. Inside a Live Canary is chirping around.)*

*(Trilby enters. She wears nothing but Great's cape. Great and Trilby look at each other.)*

TRILBY: It's the next time around.

GREAT: Both sides of the line.

*(Trilby turns out to the audience.)*

TRILBY: And in honor of the next time, we have a new act. We call it Impaled.

*(Trilby removes her cape. Underneath, she is dressed much like Great, in a nice-looking suit looking very much the magician.)*

TRILBY: *(To Great.)* Are you ready to be hypnotized?

GREAT: And willing.

*(To the audience.)*

But first, ladies and gentlemen, first let's take one moment, one simple, precious moment, to admire the beautiful and talented Elsie.

*(Great, Trilby, and Henrietta watch the Singing Magic Bird as she flies around in her cage.)*

END OF PLAY

*Note about the magic in the show

The majority of the magic in this show is performed by the actor playing Great. If this actor is not accomplished in sleight of hand, additional rehearsal time must be allotted for him to learn and get comfortable with the illusions required. The pre-show magic as well as the Paper Balls over the Head routine can be cut. (To cut Paper Balls, skip from Egypt's line "Yes, love blinds you" straight to Great's line "My grandfather used to say, go into a crowded room..."). Everything else that Great needs to do can be taught by a magic consultant as a self-working trick, but, bear in mind that even "self-working" tricks require lots of practice.

The illusions in the show which are executed by other performers (e.g. Egypt performing the Airborne Glass routine, Trilby vanishing a coin, etc.) can easily be mastered during an average rehearsal period with the help of a magic consultant.

For the central illusion (the Hypnotic Balance, i.e. Impaled) to run smoothly, it helps if the actresses playing Egypt and Trilby are short and light. The smaller the women are (and the stronger their abdominal muscles), the better the trick works. All the magic employed in the play (typed in bold when mentioned in the script) is some variation of a classic in the business. These illusions can be bought from magic warehouses, or built, or taught by experts.

In addition, directors and designers should feel free to add more illusions as they see fit. Henrietta can appear from within the locker, Great can produce Trilby's underwear from thin air, etc.

# Fit for Feet
## by Jordan Harrison

# BIOGRAPHY

Jordan Harrison's plays have been seen and developed at Perishable Theatre, Empty Space Theatre, Clubbed Thumb, Flea Theater, Present Company (Polybe + Seats) and Playwrights Horizons. His play *Kid-Simple*, first presented in the Brown New Plays Festival, was awarded the Weston Prize and was a Finalist for the Princess Grace Award. A new full-length work, *The Museum Play*, is forthcoming. Mr. Harrison is the recipient of a 2003 Jerome Fellowship from the Playwrights Center, a Lucille Lortel Playwriting Fellowship and a Djerassi Artist Residency. His plays have been published in several journals including *NuMuse*, *Factorial* and *Masque*. With Sally Oswald, he edits *Play: A Journal of Plays*. Mr. Harrison received his M.F.A. in Creative Writing from Brown University.

# HUMANA FESTIVAL PRODUCTION

*Fit for Feet* premiered at the Humana Festival of New American Plays in April 2003. It was directed by Timothy Douglas with the following cast:

| | |
|---|---|
| Claire | Holli Hamilton |
| Linda | Celia Tackaberry |
| Jimmy | Greg McFadden |
| A Prominent Dance Critic | Shannon Holt |

and the following production staff:

| | |
|---|---|
| Scenic Designer | Paul Owen |
| Costume Designers | John P. White |
| | Mike Floyd |
| Lighting Designer | Paul Werner |
| Sound Designer | Colbert S. Davis IV |
| Properties Designer | Doc Manning |
| Stage Manager | Leslie K. Oberhausen |
| Assistant Stage Managers | Michael Domue |
| | Andrew Scheer |
| Dramaturg | Steve Moulds |

# CHARACTERS

CLAIRE, late twenties, nice sweater set, pastels
LINDA, 50s, improbably blonde for her age
JIMMY, late 20s, average Joe in a baseball cap
A PROMINENT DANCE CRITIC

*Note: This play is indebted to Joan Acocella's unexpurgated edition of Nijinsky's diaries.*

Celia Tackaberry, Holli Hamilton, and Greg McFadden
in *Fit for Feet*

27th Annual Humana Festival of New American Plays
Actors Theatre of Louisville, 2003
photo by Harlan Taylor

# Fit for Feet

SCENE ONE

*Stage left. Linda and Claire in Adirondack chairs. Linda reclines, sipping an iced tea. Claire sits very straight, no iced tea.*

LINDA: Isn't this civilized?

CLAIRE: It is the ultimate goal of civilization to sit and do nothing.
*(This silences Linda for a second.)*

LINDA: How are my almost-newlyweds? How are my daughter and my wonderful new son?

CLAIRE: Jimmy thinks he's Nijinsky. The dancer. *(With added difficulty.)* Recently he's started to believe he's Nijinsky.
*(Stage right. Jimmy is sawing the heels off a pair of dress shoes. Claire can see him but Linda cannot.)*

LINDA: Does he dance?

CLAIRE: Not well, so you wouldn't think—

LINDA: I adore dancing.

CLAIRE: That really isn't the issue.

LINDA: The ballet in particular. Old World beauty. Strong male legs. *Lifting.*

CLAIRE: Listen to me. I think he might be losing his mind. He thinks he's a dead Russian.

LINDA: Might he be right?

CLAIRE: Jimmy has never been to Russia. He sits at a desk every day. He is not a dancer.

LINDA: *(Airily.)* We should go to the ballet.
*(Claire gives her a look.)*
*(Stage right. Jimmy is finished with his sawing. He tries the shoes on. Success: Ballet slippers.)*

LINDA: You might take a look at the seating chart. For the reception.
*(Pause. Claire has noticed Jimmy putting on the "slippers.")*

LINDA: Mr. Barkley is at the same table as that Arkansas woman, and you know that won't do.
*(Claire gets out of her chair and crosses to Jimmy. He is doing pliés now, his back to her.)*

LINDA: *(Calling after her.)* You might consider!
*(Linda takes a resigned sip of iced tea. Her light fades.)*

CLAIRE: Can I ask what you're doing?

*(Jimmy stops cold, but doesn't turn around. We can see that there is music in his head.)*

JIMMY: My head's full of strange names. Diaghilev, Stravinsky, Ballets Russes. Romola, Kyra, Kostrovsky. But above all, Diaghilev. How I hate that diseased dog, and love him. As I love all God's creations.

*(He begins a different exercise.)*

CLAIRE: Did anything happen recently, anything out of the ordinary?

*(He turns to her.)*

JIMMY: What is ordinary?

CLAIRE: Did you get hit on the head, did you cross a black cat, did you limbo a ladder?

JIMMY: There was the thing with the lightning.

CLAIRE: What with what?

JIMMY: I was walking along, minding my business—

CLAIRE: *(Gravely.)* That's how these things happen.

JIMMY: When out of the sky—

CLAIRE: Of course.

JIMMY: Would you mind not—

CLAIRE: Sorry.

JIMMY: Last Thursday. There hadn't been rain in the forecast, but I'm coming back from work—wouldn't you know, the sky is practically black. Jet black clouds, ions crashing in the air.

CLAIRE: Were you wearing your wedding shoes?

JIMMY: I figure I'll make it home in time if I take the shortcut through the field.

*(Claire's head in her hands.)*

JIMMY: On my way I see a cat up a tree, calico a few branches up. I start to climb, here kitty kitty, the storm all around me now. Then the Kaboom.

CLAIRE: You didn't tell me this last Thursday.

JIMMY: *(A sudden, regal change, evidenced in his posture.)* Thursday, Friday. All is the same in the great wheel of life.

CLAIRE: Why Nijinsky? That's what I don't get. Why not Nureyev, Baryshnikov, one of the other Kovs?

JIMMY: *(Speaking of himself in the third person.)* Nijinsky is the best.

CLAIRE: You're not the best.

JIMMY: Wait and see.

*(Stage left. Lights rise on Linda.)*

LINDA: You're hard on him, maybe that's it.

CLAIRE: I don't want there to be any illusions…

*(Claire returns to her chair.)*

LINDA: Wait till you're married a year. Then you can turn shrew.

CLAIRE: …Any secrets. It's destructive.

LINDA: Letting that lady minister do your vows—*that's* destructive.

CLAIRE: We can still call the whole thing off.

*(Linda removes a flask from her purse and pours something in her iced tea. She drinks deeply. Pause.)*

LINDA: You left the iron on this morning.

CLAIRE: Oopsie.

LINDA: While you were dashing out.

CLAIRE: Good thing you saw it then.

*(Stage right. Jimmy is drawing in a notebook with a crayon. Very heavily— the crayon is soon down to a stub.)*

LINDA: Exactly, good thing. Or what would have happened, Claire. You might take a moment to consider.

*(Claire doesn't take a moment.)*

CLAIRE: The house would burn, the firemen would come, we arrive home to a charred black mess. You meet a kind fireman: Big hands, a good cook. I hear those men are always good cooks. And I won't have to look after you ever again. Jimmy and I go live in some foreign, sun-dappled place. Help me find some oily rags, some lighter fluid. We'll do it right now.

LINDA: You haven't considered at all.

CLAIRE: I'm kind of preoccupied.

LINDA: Consider. Think of Muffin, for starters.

*(Sound of a yippy dog yipping. They look offstage and back, quickly.)*

CLAIRE: We would grieve.

LINDA: The photographs. Everything your memory has come to rely on, melted down to a bubbling chemical ooze-thing.

CLAIRE: A person can't live in the past.

LINDA: The CLOTHES, Claire. You have beautiful clothes.

CLAIRE: Insurance, Mother—

LINDA: —Can't replace the chenille scarf.

CLAIRE: Milan.

LINDA: That poncho doohickey.

CLAIRE: It's a *caftan*. Johannesburg.

LINDA: Earrings.

CLAIRE: Antique Market, Copenhagen. *(With special pride.)* I haggled.

LINDA: Gorgeous.

CLAIRE: I thought so.

*(Jimmy holds up his drawing, proudly, for the audience: many pairs of menacing eyes, peering out of darkness. Claire sees it and recoils.)*

LINDA: Have you considered? The absolute destruction of all you've collected, all we've amassed that makes us us. All it takes is one everyday carelessness and POOF—what do you have, who ARE you now?

CLAIRE: I guess I hadn't considered.

*(Blackout.)*


MINI-INTERLUDE

*Jimmy performs a demented little solo here between the two scenes. He begins very awkwardly, but grows in confidence, until there is a vigorous assurance to his movements. (But he never ceases to be an average guy dancing ballet. Not Nijinsky.)*


SCENE TWO

*Claire and Linda in the Adirondack chairs, as before. They are examining Jimmy's drawing.*

LINDA: Are those eyes?

CLAIRE: It's supposed to be soldiers, he told me.

LINDA: How creative.

CLAIRE: He's worse, I think. The other day I was all, "Darling, would you take a look at these china patterns?"

*(Jimmy enters. He flings off his baseball cap, a romantic gesture—his hair smoothed off his forehead. Dapper. He acts out Claire's narrative.)*

CLAIRE: He walked up to me, looking me in the eye the whole time, grabbed my wrist, said:

JIMMY: I am noise. I am youth. I am a great hammer.

CLAIRE: Normally if a guy said that to me, *especially* my husband, I'd be: "Yeah sure, you're a hammer. Now about these patterns." But he looks at me that new way and says:

JIMMY: I am a rebel angel, Romola. You are a lusterless moon. You are fit for my feet.

CLAIRE: And he holds me and calls me by that strange name and I am *happy* to be fit for his feet.

LINDA: Susan Faludi wouldn't approve, Claire.

CLAIRE: *(In his grip.)* There's more. We're still in this violent, like, erotic, like, *clench* and he says:

JIMMY: I am God in my prick. God is in me and I am in God.

CLAIRE: *(Catching her breath.)* Say that again?

JIMMY: I am in God.

CLAIRE: No, the other.

JIMMY: I am God in my prick.

CLAIRE: *(Pouncing on him.)* That's the one.

LINDA: You must be delighted.

CLAIRE: Delighted? *(Jimmy crawls out from under Claire and exits. She watches him leave.)* It's true, I can't help but find him somewhat more…magnetic these days. This new confidence. Practicing jetés instead of scratching his pits.

LINDA: I'm not sure what you're complaining about.

CLAIRE: I don't *recognize* him. We're about to tell each other for better or for worse and I don't know who he is.

LINDA: Can we ever *know* a person, really? Why not be married to someone who wakes up different every morning? Every day a surprise.

CLAIRE: I chose *Jimmy.* That's what I want to wake up to. And maybe, every now and then, the virile and commanding Russian can come to visit.

LINDA: You were always the idealist, Claire.

CLAIRE: *(To herself.)* Maybe if I knew more about him.

LINDA: You've dated for it's been years.

CLAIRE: Nijinsky, I mean. If I did some research. Maybe this would make sense, if only we knew more.

*(A Prominent Dance Critic enters. Haughty and urbane, she wears a dramatic, asymmetrical tunic. She reaches into the air and pulls down a white screen, center stage, without missing a beat. A slide of Nijinsky, in his famous* Afternoon of a Faun *garb, appears.)*

CRITIC: Tragically, we lack a celluloid record of Nijinsky in performance. But we know from first-hand accounts—among them, that of his great countryman Vladimir Nabokov—that when he leapt in the air, he seemed to hover for a moment, as if suspended by a gold thread leading out of his brow and through the roof.

Then, most remarkably, he lofted another inch before returning to Earth.

Every evening, audiences at the Ballets Russes witnessed an assault on the principles of gravity the like of which we haven't seen—unassisted by coarse machinery—since the Newtonian apple grounded mankind's Icarian fancies.

CLAIRE: What can she mean?

LINDA: Guy jumped high in the sky.

CRITIC: Next slide, please.

*(The slide changes to Nijinsky, looking quite mad now, in Stravinsky's* Petrushka.*)*

CRITIC: But if Nijinsky's leap embodied that part of us that wants to leave this world behind, it was his mind that finally carried out the dare.

CLAIRE: Pardon?

CRITIC: He went positively bonkers.

Abandoned by the ballet, the great man withdrew into the pages of his diary.

Written on three notebooks in 1919, the diary evidences a mind in which sex and war, heaven and hell simmer in the same debauched stew. A rondo of rigmarole, penned in an uneasy blend of his native Russian, courtly French, childlike scribblings, and a sort of malignantly repetitive baby-talk. Gobbledy-gook driven by a cunningly transgressive illogic. Mother Goose gone prick-mad. Muttering, proselytizing, scatologically obsessed, biting the heads off crayons, Nijinsky had become as much an animal as a God.

Is this the cost of genius? we ask the spheres.

We are still deciphering the music of their answer.

*(The Critic curtsies deeply. Her light is extinguished. The screen flies away.)*

LINDA: My head hurts.

CLAIRE: It will soon hurt more. Last night, he climbed out of bed, sleepwalking, he does that.

*(Jimmy crosses, his arms stretched out, somnambulist-style.)*

But never like this, all the way downstairs and out the front door. I put on a raincoat and followed him.

LINDA: A raincoat? With all your beautiful things…

CLAIRE: The most worrisome thing was he didn't trip once. Used to be he couldn't walk for his own shoelaces. Here he was, a bounce in his step

Sidestepping cracks, sashaying past puddles, softly snoring all the time.

Soon we're in a part of town I've never been to.

Cobblestones, steaming potholes. Can those be gaslights?

I can't even catch sight of a Starbucks.

He seems to be practicing steps.

His arms striking the air, his legs like scissors.

As I watch him, I can almost hear the music he's dancing to

And it's like he's lighter on his feet with every step.

People notice. All the motleys out at 3 A.M.:

Insomniacs with dark rings, child molesters, women with frosted hair.

*(Linda gasps.)*

They all come out of the shadows and follow him,

They don't know why. How can they not?

Soon it's a little parade of freaks, with Jimmy at the head like a drum major.

And then he takes off.

*(Stage right. Jimmy leaps into the air, hovers there, and lofts another inch before landing. Claire's hand at her mouth.)*

I'm peeking from behind a dumpster in my old raincoat,

My hair flat around my shoulders like a wet rat.

And I don't have anything to do with that brilliant thing in the air.

And he has even less to do with Jimmy.

Enough. I break the spell, I shake him awake.

He feels small in my arms, all the people watching us.

Then his eyes open on me, ash-black, and he says, "You try to keep me…"

JIMMY: *(Overlapping.)* You try to keep me down with the scalyskins and the black-eyed beasts but you are death. I am life and you are death.

LINDA: One should never wake people in the middle of dreams.

CLAIRE: Tomorrow we walk down the aisle and I'm *death*?

*(Stage left. Linda touches Claire on the knee.)*

LINDA: I'll have a talk with him, lamb.

*(Stage right. Jimmy sits at a vanity, applying thick white pancake makeup. He is not effeminate about it. Rather it is a solemn ritual—putting on war paint. Linda crosses to him.)*

LINDA: Can you believe, the big day? Wait till you see Claire, like some kind of delicious multi-leveled parfait. All that organza—

*(Jimmy turns to her, face shocking-white.)*

LINDA: Oh. *(Pause.)* Tell me my daughter's being a nervous bride. Tell me there's nothing the matter with our fine young management consultant.

JIMMY: *Je ne parle pas Anglais.*

*(Stage left. Claire putting on her wedding dress. Nervous.)*

LINDA: You just have to *parle* enough to say "I do."

JIMMY: *Je ne parle pas Anglais.*

LINDA: We don't have a lot of time. Where's your tux?

JIMMY: *Je ne parle de plus Anglais.*

LINDA: *(Trying another tack.)* *Je m'appelle Linda.* That's all I remember from high school, can you believe?

JIMMY: *(Rising.)* *Je suis boeff mes pas biffstek.*

LINDA: *Ca va bien, merci.* I'm afraid that's it, my whole bag of tricks.

JIMMY: *(Very close to her, a forceful whisper.)* *Je ne suis pas biffstek.*

*Je suis stek sans boeuf en biff.*

LINDA: Oh my my my. *Où est la Tour Eiffel?*

JIMMY: *(Slapping his thighs percussively with each "si.")* *Je ne suis je un tamboure.*

*Je suis si si si si si si si*

LINDA: *(Smoldering now.)* *Un pain au chocolat, s'il vous plait!*

*(Jimmy is elsewhere, oblivious to the game.)*

JIMMY: *Tzi tzi tzi tzi tzi tzi tzi tzi*

*Je suis ça suis ça suis ça je ça*

*ça ça ça ça ça ça ça ça ça*

LINDA: I'm afraid I lost track.

JIMMY: I am a lullabyer, I am a singer of all songs.

LINDA: *(Mischievously.)* I thought you didn't *parle Anglais*, Frenchie.

*(Jimmy jumps. This time he does not come down. Linda looks up at him in awe, mouth ajar. We can see that there is music in her head.)*

*(Claire stomps over, in full wedding dress.)*

LINDA: Excellent young man!

CLAIRE: Come down come DOWN.

*(Claire jumps after Jimmy, her arms flailing for him. After some failed attempts, she starts to take running leaps. Not even close. She continues to jump, more and more wildly. Sound of the "Wedding March" beginning.)*

*(Light fades.)*


END OF PLAY

# The Lively Lad,
## A play with songs
## by Quincy Long
## lyrics by Quincy Long
## music by Michael Silversher

# BIOGRAPHY

Quincy Long's plays include *The Joy of Going Somewhere Definite, The Virgin Molly, Shaker Heights, The Year of the Baby,* and others. They have been produced regionally by the Mark Taper Forum, Berkeley Repertory Theatre and the Magic Theatre, and in New York City by The Atlantic Theatre, Ensemble Studio Theatre and Soho Repertory. Zoo District, a Los Angeles-based company, presented *The Lively Lad* in March, 2003. Mr. Long has received new play commissions from Playwrights Horizons, South Coast Repertory, and A.S.K. Theater Projects, which commissioned *The Lively Lad.* He is currently working on a musical co-commissioned by Woolly Mammoth, The Empty Space and The Illusion. Mr. Long is from Warren, Ohio. A graduate of Yale School of Drama, he lives in New York City.

## HUMANA FESTIVAL PRODUCTION

*The Lively Lad* premiered at the Humana Festival of New American Plays in March 2003. It was directed by Timothy Douglas with the following cast:

| | |
|---|---|
| Martin (and others) | Dennis Kelly |
| Jonathan Van Huffle | Marc Vietor |
| Little Eva | Holli Hamilton |
| Dorothea | Celia Tackaberry |
| Miss McCracken | Shannon Holt |
| Jameson | William McNulty |
| Henderson (and others) | Fred Major |
| Shotworthy (and others) | Colin McPhillamy |
| Gideon | Lea Coco |

and the following production staff:

| | |
|---|---|
| Music Director/Pianist | Scott Kasbaum |
| Scenic Designer | Paul Owen |
| Costume Designer | Suttirat Larlarb |
| Lighting Designer | Mary Louise Geiger |
| Sound Designer | Colbert S. Davis IV |
| Properties Designer | Mark Walston |
| Stage Manager | Debra A. Freeman |
| Assistant Stage Manager | Michael Domue |
| Fight Director | Brent Langdon |
| Movement Coordinator | Gail Benedict |
| Dramaturg | Amy Wegener |
| Assistant Dramaturg | Susannah Engstrom |
| Casting | Jerry Beaver |
| Directing Assistants | Barbara Gulan and Gil Reyes |

# CHARACTERS

JONATHAN VAN HUFFLE, a man of means, in love with Miss McCracken; also a COURTIER

LITTLE EVA VAN HUFFLE, Jonathan's adolescent daughter

MISS McCRACKEN, a waitress and a student at the law, in love with Jonathan; also a YOUNG WOMAN and COURTIER

DOROTHEA, Jonathan's housekeeper

JAMESON, a household servant, recently released from the military

GIDEON, an adolescent boy

MARTIN, Jonathan's stockbroker; also RESTAURANT MANAGER, COURTIER, SOLDIER, and PATRIARCH

HENDERSON, a club member; also MAITRE D', COURTIER, and ATTENDANT

SHORTWORTHY, a club member; also COURTIER and ATTENDANT

# TIME
Some time ago

# SETTING
A metropolis

A stockbroker's office, the Van Huffle parlor, a bar in a gentleman's club, a tea shoppe, a restaurant, Little Eva's bed chamber, a ballroom, a dressing room backstage.

*The Lively Lad* was
Originally commissioned and developed by A.S.K. Theater Projects
Originally presented by New York Stage and Film Company and the
Powerhouse Theatre at Vassar, June 2000
Fran Webb, Creative Consultant

Celia Tackaberry, William McNulty and Holli Hamilton
in *The Lively Lad*

27th Annual Humana Festival of New American Plays
Actors Theatre of Louisville, 2003
photo by Harlan Taylor

# The Lively Lad

## ACT ONE
### SCENE ONE

*A stockbroker's office. Jonathan and Martin study stock quotes.*

MARTIN: Just look at that, Johnny. See how well it's done already, and just since June.

JONATHAN: Where?

MARTIN: What?

JONATHAN: Do I look?

MARTIN: Why, in the price per share column.

JONATHAN: Ah, yes. Here we are. Versatile Industries. Twenty six and an eighth.

MARTIN: That's *up* twenty sixth and an eighth.

JONATHAN: Oh, I see, yes. Up. Is that good, then?

MARTIN: Is that good? It's through the roof, man.

JONATHAN: Oh, I'm hopeless with all this business business.

MARTIN: Good thing old reliable's looking out for your interests, eh? So, are you in, old son, or are you insane?

JONATHAN: Oh, I don't know, Martin. What about all these stories?

MARTIN: What stories?

JONATHAN: Oh you know. Things one reads in the newspaper. All this exploitation of resources and workers and such.

MARTIN: You'll have to be a little more specific Johnny.

JONATHAN: Anyway I'm in love.

MARTIN: What?

JONATHAN: I am, yes. I say it out.

MARTIN: With whom?

JONATHAN: What?

MARTIN: Are you in love?

JONATHAN: Why her name is Miss McCracken.

MARTIN: Miss McCracken?

JONATHAN: And she's a waitress in a tea shoppe, I'm proud to say.

MARTIN: Well, now.

JONATHAN: And Miss McCracken thinks I'm quite rich enough already.

MARTIN: There is no such thing as rich enough, Johnny boy.

JONATHAN: Please don't call me Johnny.

MARTIN: But I've always called you Johnny.

JONATHAN: And I've always liked it, but Miss McCracken calls me *Jonathan.*

MARTIN: Oh, I see.

JONATHAN: Miss McCracken feels I need to become more serious, Martin; to think less about having more, and more about just where all this money comes from.

MARTIN: This is a dangerous woman.

JONATHAN: Oh, you should see her, Martin. My God, if she isn't the most gorgeous creature alive. And a woman of conscience too.

MARTIN: Apparently.

JONATHAN: Yes. Completely scrumptious, uh, scrupulous. Doesn't approve of rich living.

MARTIN: Indeed.

JONATHAN: I've given it up Martin. Renounced it. All of it. Won't even go to the club anymore.

MARTIN: Good heavens.

JONATHAN: Living much more simply all round. Even walked downtown today.

MARTIN: No.

JONATHAN: Yes, I did. Rubbing shoulders with all sorts. And as for this Versatile whatever—

MARTIN: Versatile Industries.

JONATHAN: *(Sings.)*
　　I DON'T NEED A LOT OF MONEY
　　THAT'S NOT WHAT I LIVE FOR
　　I HAVE TOO MUCH ALREADY
　　AND I DON'T NEED ANY MORE

MARTIN: Wonderful, Johnny—Jonathan—

JONATHAN: *(Sings.)*
　　I PREFER THE ADMIRATION
　　OF SHE WHOM I ADORE
　　SHE WHO'LL PROUDLY LOVE ME
　　IF I'M RICH OR IF I'M POOR

MARTIN: Lovely, yes, but what of Little Eva?

JONATHAN: Ah yes, I am glad you mention Little Eva, Martin. Miss McCracken considers her to be spoiled entirely.

MARTIN: Oh, they've been introduced then, have they?

JONATHAN: Well, not yet, no. But, I've talked endlessly to Miss McCracken about the difficulties of raising a daughter alone, and in particular about these incessant demands for *things*.

MARTIN: What things?

JONATHAN: Everything on earth it seems; clothes, and books, and baubles, and trips about, and now, of course, it's a eunuch she wants.

MARTIN: You mean to tell me Eva doesn't have a eunuch?

JONATHAN: Been hounding me practically to death to get her one for her birthday, Martin, to the point that—well, you know how much I dote on her, but—

MARTIN: But, good heavens, man.

JONATHAN: I know, I know, but Miss McCracken does not approve of castration. And, having given the matter some thought, I'm not sure I do either.

MARTIN: Well, no man does, but our girls have always had their eunuchs. And what about the Ball?

JONATHAN: Does Little Eva have to go to the Ball?

MARTIN: Not go to the Patriarch's Ball?

JONATHAN: Miss McCracken is the loveliest, most forthright woman that I've ever met, Martin, and she has never been to a ball in her life.

MARTIN: But, Miss McCracken has not been raised as Little Eva has, to chatter and go to parties and spend money. Be in love all you want, man, but don't deprive your daughter of the crowning jewel of her girlhood for the sake of some sport with a waitress.

JONATHAN: I beg your pardon, sir.

MARTIN: No offence, of course.

JONATHAN: Miss McCracken is a minister's daughter, and a student at the law.

MARTIN: The law?

JONATHAN: At the University, yes.

MARTIN: Is that entirely legal?

JONATHAN: I should think so.

MARTIN: Then, Versatile Industries would be a perfect buy for you.

JONATHAN: What?

MARTIN: Like the University and your Miss McCracken, Versatile is dedicated to fulfilling, rather than exploiting, humanity's basest, uh, most basic needs.

JONATHAN: Ahhh.

MARTIN: They're a very old, established, very exciting company, ever desirous of finding new ways of satisfying their customers.

JONATHAN: That sounds awfully good, Martin.

MARTIN: You'll be doing good, sir; and doing well besides.

JONATHAN: Really? That sounds very attractive.

MARTIN: At this price, certainly. But not for long.

JONATHAN: In that case, I'd better take a hundred shares.

MARTIN: Wise move, sir.

JONATHAN: Oh, let's make it a thousand, Martin. I'm suddenly very keen on—what? What is it I'm buying?

MARTIN: *(Sings.)*
VERSATILE VERSATILE VERSATILE

MARTIN / JONATHAN: *(Sing.)*
VERSATILE INDUSTRIES

JONATHAN: Yes! *(Signing document.)* Move when the spirit moves us, eh?

MARTIN: Absolutely.

JONATHAN: Well I should be getting along home, I suppose. Face the gathering storm of my daughter's displeasure.

MARTIN: Good luck to you, sir, and do stop by whenever you wish to delve further into the mysteries of the marketplace.

JONATHAN: Indeed I shall, Martin.

*(Jonathan exits.)*

MARTIN: *(Sings.)*
VERSATILE VERSATILE VERSATILE
VERSATILE INDUSTRIES


SCENE TWO

*The Van Huffle parlor: Dorothea, the housekeeper, is stacking birthday presents on the table. Little Eva enters.*


LITTLE EVA: Ooo, look!

DOROTHEA: Eva!

LITTLE EVA: And I saw an extra place set at table, Dorothea.

DOROTHEA: Little Eva, you're not dressed!

LITTLE EVA: And right next to my place. Who could that be for, I wonder?

DOROTHEA: I suspect your father's invited someone home to supper, hasn't he?

LITTLE EVA: He's bringing him, Dorothea! He's bringing him!

DOROTHEA: Didn't say who he's bringing now, did he? Could be the mayor.

LITTLE EVA: *(Stamping her foot.)* Do not mock me, Dorothea!

DOROTHEA: Sorry, dear. No mockin' meant. Come now. Up you go and get dressed for your party.

LITTLE EVA: Oh I'm so excited. Tell me. Tell me, Dorothea. What will he be like?

DOROTHEA: Now, don't go gettin' your hopes up, Eva.

LITTLE EVA: *(Sings.)*
WILL HE BE FAT
YES HE'LL BE FAT
AND REALLY DISGUSTING

DOROTHEA: Oh, good heavens.

LITTLE EVA: A PIG, A HOG, A SWINE, A WILD BOAR

DOROTHEA: Wild boar?

LITTLE EVA: AND HE MUST BE SMART
TERRIBLY SMART
AND TERRIBLY UGLY

DOROTHEA: Ugly indeed.

LITTLE EVA: A DRAGON, LOCH NESS MONSTER, DINOSAUR

DOROTHEA: *(Sings.)* DINOSAUR

LITTLE EVA: COMPLETE WITH WOUNDED PRIDE
AND HAUGHTY TOO AND SNIDE
AND GAUDY AS A SUGAR ALLEY WHORE

DOROTHEA: Eva!

LITTLE EVA: WILL HE BE YOUNG
NO HE'LL BE OLD
AND TERRIBLY POMPOUS

DOROTHEA: IF YOU SAY SO

LITTLE EVA: A SCHOLAR, DOCTOR, JUDGE, AND EVEN MORE

DOROTHEA: MOST PROBABLY PALE

LITTLE EVA: PALE INDEED
BUT FULL OF A BOLDNESS

DOROTHEA: BOLDER THAN BOLD

LITTLE EVA / DOROTHEA: EXPLORER, SPORTSMAN, SOLDIER, MATA-DOR

LITTLE EVA: WITH TASTE BEYOND SUBLIME
AND QUITE CAPABLE OF CRIME

LITTLE EVA / DOROTHEA: A CREATURE OF THE SORT WORTH WAIT-
    ING FOR
LITTLE EVA: OH HE COULD BE IRISH
DOROTHEA: OR CHINESE
LITTLE EVA: MAYBE FROM SPAIN
DOROTHEA: OR PORTUGUESE
LITTLE EVA: CALCUTTA BRED
DOROTHEA: OR MACEDONIAN
LITTLE EVA: COULD BE FROM CRETE
DOROTHEA: COULD BE INDEED
LITTLE EVA: OR MAYBE FROM FRANCE
DOROTHEA: OR MAYBE A SWEDE
LITTLE EVA: PERHAPS A PATAGON-ION-IONIAN
LITTLE EVA / DOROTHEA: DOESN'T MATTER WHERE HE'S FROM
    WHO HE IS OR HOW HE'S COME
DOROTHEA: JUST SO LONG AS HE IS CUNNING
LITTLE EVA: AND ABSOLUTELY STUNNING
DOROTHEA: AND RUN RUN RUN RUN RUNNING ON HIS WAY
    HERE—
LITTLE EVA: Wait! I don't see him running Dorothea.
DOROTHEA: Perhaps not, no.
LITTLE EVA: *(Sings.)* I SEE HIM CARRIED LIKE A PASHA BY HIS
    SLAVEYS
DOROTHEA: *(Sings.)* BORNE ACROSS THE WAVY SEAS BY FOREIGN
    NAVIES
LITTLE EVA: AND LIKE THE OTHERS OF HIS ILK
DOROTHEA: HE'LL BE SWATHED IN MILES OF SILK
DOROTHEA / LITTLE EVA:
    ALL STAINED WITH GREASY MEATS AND STEWS AND
    GRAVIES
LITTLE EVA: FOR THERE'S NOTHING GRANDER THAN
DOROTHEA: A HUGE BAVARIAN
LITTLE EVA: BULGARIAN
DOROTHEA: HUNGARIAN
LITTLE EVA: LIBERTARIAN, APOLLINARIAN, VULGARIAN, ANTIDIS-
    ESTABLISHMENTARIAN, CONTRARIAN
LITTLE EVA / DOROTHEA: EUNUCH
JONATHAN: *(Off.)* Little Eva!

LITTLE EVA: Oh, it's Father!

(Jonathan enters.)

JONATHAN: (Sings.) HAPPY BIRTHDAY TO WHO

LITTLE EVA: Yes! Yes! Oh, yes! Father, oh Father, where were you?

JONATHAN: My, won't you look at all these presents!

LITTLE EVA: Oh! Oh!

JONATHAN: But, we don't care that much for the ordinary present, do we?

LITTLE EVA: No!

JONATHAN: Not when there's a special surprise waiting just outside.

LITTLE EVA: Dorothea! Dorothea!

DOROTHEA: Now, now.

JONATHAN: Someone very, very special to meet.

LITTLE EVA: Oh, please!

DOROTHEA: She's not dressed, sir.

JONATHAN: That's alright, Dorothea. Little Eva, the person you are about to meet could be someone very important in your life; someone to advise you, and be your friend and—

LITTLE EVA: Father, father please!

JONATHAN: Alright, then. May I present—

(Jonathan throws open the door. Miss McCracken enters.)

JONATHAN: Miss McCracken!

MISS McCRACKEN: Hello, Little Eva.

LITTLE EVA: What?

MISS McCRACKEN: And happy birthday to you.

JONATHAN: Little Eva? Little Eva say hello to Miss McCracken.

LITTLE EVA: You must be joking.

JONATHAN: What?

LITTLE EVA: Where is my present?

MISS McCRACKEN: I spy a great big pile of presents right over there.

LITTLE EVA: Who asked you?

JONATHAN: Little Eva, please, Miss McCracken is to be your friend.

LITTLE EVA: I don't believe this. Tell me you've hidden it somewhere, Father. In the attic, or the stables, or—

JONATHAN: Eva—

LITTLE EVA: Where is my eunuch!

JONATHAN: But you don't need a eunuch. You just think you do. Tell her, Miss McCracken.

MISS McCRACKEN: It's not my place to tell her, Jonathan.

JONATHAN: Eva, dear—

LITTLE EVA: Oh, my God.

(*Little Eva begins to weep.*)

JONATHAN: Eva, Little Eva, please.

LITTLE EVA: Shut up, you liar! Just shut up! Shut up!

(*Little Eva, wailing, throws herself into Dorothea's arms.*)

MISS McCRACKEN: Oh, my.

JONATHAN: Perhaps, Dorothea, if you could show Miss McCracken to the garden and make us some tea?

DOROTHEA: Yes sir. And gladly.

JONATHAN: I'll be right along.

DOROTHEA: This way, Miss McCracken.

MISS McCRACKEN: Nice to have met you, Little Eva.

LITTLE EVA: Get out! Get out of my house! Get out! Get out! GET OUT!

(*Little Eva screams and wails. Dorothea and Miss McCracken exit.*)

JONATHAN: Now, now. Now, there. Little Eva. Please. You're going to make yourself sick if you keep this up.

LITTLE EVA: Go away! Just, go away!

JONATHAN: But look at all these lovely presents. Here's one from me. And another one from me. And yet another one from me. Oh, and one from Miss McCracken! Why don't we open Miss McCracken's gift first?

(*Jonathan holds out a present. Little Eva slaps it to the floor.*)

JONATHAN: Eva!

LITTLE EVA: Did you or did you not say that I could have anything that I wanted for my birthday this year?

JONATHAN: Yes, Little Eva, I did, I certainly did.

LITTLE EVA: Then why have you failed to bring me the one thing that I asked for, the one thing I truly wanted and needed?

JONATHAN: I'm sorry dear but, having reflected carefully upon the matter I have seen fit to, to, to—

LITTLE EVA: To what?

JONATHAN: Well, to change my mind.

LITTLE EVA: (*Cries.*)

JONATHAN: There, there now, Little Eva. It's not the end of the world.

LITTLE EVA: You promised! You promised me!

JONATHAN: I know I did darling, but—

LITTLE EVA: Am I to be the only one, the only girl in my entire circle to go into society unprotected?

JONATHAN: Perhaps you can rely upon your family to—

LITTLE EVA: Family? What family? You may as well give me away to some poor family. Or leave me out in the wilderness to die.

JONATHAN: Oh, don't be ridiculous.

LITTLE EVA: I need a eunuch for the Ball, Father.

JONATHAN: But it's only a dance, Little Eva.

LITTLE EVA: It is the Patriarch's Ball! And the expectations that await my debut are immense and terrible. I must be perfect, and with the help of my eunuch, when I get one, I shall be.

JONATHAN: But surely there are other things in life.

LITTLE EVA: What other things?

JONATHAN: Well, horseback riding, for heaven's sake. Or play acting, or the domestic arts, or, or, or—

LITTLE EVA: Or what?

JONATHAN: Well, I can remember the pleasure and satisfaction your mother derived from her charitable involvements.

LITTLE EVA: My mother enjoyed making those parvenus pony up.

JONATHAN: You are far too knowing for a—

LITTLE EVA: I am my mother's daughter, sir. And if you choose to deny me and shun your responsibilities as a parent, I shall never eat another mouthful of food so long as it is my misfortune to live under your miserable, mean-spirited roof!

JONATHAN: Ah, so that's it. Well, you will find that sort of tactic will not work with me, young lady.

LITTLE EVA: Of course it will. That is why I have fastened upon it.

JONATHAN: Oh, if you would only just talk to Miss McCracken.

LITTLE EVA: Why? What on earth does Miss McCracken know about society?

JONATHAN: Absolutely nothing. Miss McCracken scorns such matters utterly.

LITTLE EVA: Well I can assure you I do not. Who is she anyway? Her family?

JONATHAN: Well, her father is a minister.

LITTLE EVA: Oh, she's poor, then.

JONATHAN: Not poor certainly, no, Miss McCracken earns her living working as a—

LITTLE EVA: Working? She works?

JONATHAN: As a waitress in a tea shoppe, yes.

LITTLE EVA: Oh my God!

JONATHAN: More to the point, she is a lovely and principled young woman with wonderful ideas about life; and since your mother has left us—

LITTLE EVA: My mother has not left us. My mother is dead. And it is an insult to her memory for you to consort with this opportunist.

JONATHAN: Eva!

LITTLE EVA: Opportunist! I say it out!

JONATHAN: One more remark like that, Little Eva, and you will go to your room for your birthday! Do you understand?

LITTLE EVA: I understand that you mean to replace my glorious mother with a common waitress!

JONATHAN: Go to your room!

LITTLE EVA: I will not.

JONATHAN: You are spoiled and snobbish and cruel and you will go to your room until you can learn to speak and act like a, like a, like a, like a human person.

LITTLE EVA: Never! Never, never, never, never, never, never, never—

JONATHAN: Eva!

*(Jonathan raises an admonishing finger.)*

LITTLE EVA: Go ahead, strike me!

JONATHAN: Strike you? I have never struck you child, and I never will. But I will say—

LITTLE EVA: Yes?

JONATHAN: Let's just say that your mother and her circle could be terribly— well, not very kind, let us say.

LITTLE EVA: As if that were the measure of a life. Go ahead, Father. Marry your Miss McCracken.

JONATHAN: What?

LITTLE EVA: Just don't expect me at the wedding.

*(Little Eva exits.)*

JONATHAN: *(Sings.)*
WEDDING
A WEDDING
I NEVER THOUGHT OF THAT
A WEDDING WITH MISS McCRACKEN AS MY BRIDE

WEDDING
A WEDDING
ME AND MY PUSSY CAT
I'M IN HEAVEN AND I HAVEN'T EVEN DIED

I'LL BUY HER A LITTLE DIAMOND
ON A SIMPLE GOLDEN BAND
WE'LL GO AND MEET HER FATHER
I'LL ASK HIM FOR HER HAND

WE'LL BE THE AVERAGE FAMILY
ON THE AVERAGE BOULEVARD
AND WE'LL TALK ABOUT THE WEATHER
AS WE SIT IN OUR BACK YARD, OH

A WEDDING
A WEDDING
CAN YOU IMAGINE THAT
A WEDDING
A WEDDING
TO A WOMAN, NOT SOME DAMNED ARISTOCRAT
*(Dorothea enters with a tray.)*

DOROTHEA: Sir?

JONATHAN: *(Startled.)* What! Oh, Dorothea.

DOROTHEA: Your tea, sir. Supper'll be ready soon.

JONATHAN: Supper, yes.

DOROTHEA: Try not to be too hard on her, sir.

JONATHAN: Hard on whom?

DOROTHEA: Why, Little Eva, sir. I know she can say terrible rough things. But then you know how she is. Next minute she's our Little Eva.

JONATHAN: I'm afraid our Little Eva's gone a bit too far this time, Dorothea.

DOROTHEA: I know it's none of my concern, but can I speak straight from the shoulder, sir?

JONATHAN: Of course, Dorothea.

DOROTHEA: I've been talking with your Miss McCracken just now, and she's a lovely young woman, she is.

JONATHAN: Isn't she, though?

DOROTHEA: Yes sir, she certainly understands about folks, people who's got to work for a living, sir, I'll say that. And she means well, yes, but she's never had to know what Little Eva knows, has she—that she don't have to kow-tow to nobody she don't want to. Don't have to lift a finger of work. Oh, there's an awful freedom in that. And the envy and jealousy of it, and— well all I mean to say, sir, a good eunuch might be just the thing, 'cause, pardon my saying so, they're sensitive to little rich girls, somehow. It's in their power or makeup or whatever to know how to handle a person who's different. Did her mother a world of good growing up.

JONATHAN: Her mother had a eunuch?

DOROTHEA: Ephesius, yes sir. Oh, he was ever so much help to her.

JONATHAN: I never knew.

DOROTHEA: Well it's women's business, sir.

JONATHAN: Yes, of course.

DOROTHEA: Don't know if I should go bearing tales out of school, but it was Ephesius advised her to marry you, sir.

JONATHAN: You don't say.

DOROTHEA: Take that one, he said. He's the oak among the pinewood.

JONATHAN: Indeed.

DOROTHEA: Commonsensical he was, and ever so smart.

JONATHAN: Tell me Dorothea. Where's this Ephesius now?

DOROTHEA: Oh, Ephesius he went off, sir.

JONATHAN: Off? Off where?

DOROTHEA: Off in his head, sir. After the mistress settled with you and had no more need of him he became a bit lunatic and had to be put down. You can't buy that kind of loyalty no more, now can you sir? And Little Eva, she just needs someone to be with, you know, someone like Ephesius that's not family or servants, exactly, or friends even. Somebody equal in a way, but can't go getting her in no trouble, if you take my meaning.

JONATHAN: I suspect you may be right, Dorothea. But Miss McCracken has opened my eyes and heart to the fact that, well, it's rather a barbaric custom don't you think? Grotesque, even.

DOROTHEA: Most do it to themselves, I'm told. Just for the work.

JONATHAN: But doesn't that make it even worse?

DOROTHEA: Not my place to have opinions, but you're an intelligent man, sir. You'll figure it out, I'm sure.

(A knock. Jameson enters and salutes, violently.)

JAMESON: Sir!

JONATHAN: Yes, Jameson?

JAMESON: There be a woman in the garden, sir.

JONATHAN: Oh good heavens! Miss McCracken!

JAMESON: That's her!

JONATHAN: Where is she?

JAMESON: In the garden, sir.

JONATHAN: Well, bring her indoors, Jameson. Good heavens.

JAMESON: *(Saluting again.)* Sir!

JONATHAN: On second thought, I'd better go find her myself.

DOROTHEA: Good idea, sir.

(*Jonathan exits, hurriedly.*)

JAMESON: Well, ain't his feathers all aflutter.

DOROTHEA: Good to see Mister Johnny excited about a woman, I'd say.

JAMESON: Too thin for my blood.

DOROTHEA: Oh you and your blood.

JAMESON: Shed plenty for my country didn't I? 'Least there'll be no eunuchs sneakin' round here, eh? Not with the caterwaulin' I heard in here tonight.

DOROTHEA: Oh you don't know little girls.

JAMESON: All I know is any eunuch comes in this house and I gives notice.

DOROTHEA: Oh, is that so?

JAMESON: You just watch and see. I'm not treading the same stair as no eunuch.

DOROTHEA: And what harm can a poor eunuch do you?

JAMESON: What is the eunuch then, Dorothea? What?

DOROTHEA: Go on and say it; you're bursting to tell me.

JAMESON: Neither a he thing nor she thing but a torn and ruined monster full o' bitterness and gall, that's what. My old dad hisself told me, "Don't ye never turn your back on a eunuch. They're as shifty and dire a creature as ye ever want to meet, and a real man won't has nothing to do with 'em."

DOROTHEA: Ah, you weren't here before the war, Jameson. Fine eunuchs all up and down the neighborhood.

JAMESON: As like to stab ye in the back as look at ye.

DOROTHEA: Just look at the way that Miss Porter come on since she got her creature. A caterpillar to a queen she is.

JAMESON: An' I tell you there's mates o' mine out there sleepin' under bridges with one eye open just awaitin' for the signal to rise up an' slaughter the lot of 'em!

DOROTHEA: With the price a eunuch fetches these days?

JAMESON: Think what you want and say what you like, Dorothea –

(*Dorothea exits with presents. Miss McCracken enters.*)

MISS McCRACKEN: Jonathan?

JAMESON: He ain't here, ma'am.

MISS McCRACKEN: Oh, well, where is he?

JAMESON: He'd be lookin' for ye in the garden.

MISS McCRACKEN: Goodness, one could get lost forever in this house.

JAMESON: Lost, hell.

MISS McCRACKEN: I beg your pardon?

JAMESON: Slaughter's Ridge, mum. No moon. No compass. Cap'n dead. Lieutenant staggered. Wounded all about and screamin'.

MISS McCRACKEN: Good heavens.

JAMESON: That's what I call lost.

MISS McCRACKEN: Yes. Well.

JAMESON: You want, I'll reconnoiter back in the garden, Miss, and find 'm.

MISS McCRACKEN: If you would, please.

JAMESON: *(Saluting.)* Sir! Miss!

    *(Jameson exits.)*

MISS McCRACKEN: Good heavens.

    *(Jonathan enters, opposite.)*

JONATHAN: Oh. There you are. So sorry.

MISS McCRACKEN: Oh, that's quite alright.

JONATHAN: I was in the garden.

MISS McCRACKEN: And so was I, but I got turned around somehow and, well, here I am.

JONATHAN: Yes. Well. Have you been refreshed then?

MISS McCRACKEN: Yes, yes. Your man, uh …

JONATHAN: Jameson.

MISS McCRACKEN: Jameson, yes. He brought me this when I arrived. Never tasted anything quite like it I must say.

JONATHAN: Good. Good. Well, then. I must say, seeing you here in my very own home, well it does my heart good and, well, you do my heart good, Miss McCracken.

MISS McCRACKEN: Do I?

JONATHAN: Yes you do. Yes you do. Yes you do. Yes. Yes, indeed.

MISS McCRACKEN: How about a little kiss, then.

JONATHAN: Oh, may I please?

    *(They kiss. Jameson enters and salutes.)*

JAMESON: Sir!

JONATHAN: *(Startled.)* Godfrey! What? Yes, what is it Jameson?

JAMESON: There's a Miss McCracken wants to see ye.

JONATHAN: This *is* Miss McCracken, Jameson.

JAMESON: Uh huh. Ye be wantin' cocktails, then?

JONATHAN: The usual for me, yes.

JAMESON: And for the lady?

MISS McCRACKEN: More of the same, thanks.

JAMESON: Righty oh.

MISS McCRACKEN: It's so unusual. What is it?

JAMESON: Pig Wort, mum.

MISS McCRACKEN: Pig Wort?

JAMESON: Good for marchin', when the dust is filled your lung and yer spittin' up the mud.

JONATHAN: Thank you, Jameson.

JAMESON: And thankee, sir, for all who bled the blood and died the death.

JONATHAN: What?

JAMESON: Honorable you standin' up sir, not bringin' the never mind among us.

MISS McCRACKEN: The never mind?

JAMESON: Oh, nothin' but trouble they are, Miss.

JONATHAN: That'll do, Jameson.

JAMESON: My old dad, he—

JONATHAN: That will do, I say.

JAMESON: *(Saluting.)* Sir!

   *(Jameson exits.)*

MISS McCRACKEN: What a queer fellow.

JONATHAN: Mm.

MISS McCRACKEN: What was he on about?

JONATHAN: Who knows? Poor fellow's from the Veterans Hospital. Try to do my part, of course, hiring these men on, but this one's … *(Sighs.)*

MISS McCRACKEN: The trouble with having servants is having servants, I suppose.

JONATHAN: Yes. Well. Oh, my goodness, what a day. On the cross all afternoon with Martin about some company or other he's been hounding me to invest in.

MISS McCRACKEN: And did you?

JONATHAN: Did I?

MISS McCRACKEN: Invest?

JONATHAN: Oh, bought a few shares, I suppose. Just to keep him at bay, more or less.

MISS McCRACKEN: How many?

JONATHAN: What?

MISS McCRACKEN: Did you buy?

JONATHAN: Just a few. A hundred or so I think it was.

MISS McCRACKEN: Or so?

JONATHAN: A few hundred. A thousand, I think. I don't know, Miss McCracken. Good heavens.

MISS McCRACKEN: I just find it a little strange, after everything we've talked about.

JONATHAN: Well I know, but I think successful companies are most often honest companies. It's just makes sound business sense.

MISS McCRACKEN: Is that what Martin says?

JONATHAN: Martin says this is a particularly well-intentioned company, yes.

MISS McCRACKEN: And the name of this enterprise?

JONATHAN: I, uh, can't seem to recall right now.

MISS McCRACKEN: Nor what business they are engaged in, I suppose?

JONATHAN: No, no, but something very fulfilling and satisfying and, and new, he said. Yes, new.

MISS McCRACKEN: Oh, new, of course.

JONATHAN: How about another kiss?

MISS McCRACKEN: You didn't even ask to see a prospectus, did you?

JONATHAN: I'm sorry, I'm sorry, I know what we discussed, but I do not seem to have the power to resist the advice of a man whose business it is to see to my investments.

MISS McCRACKEN: We can resist most anything, Jonathan, when we are serious in our resistance.

JONATHAN: Perhaps I'm not serious then. Not serious. Not serious at all.

MISS McCRACKEN: And perhaps I make too much of things.

JONATHAN: No, no.

MISS McCRACKEN: That's what they say of me at school, you know. That I have seriosis of the brain.

JONATHAN: Oh, Miss McCracken, it isn't you, it's not, it's just my Little Eva has taken this eunuch disappointment very badly, I'm afraid.

MISS McCRACKEN: Well, did you explain your reasoning?

JONATHAN: I could not seem to remember my reasoning.

MISS McCRACKEN: Eunuchs are human beings, Jonathan.

JONATHAN: Yes. Yes, they are Miss McCracken. That's true.

MISS McCRACKEN: And human beings are not meant to be castrated and sold.

JONATHAN: Looked at that way, of course.

MISS McCRACKEN: What other way is there to look at it? Good heavens, Jonathan, how would you like it if someone were to—

JONATHAN: Don't say it. Don't say it, please. I know. You're absolutely right. But somehow, with Eva, the words just won't come.

MISS McCRACKEN: Because they're not your words, Jonathan. They're my words. And my words have no effect in her world. Because I am not of her world and never shall be.

JONATHAN: That's not so.

MISS McCRACKEN: No, no.

*(Sings.)*

YOU ARE WHO YOU ARE

I AM WHO I AM

IT WAS JUST A FANTASY

IT WAS JUST ROMANCE

LOOK AT ME

SILLINESS

LOOK AT YOU

LOOK AT THIS

LOOK AT US

IT'S JUST TOO, TOO …

JONATHAN: Yes?

MISS McCRACKEN: Oh, never mind, Jonathan. It's late, and I—

JONATHAN: No, it's not, it's—

MISS McCRACKEN: No, no, I've an early morning at work, and cases to read, and—

JONATHAN: Miss McCracken, please.

MISS McCRACKEN: Don't bother, I'll find my own way out. I hope.

*(Miss McCracken exits.)*

JONATHAN: Miss McCracken!

*(Jameson enters with drinks.)*

JAMESON: Supper's near to ready, sir.

JONATHAN: I don't care for any supper, Jameson. *(Drinks.)*

JAMESON: Tripe and cockle and hemmecker puddin' dessert, sir.

JONATHAN: Never mind. Bring me another drink.

JAMESON: How 'bout her ladyship?

JONATHAN: On second thought, never mind the drink. I'm going out.

JAMESON: Aye.

JONATHAN: Tell Dorothea I'll be at my club and that I'll be home, I'll be home, oh, goddamnit I don't know when I'll be home.

*(Jonathan exits.)*

JAMESON: *(Saluting.)* Sir!

*The bar at Jonathan's club: Charles Henderson, Bunny Shotworthy and Jonathan, all drunk.*

HENDERSON: Johnny, Johnny, face it Johnny, man in our position, yours and mine, men with daughters—

SHOTWORTHY: *(Sings.)* DIPSY DAUGHTERS.

HENDERSON: But three choices for the little darlings.

SHOTWORTHY: *(Sings.)* DOODLEY DAUGHTERS.

HENDERSON: It's horses. It's religion. Or it's eunuchs.

SHOTWORTHY: Eunuchs, yes! Or theatricals. Don't forget the damned theatricals. What was that play?

HENDERSON: You don't have daughters, Shotworthy.

SHOTWORTHY: Damn well had sisters, didn't I?

HENDERSON: *(To Jonathan.)* Ugly brutes.

SHOTWORTHY: Molly went for the stage. Ruined her. Oh, yes. But, Mary. Mary was given a eunuch and passed it to her daughter.

JONATHAN: What's your daughter fancy, Henderson?

HENDERSON: Don't give a damn what she fancies, she's getting a eunuch. Think the wife and I want stagehands, stableboys, and novices and so forth up our Jenny, do you?

SHOTWORTHY: God save us!

HENDERSON: You just be happy it's a eunuch Eva wants and not some damn jumper like my Jenny.

SHOTWORTHY: Or a romp in the pew with Brother Ha Ha!

HENDERSON: Quiet, Shotworthy. All we mean, mean to say here, Johnny, the Father needs look long and hard upon the world for his daughter's sake. No disrespect to your Miss McDougal.

JONATHAN: She's fine woman. Good woman.

SHOTWORTHY: Womanly womenly weeeee heee heee.

JONATHAN: She's just against the goddamn eunuch's all.

HENDERSON: But whyever for, Johnny? Whyever for?

JONATHAN: Oh, I don't know. Upbringing. Whatever. Thinks it's. Has a prejudice.

SHOTWORTHY: *(Signals.)* Barkeep!

HENDERSON: You just stick to your guns, Johnny. Your Miss McCutcheon'll respect you for it. 'Sides, Little Eva'll soon tire of it and you can get rid of the damn thing. Have it put down. Whatever. Hah!

JONATHAN: But, they are human after all.

HENDERSON: Human?

SHOTWORTHY: Women?

JONATHAN: Eunuchs.

HENDERSON: Legally. According to some. But in the long view. History. All relative, what's legal, what ain't. Changes by the hour. Must go back to first principles! Back to what was and was and was and has been forever!

SHOTWORTHY: *(Confidential.)* Had a eunuch in my company during the war, didn't I?

JONATHAN: What?

SHOTWORTHY: Shh. Never told anybody.

HENDERSON: Not since yesterday.

SHOTWORTHY: Damn fine fellow, actually.

JONATHAN: A eunuch?

SHOTWORTHY: Oh, yes. Brave fellow. Very brave. Had him over to the house since.

HENDERSON: Oh, Jesus.

SHOTWORTHY: Did! Damn right I did! I'll have who I want in my parlor, Henderson!

HENDERSON: Obviously.

SHOTWORTHY: Eunuch saved my life!

HENDERSON: Enough!

SHOTWORTHY: Not proud about it. But I'll drink a drink with him. Don't care what the wife says. What do they know? Women. *WOMEN!*

HENDERSON: Quiet down, Shotworthy. Quiet down, now.

SHOTWORTHY: Sorry. Sorry. Become emotional. Sorry.

HENDERSON: *(Confidential.)* Group of us, Johnny, Saturdays, behind the mar pits. Meet, discuss the eunuchs 'mongst ourselves. Men you *know*, but *don't* know, eh? Men unafraid to explore 'mongst the darker, stranger passions.

SHOTWORTHY: Xerxes, yes.

JONATHAN: Xerxes?

SHOTWORTHY: The visaged man, ha ha.

HENDERSON: Look. Look, Johnny. *(Pulls book out of his pocket.)* Look!

SHOTWORTHY: Look out! *(Laughs.)*

HENDERSON: 'Tis the Book of Eunuch, Johnny.

JONATHAN: *(Examining book.)* Hm.

HENDERSON: Tells us what there is to know about the creatures. Characteristics and such forth throughout the ages. Selection. Surgical. Hair. Life span. Powers. Propensities. All there. All you need to know.

JONATHAN: Fascinating.

SHOTWORTHY: Said the parson to the pig.

HENDERSON: See, look, drawings! The Roman, classical, castrati, Oriental. All represented. Every cut and classification.

SHOTWORTHY: Bang bang! In the brush there! Got him!

HENDERSON: Hush man! Want you with us, Johnny. Man like yourself. Our way of life.

SHOTWORTHY: Is he with us?

JONATHAN: But who is Xerxes?

HENDERSON: You are, Johnny! I am! Shotworthy here!

SHOTWORTHY: XERXES!

HENDERSON: More drink!

SHOTWORTHY: We want more drink here!

HENDERSON: More drink!

HENDERSON / SHOTWORTHY: More drink! More drink!

HENDERSON / SHOTWORTHY / JONATHAN: More drink! More drink! More drink!

JONATHAN: *(Beat.)* Cut us off, I s'pose.

HENDERSON: Niggardly bastards!

SHOTWORTHY: Rip their windpipes!

HENDERSON: Hell with the club, damn their eyes! To the Lively Lad!

SHOTWORTHY: To the Lively Lad!

JONATHAN: The Lively Lad?

HENDERSON: Club in the Vollybond!

SHOTWORTHY: Open all night!

HENDERSON: Knock three times!

SHOTWORTHY: Come along, Johnny!

HENDERSON: We'll have a pudding!

SHOTWORTHY: A pudding, yum!

HENDERSON / SHOTWORTHY: *(Singing.)*

YUM, YUM, YUM, YUM
YUM, YUM, YUM, YUM

WE'RE GOING TO HAVE A PUDDING
A PIECE OF PUMPKIN PIE
AND LINDZER TORTE
AND OTHER SPORTING PASTRIES BY AND BY

WE'LL TASTE A BIT OF STRUDEL
AND THEN THE CUMQUAT TART
AND OH THE PEACH
A PIECE OF EACH AND EACH ONE ALA CARTE

AND THEN FOR ENTERTAINMENT
TO KEEP OUR LUST AWAKE
THE GELDING OF THE SCHOOLBOY
IS THE ACT THAT TAKES THE CAKE
*(Offstage scream / Gideon.)*

HENDERSON / SHOTWORTHY: *(Singing.)*
    FEE, FI, FO, FUM
    FEE, FI, FO, FUM

    WE TAKE THE TENDER BOLLOCKS
    WE PUT THEM IN A BOX
    A SOUVENIR OF MAN'S WORST FEAR TO STIFFEN UP OUR
        COCKS

    WE PASS IT 'ROUND THE CIRCLE
    WE GAZE IN FEAR AND DREAD
    AND THEN WE DO THE THINGS THAT YOU'D PREFER TO
        LEAVE UNSAID

    OH, THE GELDING OF THE SCHOOLBOY
    THE GELDING OF THE SCHOOLBOY
    THE GELDING OF THE SCHOOLBOY
    IS THE ACT THAT TAKES THE CAKE
    *(Blackout.)*


SCENE FOUR

*The Van Huffle parlor. Jonathan enters in bathrobe, holding an ice pack to his head. Jameson enters with a drink.*

JAMESON: Here ye go then, sir.

JONATHAN: Ah! Not so loud, Jameson!

JAMESON: Sorry, sir.

JONATHAN: Heaven's sake, man.

JAMESON: Don't know me own powers sometimes.

JONATHAN: Where's Dorothea?

JAMESON: Gone out with Little Eva, ain't she.

JONATHAN: Really? What o'clock is it?

JAMESON: Near noon, sir.

JONATHAN: Noon! Good god! Aren't I meant to be somewhere?

JAMESON: Don't know, sir.

JONATHAN: I must have something to do today.

JAMESON: Better drink this down 'fore ye try anything, sir.

JONATHAN: What is it?

JAMESON: Oh ye don't want to know, sir. But it'll do the trick for ye.

JONATHAN: *(Drinks, gags.)* God, it's foul!

JAMESON: Powdered frog parts and whiskey, sir. Learnt it in the war.

JONATHAN: I'm not in a war, Jameson. I have a hangover.

JAMESON: Best thing for it too, sir. My experience. How you feelin' then? Ready for company, are you?

JONATHAN: Company?

JAMESON: Guest in the vestibule.

JONATHAN: I'm not at home to anyone, Jameson.

JAMESON: Think he's for your daughter, anyways.

JONATHAN: Little Eva?

JAMESON: Friend o' hers, I reckon.

JONATHAN: Little Eva has no friends.

JAMESON: Carryin' a case, sir. Could be a brush man, couldn't he?

JONATHAN: Oh, bring him up.

JAMESON: A juvenile type, ye know. They'll try anything.

JONATHAN: Bring him up, I said! Bring him up!

JAMESON: *(Coming to attention.)* Sir!

JONATHAN: Sorry, Jameson. Didn't mean to snap at you.

JAMESON: Oh, that's alright, sir. I had worse than that. Lost the Colonel's horse once, didn't I?

JONATHAN: Jameson—

JAMESON: Sergeant Major throwed a jug at me.

JONATHAN: That's enough.

JAMESON: And it were full, too!

JONATHAN: For god's sake, Jameson!

JAMESON: *(Saluting.)* Sir!

*(Jonathan exits. Jameson exits oppositely and re-enters with an adolescent boy. The boy has an envelope pinned to his coat. He carries a suitcase in one hand and a small wooden box in the other.)*

JAMESON: Right this way. The Cap'n, he'll be down directly to interrogate ye proper. He's in a temper, too, I can tell ye. From the drink. I give up drink myself on account o' Sergeant Major. No I don't touch drip nor drop no more, except upon occasion, and cook, she went to town with Little Eva, so. *(Pulls out a flask.)* She's a reg'lar head wound, that Little Eva. *(Toasts.)* To Sergeant Major. *(Drinks)* Have one, won't ye? *(Boy drinks and drinks again.)* Hey, hey, now! *(Takes flask.)* Leave a drop for Jameson, for he needs another, don't he? Yes I do. *(Drinks.)* For I were in the wars, and seen bad business. Rockaloo Ridge. Lookers Hole. Pinned down two months at Rickety Run, we were, without our winter hose.

*(Jonathan enters, dressed.)*

JONATHAN: Thank you, Jameson.

JAMESON: *(Coming to attention.)* Sir! I was just tellin' the prisoner here about the time we—

JONATHAN: That will be all.

JAMESON: *(Salutes.)* Sir!

*(Jameson exits.)*

JONATHAN: I apologize for my man. He can go on sometimes about … things, yes. So, now then, who are you and what do you want here?

BOY: …

JONATHAN: What's your name, I say?

BOY : …

JONATHAN: *(Sees envelope.)* What's all this about? *(Reads envelope.)* "To Johnny." Hm. *(Opens envelope and reads enclosed message.)* "A lively lad for Little Eva on her birthday, compliments of Xerxes." What on earth? *(To boy.)* Is this some kind of joke?

BOY : …

JONATHAN: Listen, I hope this, uh … I'm afraid you have rather the advantage of me here, for last night, last night I was, uh, I had rather a lot to drink, and was, well, potted, actually, and I have no recollection of any Xerxes, or anything at all, frankly, past an argument with Miss McCracken, a lovely young woman whom you probably don't … then a drink or two at my club and then … what's in the box?

*(Boy holds up box. Jonathan takes it, opens it, looks inside.)*

JONATHAN: AH!

*(Jameson re-enters.)*

JAMESON: Sir!

JONATHAN: *(Startled again.)* AH!

JAMESON: Everything alright in here?

JONATHAN: Yes. Yes. Yes. Fine, Jameson. Everything's fine.

JAMESON: I heard a shoutin', sir.

JONATHAN: No. Yes. Just—just bring me a drink.

JAMESON: *(Saluting.)* Sir! *(Offers his flask.)*

JONATHAN: Thank you. *(Takes flask and drinks, drinks again and hands it back.)* That will be all, then.

JAMESON: *(Salutes.)* Sir!

*(Jameson exits.)*

JONATHAN: Oh, my God. A eunuch. I don't want a eunuch. Never wanted a eunuch. You cannot be a eunuch!

BOY : *(Looks at Jonathan.)*

JONATHAN: Oh, what on earth am I to—I'm sorry, I'm sorry, I can't—oh I just cannot bear this. *(Calling off.)* Jameson! Jameson! ... Wait! Who should I say you—What should I call you? Oh, I know! What's his name? Boy at school, used to eat *pate de foie gras* to the sound of trumpets?

*(Jameson enters, saluting.)*

JAMESON; Sir!

JONATHAN: *(Startled.)* AH!

JAMESON: Sorry sir, I were in the latrine!

JONATHAN: Never mind, Jameson. This is my, uh, uh, my nephew.

JAMESON: Nephew, sir?

JONATHAN: My brother's boy. My brother lives on a farm. In the, uh, country, yes. He'll be staying on with us a bit.

JAMESON: Your brother?

JONATHAN: No. His son, here. *(Remembering suddenly.)* Gideon! Gideon. Gideon, his name was, is, and he's come to town to, to—

JAMESON: See the sights, eh?

JONATHAN: What? Yes!

JAMESON: Us country boys makes hellish fighters, Gideon. When I were in the war, I cut arms an' legs an' heads off with a scythe.

JONATHAN: Jameson—

JAMESON: Blood squirtin' every whichaways! Whoooee!

JONATHAN: Jameson, please!

JAMESON: *(Saluting.)* Sir!

JONATHAN: And will you stop that infernal saluting!

JAMESON: Yes, sir. Sorry, sir. Habit, sir. Sergeant Major, he were always on me for forgettin', so—

JONATHAN: Never mind, never mind. Listen, it's a bit of a surprise, Gideon's visit. Little Eva is not aware she has a cousin from the country.

JAMESON: No?

JONATHAN: Bit of a black sheep, my bother, uh, brother.

JAMESON: Oh, I knows the type, sir.

JONATHAN: Yes, so, let's keep this quiet for now, alright?

JAMESON: Just like Pelican Bridge, eh?

JONATHAN: What?

JAMESON: Hush hush it were. Not even Sergeant Major knew. Had the element a surprise right up to the—

JONATHAN: Yes. Exactly like that. Now, I'm going downtown for a bit, to, to, to— Just take Gideon's case upstairs would you. A quiet room in the back. And bring him anything he requires. Anything at all.

JAMESON: Yes sir, I will. And hush hush be the word about it, too.

*(Jameson exits with Gideon's suitcase.)*

JONATHAN: I'll be back shortly, Gideon, I will, and we'll, we'll … yes.

*(Jonathan exits. Pause. Gideon sings.)*

GIDEON:

THE LONELY SHEPHERD FOUND HIS FLOCK
AND DROVE THEM TO THE STREAM
AND STRETCHED OUT FULL UPON THE BANK
AND THERE DID HAVE A DREAM

HE DREAMED HE WAS FORSAKEN
DREAMED HIS GOD HAD FLED
HE WOKE IN FEAR AND TREMBLING
WISHING HE WERE DEAD

*(Jameson re-enters.)*

JAMESON: Hey, now. That's a nice singin' there.

GIDEON: Just a little country air.

JAMESON: Well, me I'm from the country, like I said, and we don't put on airs like that.

GIDEON: Oh?

JAMESON: No sir, that sounded high sung to me like eunuchs done at the hospital, nights. Singin' together in the shithouse there. Like to drove me insane.

GIDEON: You were in the insane hospital?

JAMESON: I were not! I caught a round at Philmore's Grove!

GIDEON: Oh, you must have been with the 455th.

JAMESON: You know the 455?

GIDEON: *(Remembering a snatch.)*
   A RUM TITTLE TITTLE
   AND A RUM TITTLE RUM …

JAMESON: *(In answer, amazed.)*
   WE DANCE TO THE FIDDLE
   AND WE MARCH TO THE DRUM …

GIDEON / JAMESON: *(Singing.)*
   A RUM TITTLE TITTLE
   AND A RUM TITTLE RYE
   WE STAND FOR OUR COUNTRY
   AND WE FIGHT TIL WE DIE

   THE 455
   HEY THE 455
   WE'RE THE 455 FOREVER
   THE 455
   YES THE 455
   AND WE NEVER GIVE UP
   NO NEVER

JAMESON: *(Laughing.)* Oh my gracious, I ain't sung that in forever.

GIDEON: The 455th captured Hilliard at Eagle's Bluff.

JAMESON: Found him myself, didn't I, hidin' in the cellar, drunk.

GIDEON: General Hilliard?

JAMESON: Pissed his britches, too. Come on in the kitchen, friend. We'll have another whiskey an' I'll tell ye all about it.

   *(Jameson and Gideon exit.)*

# SCENE FIVE

*A tea shoppe. Maitre d' seats Dorothea and Little Eva.*

DOROTHEA: Well, my mother told me a youngster without breakfast is a pistol without powder.

LITTLE EVA: I don't care to hear any more of your mother's idiotic wisdoms, Dorothea.

DOROTHEA: Well, I never.

LITTLE EVA: And I don't intend to eat ever again. Certainly not in a place like this, anyway. I don't see her, do you?

DOROTHEA: No, and I don't think your father would like us being here.

LITTLE EVA: I don't like being here myself, Dorothea, but something has to be done. Ugh, what a hideous decor.

DOROTHEA: Oh, I don't know.

LITTLE EVA: It looks like a Swiss brothel, Dorothea.

DOROTHEA: And what would you know about things like that?

LITTLE EVA: *(Pointing.)* There she is. *(To Maitre d'.)* That waitress over there. Send her over, please.

MAITRE D': I am sorry Miss, but this is not her station.

LITTLE EVA: Dorothea, give him some money.

DOROTHEA: Good heavens, child.

*(Dorothea gives Maitre d' money. Maitre d' exits.)*

LITTLE EVA: Dear lord, give me the words with which to cudgel mine enemies.

DOROTHEA: Little Eva—

LITTLE EVA: Oh, spare me.

*(Miss McCracken enters.)*

MISS McCRACKEN: Little Eva!

LITTLE EVA: Miss McCracken, there is something I wish to say to you.

MISS McCRACKEN: I'm sorry, but we're very busy right now.

LITTLE EVA: You'll remember Dorothea?

MISS McCRACKEN: Hello, Dorothea.

DOROTHEA: Miss.

LITTLE EVA: Briefly, Miss McCracken. As you know, my father wishes to marry you.

MISS McCRACKEN: I know nothing of the sort.

LITTLE EVA: Well, if you don't you're a bigger fool than he is.

DOROTHEA: Oh, good heavens.

LITTLE EVA: He means to marry you alright. And I made no secret of my opposition last evening.

MISS McCRACKEN: I'm not sure that matters much.

LITTLE EVA: Oh, I think I hold some sway over my father yet, Miss McCracken.

MISS McCRACKEN: Indeed, he's completely under your control. But you needn't worry, your father and I are no longer friends.

LITTLE EVA: That's not how things looked last evening. And if you have quarreled with him since, it is merely to serve your getting closer. That is the way these things progress.

DOROTHEA: Little Eva, I think that we should mind our own business.

LITTLE EVA: If ever there was a business that's mine to mind, Dorothea, this is it.

MISS McCRACKEN: If you'll excuse me.

LITTLE EVA: You don't want me to have a eunuch do you?

DOROTHEA: Shh. Not here.

MISS McCRACKEN: I don't approve of the idea, no. I don't see why a normal, healthy girl should want a eunuch for company.

LITTLE EVA: Miss McCracken, I am neither normal nor healthy and have as little inclination toward that blessed state as I have chance of achieving it. Still, there are opportunities for me in this world, and to take advantage of them, I require the services of a eunuch.

MISS McCRACKEN: My, but you're a piece of work, aren't you?

LITTLE EVA: Admire me or not, it's best to join me, Miss McCracken. Believe me, you do not want me for an enemy.

MISS McCRACKEN: I don't want anyone for my enemy. Least of all the daughter of a man in whom I ... well, I ... nevertheless, I have scruples about the exploitation of eunuchs, Little Eva.

LITTLE EVA: I'm sure they can be easily got 'round.

MISS McCRACKEN: I'm not so sure. But, if you want to talk with me later—

LITTLE EVA: Later is too late. I have decisions to make, important decisions regarding a social and artistic strategy for the Ball. Mine is a treacherous path, Miss McCracken. One misstep and I am ruined. Now, I am offering you the hand of friendship. Please. Won't you accept it?

(Maitre d' re-enters.)

MAITRE D': I believe you have other customers, Miss.

LITTLE EVA: Oh, leave her alone a moment, won't you?

DOROTHEA: Eva!

LITTLE EVA: Well, he's just a grotty little maitre d', for heaven's sake. Give him some money. Let him go on about his business.

MISS McCRACKEN: Sir, I'm so—

*(Maitre d' exits.)*

MISS McCRACKEN: *(Continued.)* You will not talk to me or my superiors this way in my place of business, Miss Eva. I don't care who you are. I won't permit it.

LITTLE EVA: It is not yours to permit me anything, Miss McCracken. You are not my mother. Not yet.

*(Maitre d' re-enters with coat. Holds it out to Miss McCracken.)*

MAITRE D': Your coat, Miss.

MISS McCRACKEN: I'm fired?

MAITRE D': The apron please. And settle up with the cashier on your way out.

*(Maitre d' exits.)*

DOROTHEA: Oh Miss McCracken. I'm so sorry.

LITTLE EVA: She's too good for this wretched tea shoppe, I'd say.

MISS McCRACKEN: You are a horrid, horrid little girl!

LITTLE EVA: Does this mean we cannot be friends?

MISS McCRACKEN: Go away, please. Just, go away!

LITTLE EVA: Very well. Do stop by the house if you need anything.

MISS McCRACKEN: Oh!

LITTLE EVA: Anything at all.

*(Miss McCracken exits.)*

LITTLE EVA: You're welcome. Come along, Dorothea.

*(Little Eva and Dorothea exit.)*


SCENE SIX

*The Van Huffle parlor. Jonathan enters, taking off his overcoat.*

JONATHAN: Jameson!

*(Jameson enters, saluting.)*

JAMESON: Sir! *(Slapping his own hand down.)* Sorry sir. I'll mend that habit, I will.

JONATHAN: Never mind that now. *(Whispering.)* Where is Gideon?

JAMESON: Who?

JONATHAN: Gideon, Gideon, the eu—my nephew.

JAMESON: Don't have no idea who you're talking about, sir.

JONATHAN: Gideon! Gideon, damnit all! You were to take him upstairs.

JAMESON: Oh, that's secret, that is, sir. I ain't authorized to speak nothin' about it.

JONATHAN: You can speak about it to me, Jameson.

JAMESON: Yer the cap'n, sir. He's restin' quiet.

JONATHAN: And Dorothea and Little Eva? Where are they?

JAMESON: Little Eva's she's at school, sir, and Dorothea's in the kitchen with her duck.

JONATHAN: Duck?

JAMESON: She's cookin' a duck, sir.

JONATHAN: Oh.

JAMESON: For dinner.

JONATHAN: Yes, yes. Alright, then. Quickly. Bring him to me.

JAMESON: The duck?

JONATHAN: No! No! Gideon!

JAMESON: Oh, I don't call him that, sir, no. In my mind I think of him as Mister Pyjamas.

JONATHAN: Mister Pyjamas?

JAMESON: Kind of a code, sir. So as not to give anything away accidental, don't ye know.

JONATHAN: Just go upstairs and fetch him down, please. Quickly now!

JAMESON: He ain't upstairs, sir.

JONATHAN: You said he was in his room.

JAMESON: I said he were restin' quiet, sir. Put him in the root cellar, didn't I.

JONATHAN: The root cellar?

JAMESON: The way he was singin' and carryin' on—

JONATHAN: What is going on here, Jameson?

JAMESON: Why after you left, sir, we was in the pantry tellin' war stories an' drinkin' whiskey—he was. You know I ain't touched a drop since Sergeant Major—

JONATHAN: Yes, yes, I know all that. Go on.

JAMESON: Well, Mister Pyjamas got to wavin' the meat knife about and yellin' about revenge an' all, an' next thing is he's down, sir, right in his own heave ho, and passed out. Don't drink so good for a military man.

JONATHAN: He's a soldier?

JAMESON: He's a cadet, sir. An' a good one too, I reckon. But you'd know better than me about that, bein' yer his uncle.

JONATHAN: Oh, yes, of course. He's a model cadet. And he certainly doesn't belong in the damp basement.

JAMESON: Oh, it ain't so bad, sir. We was bivouacked out to Burnt Dog Cove one winter—

JONATHAN: Yes, yes. Just bring him up here, Jameson.

JAMESON: But—

JONATHAN: Immediately!

JAMESON: Sir! *(Salutes.)* Goddamnit! Ooops. Sorry. Pardon my language, Cap'n. I mean—ah hell, I don't know what I mean. I'm all confangled without my salute, sir!

JONATHAN: Salute! Salute, then! Salute all you want! Just—

JAMESON: Thankee, sir!

JONATHAN: Just, just, just—

JAMESON: *(Saluting.)* Sir!

*(Jameson exits as Dorothea enters opposite.)*

DOROTHEA: Mister Van Huffle, sir.

JONATHAN: Yes, Dorothea. What is it?

DOROTHEA: Well, I just wanted to say I'm awful sorry sir, what happened at the tea shoppe.

JONATHAN: Tea shoppe? What tea shoppe?

DOROTHEA: I told her it was wrong to go, but Little Eva—

JONATHAN: Little Eva went to Miss McCracken's tea shoppe?

DOROTHEA: Yes sir.

JONATHAN: Oh, my God.

DOROTHEA: And she got the poor woman fired from her job!

JONATHAN: Oh, that wretched girl!

DOROTHEA: She's horrible, sir. I coulda died with the mortification of it.

JONATHAN: Actually, actually, this may work out for the best, Dorothea. You see, I've just returned from the Vollybond.

DOROTHEA: You sir? In the Vollybond?

JONATHAN: I had a desperate errand there, as you may well imagine.

DOROTHEA: Can't imagine you in the Vollybond 't all, sir.

JONATHAN: Nor can I. Normally. And I quite failed in my mission, but I did find this. *(Shows Dorothea a ring.)*

DOROTHEA: Oh, it's beautiful, sir.

JONATHAN: I was approached by a one-eyed peddler gifted with a second sight, it seems.

DOROTHEA: How so, sir?

JONATHAN: Well, now that Miss McCracken has no job of work, she has every reason to accept my proposal of marriage.

DOROTHEA: Oh.

JONATHAN: What? Is something the matter?

DOROTHEA: No sir, no, not a bit of it. It's just—

JONATHAN: Go ahead, Dorothea. You may speak freely.

DOROTHEA: Well sir, it's just that Miss McCracken, nice as she is, pretty as she is—

JONATHAN: Is not a lady?

DOROTHEA: No sir, she's ... not.

JONATHAN: Well, thank heaven, I say.

DOROTHEA: Well sir, I can get used to that and help her, but I just think there's going to be no end of trouble with her and Little Eva over the eunuchs.

*(A knock at the door.)*

JONATHAN: Speaking of which.

JAMESON: *(Off.)* Sir!

JONATHAN: *(Calling off.)* Bring him in Jameson.

*(Jameson enters with Gideon, who is drunk and barefoot.)*

JAMESON: Has her been sworn to silence sir?

JONATHAN: Just bring him in.

JAMESON: Yes, sir!

DOROTHEA: Oh my heavens! The smell of him!

JONATHAN: That will be all, Jameson.

JAMESON: He ain't too steady on his pins yet, sir.

JONATHAN: Then let him sit.

JAMESON: He ain't too clean, neither.

JONATHAN: Then let him sit on the floor.

*(Jameson lowers Gideon to the floor.)*

JAMESON: Had to leave his footwear to soak in the sink, sir.

GIDEON: Ohhhh.

JAMESON: Steady on there Mister Pyjamas.

JONATHAN: Thank you, Jameson.

JAMESON: D'you know this fella knows every battle of every campaign me and my regiment ever fought in?

JONATHAN: Thank you, Jameson!

JAMESON: An' every other regiment and naval battles, too?

JONATHAN: Go away!

JAMESON: *(Saluting.)* Sir!

> *(Jameson exits. Gideon lies down.)*

DOROTHEA: Excuse me sayin' this, but I didn't know better sir, I'd say you gone and brung a eunuch in the house.

JONATHAN: That is exactly what I've done, Dorothea.

DOROTHEA: Oh sir, I knew you'd come 'round!

JONATHAN: I have not come round to anything. I intend to marry Miss McCracken, and Miss McCracken cannot abide the idea of eunuchs. Ergo, there will be no eunuchs in this house when next she comes. If she comes.

DOROTHEA: Oh, but once he's sobered up and preening, sir, he'll be the making of Little Eva and this household, just you wait and see.

JONATHAN: Little Eva is to know nothing of this, Dorothea.

DOROTHEA: Oh.

JONATHAN: Now bring some coffee, please.

DOROTHEA: Very good, sir, but—

JONATHAN:: Strong, black coffee and right away.

> *(Dorothea exits.)*

JONATHAN: Gideon. Gideon?

GIDEON: *(Groans.)*

JONATHAN: Wake up, now. Wake up. Gideon! We must discuss your situation here.

GIDEON: Father?

JONATHAN: What?

GIDEON: Oh Father, is that you?

JONATHAN: I am not your father.

> *(Dorothea re-enters with coffee.)*

DOROTHEA: Here's the coffee, sir.

JONATHAN: Thank you, Dorothea. And draw him a bath, please.

DOROTHEA: Yes sir.

> *(Dorothea exits.)*

JONATHAN: Gideon? Gideon?

> *(Jameson enters with slippers.)*

JAMESON: Sir!

JONATHAN: *(Startled.)* Ah!

JAMESON: I brought thy nephew down some slippies.

JONATHAN: Not now, Jameson.

JAMESON: *(Putting slippers down.)* Puked all over yer own footgear, didn't ye Mister Pyjamas?

JONATHAN: Jameson, please! I am trying to talk with Gideon.

JAMESON: Better hurry up, sir.

JONATHAN: Why so?

JAMESON: 'Cause of Miss Eva's comin' up the stair.

JONATHAN: You said she was at school!

JAMESON: Well, she was.

JONATHAN: Oh my God! Oh my God! Get him, get him up!

JAMESON: Yes sir.

    *(Jameson picks up Gideon.)*

GIDEON: Ohhhh.

JONATHAN: Take him. Put him—

LITTLE EVA: *(Off.)* Father! Father!

JONATHAN: Give him to me!

    *(Jonathan exits, dragging Gideon. Little Eva enters.)*

LITTLE EVA: *(Looking about.)* Where is my father, Jameson?

JAMESON: I don't know, Miss. He was just here talkin' to somebody.

LITTLE EVA: Talking to whom?

JAMESON: Oh, just some man. Businessman it were.

LITTLE EVA: Don't be silly. My father knows nothing of business. *(Calling out.)* Father!

JAMESON: Musta gone downtown, I guess.

LITTLE EVA: *(Noticing overcoat.)* Without his coat? What's that smell?

JAMESON: *(Seeing coffee cup.)* Coffee?

LITTLE EVA: Like vomit or something. And what are those doing there?

JAMESON: Which is that, Miss?

LITTLE EVA: On the floor, there.

JAMESON: Oh. Them are slippies.

LITTLE EVA: I can see that. Whose are they? What are they doing in here?

JAMESON: They're, uh, they're for my dog.

LITTLE EVA: Your dog?

JAMESON: For to chew on, yeah.

LITTLE EVA: You haven't any dog.

JAMESON: Always wanted one, didn't I? No, it's yer father got a dog, is what it is.

LITTLE EVA: What?

JAMESON: Yes he did, Miss Eva, and just for you.

LITTLE EVA: Oh, no!

JAMESON: A surprise, yep. Please don't tell I told ye.

LITTLE EVA: But, I don't want a dog!

JAMESON: Ohh, you'll like this one. Yes, you will. He's such a handsome little doggie, isn't he, Miss, with a bright little tail and big brown spots, an' tricks he does, as well.

LITTLE EVA: Tricks?

JAMESON: He can sing and dance and drink the whiskey, too.

LITTLE EVA: I don't believe you. What's his name?

JAMESON: His name?

LITTLE EVA: I thought so. There is no dog.

JAMESON: Is too. He's called Mister Pyjamas.

LITTLE EVA: Mister—

JAMESON: Pyjamas, yep. *(Holding slippers up.)* And these are for to chew on, so that he don't chew the—

LITTLE EVA: Ugh! Take those nasty things away!

JAMESON: Righty oh.

*(Jameson exits with slippers. Jonathan enters opposite.)*

JONATHAN: Little Eva.

LITTLE EVA: Oh Father, where were you?

JONATHAN: Never mind about me. You're supposed to be in school, young lady.

LITTLE EVA: Oh Daddy, I couldn't stay. That horrible Meenie Pomeroy's father has rented the ballroom at the Belvedere for her rehearsals.

JONATHAN: The entire thing?

LITTLE EVA: Well of course. Do you think she'd be content with half? The little trollop.

JONATHAN: Eva!

LITTLE EVA: Meenie Pomeroy is disgusting Father. So disgusting. And ugly and stupid and not one person likes her except Ernald Percher and he's as ugly and stupid as she.

JONATHAN: Meenie Pomeroy is perfectly—

LITTLE EVA: Now the Regal Room is still available, Father. And if you act immediately you can secure it for me.

JONATHAN: I am not going to rent you the Regal, Eva.

LITTLE EVA: *(Cries.)* But why?

JONATHAN: Why? Because it's ridiculous! Have you no idea of the cost of things?

LITTLE EVA: You cannot afford it, then?

JONATHAN: Of course I can afford it. That is hardly the point.

LITTLE EVA: What is the point, then, to deny me for the sake of denying me?

JONATHAN: To illustrate a moral lesson, Little Eva.

LITTLE EVA: Oh you make me sick! Earnestly sick!

JONATHAN: Well I'm sorry for that, but if that is what it takes then I must pay the price of your displeasure.

LITTLE EVA: Oh, you have not begun to feel the sting of my displeasure. I will find the money myself.

JONATHAN: You are welcome to try.

LITTLE EVA: I will sell my things. My dresses. My baubles. My books. My body, if necessary.

JONATHAN: Eva!

LITTLE EVA: A common whore in Sugar Alley!

JONATHAN: Don't you dare say such a thing. Don't you dare to even think it.

LITTLE EVA: Then give me what I want!

JONATHAN: Eva, please. Give my way a try. There will be rewards aplenty, I promise you.

LITTLE EVA: Like Mister Pyjamas, I suppose.

JONATHAN: What?

LITTLE EVA: Jameson told me all about him.

JONATHAN: He didn't!

LITTLE EVA: Of course he did.

JONATHAN: Oh that fool, that idiotic fool!

LITTLE EVA: Indeed.

JONATHAN: Well, the secret's out, I suppose.

LITTLE EVA: Yes it is, and I don't want him, Father.

JONATHAN: You—you don't want him?

LITTLE EVA: No. What in the world would I do with him?

JONATHAN: But you've been begging me for a eunuch for weeks and weeks!

LITTLE EVA: A what?

JONATHAN: Making my life miserable! Threatening my very happiness! And now you don't want him?

LITTLE EVA: A eunuch?

JONATHAN: Yes, and a nice one, too.

LITTLE EVA: But, Jameson said it was a dog!

JONATHAN: A dog?

LITTLE EVA: *(Throwing her arms around Jonathan.)* Oh, Daddy! Such a good, good daddy you are! The very best daddy in the world to Little Eva!

JONATHAN: Stop, Eva! Heavens!

LITTLE EVA: Where is he, Father? I must see him!

JONATHAN: Now, now.

LITTLE EVA: Immediately, please!

JONATHAN: Dorothea's giving him a little cleanup in the kitchen.

*(Little Eva starts for the door just as Gideon enters running from Dorothea.)*

LITTLE EVA: *(Startled.)* Ah!

GIDEON: *(Startled.)* Ah!

*(Gideon turns. Dorothea grabs him.)*

DOROTHEA: Gotcha!

GIDEON: Let me go, you! Let me go!

JONATHAN: It's alright, Dorothea. It's alright. Little Eva, meet your Gideon.

LITTLE EVA: Gideon?

*(Little Eva approaches Gideon shyly, examines him, then runs behind her father.)*

LITTLE EVA: Oh, Father!

JONATHAN: What?

LITTLE EVA: Oh!

JONATHAN: What's the matter, Little Eva? You don't like him?

LITTLE EVA: *(Sings.)*

HE'S PERFECT, PERFECT, PERFECTLY PERFECT
PERFECT BEYOND PERFECT DREAM
PERFECT, PERFECT, PERFECTLY PERFECT
WONDERFUL WONDER SUPREME

MORE THAN I EVER EXPECTED
BETTER BY FAR THAN THE BEST
I DOUBTED NOW I STAND CORRECTED
I'M COMPLETELY ENTIRELY IMPRESSED

BRILLIANT, BRILLIANT, BRILLIANTLY BRILLIANT
BRILLIANT BEYOND BRILLIANT CHOICE
SO SPLENDID AND SPLENDID AND SPLENDIDLY SPLENDID
OH JOY AND MORE JOY AND REJOICE

*(A knock at the door. Jameson enters, saluting.)*

JAMESON: Sir!

*(Miss McCracken enters.)*

JONATHAN: Miss McCracken?

JAMESON: Miss McCracken's here!

LITTLE EVA: Apparently.

*(Jameson and Dorothea exit.)*

JONATHAN: Uh, what, what, what—

MISS McCRACKEN: Is something wrong, Jonathan?

JONATHAN: No. Not. Nothing. No.

MISS McCRACKEN: Should I not have come by unannounced?

JONATHAN: *(Covers Gideon with overcoat.)* No, no. Please.

MISS McCRACKEN: I know it's not what's done.

JONATHAN: No, I want to see you. Very much, in fact.

LITTLE EVA: *(Taking Gideon by the hand.)* If you'll excuse us, please.

JONATHAN: Yes, of course.

MISS McCRACKEN: Just a moment, Eva.

LITTLE EVA: I'm sure you and my father have a great deal to talk about, Miss McCracken.

MISS McCRACKEN: I came to talk to both of you, actually.

LITTLE EVA: I'd love to chat, really, but I'm rather busy as you can see.

MISS McCRACKEN: Your daughter came to see me today, Jonathan.

LITTLE EVA: I was trying to help.

MISS McCRACKEN: Your rich, spoiled daughter came into my place of employment and had me sacked.

JONATHAN: Oh, I'm terribly sorry.

MISS McCRACKEN: That's all well and good, but what are you going to do about it?

JONATHAN: Well—

MISS McCRACKEN: That was my living, Jonathan, and my schooling as well.

LITTLE EVA: Give her some money Father, and send her away.

MISS McCRACKEN: That's your answer to everything isn't it?

LITTLE EVA: It's what you want, isn't it?

MISS McCRACKEN: I want satisfaction.

LITTLE EVA: And I'm sure you'll get it. Come along, Gideon.

MISS McCRACKEN: No, I'd like your friend to hear this.

LITTLE EVA: He's not my friend.

JONATHAN: No, Gideon, Gideon is, Gideon is our visitor. He's my brother's wife.

MISS McCRACKEN: Wife?

JONATHAN: Boy. My brother's boy.

MISS McCRACKEN: What brother? What are you saying?

JONATHAN: Nothing! Nothing! I'm saying nothing! Can't I have a brother? A black sheep? He's an opium, alright! A mental person I choose not to talk about!

LITTLE EVA: He's a eunuch, Miss McCracken.

MISS McCRACKEN: Your brother?

JONATHAN: Yes! There it is! The secret's out! Take Gideon upstairs, please, Little Eva, while I explain to Miss McCracken.

LITTLE EVA: Very well, Father.

*(Little Eva and Gideon exit.)*

MISS McCRACKEN: I'm very confused, Jonathan.

JONATHAN: And so am I. It's been a wretched night and day since I've seen you, Miss McCracken.

MISS McCRACKEN: But, I don't understand. How could your brother be a eunuch?

JONATHAN: Well, he, he was, uh, he was born that way. A congenital eunuch, yes.

MISS McCRACKEN: But he has a son.

JONATHAN: Yes, yes, yes, yes he does, yes, but that's not his son, you see, because Gideon, after all, is, is—*my* son.

MISS McCRACKEN: You have a son?

JONATHAN: Oh, it's a long and tangled tale, Miss McCracken. And one that I'm hardly proud of, as you can well imagine.

MISS McCRACKEN: Nonetheless, I should like to hear it.

JONATHAN: But, it all happened so long ago. I can barely remember. A youthful indiscretion.

MISS McCRACKEN: But that's so irresponsible, Jonathan!

JONATHAN: But I am taking responsibility now, Miss McCracken. That is why Gideon is here with us. My brother—my brother has died, you see.

MISS McCRACKEN: Died?

JONATHAN: One moment he's there. The next he's not. So sudden, these things.

MISS McCRACKEN: Oh, I'm so sorry, Jonathan.

JONATHAN: It was a blessing, given his infirmity, and it allows me to, to, to, well, to take Gideon in, do the right thing and claim him for my own at last.

MISS McCRACKEN: Oh, but that's wonderful, Johnny.

JONATHAN: Johnny! You called me Johnny!

MISS McCRACKEN: It was—I certainly did not mean to.

JONATHAN: But you did! You did! Oh, this makes me so happy! I cannot tell you!

MISS McCRACKEN: Well, I'm fond of you, truly I am, though for the life of me I don't know why.

JONATHAN: Fond?

MISS McCRACKEN: Well, more than fond, but that's enough for now.

JONATHAN: Oh, Miss McCracken, I want to spend my life with you!

MISS McCRACKEN: What?

JONATHAN: And if you won't have me, I swear I will die! We will both die! And it will be entirely your fault!

MISS McCRACKEN: Oh Jonathan, what are you talking about?

JONATHAN: *(Shows her the ring.)* This!

MISS McCRACKEN: Oh.

JONATHAN: I was passing through the Vollybond—

MISS McCRACKEN: The Vollybond!

JONATHAN: Entirely by accident. I'd taken a wrong turning in my torment and, and, and, confusion, and suddenly, there he is, a one-eyed man, looking, staring directly, intently, right at me, and holding out this ring. Suddenly I knew my mind, knew that I had grasped the solution to my problems. And now to your, uh, employment problems. Why to all our problems. And the answer is bliss!

MISS McCRACKEN: I wish it were so easy.

JONATHAN: Can I slip it on your finger?

MISS McCRACKEN: No, no.

JONATHAN: Please, just—

MISS McCRACKEN: Jonathan—

JONATHAN: Johnny, please.

MISS McCRACKEN: There are unwholesome things at work here in this house. I know it. I can feel it.

JONATHAN: *(Kneeling.)* I can only hope—

MISS McCRACKEN: Get up Jonathan, please.

JONATHAN: I can only pray that you will have the fortitude and patience to bear with both me and my daughter—and my new son. To come into our home and balance the scale of our moral economy. To love us unto health and happiness. For without you, I fear none of us has a chance.

MISS McCRACKEN: Oh, what can I say?

JONATHAN: You can say yes.

MISS McCRACKEN: But this eunuch business.

JONATHAN: Eunuch? What eunuch? There is no eunuch! There will be no eunuchs!

MISS McCRACKEN: Can you promise me that?

JONATHAN: I can promise you anything! As I can promise that this ring shall be a perfect fit.

MISS McCRACKEN: And if it is not?

JONATHAN: Then we are not meant for each other.

(*Beat. Miss McCracken extends her hand. Jonathan slips the ring upon her finger.*)

MISS McCRACKEN: Oh!

JONATHAN: (*Sings, to audience.*)
IT FITS
IT FITS
BEHOLD THE WEDDING BAND
IT FITS UPON THE FINGER
ON THE FINGER OF THE HAND
THE HAND THAT I HAVE LIED FOR
THE HAND THAT I DESIRE
THE HAND THAT MAKES MY HEART BEAT
AND SETS MY LOINS AFIRE

MISS McCRACKEN: (*Sings, to audience.*)
IT FITS
IT FITS
BEHOLD THE WEDDING BAND
IT FITS UPON MY FINGER
LIKE THE LAW UPON THE LAND
THE LAW THAT SNIFFS THE TRUTH OUT
THAT JUSTICE MAY BE DONE
THE LAW THAT BATTLES EVIL
UNTIL THE BATTLE'S WON

JONATHAN / MISS McCRACKEN: (*Sing to audience.*)
THE LIAR AND THE LAWYER
OH, IT WAS EVER THUS
THE ESSENCE OF ATTRACTION
THE CAUSE OF ALL THE FUSS

BUT EACH ONE CRAVES THE OTHER
THAT MUCH WE ALL KNOW
FOR OTHERWISE OUR STORY
WOULD HAVE NOWHERE TO GO

END OF ACT ONE

# ACT TWO
SCENE ONE

*A stockbroker's office. Martin and Jonathan.*

JONATHAN: Well, yes, dreadfully happy, Martin, except that Miss McCracken keeps asking when I expect to adopt this boy.

MARTIN: Oh, that's rich, that's really rich.

JONATHAN: It's not funny, Martin. He's not a boy, he's a eunuch; and I'm in torment about all of this.

MARTIN: You're in torment for the moment, Jonathan, but look upon the bright side of things why don't you?

JONATHAN: For example.

MARTIN: Well, your Versatile is doing quite well.

JONATHAN: My what?

MARTIN: Up fifty-six and an eighth; and up is good, remember?

JONATHAN: As if that mattered.

MARTIN: Gather in your good news where and while ye may, Jonathan.

JONATHAN: Oh, call me Johnny, please.

MARTIN: But I thought that your beloved—

JONATHAN: Miss McCracken prefers Jonathan, yes, but I cannot get the hang of it, Martin.

MARTIN: The bloom is off the rose, I take it?

JONATHAN: Not at all, no. I am more in love with Miss McCracken than ever. It's just that, well, I find the moral obligations associated with always being a Jonathan oppressive upon occasion.

MARTIN: I'm not surprised.

JONATHAN: All I mean to say, Martin, is that Miss McCracken, relieved from the pressures of her employment at the tea shoppe, has begun asking rather a lot of questions.

MARTIN: Questions? What questions?

JONATHAN: Speaking of which, may I ask you something, Martin, just between ourselves?

MARTIN: Of course.

JONATHAN: Something that's been bothering me in all this. Do you know of any person, or organization, called Xerxes?

MARTIN: (Beat.) Xerxes?

JONATHAN: Yes.

MARTIN: Sounds like a laundry soap.

JONATHAN: I don't know what it is.

MARTIN: Never heard of it. Is this what Miss McCracken asked about?

JONATHAN: You see, this eunuch came to Little Eva as a gift from Xerxes.

MARTIN: Don't know anything about any Xerxes. Heavens.

JONATHAN: Anyway, I'm throwing a luncheon party for Miss McCracken and myself at the Marmadon this afternoon.

MARTIN: I thought restaurants like the Marmadon were not Miss McCracken's preferred milieu.

JONATHAN: Well, they're not, of course, but we are engaged to be married and these are my friends.

MARTIN: Johnny, are you certain this is wise?

JONATHAN: Why, whatever do you mean?

MARTIN: Only that these mixed marriages are so seldom successful in the long run. Why don't you just take a little love nest in the Vollybond and make certain of each other before you leap into the abyss?

JONATHAN: I have leapt into the abyss already in proposing to Miss McCracken, Martin, and will be happy in her clam to be—happy *as* a clam in her—Godfrey! Most *content* with her, I mean to say.

MARTIN: I see.

JONATHAN: No, my only problem is what to do about this blessed eunuch, though he seems a pleasant enough little fellow.

MARTIN: He and Little Eva getting on then, are they?

JONATHAN: She seems quite taken with him.

MARTIN: Oh, I'm so pleased.

JONATHAN: He was a bit morose at first, but—

MARTIN: A little difficulty in accepting his reduced status, I would imagine.

JONATHAN: Yes, but he's been out and about lately, getting to know some of the more established eunuchs in the neighborhood.

MARTIN: Good, good.

JONATHAN: They gather evenings by the river, exchanging gossip for and about their mistresses; singing their laments. Quite haunting, actually. Anyway, it would appear he's thrown himself completely behind Little Eva's aspiration to be queen of the Ball.

MARTIN: Wonderful.

JONATHAN: Always plotting one thing and another, the two of them. I've never seen Little Eva so happy.

MARTIN: It's a wonderful thing for a girl, Johnny. Which is why I must recommend another round of Versatile.

JONATHAN: More Versatile, eh?

MARTIN: For her future, yes.

JONATHAN: Perhaps I might see a prospectus then?

MARTIN: A prospectus? He wants to see a prospectus?

JONATHAN: I know it's an absurd precaution, Martin, but I feel I should.

MARTIN: And I would show it to you at once if I had one, Johnny, but Versatile has been so successful of late they are a bit behind in the printing of prospecti.

JONATHAN: Is that regular?

MARTIN: Entirely so, when you're making money hand over fist.

JONATHAN: Well … in for a penny in for a pound, I suppose.

MARTIN: Good. Shall we say a thousand?

JONATHAN: Up fifty-six and a what, an eighth, did you say?

MARTIN: You remembered!

JONATHAN: Ten thousand, then!

MARTIN: Ahoy! There's the backbone showing! *(Presenting document.)*

JONATHAN: *(Signing.)* Must do *something*, musn't I?

MARTIN: You must and you have, and may I say, you'll not regret it.

JONATHAN: I will if Miss McCracken finds out about it before we're well and truly wed.

MARTIN: And well and truly provided for, thanks to you taking your financial responsibilities seriously, sir.

JONATHAN: Isn't it strange, the both of you wanting so much that I should take this life more seriously.

MARTIN: That's all I've ever wanted for you, Johnny, which is why I—no, I shouldn't say it.

JONATHAN: What, Martin?

MARTIN: Oh Johnny, I have learnt from long and painful experience never to insert myself between my friends and their infatuations, but it's so painful for me to sit here knowing that—no, I mustn't.

JONATHAN: Say it out, Martin, please.

MARTIN: Very well, then. Johnny, just how well do you know this Miss McCracken?

JONATHAN: How well do I know her?

(*Sings.*) I'VE KNOWN HER ALL MY LIFE
HAVEN'T I?
WE WERE CHILDREN ON THE BEACH
WEREN'T WE?
WEARING ONLY SUN AND SAND
BARING ALL OUR SECRETS AND
SHARING IN A SECRET WONDERLAND

(*Speaks.*) I know her.

MARTIN: Then you know that she is a member of the Freudian Circle?

JONATHAN: The what?

MARTIN: I thought not.

JONATHAN: What on earth is the Freudian Circle?

MARTIN: I suggest you ask your intended.

JONATHAN: But, how do you know of her involvement in this, this—

MARTIN: The University is a favored client, Johnny, and the Chancellor a particular friend. He regards these Freudians as a dangerous and pernicious influence and their presence on his campus as a blight upon University life. And that is all that I will say upon the matter.

JONATHAN: But Martin, you cannot keep me in the dark as to the intentions of this terrible—

MARTIN: Ignorance, in this case, is your best defense, believe me, Johnny. You do not want to know the things they talk about. And in mixed company!

JONATHAN: But men and women discussing things together, this is the modern way, after all.

MARTIN: Not when men and women together is the very subject of their discourse!

JONATHAN: What?

MARTIN: And men and men! And women and women! And both with the animals, and in the most heinous postures imaginable!

JONATHAN: Stop, Martin!

MARTIN: As I understand it from the Chancellor. And God knows what they get up to in this infernal Circle when they stop talking!

JONATHAN: Stop! Stop it! You are terrifying me!

MARTIN: Believe me, I—

JONATHAN: No, no, you—

MARTIN: Your happiness is—

JONATHAN: Happiness? What happiness could I possibly enjoy if this were true? Freudian Circle! Oh, Martin! It cannot, must not be true!

MARTIN: Johnny, don't take my word for it, please. Ask your Miss McCracken if what you hear is true. Perhaps the Chancellor is mistaken in some way. And if he is not, perhaps she will renounce her participation in this Circle when confronted with the heat and light of your most passionate disgust.

JONATHAN: Of course she will.

MARTIN: Before the police become involved.

JONATHAN: The police!

MARTIN: Your waitress and her Circle are distributing pamphlets among the populace calling for the end of castration and the overthrow of the Patriarch!

JONATHAN: What?

MARTIN: Depicting our Patriarch in crude cartoons as a drooling monster with a knife in one hand and a sack of bloody testicles in the other!

JONATHAN: Miss McCracken?

MARTIN: Oh, you really know how to pick 'em, Johnny.

JONATHAN: Oh, I must confront her, Martin! And at once!

MARTIN: I am so sorry, Johnny.

JONATHAN: No, no, Martin.

MARTIN: To have allowed you to drag this news from me.

JONATHAN: You have only done your duty as my friend and advisor.

MARTIN: Good luck to you, sir.

JONATHAN: Good day, Martin. And thank you.

(Jonathan exits.)

MARTIN: (Sings.)
VERSATILE VERSATILE VERSATILE
VERSATILE INDUSTRIES


SCENE TWO

The Van Huffle parlor. Little Eva and Gideon enter, dancing, Little Eva somewhat awkwardly.

GIDEON: Step, two three, step, two three, (She steps on his foot.) ouch, two three, step, two three. I bow to your curtsey, and back two three. Wait.

No, back two three, up two three, half to the left—my left—I salute and you … curtsey, and half to the left and then swallow the hole, and we stagger, stagger, dip, dip, recede—

LITTLE EVA: No!

GIDEON: Yes, we recede here before the promenade.

LITTLE EVA: We do not recede! We turn and dip toward one another at this point, and then I turn and raise my fan to the judges, and then we recede to begin the promenade.

GIDEON: Not this year.

LITTLE EVA: What do you mean?

GIDEON: I have it upon reliable authority that the rules regarding the Pretorian Waltz are to be rigorously enforced as written.

LITTLE EVA: According to whom?

GIDEON: I got it from Miss Priscilla's eunuch.

LITTLE EVA: Phooey! You cannot trust him! Priscilla Worthington would like nothing better than to see me ruined by a misstep.

GIDEON: Her eunuch has shown particular friendship for me. I would entrust him with my life and yours.

LITTLE EVA: And how did he find this out?

GIDEON: He is friendly with Mrs. Throckmorton's steward, who overheard it while serving his lady's luncheon meeting with the judges.

LITTLE EVA: I see. Let's do it again, then.

GIDEON: There's something we need to discuss.

LITTLE EVA: But I haven't got it right, yet.

GIDEON: You haven't got an escort yet, either.

LITTLE EVA: I don't wish to talk about it.

GIDEON: I may have some news on that front.

LITTLE EVA: What? Who?

GIDEON: Well, it isn't certain yet, but—

LITTLE EVA: Tell me, tell me, Gideon! Is it to be Jocko Malloway? Oh, do let it be Jocko!

GIDEON: Not Jocko, no, but, the eunuch with the Percher family—

LITTLE EVA: Ernald Percher?

GIDEON: Titi's brother, yes.

LITTLE EVA: Oh, no!

GIDEON: Master Percher has his drawbacks, but—

LITTLE EVA: Drawbacks! He is hideous! Hideous! *(Weeps.)* Oh, my God! Ernald Percher! I cannot go to the Ball with him! You must find me someone else!

GIDEON: But everyone else is taken.

LITTLE EVA: What about the Appleby boy.

GIDEON: Taken.

LITTLE EVA: And Zachery Trent-Locken? He can be amusing, certainly.

GIDEON: Going with Miss Hillary Lamb.

LITTLE EVA: The second tier, then. Deter Percy? Egan Archer?

GIDEON: There is very little time, Little Eva. I suggest that you settle upon Master Percher and make do.

LITTLE EVA: I will die first, or, or, or—

GIDEON: Or what?

LITTLE EVA: Or I will go alone!

GIDEON: I'm afraid there is no precedent for that.

LITTLE EVA: Then I will set one!

GIDEON: Daring idea, yes. General Pilates was certainly of that school. He sent his horsemen in advance of his bowmen at the Battle of Thermadon to stunning effect.

LITTLE EVA: Well, there you are.

GIDEON: The stunning effect being that his army was annihilated.

LITTLE EVA: *(Weeping.)* Oh, my God!

GIDEON: Do you want to address the problem or do you want to weep?

LITTLE EVA: But what can I do?

GIDEON: Little Eva, how is Ernald Percher viewed in this community?

LITTLE EVA: As a stupid, ugly clown!

GIDEON: Very well, and how are *you* perceived in the community?

LITTLE EVA: Who cares how I'm perceived? I'm better than they are and they know it. And once the judges are convinced, my perfection will be certified, and I will be presented to the Patriarch as his perfect Junior Miss to receive his blessing, and be seated at his table at the feast, and have my portrait hung in the Gallery of Girls, and have my story told forever and ever throughout the land, and be given whatever I want.

GIDEON: Which is ... what?

LITTLE EVA: None of your business, eunuch. Now get out there and find me someone suitable.

GIDEON: I cannot.

LITTLE EVA: You will not.

GIDEON: There is no one but Master Percher and even he has expressed reservations.

LITTLE EVA: Liar!

GIDEON: I assure you –

LITTLE EVA: You're a liar! *(Calls off.)* Jameson! Jameson!

*(Jameson enters and salutes.)*

JAMESON: Miss!

LITTLE EVA: Take this lying eunuch to the basement and give it a beating.

JAMESON: Eunuch? Which eunuch?

LITTLE EVA: This eunuch, fool!

JAMESON: Why, this ain't no eunuch, Miss; that's your cousin Gideon. He'll be mad at ye, ye call him eunuch.

LITTLE EVA: He is not my cousin. He is my eunuch. And you are insane. Take him to the cellar and flog his skin off!

JAMESON: But, how can he be eunuch when your daddy says Gideon were his brother's boy, come to town to see the sights. No, t'was *I* said that, come to think on it. Why *did* ye come down from the country, Master Gideon?

GIDEON: I didn't, Jameson. I came from the Vollybond.

JAMESON: But—but yer a cadet!

GIDEON: I *was* a cadet. I was many things, once upon a time, and wanted to be more. Now, I am but one thing, and that one thing, as far as you or any-one else is concerned, is eunuch.

JAMESON: No, don't say it! I can't believe! Won't believe it! I know a eunuch when I see it, an' I don't see it!

LITTLE EVA: Show him, Gideon.

*(Gideon takes the wooden box from his pocket, opens it and shows it to Jameson.)*

JAMESON: Ahhhhh, it's a eunuch! A eunuch!

LITTLE EVA: And a nasty, disobedient eunuch at that. Take him down, Jameson.

JAMESON: No sir, no Miss, I ain't touchin' eunuchs.

LITTLE EVA: What?

JAMESON: Not fer all the guns an' ammo in the world! *(To Gideon.)* An' I take back the drinks I give ye, liar! An' all them oaths we swore? I take mine back as well! For ye've deceived me in my heart of hearts, my regiment an' pride.

GIDEON: I'm sorry, for I enjoyed your company, Jameson.

JAMESON: An' I liked ye too, but ye turned eunuch now, and that I can't abide.

GIDEON: So, I should take you off my list, then?

JAMESON: What list is that, yer eunuch lovers list?

GIDEON: The list for Miss Eva's Honor Guard.

JAMESON: Honor Guard?

LITTLE EVA: What Honor Guard?

GIDEON: I'm looking for a model soldier, someone who'd look smart in a uniform.

JAMESON: You mean regulation?

GIDEON: Cross piniomed with brass foliards.

JAMESON: Like the officers have!

GIDEON: Something like, only a bit fancier. But I can understand your not wanting to participate.

JAMESON: Hold on! Hold on, now! I didn't know about no Honor Guard!

LITTLE EVA: Nor did I! An Honor Guard!

GIDEON: The Guard is not for you, per se, Little Eva. It's for the character that you would personify in your display, if you choose; a character from history, a famous general.

JAMESON: A soldier man?

GIDEON: Joan of Arc.

JAMESON: Joan o' who?

LITTLE EVA: Be quiet, Jameson. Continue, please.

GIDEON: I suggest you re-enact a scene from Joan's life by means of a tableaux vivant or pantomime; specifically, the scene in which Joan is brought to court to meet the dauphin and future king, a boy her own age, whom she's never before seen.

JAMESON: Would I get to kill somebody?

LITTLE EVA: Jameson!

JAMESON: Yes'm.

GIDEON: In order to fool the Maid, and amuse the dauphin, his courtiers put a soldier—Jameson, say—on the throne, dressed as the dauphin and wearing the crown of France, while the real dauphin hides in the crowd, watching. Joan enters, and ignoring the imposter on the throne, goes straight to the dauphin and kneels before him.

JAMESON: So, I'd be Honor Guard an' dauphin, both?

GIDEON: If you can bring yourself to take orders from a eunuch.

JAMESON: Oh, I don't know. Sergeant Major wouldn't like it, no. But Sergeant Major he ain't here to guide me in civilian ways. Hm. If ye was maybe to keep yer distance say, an' not be openin' that box at me, nor flauntin' yer nasty scar about, I reckon I might maybe can stand it.

GIDEON: What a brave fellow.

JAMESON: I were in the war!

LITTLE EVA: We know all that.

JAMESON: I were wounded at Philmore's Grove!

LITTLE EVA: I don't care about the stupid war, Jameson! I care about the Ball! Do you want the uniform or not?

JAMESON: *(Beat.)* I got to have it!

LITTLE EVA: Very well, it's yours.

JAMESON: But, how do Honor Guards salute?

GIDEON: Like so. *(Demonstrates.)*

JAMESON: Ohhhh, uh huh. I best go and practice. *(Salutes.)* Sir! *(Salutes.)* Miss! *(Jameson exits.)*

LITTLE EVA: Alright then, who was this Joan of Arc?

GIDEON: She was a soldier saint, who drove the English out of France.

LITTLE EVA: She was triumphant, then.

GIDEON: She was burnt.

LITTLE EVA: Burnt?

GIDEON: At the stake, yes.

LITTLE EVA: Well, that's the scene we should do, for heaven's sake!

GIDEON: I would like for you to be distinguished for your restraint, Eva.

LITTLE EVA: I wish to suffer and be burnt at the stake!

GIDEON: I strongly suggest the recognition scene.

LITTLE EVA: I wouldn't get to shriek or scream or rend my garments or exhort my troops or anything!

GIDEON: Exactly.

LITTLE EVA: But, all the other girls—

GIDEON: I've heard what the other girls do. Their eunuchs are bored to death.

LITTLE EVA: I wish to be burnt at the stake, Gideon.

GIDEON: Very well.

LITTLE EVA: It will be magnificent. You will see to the arrangements.

GIDEON: And do you wish me to approach the Percher family?

LITTLE EVA: No. I will not go to the Ball with Ernald Percher.

GIDEON: Then who will be your escort?

LITTLE EVA: You will.

GIDEON: Me?

LITTLE EVA: You can dance.

GIDEON: I'm your eunuch, Little Eva.

LITTLE EVA: You are my cousin from the country, and I will go with you and no one else but you. Even if my horsemen are all killed and my army annihilated.

GIDEON: I'll consider it.

LITTLE EVA: You will do it. Or you will be put down. And don't imagine that I wouldn't see it done.

GIDEON: And don't imagine that I wouldn't find it welcome.

LITTLE EVA: *(Beat.)* Still, we must practice.

GIDEON: Very well.

*(Little Eva and Gideon exit, dancing.)*

GIDEON: Step, two three, step, two three, step, two three, step, two three.


SCENE THREE

*The Marmadon, a restaurant. Jonathan, Miss McCracken, Henderson and Shotworthy, at an otherwise empty table. Beat.*

HENDERSON: Rather quiet, isn't it?

SHOTWORTHY: Yes. Like election day at the polls the time you stood for … what was it then?

HENDERSON: "Firm Hand and a Handshake."

SHOTWORTHY: Yes, yes. Sad to see such a sorry turnout, Johnny.

JONATHAN: It's alright, old man.

SHOTWORTHY: What comes of marrying a nobody, I suppose.

HENDERSON: Do get on with it, Bunny.

SHOTWORTHY: Yes, of course. *(Taps glass with utensil, stands, clears throat.)* Ladies. Gentlemen. Assorted hangers on. Time has come to offer my solemn benediction upon the blessed couplet. Prepared some remarks, of course. *(Looks in jacket pockets.)* Sorry, must of left them in my other … had a stain upon the … Where was I?

HENDERSON: God knows.

SHOTWORTHY: Oh yes, to my good friend Johnny and his brand new broad— bride. Distinctly remember offering similar services to you and the first whiff—wife—woof! Woof! Ha ha!

HENDERSON: *(Toasts.)* Loved her well and miss her so!

SHOTWORTHY: And now the new one. What's her name, then? Little trouble. Names and such. Places … faces … lists! Lists! Make a list and stick to her! That's what my Margaret and I have done, and it ain't turned out so badly, has it now?

HENDERSON: Sit down, man.

SHOTWORTHY: Soon as I deliver a few remarks I've put together for the occasion. *(Looking in pockets.)* Somewhere …

HENDERSON: Dear sweet Jesus!

SHOTWORTHY: *(Finds speech.)* Ah, here it is.

*(Reads.)* BOLD MEN
BROAD MEN
MUSCULAR AND WIDE
STRIDING FORTH UPON THE GAMBIT
FEAR AND FAME BETIDE

HENDERSON: What the devil!

SHOTWORTHY: Sorry. Sorry. That's for Xerxes, isn't it?

HENDERSON: Sh!

JONATHAN: What?

MISS McCRACKEN: Xerxes?

SHOTWORTHY: I am to be master of revels this annum, yes.

HENDERSON: Tell the world, why don't you?

MISS McCRACKEN: You are members of Xerxes?

SHOTWORTHY: Shhh. *(Giggles.)* Secret.

HENDERSON: It was.

SHOTWORTHY: Xerxes is here to stand by our brother in his wedding toils.

MISS McCRACKEN: Jonathan?

JONATHAN: I'm not a member of any Xerxes.

SHOTWORTHY: Our newest, yes. And finest yet.

HENDERSON: Richest anyhow.

JONATHAN: I don't even know what Xerxes is!

HENDERSON: We are what we are, sir!

MISS McCRACKEN: The most despicable group in the city!

SHOTWORTHY: Yes, and here's your name, Johnny. *(Points to paper.)* See? Right there next your eunuch's.

MISS McCRACKEN: Your what?

JONATHAN: No!

HENDERSON: Not a member 'til you got a eunuch.

MISS McCRACKEN: Jonathan!

SHOTWORTHY: Eunuch's name is … can't make this out, Henderson.

JONATHAN: I didn't buy a eunuch, Miss McCracken! I did not! I swear it!

HENDERSON: *(Reading.)* Gideon, it says.

MISS McCRACKEN: Gideon?

JONATHAN: No!

MISS McCRACKEN: Your son!

JONATHAN: No, no, you don't understand!

MISS McCRACKEN: Oh, but I do! I certainly do! *(Stands.)*

SHOTWORTHY: May I kiss the bride?

MISS McCRACKEN: Where is my wrap?

JONATHAN: Miss McCracken, please!

SHOTWORTHY: Something wrong, Johnny?

JONATHAN: Nothing, no. She doesn't understand the joke. They're joking.

MISS McCRACKEN: Joking?

JONATHAN: Teasing, yes. It's just our way. Diddling the groom, so to speak. Old tradition amongst us.

SHOTWORTHY: Hands up! Pants down!

JONATHAN: That's it!

HENDERSON: Who's in the kitchen?

JONATHAN: Ha ha!

MISS McCRACKEN: These men are not joking, Jonathan!

SHOTWORTHY: Let's play Boogley Bush!

MISS McCRACKEN: They are fools and drunkards and much, much worse!

JONATHAN: Oh, not like your friends, I suppose.

MISS McCRACKEN: Which friends?

JONATHAN: You and your French Circle!

MISS McCRACKEN: What?

HENDERSON: What's that?

SHOTWORTHY: Who's French?

JONATHAN: I have it upon reliable information that you are a member of the French Circle, and that you talk about things that are not to be talked about!

MISS McCRACKEN: You aren't, by any chance, referring to my Freudian Circle?

JONATHAN: Yes! That!

MISS McCRACKEN: Well, your informant must be mistaken. I am not a member of the Freudian Circle.

JONATHAN: I knew it! Thank heaven!

MISS McCRACKEN: I am the *leader* of the Freudian Circle!

JONATHAN: Oh, ye gods!

HENDERSON: What's that, then?

MISS McCRACKEN: The Freudian Circle, Mister Henderson, is a collective intelligence. Our symbol is the double-bladed axe, and our mission is nothing less than the severing of the Gordian Knot that binds society to its pathology.

SHOTWORTHY: Lovely.

HENDERSON: Undifferentiated couplings with one another and with beasts!

SHOTWORTHY: Hooray!

HENDERSON: Not to mention seditious misbehavior!

MISS McCRACKEN: These things don't frighten us so much, Mr. Henderson. We are, however, deeply disturbed by the activities of your Xerxes.

SHOTWORTHY: Hear! Hear!

HENDERSON: Hush! *(Pinches Shotworthy.)*

SHOTWORTHY: Ow! Stop that!

MISS McCRACKEN: Mister Shotworthy, you do not seem to appreciate that my Freudian Circle and your Xerxes are bound to be sworn enemies.

SHOTWORTHY: But I am entirely in agreement with you! They are louts, these fellows! Bullies and louts! They do not listen, and they have nothing on their minds, not a single thing!

HENDERSON: Leave off, Bunny!

SHOTWORTHY: Nothing but eunuchs and poker!

HENDERSON: Shut up!

SHOTWORTHY: You shut up!

MISS McCRACKEN: I wish to go home.

SHOTWORTHY: So do I. Hate these things, don't you, Johnny?

MISS McCRACKEN: *(Removing her ring and holding it out.)* Jonathan …

JONATHAN: Oh, Miss McCracken, no.

MISS McCRACKEN: Take it, please, and goodbye.

JONATHAN: No, I gave you that ring for life. I'll not take it back. I'd sooner throw it in the river. I'd sooner throw myself in the river and drown!

MISS McCRACKEN: Then you take it, Mister Shotworthy. *(Gives Shotworthy the ring.)* And give it to your friend, Jonathan.

SHOTWORTHY: Who's Jonathan?

MISS McCRACKEN: My question exactly. What on earth was I thinking?

SHOTWORTHY: *(Looking at ring.)* Wait a moment, this is my Margaret's ring.

MISS McCRACKEN: What?

JONATHAN: I beg your pardon.

SHOTWORTHY: My wife Margaret's ring! Stolen at carnival last season!

MISS McCRACKEN: Oh, good lord!

HENDERSON: Let me see that. *(Looks at ring.)*

JONATHAN: There must be some mistake.

SHOTWORTHY: You think I don't know my own wife?

JONATHAN: Not at all, but—

HENDERSON: It *is* her ring, Bunny.

SHOTWORTHY: Police!

JONATHAN: Wait a moment, Bunny! Please!

SHOTWORTHY / HENDERSON: Thief! Police!

MISS McCRACKEN: Oh, if this isn't the very limit!

> *(Manager enters.)*

MANAGER: Is there a problem here?

SHOTWORTHY: This woman has stolen my wife!

MANAGER: Your wife, sir?

SHOTWORTHY: My wife's ring, damnitall!

HENDERSON: She is a jewel thief!

SHOTWORTHY: Take her away!

MANAGER: This is your wife's ring, sir?

SHOTWORTHY: Registered at Peabody's, praise God.

MANAGER: If you'd come with me to the office, Miss, we'll sort this out.

> *(Manager takes Miss McCracken's arm.)*

JONATHAN: Wait!

MANAGER: Stand off, sir.

MISS McCRACKEN: Jonathan, please.

MANAGER: Let's not have any disturbance now, shall we?

JONATHAN: But, this is so easily explained. It's all my fault, you see.

MANAGER: You, sir?

SHOTWORTHY: Oh, don't be ridiculous, Johnny. You didn't do anything.

JONATHAN: But I bought that ring myself, Bunny.

HENDERSON: Then she has accepted stolen property?

JONATHAN: No, no. Well, yes. Technically. But only because—

HENDERSON: Oh, this could prove to be very serious, Johnny.

SHOTWORTHY: Yes, best leave it to the authorities.

MANAGER: Come along then, Miss.

> *(Manager leads Miss McCracken offstage.)*

JONATHAN: Oh, dear God.

HENDERSON: Indeed.

SHOTWORTHY: Yes, congratulations, Johnny. Seems a lovely girl.

HENDERSON: Let's hear that speech again, shall we?

SHOTWORTHY: My Xerxes speech?

HENDERSON: Yes, I liked the thrust of it.

SHOTWORTHY: Did you? Well, I have it right here, don't I … *(Searching pockets.)* … somewhere …

> *(Henderson and Shotworthy exit.)*

## SCENE FOUR

*The Van Huffle parlor. Jonathan sits, alone. Cloaked figures sing in the shadows.*

EUNUCHS: *(Singing.)*
> MOONLY MOON
> ONLY MOON
> SUN IS GONE AWAY
>
> RESTLESSLY
> ENDLESSLY
> WE RECALL THE DAY
>
> WHEN WE WERE IN FLOWER
> WITH OUR MANLY POWER
>
> GOD ABOVE
> TURN OUR LOVE
> FROM OUR LOSS TO YOU

JONATHAN: *(Sighs.)*

*(A knock at the door.)*

JONATHAN: Yes.

*(Gideon enters.)*

GIDEON:: May I speak with you a moment, sir?

JONATHAN: Am I a bad man, Gideon?

GIDEON: A bad man? No, sir.

JONATHAN: I'm not a bad person, in your judgment?

GIDEON: You've been kind to me, sir. Most kind, for a man in your position.

JONATHAN: A wealthy man, you mean? A monster of economic possession, or some such?

GIDEON: You wish to discuss your character with me, sir?

JONATHAN: No, but listening to the lamentations of the eunuchs just now, I— well, I'm just saying aloud what Miss McCracken would say were she here to chastise me in person.

GIDEON: It's Miss McCracken I came to speak to you about, sir.

JONATHAN: Oh, Gideon, I know she's only a waitress and that she goes on and on about my faults and society's faults, but damn it all, I miss her, and don't care to see her humiliated over some silly mistake.

GIDEON: Humiliated?

JONATHAN: Miss McCracken is to spend the night in jail and it's all my fault.

GIDEON: Miss McCracken is to be burnt, sir.

JONATHAN: Burnt?

GIDEON: For treason, yes, and the eunuchs are most upset by it.

JONATHAN: You cannot be serious!

GIDEON: It has not yet been announced, but the Patriarch himself has decreed it.

JONATHAN: But, how do *you* know of this?

GIDEON: Eunuchs know most everything, sir, and Miss McCracken is revered among us for the stand she and the anti-castrationists have taken against Xerxes.

JONATHAN: Xerxes again! Who or what the devil is this blessed Xerxes?

GIDEON: Xerxes is a secret society which preys upon lads who speak out against the Patriarch, sir, castrating them and selling them into eunuchdom.

JONATHAN: But why?

GIDEON: Why?

JONATHAN: Why on earth would you speak out against the Patriarch? Surely you must have a father, a family, someone to teach you—

GIDEON: I have a father, sir, but no family.

JONATHAN: How can that be?

GIDEON: *(Chants.)* I AM THE LOVE CHILD OF THE PATRIARCH

JONATHAN: Oh.

GIDEON: PROOF IN THE FORM OF A LETTER WAS GIVEN ME BY MY MOTHER ON HER DEATH BED

JONATHAN: Good lord.

GIDEON: BUT WHEN I TRIED TO MEET HIM
MEET WITH MY FATHER THE PATRIARCH
I WAS REBUFFED
TAKEN OFF TO MILITARY SCHOOL
TRAINED UP AS AN OFFICER IN HIS GUARD
AND WHEN I EXCELLED AT ARMS
AND AT MY STUDIES
I KNEW THAT I WAS READY
WORTHY AT LAST TO MEET WITH MY FATHER THE
PATRIARCH
I DEMANDED AUDIENCE
BUT AGAIN I WAS REJECTED

AND SO BECAME DISHEARTENED
UNDISCIPLINED
REBELLIOUS
AND WAS EXPELLED FROM THE ACADEMY
MY HONOR BLACKENED
CONDEMNED TO ROAMING THE STREETS
CRYING AND BLASPHEMING MY FATHER THE PATRIARCH
UNTIL FINALLY HE DID HEAR ME
AND SEND FOR ME
AND CUT ME

JONATHAN: The Patriarch?

GIDEON: DO NOT PITY ME, SIR
FOR I HAVE FOUND A BAND OF BROTHERS
MEN WHO ARE NOT MEN BUT MORE THAN MEN
MEN WHO HAVE SHOWN ME THAT POWER LIES NOT
BETWEEN OUR LEGS BUT IN OUR HEARTS AND MINDS
WHO REMIND ME THAT IT MATTERS NOT WHAT HAPPENS
  TO US
SO MUCH AS HOW WE BEAR IT
AND WHAT WE DO WITH IT
I AM CONTENT TO BE OF SERVICE NOW
I AM CONTENT
AND HAPPY SOMETIMES, WHERE I NEVER WAS BEFORE
HAPPY WHERE I NEVER WAS BEFORE

JONATHAN: I—I don't know what to say, Gideon. I have always believed in
the Patriarch.

GIDEON: It's hard not to, sir.

JONATHAN: Oh, that ring, that confounded ring!

GIDEON: You should know, sir, that the one-eyed man who sold you that ring
is employed by Xerxes.

JONATHAN: What!

GIDEON: These are the Patriarch's friends sir, Mr. Henderson and Shotworthy,
and others whom you would never suspect. Think only of your broker.

JONATHAN: Martin, a member of Xerxes?

GIDEON: And taking advantage of you as well.

JONATHAN: Versatile Industries!

GIDEON: International traders in eunuchery of all sorts.

JONATHAN: Dear God, Miss McCracken!

GIDEON: If you mean to help Miss McCracken, sir—

JONATHAN: Indeed I do, Gideon! I must!

GIDEON: Then you'll need a plan of action, and a good one.

JONATHAN: Oh. Not my strong suit, I'm afraid.

GIDEON: Leave that to me, sir. Strategies and tactics are the very air I breathe.
But for now I must help Little Eva with her preparations for the Ball.

JONATHAN: Go then, Gideon. And do please think of something.

GIDEON: Not to worry, sir. I'll have a plan in mind before I reach the top of
the stair.

JONATHAN: But what should I do, meantime?

GIDEON: To begin with, I should practice my Latin.

JONATHAN: Latin?

GIDEON: And I would get rid of my Versatile.

JONATHAN: Indeed.

GIDEON: *Rebellio Eunuchus!*
*(Gideon exits.)*

JONATHAN: Godfrey!
*(Blackout.)*
*(Sound cue: Drumbeats. Wailings. Screams.)*


## SCENE FIVE

*Little Eva's bedchamber. Little Eva, wearing sackcloth, stands on the bed,
trussed to the bedpost, screaming. Jameson, costumed as a soldier, thrusts a
homemade crucifix at her, as though through flames. Dorothea, dressed as a
peasant woman, kneels to one side, lamenting, and working a small smoke
pot and drum.*


JAMESON: Repent, ye witch! Repent!

LITTLE EVA: Oh, how the fire works me! Severing breath from life, spirit from
flesh! Bringing me closer and closer and closer to God!
*(Gideon enters.)*

LITTLE EVA: Where have you been?

GIDEON: Your Father wanted to speak with me.

LITTLE EVA: While I've been tied to the stake, shrieking myself hoarse? Untie
me at once.

GIDEON: *(Untying her.)* I've terrible news, I'm afraid. They're planning to burn
some unfortunate woman the night of the Ball.

LITTLE EVA: What?

DOROTHEA: Oh, that's awful.

LITTLE EVA: But how could they? How is it going to look for me to be burnt at the stake in some silly tableau when there's going to be a real woman burnt?

GIDEON: I hadn't thought of that.

LITTLE EVA: I'll look ridiculous.

GIDEON: Perhaps you're right.

LITTLE EVA: But, everything is planned—all my sets and costumes, my super-numeraries!

GIDEON: We must think of something else to do, Little Eva.

LITTLE EVA: But, there's no time! Oh, everything is ruined! Ruined!

GIDEON: On the contrary, Little Eva. Everything is going completely according to plan.

LITTLE EVA: What plan? Whose plan? Certainly not my plan.

GIDEON: If you would but allow it.

LITTLE EVA: Don't you dare be enigmatic with me, eunuch.

GIDEON: What is a eunuch for, if not to be enigmatic? And resourceful, hm? Come now, do you really think I'd allow you to fail?

LITTLE EVA: Yes. No. I don't know. Oh, what kind of woman would steal the limelight at the very moment of my triumph!

GIDEON: She's been accused of treason, they say.

LITTLE EVA: Oh, how grand.

DOROTHEA: Well, I think it's a shame.

LITTLE EVA: You would. We'll mount a battle scene instead, Gideon. Say the storming of the walls at Orleans. Bloody war certainly trumps treason.

GIDEON: Not time enough, I'm afraid.

LITTLE EVA: Well, something from *Marry Harry!* then.

GIDEON: I wouldn't recommend it.

LITTLE EVA: But it's fun!

GIDEON: How many more renditions of *Mama's Red Stocking* can the audience bear? Besides, you'd need all new costumes.

LITTLE EVA: Well, what am I going to do, then!? What am I going to do?

GIDEON: May I suggest the scene at court in which Joan recognizes the dauphin.

LITTLE EVA: It lacks drama!

GIDEON: It lacks extravagance.

LITTLE EVA: Oh, I don't know, I don't know, I don't know!

JAMESON: Do I be pokin' at ye with the cross, now, Missy?

LITTLE EVA: Put that down, Jameson. Dorothea take it away from him!

DOROTHEA: Jameson, behave!

GIDEON: Jameson, sit here and play the part of Charles, would you?

JAMESON: Can't do that.

LITTLE EVA: What?

JAMESON: I don't do nothing but a soldier man and dauphin.

LITTLE EVA: Oh, my God.

DOROTHEA: Charles is the dauphin's name, Jameson.

JAMESON: Whyn't ye say so, then?

GIDEON: Just sit down.

JAMESON: Yes sir.

> *(Jameson sits.)*

GIDEON: Meanwhile, the real dauphin is hiding over here amongst his courtiers.

JAMESON: I don't see nobody.

GIDEON: Now, Joan enters. Wait. Your sword. *(Grabs Jameson's wooden sword.)*

JAMESON: Hey!

GIDEON: Here is the sword that you found buried behind a tomb exactly where God told you that it would be.

> *(Little Eva takes "sword.")*

GIDEON: Now, you enter the court … nervously, Little Eva. You're a peasant girl.

LITTLE EVA: Ugh!

GIDEON: You've never been to court. Never been out of your little town for that matter.

> *(Little Eva walks slowly, eyes downcast.)*

GIDEON: That's right. Now, Dorothea, you're a very grand lady.

DOROTHEA: Oh, I don't know.

GIDEON: Mistress of the court.

DOROTHEA: Oh, master Gideon!

GIDEON: And you step out from among the courtiers and lead Joan to the false dauphin.

JAMESON: Do I stand up?

GIDEON: No, just sit there. Joan will approach you.

JAMESON: Oh, then I bow the knee?

GIDEON: No.

JAMESON: I don't stand nor bow nor nothin'?

GIDEON: Nothing, no.

JAMESON: But, she'll be mad if I just set here like a—

LITTLE EVA: Of course I won't be mad, you fool!

JAMESON: Ye see?

GIDEON: Just sit there, Jameson.

JAMESON: Yes sir.

GIDEON: Alright, Dorothea, enter.

*(Dorothea leads Little Eva to Jameson.)*

DOROTHEA: This is Joan of Arc, Mister Dauphin. She's a very nice girl come from the country to—

GIDEON: Sh, sh. No words.

DOROTHEA Oh.

*(Little Eva looks at Jameson, shakes her head and looks elsewhere.)*

GIDEON: And now you look right at the true dauphin.

JAMESON: Here I am!

DOROTHEA: Shh!

*(Little Eva looks around, sees Gideon, crosses to him and kneels at his feet.)*

GIDEON: Very good.

LITTLE EVA: That's all?

DOROTHEA: Oh, Miss Eva. I liked to cried you was so humble.

LITTLE EVA: You'd cry over anything. I want to cry. I want something exciting to happen.

GIDEON: Don't worry, there's more to the scene, Little Eva. After Joan has recognized him, the dauphin dismisses the court ... *(Waves.)*

DOROTHEA: That's us, Jameson.

JAMESON: What?

DOROTHEA: He's dismissing us. Waving his arm about, see.

JAMESON: Oh, like "*Diss*-missed!"

GIDEON: That's right.

*(Dorothea and Jameson step back.)*

GIDEON: Now, the dauphin says something to the effect of, "Alright, you've recognized me Joan, but that could be a trick. How can I trust that you are truly come from God?"

LITTLE EVA: And Joan says ... ?

GIDEON: She tells the dauphin a secret.

JAMESON: A secret?

LITTLE EVA: What secret?

GIDEON: Something about the dauphin that only God could know.

JAMESON: Ohhh.

LITTLE EVA: Alright. *(As Joan.)* God knows all our secrets, dauphin, and he has vouchsafed your terrible secret unto me in a dream …

JAMESON: *(Whispers.)* Ahh, ain't she something.

DOROTHEA: Yes.

JAMESON: Who is that?

DOROTHEA: *(Whispers.)* Shh. That's Joan of Arc.

LITTLE EVA: And this terrible, terrible secret, this dark and dreadful thing that you don't want anybody on earth ever to know about, is … *(As Little Eva.)* What? What is the dauphin's awful secret?

JAMESON: I know!

DOROTHEA: Hush!

JAMESON: Yer secret is that ye're a coward!

DOROTHEA: What?

JAMESON: And ye never went to war! Ye was just a orderly at hospital, an' a coward to boot, an' they called ye—they called ye Mister Bedpans!

LITTLE EVA: Mister Bedpans?

JAMESON: 'Cause of ye was scared! So scared ye stained thy bunk nights! *(Weeps.)*

DOROTHEA: Now, now.

JAMESON: Ain't that a secret worth to kill an' die for?

LITTLE EVA: Oh my God! Take him away!

DOROTHEA: Ah, Jameson, now. *(Comforting him.)*

JAMESON: Keep thy hands to yerself, woman!

DOROTHEA: Come down the kitchen, why don't you, for some nice hot cocoa.

JAMESON: Cocoa?

DOROTHEA: Um hm.

JAMESON: I like the cocoa.

DOROTHEA: Come on, then.

*(Dorothea leads Jameson off.)*

LITTLE EVA: Oh, I am doomed!

GIDEON: Eva—

LITTLE EVA: Doomed! I cannot rely upon these fools, these idiots, these amateurs! I'll be the laughingstock of the Ball!

GIDEON: You know, I've heard from a friend something he does to soothe his mistress when she is upset.

LITTLE EVA: I am not upset!

GIDEON: Alright, then.

LITTLE EVA: What is it?

GIDEON: It is called various things. Standing Dog, Paku Paku, The Light of the Illataluma. Would you care to experience it?

LITTLE EVA: No!

GIDEON: Very well.

LITTLE EVA: You will explain it to me.

GIDEON: Well, from what I understand, the eunuch begins by rubbing his mistress all over, both lightly with fingertips and more severely with the meat of the hands.

LITTLE EVA: Yes?

GIDEON: Gently, gently, then hard and harder, hands and feet, legs, arms, back and neck, the nether parts and buttocks.

LITTLE EVA: Yes, and then what?

GIDEON: When she is soothed to a degree, and ready, the mistress lifts her skirts and mounts her eunuch.

LITTLE EVA: Like a horse?

GIDEON: Something like. She grasps the Horn of Rancor—

LITTLE EVA: Horn of Rancor? What is that?

GIDEON: What is left the goat when he's gelded.

LITTLE EVA: I don't understand.

GIDEON: Well …

LITTLE EVA: You're turning all red, Gideon!

GIDEON: My friend gave me a picture. *(Removes parchment from his jacket.)* It's an ancient illustration.

LITTLE EVA: Well, let me see it.

GIDEON: Perhaps we shouldn't.

LITTLE EVA: No, no, no, no, no. Let me look. Let me see. *(Taking drawing.)* Oh my God! Look at that! Oh, and here's an inscription. It says, *(Reading.)* "And then, taking her eunuch's horny wrath inside her, she rides far into the darkening desert, rocking back and forth, back and forth, until at last a violent excitement breaks forth from deep inside her, releasing her from herself for a moment of eternity." Hm.

GIDEON: It is perfectly safe, my friend says, and quite pleasant after awhile.

LITTLE EVA: And what's it called again?

GIDEON: Whatever you like.

LITTLE EVA: Well, perhaps we should try it.

GIDEON: If you wish.

LITTLE EVA: And then we'll rehearse?

GIDEON: As much as you like.

(Gideon rubs Little Eva gently with fingertips.)

LITTLE EVA: We must be perfect, Gideon.

GIDEON: Of course.

LITTLE EVA: Perfectly perfect. Mmm.

GIDEON: (Sings.)
SOON THE STORY WILL BE TOLD
OF THE GIRL WHO'S GOOD AS GOLD
SHE'S THE BEST GIRL AT THE BALL
HER PICTURE HANGING ON THE WALL

GIDEON / LITTLE EVA:
SHE'LL BE KNOWN BOTH FAR AND WIDE
IN THE TOWN AND COUNTRYSIDE

LITTLE EVA: FROM THE ROOFTOPS

GIDEON: THEY'LL PROCLAIM

GIDEON / LITTLE EVA:
OUR GOLDEN GIRL'S GOLDEN NAME

LITTLE EVA: (Calling.) LITTLE

GIDEON: (Calling.) EVA

LITTLE EVA: (Calling.) LITTLE

GIDEON: (Calling.) EVA

LITTLE EVA: YES! YES! YES! YES! YES! YES!

GIDEON / LITTLE EVA: THE BEST

(Music cue: Waltz. Little Eva and Gideon dance.)


SCENE SIX

*Light/scene change: Transition into ballroom as Gideon and Little Eva dance. Gideon and Little Eva exit oppositely. Matron enters.*

MATRON: And our finalists are: Miss Angela Loringer, Miss Bernadette Fife, Mary Princess Rachenholler, Miss Gertrude Stanbro, Miss Theresa Sweringen, Miss Ellen Walker-Wells, Miss Edwina Hawkins, Miss Corinthia Jennings, Miss Annabella Beardsley, Miss Dorcas Tanner Hunt and Miss Eva Van Huffle. On behalf of the judges, I congratulate these young ladies who have danced their way into our hearts and into the final competition, the Talentoria, which our Patriarch himself will judge. To the stage, young ladies. To the stage. And don't forget to thank your gentlemen.

*(Matron exits. Edwina Hawkins, a young woman, played by the accompanist, stands and recites.)*

EDWINA HAWKINS / ACCOMPANIST: …But in the end, she longed to see Demeter, her loving mother, and hope charmed her great mind, despite her grief. The peaks of the mountains and the depths of the sea resounded with her immortal voice, and at last, her mighty mother heard her!

*(Offstage applause. Little Eva, as Joan of Arc, and Dorothea, as Lady at Court, enter as if backstage. Dorothea helps Little Eva with her costume.)*

MATRON: *(Offstage, as if onstage addressing audience.)* Miss Edwina Hawkins, ladies and gentlemen. That was Miss Edwina Hawkins with her Selections from the Mysteries of Thrace. Clear the stage please, Miss Hawkins. Clear the stage.

LITTLE EVA: Oh, Dorothea, hurry!

DOROTHEA: Going as fast as I can, Eva.

LITTLE EVA: Do you think the judges liked us?

DOROTHEA: Oh, you should have seen the looks on their faces, Eva. They'd never seen anything like the pair of you, I'm sure.

LITTLE EVA: He dances well, doesn't he?

DOROTHEA: For a eunuch, yes indeed.

LITTLE EVA: For anybody.

DOROTHEA: I'm sure he does, dear, yes.

MATRON: *(Offstage.)* And finally, for the pleasure of the Patriarch, we wish to present Miss Eva Van Huffle—

LITTLE EVA: Oh, my God!

MATRON: *(Offstage.)*—performing a scene from the life of Saint Joan in which the Maid presents herself at court and proves to her sovereign that she has been sent by God to save France.

LITTLE EVA: *(Over Matron.)* But, I'm not ready! Dorothea!

DOROTHEA: *(Over Matron.)* You're ready, Miss!

*(Joan exits as several masked Courtiers and a Second Soldier enter with a throne and place it center stage. Dauphin sits on throne, head in hands, bored. Courtiers take up languorous positions around him. Second Soldier stands at attention. Lights rise, creating "onstage" as pantomime begins.)*

*(DEAR READER: All cast members participate in the following pantomime— both moving and hilarious—in which the Dauphin attempts to fool the*

*recently-arrived Joan of Arc by switching costumes with a dim soldier, played by Jameson. Joan recognizes the Dauphin and, after he dismisses the court, sings a duet with him in which she proves to the Dauphin that she has been sent by God.)*

*(Sound cue: Metronome ticking. Beat. Soldier [Jameson] enters, saluting, and gives message to First Courtier, who reads message with other Courtiers. Courtiers do double take, mime laughter. Dauphin looks up. First Courtier shows message to Dauphin. Dauphin reads, yawns. Courtier yawns, Soldier yawns, covering mouth and dropping battleaxe. Noticing this, First Courtier mimes getting an idea, then whispers in Dauphin's ear, miming idea for a switch. Beat. Dauphin mimes laughter and stands, leaving royal robe on throne. First Courtier takes Soldier's helmet, cloak and battleaxe, tossing them one by one to Second Soldier, who helps Courtier put them on Dauphin. First Courtier points to throne, indicating Soldier should sit. Soldier shakes head in refusal. All Courtiers point to throne, indicating that Soldier should sit. Soldier shakes head more vehemently. In rapid movement: Dauphin stomps in exasperation and points to throne; Second Soldier knocks floor with lance butt; Soldier stamps foot and crosses his arms; Courtiers seize Soldier, set him on the throne and wrap him in Dauphin's royal robes. Again in rapid movement, Soldier attempts to rise three times; First Courtier puts hand on his shoulder and seats him each time. The third time, Soldier signals a rise, but does not, causing First Courtier to stumble awkwardly as he tries to seat him. Soldier points and smiles a "gotcha.")*

*(Music cue: Dauphin quickly passes crown to Courtiers, who place crown on Soldier's head. They all assemble in dignified positions in front of Dauphin, now appareled as Soldier. Fanfare: Enter Joan of Arc [Little Eva] in the company of Lady at Court [Dorothea]. Joan looks about timidly as the Lady guides her to False Dauphin. Lady at Court curtseys deeply to False Dauphin and indicates Joan do likewise. Joan looks puzzled and shrugs. Lady at Court repeats curtsey and indicates again, more insistently, that Joan do likewise. Joan shakes her head. Lady at Court claps her hands. The other Courtiers do the same, and an angry, rhythmic clapping builds. Joan looks about her, intimidated for a moment, then thrusts her hand out, sternly. The clapping stops. Joan searches the room, then pushes through the mass of Courtiers as music swells, to reveal, at last, the True Dauphin, disguised as a Soldier. Joan looks into the True Dauphin's eyes and kneels at his feet. The True Dauphin extends a hand to Joan, helping her to her feet. The Courtiers gasp. The Dauphin dismisses the Courtiers and Second Soldier, who exit, shaking their*

*heads and mumbling to one another. The Soldier gives Joan the crown, snatches his helmet, battleaxe and cloak from the Dauphin and exits.)*
*(The Dauphin sings.)*

DAUPHIN: YES YOU HAVE FOUND ME OUT
YOU'VE SEEN THROUGH MY DISGUISE
I SEE THAT YOU ARE HONEST
I SEE THE TRUTH IN YOUR EYES
BUT HOW CAN I HOW CAN I HOW CAN I KNOW
THAT YOU COME FROM GOD

JOAN: *(Sings.)* THE GOD YOU CANNOT SEE
HAS TOLD ME WHAT YOU LACK
YOU THINK YOU ARE A COWARD
THAT YOU'RE AFRAID TO ATTACK
BUT YOU CAN BE YOU CAN BE YOU CAN BE SURE
GOD IS ON YOUR SIDE

DAUPHIN: BEHOLD MY DEEPEST WISH
MY DOUBT IS LAID TO REST
I DARE NOW TO BELIEVE YOU
AND ASK YOUR AID IN MY QUEST
NOW DO I NOW DO I NOW DO I KNOW
THAT YOU COME FROM GOD

JOAN / DAUPHIN: TOGETHER WE'RE FOR FRANCE
ON THAT YOU CAN DEPEND
COMPANIONS AND FOREVER
AND FAITHFUL RIGHT TO THE END
HOW DO WE HOW DO WE HOW DO WE KNOW
GOD HAS TOLD US SO
GOD HAS TOLD US SO

*(Little Eva and Gideon bow to the audience. Jameson and Dorothea enter as Soldier and Lady at Court. All four bow.)*

OFFSTAGE VOICE: Enter the Patriarch.

*(The Patriarch enters, sits on the throne and addresses the audience.)*

PATRIARCH: Well, our gallant girls have done us proud once again, have they not? So much talent. Such beauty. But among the fair there is a fairest; among the rare, the rarest. Of all our wonderful girls there is *the* girl, is there not? And who is she this year? She is … Miss Edwina Hawkins!

*(Offstage cry. Polite applause.)*

LITTLE EVA: What?

PATRIARCH: Miss Edwina Hawkins, who graced and improved us with her readings from antiquity.

LITTLE EVA: I didn't win?

PATRIARCH: Is Miss Hawkins here?

LITTLE EVA: I can't believe this! I am the Greatest Girl!

GIDEON: Little Eva—

LITTLE EVA: I am! You know I am! *(To audience.)* Is no one going to protest?

PATRIARCH: Miss Hawkins?

LITTLE EVA: *(Yells offstage.)* Don't you dare come out here, Dweenie!

PATRIARCH: Do we have a problem?

LITTLE EVA: May I address the Patriarch?

PATRIARCH: Little Eva, isn't it?

LITTLE EVA: Yes!

PATRIARCH: Approach us.

LITTLE EVA: I have always revered the Patriarch and have dedicated my life to one day receiving the ribbon for Greatest Girl from his hand.

PATRIARCH: Sometimes, Little Eva, our plan of battle may be brilliant, our execution flawless, but owing to some accident of fate—

LITTLE EVA: Something is going on here, something other than the workings of fate, and as a loyal subject I demand to know what it is!

*(The Patriarch motions offstage.)*

PATRIARCH: And soon you shall, my child.

*(Jonathan enters, disguised as a priest.)*

LITTLE EVA: Who are you?

PATRIARCH: Father comes to set the seal of the church upon a certain melancholy act of state. You may proceed.

*(Jonathan swings a smoking censer and chants.)*

JONATHAN: *(Chants.)* HOMINES DOMINUS SANCTUS BENEDICTUS

*(Attendants push on platform bearing Miss McCracken, tied to a stake and hung with placards proclaiming her to be Thief, Freudian and Eunuch Lover.)*

LITTLE EVA: Miss McCracken?

PATRIARCH: Do you see now, child?

LITTLE EVA: See what? See how my chances to be Greatest Girl have been ruined forever by my father's infatuation with this wretched waitress?

PATRIARCH: Read out the Holy Catalogue of Crimes, Father.

GIDEON: First, we would see the Patriarch reunited with his son.

PATRIARCH: Son? What son?

GIDEON: *(Chants.)* I AM THE LOVE CHILD OF THE PATRIARCH

LITTLE EVA: Gideon?

GIDEON: *(Holding up letter.)*
I HAVE HERE A LETTER
A LETTER TO MY MOTHER
ACKNOWLEDGING THAT THE PATRIARCH IS MY FATHER

LITTLE EVA: Of course he's your father, Gideon. He's everyone's father. He's the Patriarch for heaven's sake.

PATRIARCH: Indeed. Proceed with the Execution of Justice, priest.

JONATHAN: I—I cannot, sir!

PATRIARCH: What?

JONATHAN: *(Chanting.)* INNOCENTUS FECUNDUS

PATRIARCH: What is he saying?

JONATHAN: *(Chanting.)* MAXIMUS WOMANUS INNOCENTUS

LITTLE EVA: She is *not!* She is *not* innocent! She is a social-climbing fraud who will stop at nothing, *nothing* to win her place in society, *and* at my expense, and I will never forgive her for it! Never, never, never, never, never, never, never!

PATRIARCH: Perhaps then, Little Eva, it is meet and right that you be the one to light the Bonfire of the Patriarch.

LITTLE EVA: Oh.

PATRIARCH: Yes, and that you be known not as Greatest Girl, no, but as the Greatest Girl Who Ever Lived, and that a statue be raised in your honor to stand forevermore in the Gallery of Girls.

LITTLE EVA: Oh, my.

GIDEON: *(Sings.)* EVA

PATRIARCH: Think about it.

JONATHAN: *(Sings.)* EVA

LITTLE EVA: My truest heart's ambition.

MISS McCRACKEN: *(Sings.)* LITTLE EVA

LITTLE EVA: What!?

GIDEON: *(Sings.)* YOU MUST BE, YOU MUST BE, YOU MUST BE SURE

LITTLE EVA: *(Covering her ears.)* No!

GIDEON / JONATHAN / MISS McCRACKEN: *(Sing.)* IS THIS WHAT YOU WANT

LITTLE EVA: The voices!

GIDEON / JONATHAN / MISS McCRACKEN: *(Sing.)* IS THIS WHAT YOU NEED

PATRIARCH: Voices?

GIDEON / JONATHAN / MISS McCRACKEN: *(Sing.)* THERE MUST BE NO DOUBT

LITTLE EVA: Oh leave me alone! I want my fame! A unique and abiding fame like Joan of Arc! *(Raising her sword.)* Joan of Arc, who spoke out against the enemies of her dauphin, and the enemies of her country, and the enemies of her church and her God and her truth and was reviled and burned at the stake, like— *(Sees that her sword is pointing directly at Miss McCracken.)* Oh.

JONATHAN / GIDEON / MISS McCRACKEN: *(Sing.)* OHHHHHHHHHHH

LITTLE EVA: Like Miss McCracken, who is always speaking out like Joan of Arc.

JONATHAN / GIDEON / MISS McCRACKEN: *(Sing.)* AHHHHHHHHHHH

LITTLE EVA: Miss McCracken speaks out against privilege! Miss McCracken speaks out against injustice! She speaks out against castration and the use of eunuchs! Miss McCracken—oh my goodness! She speaks out against—

PATRIARCH: Enough!

JONATHAN: *(Throwing off disguise.)* She speaks out against Xerxes!

LITTLE EVA: Father?!

JONATHAN: They are guilty of heinous crimes!

PATRIARCH: Enough, I say! The people—

MISS McCRACKEN: You are castrating the people!

PATRIARCH: I am not.

MISS McCRACKEN: And your power is founded on shit!

LITTLE EVA: Miss McCracken!

MISS McCRACKEN: Shit and lies!

PATRIARCH: You! Soldier!

JAMESON: Me, sir?

PATRIARCH: Light her on fire!

JAMESON: But, that's Miss McCracken, sir.

PATRIARCH: And I'm your Patriarch! Burn her!

JAMESON: Well, I don't know, sir, I—I don't have a match.

PATRIARCH: Burn her, you coward!

JAMESON: I ain't a coward!

PATRIARCH: You are a coward! You belong in the hospital for the cowardly insane!

JAMESON: No!

PATRIARCH: Emptying the bedpans of all the other cowards who haven't the courage to obey their Patriarch! Now burn the goddamn waitress!

JAMESON: *(Beat.)* AHHHHHHHH!

*(Jameson rushes the Patriarch and buries the double-bladed battle axe in his breast. Shocked pause.)*

JAMESON: He shouldn'ta said that.

DOROTHEA: Oh, Jameson.

JAMESON: Not in public anyway.

*(Gideon approaches dying Patriarch.)*

GIDEON: Father? I have something for you, Father. *(Holds up wooden box.)* A small token. *(Opens box and shows contents to Patriarch.)*

PATRIARCH: Ah!

*(Gideon closes box and gives it to Patriarch.)*

PATRIARCH: *(Sings.)*
FROG HOP
LITTLE HOP TOAD
HOP FOR YOUR MASTER
HOP DOWN THE ROAD
*(Patriarch dies.)*

ATTENDANTS: The Patriarch is dead! Long live the … ! Long live … !

*(Attendants push throne and Patriarch offstage. Pause.)*

ALL: *(Sing.)*
OUR PATRIARCH IS GONE
OUR PATRIARCH IS DEAD
HE WAS HERE AND NOW HE'S NOT
THE FUTURE YAWNS AHEAD

OUR PSYCHES ARE UNSTEADY
WE CANNOT COMPREHEND
WE'RE GOING TO TAKE A LITTLE PAUSE
THEN TELL YOU HOW THINGS END
*(Musical interlude as Jonathan removes disguise and Miss McCracken steps down from the stake. They join Little Eva and Gideon and Dorothea and Jameson in a tableau. Martin, Henderson and Shotworthy, shackled and hung with placards labeling them as Castrators and Members of Xerxes, Enter as Barbershop Trio.)*

ALL: *(Except Xerxes.)*
WE'RE ALL SORTED OUT NOW
OUR LIVES RE-ORGANIZED
OUR FEARS ARE IN THE DISTANT PAST
OUR FUTURES REALIZED

XERXES: YES REALIZED

JONATHAN: I'VE GOT MY MISS McCRACKEN

MISS McCRACKEN: JUDGE McCRACKEN PLEASE

JONATHAN / MISS McCRACKEN:
>     XERXES IS A MEMORY
>     BROUGHT RIGHT TO ITS KNEES

XERXES : RIGHT TO ITS KNEES

LITTLE EVA: GIDEON'S GOT HIS FREEDOM

GIDEON: LITTLE EVA HER CAREER

LITTLE EVA / GIDEON:
>     WE DO OUR SHOWS AT THE LIVELY LAD
>     THE PEOPLE STOMP AND CHEER

XERXES : OH HOW THEY CHEER

JAMESON: ME I PLUCK THE PIG WORT

DOROTHEA: AND I STILL BREW THE TEA

XERXES : TEA

ALL: *(Except Xerxes.)*
>     WE'RE WELL ADJUSTED AND CONTENT
>     OUR LIVES IN HARMONY

XERXES : SWEET HARMO

ALL: NYYYYYYYY


END OF PLAY

# Omnium Gatherum
## by Theresa Rebeck and
## Alexandra Gersten-Vassilaros

## BIOGRAPHIES

Theresa Rebeck's plays include *The Butterfly Collection* (Playwrights Horizons), *View of the Dome* (New York Theatre Workshop), *The Family of Mann*, *Loose Knit* and *Spike Heels* (Second Stage), *DollHouse* (Hartford Stage), *Sunday on the Rocks* and *Abstract Expression* (Long Wharf). She has also had plays produced at Actors Theatre of Louisville, Victory Gardens, Source, Seattle Repertory, New York Stage & Film and South Coast Repertory. Ms. Rebeck's collection of short plays, *Rebeck Revisited*, enjoyed a nine-month run at Theatre Neo in L.A. Her plays have been published by Samuel French as well as Smith and Kraus, who in addition to publishing her collected plays, have included her work in the *Best Plays by Women* series five times. Ms. Rebeck is a member of Naked Angels, New York Theatre Workshop's Usual Suspects and HB Playwright's Lab.

Alexandra Gersten-Vassilaros' plays include *My Thing Called Love*, Steppenwolf Theatre (Jefferson Award), Broadway; *Supple in Combat*, Steppenwolf Theatre; *I Never Told Anyone*, a short play, McCarter Theatre; *The Mimi Variations*, Steppenwolf Theatre, Williamstown Theatre Festival in Summer 2003 (director Nicholas Martin); *Omnium-Gatherum* workshop, New York Stage & Film. As an actress, she has appeared in productions in New York at E.S.T., Second Stage, Primary Stages, HOME and on Broadway. She's acted regionally at Yale Repertory, Center Stage, Sundance, New York Stage & Film and the Williamstown Theatre Festival. Ms. Gersten-Vassilaros is a graduate of NYU's Tisch School of the Arts, a member of The Actors Studio, a member playwright at HB Playwrights Foundation (where six of her short plays have been presented), and will soon be published in a collection by Smith and Kraus.

## HUMANA FESTIVAL PRODUCTION

*Omnium Gatherum* premiered at the Humana Festival of New American Plays in March 2003. It was directed by Will Frears with the following cast:

| | |
|---|---|
| Suzie | Kristine Nielsen |
| Roger | Phillip Clark |
| Lydia | Roma Maffia |
| Julia | Melanna Gray |
| Khalid | Edward A. Hajj |
| Terence | Dean Nolen |
| Jeff | Richard Furlong |
| Mohammed | Robert Lee Simmons |

and the following production staff:

Scenic Designer . . . . . . . . . . . . . . . . . . . . . . . . . . . . . . Paul Owen
Costume Designer . . . . . . . . . . . . . . . . . . . . . . . Lorraine Venberg
Lighting Designer . . . . . . . . . . . . . . . . . . . . . . . . . . . . Tony Penna
Sound Designer . . . . . . . . . . . . . . . . . . . . . . . . . Vincent Olivieri
Properties Designer . . . . . . . . . . . . . . . . . . . . . . . . Mark Walston
Stage Manager . . . . . . . . . . . . . . . . . . . . . . . . . . . . . Kathy Preher
Production Assistant . . . . . . . . . . . . . . . . . . . . . . Justin McDaniel
Fight Director . . . . . . . . . . . . . . . . . . . . . . . . . . . Brent Langdon
Dramaturg . . . . . . . . . . . . . . . . . . . . . . . . . . . . . Sarah Gubbins
Assistant Dramaturg . . . . . . . . . . . . . . . . . . . . . . . . . . Claire Cox
Casting . . . . . . . . . . . . . . . . . . . . . . . . . . . Orpheus Group Casting
With special assistance from Billy Hopkins
Directing Assistant . . . . . . . . . . . . . . . . . . . . . . . . . Devon Higby

## CHARACTERS

SUZIE

ROGER

LYDIA

JULIA

KHALID

TERENCE

JEFF

MOHAMMED

## SETTING

An elegant dinner party

## TIME

The present, or somewhere around there

*Omnium Gatherum* was first read at Actors Studio, New York City,
March 2002.

Developed at New York Stage & Film, Poughkeepsie, New York, July 2002.

Workshopped at Naked Angels, New York City, January 2003.

Roma Maffia, Kristine Nielsen and Dean Nolen
in *Omnium Gatherum*

27th Annual Humana Festival of New American Plays
Actors Theatre of Louisville, 2003
photo by John Fitzgerald

# Omnium Gatherum

## ACT ONE

*A beautifully set table dominates the room. There is a chandelier overhead. The set imperceptibly turns during the course of the play. Everyone is seated and quickly ending a lively conversation about rhubarb.*

TERENCE: *(Declaring.)* Rhubarb.

JULIA: *(Agreeing.)* Rhubarb.

JEFF: I love rhubarb.

SUZIE: No, it's a moody fruit. You can only use it in combination. Go on, Khalid.

KHALID: As I was saying—If we could but shrink the earth's population to a village of precisely 100 people—

ROGER: Oh, no. Is this that?

LYDIA: Let him finish.

KHALID: With the existing human ratios—

ROGER: *(Overlap.)* We all got this on the internet!

TERENCE: *(Overlap.)* I didn't!

KHALID: Oh—perhaps, then, if people already know—

TERENCE: I don't!

SUZIE: *(Overlap.)* No no, we're listening, recap, recap—
*(She goes around the table, placing little plates with tiny silver bubbles on them before all her guests.)*

KHALID: All right then. Simply: there would be fifty-seven Asians, twenty-one Europeans—

SUZIE: *(To Terence, overlap.)* Don't peek—

TERENCE: *(Overlap.)* But I am anxious, desperate anxious—

KHALID: Fourteen from the Western Hemisphere, both north and south, eight Africans—

SUZIE: *(Overlap.)* This is very important what he's saying, it's absolutely the right place to start—

KHALID: Fifty-two would be female—

LYDIA: A majority, ha ha ha ha!

SUZIE: *(Setting down a bubble.) Amuse bouche,* to amuse your mouth!

KHALID: Forty-eight would be male. Seventy would be non-white.

SUZIE: Non-white, meaning—?

JULIA: Uh. Not, uh, white.

SUZIE: *(Laughs.)* Oh I see, of course, go on!

*(She laughs, Julia laughs, and then everyone laughs.)*

KHALID: Seventy would be non-Christian. Thirty would be Christian. Eighty-nine would be heterosexual, eleven would be homosexual.

SUZIE: Stop that. I'll tell you when you can look.

*(Suzie slaps Terence's hand, as he tries to peek.)*

KHALID: Shall I keep going?

LYDIA: Yes, please.

SUZIE: Yes yes, we're fascinated.

KHALID: Six people would possess 59 percent of the entire world's wealth and all six would be from the United States.

JULIA: Oh, my dear god. That's horrifying.

ROGER: Not to me.

KHALID: Eighty would live in substandard housing. Seventy would be unable to read. Fifty would suffer from malnutrition.

SUZIE: *(Clanging on a little triangle.)* Could I interrupt for a moment. Merely a taste treat, *(A very bad French accent.)* a "pre-apetiser," ladies and gentlemen—you may lift your thingies!

*(They lift the silver hoods and on everyone's plate is a very tiny portion of something.)*

JULIA: My oh my. It's the size of a jellybean.

ROGER: What is it?

SUZIE: It's a marvelous mini beet tartar thingiedo made of thinly sliced—Not yet, Terence!—Golden and Candy Cane beets, tossed with peppery icicle radish tops and finished with a vivacious drizzle of tangy tangerine oil.

JULIA: *(A gasp.)* Oh my.

SUZIE: Carry on, with your list, Khalid, dear.

KHALID: *(As everyone eats.)* There's not much more to it. One would be near death.

JEFF: This is—amazing.

TERENCE: Oh my gracious—

ROGER: Whoa—Suz—

*(All are moaning with delight at the taste of the thing.)*

KHALID: One would be near birth.

LYDIA: *(A shout of delight.)* Ohhh! This is unbelievable.

KHALID: Only one would have a college education. One! When you consider our world from such a compressed perspective, the need for acceptance and understanding is so urgent, my friends. So urgent.

JEFF: Can I ask for another?

TERENCE: Me too!

SUZIE: Only one per person. Don't worry. There's food aplenty. I'll be right back.

(*Suzie disappears into a smoking red hole in the ground. Roger stands up, startled.*)

JEFF: I think that was good, but there was so little of it it's kinda hard to tell.

ROGER: Whoa! What the hell is that?

JULIA: I'm resisting the urge to lick the plate.

ROGER: Suz? Suzie? Sukie, honey? Anybody else see that?

SUZIE: (*Reentering from trap door, holding a bottle up as she enters.*) Cheers! Everyone! I nearly forgot! Ta ta ta ta!!! This is an exquisite Tenuta dell Ornellaia from the house of Something, the year, let's see, squinting, squinting, nineteen hundred and eighty-five.

TERENCE: Pass it down, dear, I'll do the honors.

SUZIE: Yes, please, unleash the elixir! I was feeling so badly after the attacks I bid on two cases of this stuff.

(*Terence starts to uncork two bottles while Suzie puts several others on the sideboard.*)

KHALID: Another example of the unquestioning American drive for acquisition.

ROGER: Don't knock capitalism. That's the only way this country will recover. Get the money flowing. Create wealth.

SUZIE: No that's not what I was doing, I was just thinking about getting a little tipsy with my favorite people.

TERENCE: Ah, the bouquet, it's exquisite. How much was this?

JULIA: Is there anybody else who is worried by that, the idea that our spiritual response to any catastrophe should be to go out and shop?

ROGER: No, it's a good idea. I'll be damned if I'd spend my money on French wine, but—

SUZIE: Okay, you can just drink it. There's nothing wrong with a little retail therapy, is there, Khalid?

KHALID: I have reservations but perhaps I've already said too much.

TERENCE: There he goes, down into his own little existential hell.

SUZIE: Already?

TERENCE: Don't worry, he comes right out. I've known him for years. It's the discrepancies he finds so howlingly alarming. *(Holding up his glass.)* Cheers, mates! Here's to discrepancies! *Le monde se lon l'homme!*

JULIA: I'd like to bless the meal.

SUZIE: *(Surprised.)* Oh!

*(Julia stands, lowers her head, and prays. Everyone follows suit.)*

JULIA: We have come together tonight in the hope of understanding and fellowship. Suzie has generously shared her gifts with us by creating this beautiful feast, a plenty of nourishment for our souls and our bodies. We thank her for that. Bless this food. Bless this moment, and everyone here. Bless the life that fills this room, and holds us in harmony with the living universe. Amen.

ALL: Amen.

SUZIE: Thank you, Julia. That was lovely.

TERENCE: *(Any chance to celebrate.)* Splendid! Hear hear!

KHALID: Yes, very beautiful sentiment to be sure.

SUZIE: And now it's time for the first course!

*(A tray full of food suddenly appears in a doorway.)*

LYDIA: I'm starved.

JEFF: Me too.

SUZIE: This is a beautiful Wild Salmon, caught in the deep waters of the Columbia River, which has been pan-roasted and ingeniously served with a confit of tomato and fennel on a tower of sliced ruby crescent fingerlings. *(Plainly to Roger, who doesn't get it.)* Potatoes.

TERENCE: That's astonishing.

SUZIE: The whole meal has been designed by Alfred Portale. We go way back. Not as far back as some people— *(Off Roger.)* But there was one night, in Rome—oh, I can't tell you everything! This on the side, is a lovely warmish sauce made from lobster stock, champagne vinegar, and young shallots.

LYDIA: In America, even our shallots are young.

*(Everyone laughs, or not.)*

SUZIE: *(Serving Jeff.)* Here you go, sweetheart.

JEFF: Thanks, Suzie.

SUZIE: *(To someone near.)* He's a fireman.

KHALID: Perhaps I might explain why that list was so provocative to me.

JEFF: Is there anything on tap?

SUZIE: We have imported water! Water pitcher! Could you pass this down, pass this down—

*(She hands them water pitchers, which get passed down both sides of the table.)*

KHALID: Unbridled capitalism has long been a concern to the global community—

SUZIE: *(To Julia.)* I love your jacket, is that Donna's?

KHALID: Warnings have been made again and again and the resistance in America—

JULIA: I got it at Lohman's. They cut the tag out.

KHALID: —to the simplest examination of this basic question has been rather absolute. We must reflect.

LYDIA: Americans, reflect?

ROGER: Hey. You don't get to criticize us after you blew up the World Trade Center.

*(They all protest at once.)*

JULIA: He didn't—

JEFF: No, no, now—

SUZIE: Oh, no, we can't—

TERENCE: He didn't—

LYDIA: He didn't do it—

SUZIE: How can you say that?

JULIA: We have to be sensitive to racial issues.

ROGER: I'm not going to defend myself! I'm sorry, Suzie. I thought I was coming to a dinner party. I thought there would be a band or something, and now I'm stuck in the same old argument. People don't like capitalism, so lunatics get to come over here and blow things up? Sorry.

JULIA: I don't think that's what he—

ROGER: It makes me sick. Sukie. Let's put on some music, huh?

SUZIE: But we're debating!

ROGER: You can't debate with half-wits.

*(Julia, Terence and Lydia protest this.)*

KHALID: *(Overlap.)* You cannot just brush this away! These events cannot be seen as unrelated!

TERENCE: *(Overlap.)* Yes Khalid, but—lord I am loathe to second my conservative friend—

ROGER: Can I have the wine?

JULIA: Is there white? I don't want to overwhelm the salmon, it's exquisite by the way.

TERENCE: But you have to ask yourself—

SUZIE: White! Where is my head? Where is my head!!!?

TERENCE: Don't worry about it, Suzie dear, wild salmon stands up to red, it really does—

SUZIE: Oh dear, oh dear, oh dear!

*(She rushes to the trap, opens it.)*

TERENCE: *(Continuing.)* Suzie, really, darling—oh well.

KHALID: *(To Terence.)* Carry on.

TERENCE: As I was saying, Khalid, you must ask yourself if a causal relationship in this situation actually supports your thesis.

*(Suzie disappears in the trap. Julia watches, fascinated.)*

TERENCE: *(Continuing.)* The proposition that mass murders committed by the most reactionary world actors are an expression of international outrage against the American marketplace, actually sabotages your argument in its nascency.

LYDIA: Whoa. What?

TERENCE: Cambridge, darling, you had to keep up. These men are madmen, you'd say they were psychotic, if that wasn't an insult to psychotics everywhere. If you link all critical analysis of the capitalist project to the destruction of the twin towers, you associate the horrific violence of one particular act with a much more benign set of goals—social justice, say, or the diminishment of poverty worldwide.

JULIA: They taught you that at Cambridge?

TERENCE: Yes, but what can you do with it, other than show off at dinner parties?

KHALID: I understand what you are saying—

JEFF: I don't.

KHALID: —but it is naive to ignore the fact that everywhere in the world this association is being made.

*(Suzie returns with many bottles.)*

SUZIE: Here's the white! The white!! Roger, do the honors—

*(She hands him a bottle.)*

TERENCE: That doesn't stop it from presenting a version of reality which is every bit as mind-numbingly idiotic as everyone out there waving flags and saying God Bless America.

JEFF: I don't think that's idiotic.

TERENCE: Not idiotic then. Let's say unnerving.

LYDIA: Can I have the water, please?

SUZIE: Absolutely! Oh, you didn't eat your salmon.

LYDIA: I'm a vegan.

SUZIE: Oh. Oh—ah—I wish I had known that—

JEFF: Can I have your salmon, I mean, if you're not going to eat it?

LYDIA: Absolutely.

JEFF: This stuff is incredible. You should try it.

LYDIA: I can't.

TERENCE: What is a vegan? I mean, precisely?

LYDIA: I can't eat anything with a face.

JEFF: Fish don't have faces.

LYDIA: They most certainly do.

ROGER: Fish don't have beards.

TERENCE: They have faces but they don't have a nervous system.

JULIA: That's lobsters.

TERENCE: Lobsters and shellfish have exoskeletons.

KHALID: Shells but no nervous systems.

LYDIA: *(Getting defensive.)* Then why do they scream when you put them in boiling water?

SUZIE: That's not the lobster, that's the steam that's trapped in the shell, dear.

LYDIA: How do you know?

SUZIE: I think I would know.

JULIA: I think he's right, I don't think fish have nervous systems either.

LYDIA: I don't care about the nervous system. I'm not eating anything with a face!

JULIA: Shellfish don't have faces.

LYDIA: Yes they do. Shrimp have eyes and tails.

TERENCE: Tails aren't faces.

LYDIA: I didn't say they were.

JEFF: Scallops! Scallops, clams and mussels have no faces.

ROGER: Scallops have faces. I had a pet scallop once.

SUZIE: Quahogs!

TERENCE: A quahog is a clam.

LYDIA: *(Finally.)* So, if this was a clam, I might eat it, but it's not a clam, it's salmon.

SUZIE: Do Arabs eat shellfish?

KHALID: I'll have to check my notes.

JEFF: Is there bread?

SUZIE: Oh no no. Bread is over!

JEFF: Over?

SUZIE: All that starch just interferes with the complexity of the meal. Besides, it's very bad for you.

*(She slaps his hand.)*

ROGER: Could I have the red, or is that your personal stash?

TERENCE: *(Lining up the bottles before him.)* I drink to make other people interesting.

JEFF: The white is really good.

JULIA: You know, a lot of times people in my congregation come to me, especially now, and they're feeling overwhelmed, and they want to know, What am I doing with my life? Is what I'm doing enough? I mean, when do we question our usefulness?

TERENCE: Never. Ever!

SUZIE: I'm useful! I've found a way to help women and men all over the world find their creative souls by embracing the domestic arts. I was just a caterer!

ROGER: *(Gracious and gruff.)* Suzie, there is nothing "just" about you. Then, or now.

SUZIE: Thank you, you old fatty. *(To others.)* We go way back.

JEFF: You started as a caterer?

SUZIE: Yes!

ROGER: She sure did!

SUZIE: I was working out of my basement! The immediate response was terrific, well back then there weren't very many people doing it, word of mouth was really all you needed.

JULIA: How does that work? You go to people's houses and cook for them, or do you cook somewhere else and bring it—

SUZIE: That never works. Everything dries out.

ROGER: How about that catalogue food? Is that any good?

TERENCE: Exquisitely prepared filet mignon, just appearing at your doorstep, I confess I've fantasized about that.

JEFF: Those pictures, they look so delicious.

LYDIA: Can I just say that red meat from a catalogue sounds—

ROGER: Stop it right there, we're not interested.

SUZIE: No, don't do it. Catalogue food. Just don't do it.

JEFF: *(Prompting Suzie.)* So the catering business took off.

SUZIE: Yes. And I realized—well, that people were looking for beauty in their lives. "Esthetic Serenity," I call it. And delicious food!

LYDIA: But this isn't like, spiritual. You know that, right?

SUZIE: No darling, really it is. That's what I'm saying.

ROGER: Don't criticize the hostess.

LYDIA: I wasn't criticizing, I was asking a question! You're the one, you were absolutely rude to me before—

SUZIE: A lively, contentious debate is the heart and soul of every dinner party but I do think we should wait until the main course is served, don't you?

*(There is the loud sound of a helicopter passing overhead. They look up.)*

SUZIE: *(Continuing; oblivious, to Jeff.)* Let me refresh your glass, dear. Anyone else?

*(Lydia holds her water glass up, as do several others. Suzie pours.)*

KHALID: I agree with Lydia.

LYDIA: How can you agree? I didn't get to finish my point.

ROGER: You implied. Your tone of voice—

LYDIA: My what?!?

KHALID: Suzie has had an entitled American experience. For you, this is a dream come true.

SUZIE: Oh yes!

KHALID: You pray at night and God answers your prayers, or seems to. Perhaps your secret terror is that it will vanish.

SUZIE: No.

KHALID: It will change.

SUZIE: No.

KHALID: You may have to share more.

SUZIE: *(Startled.)* Share more with whom?

*(There is a slight, but deadly, pause. Terence clears his throat.)*

TERENCE: Perhaps he's suggesting, and I hope you don't take it as an offense that I bring this up, but while you employ people all over the world, Suzie, and by the way, god this is monstrously good—

JULIA: Just delicious.

JEFF: I've never tasted anything ever I've liked so much.

*(All demur.)*

LYDIA: You were saying...

TERENCE: And I hope you don't think this is said in anything except the spirit of dinner party bonhomie, but the fact is—

ROGER: Can't you just get to the point?

TERENCE: Ah, but who can remember what it is?

*(He laughs and reaches for the wine.)*

LYDIA: Standard of living. That's where you're going.

TERENCE: Was I?

LYDIA: Weren't you?

TERENCE: They also taught discretion at Cambridge, darling.

SUZIE: No no, I want to know. What about my standard of living?

LYDIA: Not yours. The people who work for you.

SUZIE: What about them?

LYDIA: You don't pay them enough.

SUZIE: Oh, but I do. I'm sure I do.

LYDIA: How much do you pay them?

SUZIE: *(Suddenly forgetting.)* Pay who?

LYDIA: All the cookware and the kitchen mitts and the matching tablecloths and napkins and ironing boards have to come from somewhere, Suzie— *(Suzie stands, annoyed, and passes around the salmon again.)*

SUZIE: How could I keep all those facts and figures running through my head. I'd have to be a one-man band. *(To Jeff.)* Would you like more? You worked so hard and we are so grateful for what you've done, have as much as you like.

JEFF: It's very good.

SUZIE: And so well-mannered.
*(She shoots Lydia a look.)*

JULIA: All the pieces of the puzzle are so complex.

KHALID: Yes, yes, it is overwhelming to even begin, to approach—

ROGER: What are we supposed to do? Spend all our time worrying about the complexities? Listen to me. We don't *have* time. We're at war. So I'm not getting involved in all this hand-wringing. We have to get a little crazy on everybody, is what we have to do.

LYDIA: "Getting crazy on 'em," there's a sophisticated position.

ROGER: When they're getting crazy on us it's not time to be sophisticated!

SUZIE: *(Trying meekly to get attention.)* Um. Excuse me…

ROGER: I'm not arguing for oversimplification, I'm just making it easy for the boob mentality.

LYDIA: "Boob" mentality?

JULIA: No, no. That's banal.

ROGER: "Banal"?

JULIA: The banal language of combat—I don't mean to insult, but—

ROGER: *(Overlap.)* There is what is right, and what is unfortunately necessary.

LYDIA: *(Overlap.)* No, no, she's right, that's just reductive and disgusting.

ROGER: *(Overlap.)* It's a code of war.

JULIA: Next thing you'll be saying "Let's smoke 'em out—"

ROGER: Yes, and get 'em running—

SUZIE: *(Quietly.) Pardon.*

JULIA: Do you know what that is? That's the language of lynching. Do you even know that—

ROGER: You know that's not—

JULIA: Or Amos and Andy. Tonto and the Lone Ranger—

JEFF: Is there something wrong with them, too?

ROGER: No!

JULIA: Yes!

LYDIA: There is if that's what you think life is. That's what you think it all boils down to.

ROGER: *(Overlap.)* Don't pull that crap. I'm grateful that someone in this country is thinking about consequences. You should be too.

SUZIE: *(Hand raised.)* Excuse—

ROGER: Because if you don't like it here, if it's not evolved enough for you, find a better place! No I mean it!

LYDIA: *(Overlap.)* "Love it or leave it," it's the perfect answer to anyone suggesting we actually work at being a better nation—

ROGER: *(Overlap.)* Go to Baghdad. Go to Afghanistan for that matter, let the Taliban cover you in a sheet and throw you in an open grave for a couple weeks, then give me a call!

SUZIE: *(Finally!)* But what about me? What about my feelings? I mean, can I just say I feel a little itty bitty bit attacked? I appreciate what you're all saying but I do the best I can with what I have!! I give a heck of a lot of money away! I'm aware of my wealth. I used to be middle-class. I know how that feels.

ROGER: *(Pointedly re: Lydia.)* You're a *nice* person.

SUZIE: I'm trying. It's complicated. We're none of us, just one thing or another. Good or bad.

JULIA: You're right, Suzie. And that's why we fall into absolutism. Just pretending we're right and they're wrong, like there's security in that.

KHALID: So we are then, all of us seeking let's say, a false oneness to pull us through the demanding duality of life.

JULIA: Yes, it's so cunning how we do it. How we all judge and compare constantly.

TERENCE: But judgement is so relaxing. And fun!

JULIA: Yes, but it offers an utterly unreal feeling of power and security. And elitism. In fact, there's nothing real about it.

ROGER: There's nothing real in identifying an enemy?

JULIA: Enemy? See, that word is what I'm talking about—

ROGER: They're flying planes into buildings! What am I supposed to call them? What they did is pure evil! And I'm sick of hearing everyone make excuses!

JULIA: *(Overlap.)* "Evil," there's another one of those words.

ROGER: Oh, brother—

LYDIA: No, she's right. You all pull out words like "evil" to trick people into subscribing to your political agenda.

SUZIE: *(To Jeff.)* Do you need more white?

ROGER: Oh, so that's what I'm doing.

LYDIA: You're stealing from the Nazi playbook! They invented this kind of reckless dissemination of hysterical propaganda.

ROGER: Great, now I'm a Nazi.

TERENCE: I do think it was the Stalinists, darling—

SUZIE: White? White?

JULIA: Perhaps we should try to set reactivity aside, in our search for meaning.

SUZIE: White? White?

ROGER: She called me a Nazi!

JULIA: How do we stop arguing long enough to give ourselves half a second to find it?

SUZIE: Find what, I'm sorry?

TERENCE: Meaning dear. Meaning.

SUZIE: Ohhhhh.

ROGER: You think those mullahs over there developing nuclear bombs and biological who-knows-what are looking for meaning?

LYDIA: *(Edgy.)* I think the point is that we should *all* be looking for meaning.

ROGER: You know, there's that tone again.

LYDIA: *(High, soft Marilyn voice.)* "Oh I'm sorry. Is this better?"

ROGER: Yes.

SUZIE: Try to get along! That's what Julia's saying.

*(Suzie taps her water glass, aggressively.)*

SUZIE: *(Continuing.)* What can we agree on, that's the question!!

TERENCE: The wine is in my glass. The table is hard. The food is superb. Roger is an idiot. Sorry, sorry, just slipped out.

ROGER: I need a smoke.

LYDIA: No smoking!

SUZIE: *(Dinging glass.)* Agree! Agree!

ROGER: He called me an idiot!

KHALID: This reminds me of my childhood.

JULIA: We can agree that the food is delicious!

ROGER: Alright. Fine. Agreed.

JULIA: That we need the food—

SUZIE: We can agree on that, can't we?

LYDIA: I'm a vegan, so I actually do have issues here.

JULIA: You're a "vegan," but you need food.

LYDIA: Not meat! I don't need meat, and neither do you.

ROGER: I need meat, goddammit, it's protein. Only a fool doesn't eat protein.

LYDIA: But it's blood, you're eating blood!

TERENCE: *(Lifting his wineglass.)* Wine, the blood of you know who, does that count?

LYDIA: We don't need blood!

KHALID: Could you pass the wine?

ROGER: You're probably one of those Pita people.

LYDIA: Peta! Peta!

SUZIE: Bread is pita, this is Peta. Pita, Peta. Pita, Peta. Although all bread, as we know, is over!

ROGER: *(Re: Lydia.)* Why is she here? I've spent my whole life trying to keep these people out of earshot.

SUZIE: It's a dinner party!

ROGER: Where's the music?

JULIA: This is the exercise. This is the meat of life.

TERENCE: Oh no, don't bring meat up again, please. Refills, anyone?

> *(He goes to the sideboard to open more wine. There is another sound of explosion, in the distance. People look around.)*

SUZIE: Oh, I just wish that would stop!

KHALID: Do you know what it is?

SUZIE: No idea. None whatever.

JULIA: Is it something we should be worried about?

SUZIE: I certainly hope not.

JEFF: You want me to go look?

SUZIE: No, sit! Enjoy your meal!

ROGER: Here's what I have to say to all of you: *JIHAD*.

LYDIA: Meaning what?

ROGER: Meaning, look alive! You're talking about bread and meat and whatever—I wrote a huge bestseller about this!

SUZIE: *(Rising to escape Roger's story.)* Let me take that for you.

ROGER: And I mean, I won't go into the whole plot but—

JULIA: Can I give you a hand?

SUZIE: No, I'm fine.

ROGER: But after a catastrophic nuclear terrorist attack over in another part of the world in Chapter One—

JULIA: Let me help you—

*(They both start to clear plates. Roger continues over the noise.)*

ROGER: It becomes obvious in Chapter Two, that the fate of the whole world can only be secure under the leadership of a kind of new world governance.

SUZIE: Don't forget the forks, dear—

ROGER: Which is run by, and here's where it gets interesting, the President of the United States of America of the World.

TERENCE: Oh bully for everyone!

SUZIE: Would you mind passing me that platter?

ROGER: And by Chapter Four—

SUZIE: Uh huh. Listening. Listening.

LYDIA: May I have some red? Just a splash—

ROGER: No, no, I mean Chapter Six—

TERENCE: Take the white, the red is mine.

ROGER: A war begins between the International Terrorist Party and the M.I.E.C.

LYDIA: What's M.I.E.C.?

ROGER: Military Industrial Entertainment Complex. Which is really the shadow government, see? With underground cities all over the world. And the Terrorist Party is trying to infiltrate it by having sex with—well, it's really a spy novel when you get down to it, but the point is, the point is…

TERENCE: *(Demonstratively impatient.)* Yeeeeeees?

ROGER: The point is that all the people, like you, had no goddamn imagination and then it happened! See, I wrote that years ago! I'm not just a good novelist, I'm fucking psychic!

TERENCE: Egads! Why didn't you call and warn them, man?

ROGER: You'll see. Ask him how it feels.

*(He indicates Jeff. All eyes turn.)*

JEFF: It feels….

*(After a moment, he shakes his head.)*

ROGER: That's right. He can't even say. So do we have the right to stop them before they come at us again? You bet we do. As far as I'm concerned, the world is just a bunch of spoiled teenagers. They want us to watch over them, help 'em out, and politely stand by while they complain and criticize us. Christ! If there's gonna be a goddamn world power, I'm glad it's us!

SUZIE: But why does there have to be a world power at all?

ROGER: Oh, grow up.

SUZIE: Rog!

ROGER: Oh. Sorry, Suz. It's just that if we let go of our power, someone else is just going to step up. And who is that going to be? Russia? China? Korea? *(To the others.)* See what I mean? See what I mean?

TERENCE: Another point, brilliantly made.

ROGER: Damn right. I need a smoke.

SUZIE: *(Clanging on the triangle.)* You don't have time for that!
*(Another tray full of food appears.)*

SUZIE: *(Continuing.)* The main course *sont arrivez*. You're really going to enjoy this one! This, my friends, is a dish from the South of Pakistan, a favorite among moderate Shiites— *(To Roger.)* Not one word! *(Continuing to the group.)* Comprised of freshly blessed lamb…
*(She reaches for a plate and starts to serve the lamb.)*

LYDIA: Lamb?

SUZIE: *(Quick, overriding her serving another dish.)* Rubbed and marinated in rock salt, lemon, indigenous cinnamon and the blackest of pepper.

TERENCE: Oh my, oh my.

SUZIE: Roasted and served with coush coush, that's its correct pronunciation, "coush coush," dotted with figs, Majool dates, cilantro and green onion.

JEFF: What's that stuff on the side?

SUZIE: Hot curried corn, which I use as a kind of, well, relish, which means you can skip it, if you like. My grandmother suffered from colitis so corn is always optional with me.

LYDIA: What is colitis?

SUZIE: I'll explain it later. It's not exactly dinner table conversation.

KHALID: My mother had colitis. It was excruciating for her, so very painful. And she loved food so much, she could deny herself nothing, the nuts and the strawberries, she finally died from it.

SUZIE: I'm so sorry.

LYDIA: But what is it?

JULIA: Excuse me. Where is the rest room?
*(Suzie points her to the pit. Julia goes.)*

ROGER: The lining of the bowels gets inflamed, infected, so any kind of food that gets stuck down there causes terrible intestinal distress. Especially things like corn. *(Offers food to seatmate.)* Careful, it's hot.

TERENCE: No, that's not colitis. That's diverticulitis. Colitis is—

LYDIA: *(Appalled now.)* Oh no, oh, god, please! I'm so sorry I asked.

*(In the corner, Julia opens a hatch. A huge waft of smoke, red light, appear.)*

JULIA: Oh my. Oh my. Is this right?

SUZIE: Yes, yes, go on, it's down the steps and around the corner, a sharp left, you'll see! Who needs wine?

*(Perplexed, Julia goes. The conversation continues. Suzie serves wine.)*

TERENCE: I'm speaking there.

LYDIA: Where?

TERENCE: The Colitis Foundation of America has asked me to speak. Muhammad Ali was there last year.

SUZIE: A Muslim.

LYDIA: He had colitis?

TERENCE: An American Muslim with colitis, yes.

LYDIA: Why did they ask you?

TERENCE: You know, it's a foundation, darling. They need people of a certain stature, I suppose.

LYDIA: Stature, you have stature?

TERENCE: Well… a little stature goes a long way these days. Cheers!

*(He drinks.)*

SUZIE: Don't be ridiculous, you're very famous. He's famous, just like the rest of you.

LYDIA: I make no claim to be famous.

SUZIE: Well, I'm famous.

JEFF: I'm not famous.

SUZIE: You are now!

TERENCE: I was famous once. Fifteen minutes, or perhaps it was a little less than that.

ROGER: I'm famous. I'm the most famous person here.

SUZIE: Has anyone read Roger's latest novel? He writes one a year. They make big movies out of them. Blockbusters! President Reagan once said Roger was his favorite novelist.

ROGER: Now he doesn't know who the fuck I am, but I still get invitations to things.

LYDIA: And who are you?

KHALID: I'm mere. I'm just a man. A simple man with a simple cause.

SUZIE: Khalid is a scholar and an esteemed specialist in Middle Eastern studies.

ROGER: So?

TERENCE: Well, more wine, anyone? *(Stopping, stunned.)* Good Lord, Suz, this is a terrific bottle. *(Kissing the bottle.)* I'm undone.

SUZIE: How's the lamb everyone?

*(Everyone but Lydia applauds the lamb.)*

LYDIA: *(Concerned and hungry.)* Isn't there any uh, salad or anything?

SUZIE: Not until after the main course. Have some of this.

*(She takes the wine away from Terence and pours it for Jeff. The trap opens, and Julia reappears. She approaches the table, takes her seat.)*

JULIA: I found it. My God, It's kind of remarkable really—

SUZIE: It's an experience, isn't it?

JULIA: Well, first of all, it's very, how shall I put it…Big. And My God! All those endless mirrored walls and ceilings and then on the floor, what was that?

SUZIE: Burnished Venetian amber.

JULIA: Which is all back-lit, you know, so everything just sort of glows.

LYDIA: This sounds incredible.

JULIA: *(Charged, a little angry.)* Girl, you have to see it! I mean, it's big!

SUZIE: It's very special, if I say so myself!

JULIA: There I was, all by myself, you know, and I suddenly became aware of this kind of infinite chorus line reflection of me in every single mirror! I mean, I was just surrounded by ME, hundreds of "ME"s just sitting there. And, well, I started to feel sorry, so sorry, like I wanted to apologize but I didn't know to whom. *(Suddenly indicting.)* I mean, it's really less of a bathroom and more of a shrine to our own shit, isn't it?

TERENCE: Wowwee!

SUZIE: No no, it's fine, she's overwhelmed. Is that it, you're overwhelmed by the bathroom?

JULIA: Yes, that's exactly—could I have some of that? *(Recklessly pouring herself wine as she talks.)* I was down there and I thought of my mother and the little excursions we'd take to Bloomingdale's. We'd go up to the eighth floor where there were these little mock rooms, all decorated to the hilt, and she'd oohh and ahhh, I mean this was way better than a trip to the museum for her, it was more like an archeological foray into white people's lives only you didn't have to make small talk and pretend you were cozy. See, she wished that all that luxury could be mine one day, 'cause that was a sign of real achievement to her. But for me, hanging out in that ballroom you call a bathroom, well, it just made me feel so far away from her and so far away from anything real—look, no offense, Suzie, but don't you think having a gloriously appointed bathroom is the strangest barometer of fulfillment you could ever imagine?

*(Cell phone rings. Everyone panics, wondering if it's theirs. It's Roger's.)*

SUZIE: Cell phones *Verboten!*

*(Some people turn theirs off.)*

ROGER: Sorry. It'll only be a moment…

*(He steps away from the table to talk.)*

JULIA: *(Still angry.)* I'm just upset. Sorry. I'm upset. You're all staring at me. Suddenly, I feel like the only black person in the room.

JEFF: You are the only black person in the room.

SUZIE: I invited Denzel but he cancelled at the last minute. ROG!!!

ROGER: It's my mother!

KHALID: *(To Julia.)* I'm golden. But in the sun I turn black too.

SUZIE: I'm sorry my bathroom upset you so much. That decorator told me the floor thing would be soothing.

JULIA: *(The truth.)* Forget it. I'm sorry. I just feel so alone, sometimes, in situations like this.

SUZIE: What would make you feel better? Would you like to sing?

JULIA: Oh—no.

SUZIE: A little gospel tune or something? A Whitney Houston song, I love her, although really, she should eat.

JULIA: It's okay, Suzie. I'm really not much of a singer.

SUZIE: I'm sure you're wonderful!

JULIA: No, I'm not. *(Ironic.)* I'm the only black person on earth who can't sing.

SUZIE: *(Not getting it.)* I'm sure that's not true!!

KHALID: I love music. You don't like to sing?

JULIA: Well, actually, I do, I've always loved it. I'm just, really, I'm not very good at it.

SUZIE: Who told you that?

JULIA: Mrs. Gambi, who led the choir in grade school. My cousin Frank. Three separate boyfriends in college.

SUZIE: Well, you can't let them silence you! No no no, listen: If I listened to everyone who told me I was a dingaling, I would never have all this!

ROGER: She's right about that. Nobody believed in her. Except for me, I saw the genius before anybody.

SUZIE: He was heroic. *(To Rog, back story.)* You were. *(To Terence.)* He was!

JULIA: I think that's different.

LYDIA: No it's not.

KHALID: Why would that be different?

JULIA: Well, because because….you want me to sing?

*(Everyone agrees they do.)*

SUZIE: Don't you want to?

*(Julia thinks about this. The idea has an odd, friendly appeal to her.)*

JULIA: Actually, I think it would make me feel better.

SUZIE: Well, then you must! Give her room, give her room—

*(They encourage her, applauding. She stands, to sing, and then starts.)*

JULIA:

"I believe that children are our future.

Teach them well and let them lead the way.

Let them see the beauty that they have inside!

Give them a sense of pride, ta da da da.

I decided long ago, never to walk in anyone's shadow.

If I fail, if I succeed, at least I'll live as I believe,

no matter what they think of me,

they can't take away my dignity!

Because the greatest love of all is happening to me.

I found the greatest…love of all inside of me."

*(She stops. She is truly a terrible singer. The group is silenced for a moment by how awful she is.)*

ROGER: That was terrific.

*(The group all struggles valiantly to enthusiastically agree.)*

TERENCE: Really, just splendid. Who was that who told you you couldn't sing? Complete nonsense.

JULIA: Thank you. You're right, Suzie, I feel a lot better.

KHALID: *(Pouring wine.)* Yes, wonderful, wonderful. I was transfixed.

JULIA: I'm sure.

KHALID: *(Reassuring her.)* You are exquisite. Have some lamb, you must be hungry, and our hostess has outdone herself.

SUZIE: Thank you, sweetheart.

JEFF: And that coushcoush stuff, unbelievable. *(To Lydia.)* Can you have that?

LYDIA: I could if it weren't drenched in lamb fat.

JEFF: Well, it's real good.

TERENCE: I would like to pose a question, and god knows I don't mean to rile or provoke, but why peace? I mean, indeed. Why?

LYDIA: "Why peace?"

TERENCE: Historically it is an anomaly. I think we need to examine the possibility that peace is not a beneficial or desirable condition for the human race. If it were, it would have been more readily embraced by now.

JULIA: I disagree.

JEFF: There it is!

TERENCE: Hear me out.

KHALID: Oh dear. Is this a fly in my glass?

SUZIE: *(Gasping.)* Oh no! Oh no no, oh no—

*(She grabs the glass and takes it off.)*

LYDIA: So peace is still a sort of…

KHALID: Chimera…

LYDIA: A chimera, yes, is that what you mean?

*(Suzie returns, giving Khalid a new wineglass.)*

TERENCE: More along the lines of a child's fairy tale. Happily ever after, the imagined state of bliss which can never be fully or even partially described within the story itself because it is in fact a fantasy.

LYDIA: So, the human race, people, women, when we say we want peace we don't really mean it.

TERENCE: Perhaps peace is a romantic assumption that has no grounding in a post-modern utopia.

LYDIA: Hey. Enough with the British superiority, everything is so articulate and calming and dismissive when the fact is, this is just another version of some imperialistic old world excuse to be the right one in the room.

TERENCE: Well. *En garde.*

LYDIA: *(Riled and direct.)* We don't want peace? Let me tell you something. Women and children want peace and this is, you know, male narcissism, this global male narcissm, that we are all like you, want what you want, greed, winning, well, that's not what's driving the rest of us and the fact is some of us really do want the world to survive. What men want is not what everyone wants.

SUZIE: I'm an incest survivor, too.

LYDIA: No no. Don't do that. We're not victims together here, I'm not a victim and I have no interest in participating in some ludicrous victim identity. Everyone else seems to be really interested in that and I'll tell you something: I am not.

KHALID: Who are you in community with? You must be very lonely.

LYDIA: Because I don't identify myself as a victim, I'm lonely?

SUZIE: I'm never lonely.

KHALID: I'm lonely all the time. Which is why, you see, without community we have no container for our lives.

ROGER: Oh for god's sake. I'm not in community with you. I agree with her.

LYDIA: Don't agree with me. I am so not in community with you.

JEFF: God, this is good.

SUZIE: Thank you. I had help! Thousands of slaves!

TERENCE: Stunning. Bravo.

SUZIE: And wait till you see what else is coming!

TERENCE: Don't tell!

SUZIE: I won't! I won't!

JEFF: Are you going to have any?

LYDIA: No, you can have it all.

JEFF: You could have the corn stuff.

SUZIE: It's relish, dear. Relish.

LYDIA: What's in it?

SUZIE: Fresh September corn off the cob, red pepper and curried spices.

LYDIA: Fine. I'll take it.

*(She takes the bowl.)*

KHALID: Couldn't I have a drop of something, something hard, such as whiskey or scotch…

SUZIE: *(Already on her way to the trap door.)* Say no more! Scotch with the meal, *muy* macho.

*(She disappears.)*

KHALID: I need a little hard stuff on occasion. Helps me to forget.

TERENCE: *(Toasting.)* Here's to forgetting.

LYDIA: Forgetting what?

KHALID: Oh, you know. Pain. Loss. Death.

ROGER: Whoa!

TERENCE: Bravo! It isn't a dinner party until someone mentions the Grim Reaper, that's when you know you've really hit your stride.

KHALID: But death, that is not a metaphor! There is real danger here! You are being cast as enemies of god! If this is the perception, the call to fatwa is holy!

TERENCE: All right then, let me just say it: I detest all Abrahmic religions. Everyone killing in the name of God, please.

*(He picks up the lamb, starts to serve it, without skipping a beat.)*

ROGER: I'm not killing anybody in the name of God. I'm just defending myself.

JULIA: Yes, but it's logic like that which has us talking about nuclear war again. Could you pass the relish?

LYDIA: Okay, but I need it back!

ROGER: What are we supposed to do, just sit there?

TERENCE: Wait wait wait. I want some of that.

*(He intercepts the relish.)*

JULIA: That's what Ghandi did. That and organized peaceful protest.

LYDIA: You don't want that, it's not that good.

ROGER: As part of a strategy.

JULIA: *(Angry now.)* As part of true belief! Come on! If you guys are saying "nuclear war" and Ghandi is saying "peaceful protest," well, I'm going to go stand over here, with Ghandi! *(Furious.)* Give me the relish!

TERENCE: All right, all right!

JULIA: Sorry. It's just, there comes a point when peace isn't some crazy ideal, it's just common fucking sense!

LYDIA: Can I have that back? It's the only thing without a face.

ROGER: You can't just ask for peace! It's too simple!

JULIA: Why?

JEFF: I'd like some of that, too.

LYDIA: Too late!

ROGER: You can't just talk about a paradigm for peace with people as nuts as Hitler!

JULIA: Oh, and we're not nuts? We're enslaved to oil, we're poisoning the planet, and we're ready to kill our own children, send them into battle, to preserve our right to do that!

ROGER: That's simplistic.

JULIA: No it's not! It's fucking not!

SUZIE: *(Re-emerging.) Et voilà.* Bourbon! *Pour Monsieur Khalid.*

TERENCE: Our buds of taste are all aflutter, dear Suzie. You missed death, global annihilation—

JULIA: Ghandi.

TERENCE: And Hitler.

LYDIA: *(Pointing to Roger.)* He brought him up, not me.

SUZIE: Good. Oh, good!

TERENCE: I can't remember the last time something tasted so good. I did have a marvelous white rat at the Royal Palace in Constantinople.

ROGER: I ate there once. Chocolate fucking bugs and shit.

*(He pulls out a pack of cigarettes.)*

LYDIA: *(Reacting.)* Hey, hey, hey!!!

ROGER: Oh, here it comes—

TERENCE: Tremendous! Smoking at the dinner table, we'll have our own little world war three. *(He pulls out his own pack.)*

LYDIA: I'm not kidding about this. This is not good!

ROGER: Look. I don't care! I grew up in a different time.

SUZIE: We all did, dear Roger. Terence!

ROGER: It was considered civilized!

LYDIA: So was the atom bomb!

ROGER: The atom bomb ended the war! Truman was our greatest president!

LYDIA: He dropped the bomb!

SUZIE: *(Springing up.)* But the problem is, you can't smoke in here because it will destabilize the air quality. Because of that nasty eternal fire, I have to have my air flown in. Now, come on, Roggie, you can smoke down here.

ROGER: *(As they go.)* I just thought this would be a little more relaxing, honey. You know. Sinatra. A band.

SUZIE: Just wait until you see what's coming later!

ROGER: Is it a band?

*(They exit through the trap. Lydia watches, while the others eat.)*

LYDIA: Wait a minute. So it's burning, but the air is pure? Is anyone else having trouble with this?

KHALID: Paradox. Like America itself. Which is at once both the thing and its opposite.

TERENCE: Hats off to paradox. *(He lights up.)*

KHALID: *"Aureo Apprehensio."*

JULIA: Golden Understanding.

TERENCE: Enlightenment.

JULIA: Faith.

TERENCE: Faith, oh no no, please, God. Faith. What the devil is it, faith?

JEFF: It's just—faith.

KHALID: Faith replaces the cynical ambivalence we all feel as a defense to the world.

TERENCE: You haven't a clue then.

JULIA: Yes I do. The universe makes perfect sense, just not to us.

TERENCE: Oh good. That clears it up then, clears it right up.

JULIA: Faith gives us the stamina to accomplish the difficult task of being human.

*(Suzie and Roger emerge.)*

JULIA: *(Continuing.)* You know, The Bible says—

TERENCE: Oh, god. The Bible. Here it comes, here it comes, a gentle segue into biblical topics leading straight into the Promised Land and the Chosen people!

ROGER: *(Beginning to exit again.)* You should have let me finish that cigarette.

TERENCE: Bloody Israel!

SUZIE: No, no, no you can't keep leaving!

ROGER: Don't start in on Israel!

TERENCE: My mother is Jewish. I can say whatever I want.

JEFF: Is there any salad?

SUZIE: Yes dear, you're so right.

LYDIA: Oh good, oh good.

*(Terence pulls out a cigarette.)*

SUZIE: Terence!

*(Another table appears in the doorway. This one sports salad.)*

ROGER: Look here, Israel is America's moral and philosophical partner, and its founders were people like us, fleeing oppression, and their democracy is the only one in the region, based on freedom and tolerance.

KHALID: Tolerance?

TERENCE: Yes, yes, I've heard all about it. My mother wanted to go to Palestine, a.k.a., "Israel," very badly at one point.

ROGER: Good for her.

TERENCE: Well I told her, "Mum, dear, it's a bad bloody idea. An overzealous, messianic shithole of an idea, oh, and by the way, what do you suppose we're going to do with all those Arabs after we take their land away from them?"

ROGER: Take it away? Israel was deemed a Sovereign State by the United Nations in 1948.

TERENCE: Take it away and give it to a whole bunch of sophisticated Jews so that they can suddenly turn themselves into peasant farmers, what kind of an idea is this?

ROGER: They turned a desert into a garden for crying out loud.

TERENCE: They stole the fucking water! Besides which the occupation—

ROGER: Here we go—

TERENCE: And I don't give a shit! That is precisely what it is—

ROGER: It's their Goddamn Biblical Homeland!!

TERENCE: Not the State, the *occupation*, presents a guaranteed injustice—

ROGER: Golan Heights, the Sinai Peninsula, the West Bank were all gained after Israel was attacked in a war!!!

TERENCE: May I finish!! Injustice against the Arabs—

ROGER: They didn't even want that land—

TERENCE: Let me finish. And now, to add insult to injustice, this fence—this *wall*—

ROGER: Mark Twain went there at the end of the nineteenth—The Balfour Declaration! Ah, you don't know your history! There were Jews already there! But as soon as they claimed it as their homeland, every Arab in the world bragged—bragged!—that they would drive them into the sea!

TERENCE: Four decades of Arabs suffering under the most humiliating and degraded conditions—

ROGER: Humiliated by fellow Arabs who never lift a finger to help their own—

TERENCE: Children murdered in the streets by Israeli soldiers—

ROGER: Palestinian maniacs blowing themselves up—

TERENCE: Nobody's hands are clean over there! Nobody's hands are clean! And now, the world's finally recognizing the disastrous error behind the whole bloody thing! And as far as I'm concerned anyone who doesn't agree with me is a fucking idiot!

ROGER: There's no need to lose your temper.

TERENCE: Look here, the point is, if Jews born in Yonkers, or Los Angeles or Cleveland for godsakes, have a right to a blasted bloody state in Palestine, then it should follow Palestinians born in Jerusalem also have a right to a state in Palestine, or how about some carved up Palestinian settlements smack in the middle of West Palm Beach or East Hampton for that matter!! *(To Khalid.)* Any time you want to leap in, be my guest.

KHALID: No, you're doing just fine.

ROGER: The world will always use a double standard toward the Jews because they hate Jews.

SUZIE: Wonderful! What a wonderful point! I'd like to turn your attention, if I may, to the salad!

ROGER: This is the prelude to another holocaust.

TERENCE: Oh the big H. I knew you were going to say that!

ROGER: Arabs want a final solution, not just to Israel. But to Jews! All Jews, everywhere!! *(Pointedly.)* And that means you!!

KHALID: Stop. Stop, please. Your position is so cruel and demeaning to all of us. To my people, to your people.

ROGER: Your leaders support Saddam Hussein.

KHALID: So did yours!

ROGER: They supported Bin Laden.

KHALID: So did yours!

ROGER: At the moment when Israel was ready to make peace, they declared war.

KHALID: A Jewish extremist murdered his own peacemaker! You see, tragic mistakes have been made by both sides, but we must not despair. Please.

SUZIE: Such a lively debate. Wonderful, really, bravo to everyone. Now, for the salad. I, for one have never been a fan of frisee. It's too wild on the plate. I do a nice melange of Belgian endive, radicchio and watercress in a light vinaigrette tossed with whole toasted walnuts.

LYDIA: Walnuts!! I'm fucking allergic to walnuts. I'm sorry, I'm sorry, I'm so so hungry. And aside from the relish and that thingiedo which was the size of a pea, I can't eat anything.

SUZIE: *(Annoyed.)* Well, you could just pick the walnuts out dear, if you must. Julia, could I impose on you?

JULIA: Of course.

SUZIE: You really are the perfect dinner guest.

*(They clear the table. Suzie starts to serve.)*

JEFF: Uh, sorry, where's the dressing?

SUZIE: It's totally dressed! And everything picked fresh from my own little hydroponic greenhouse.

ROGER: She does it all. She's a goddamn renaissance mogul.

SUZIE: You have such a way with words.

JULIA: I love to garden.

SUZIE: I'm just about to launch a great gardening website.

TERENCE: *(Pouring.)* Vino vite in vitro wino—

KHALID: Slow down, man.

SUZIE: You can literally create a garden of your own design, whatever you fancy—

TERENCE: No no, what is it, in vino vino?

KHALID: *In vino veritas.* Give me some of that.

SUZIE: *(Overlap.)* Formal English—

TERENCE: In weeno-weri-what?

SUZIE: Rustic Americana—

KHALID: Yes, that's it—

SUZIE: Or even a sort of pan-Japanese reflecting pool—

TERENCE: That's what?

SUZIE: And surrounding serenity garden. And all virtual!

KHALID: What?

TERENCE: What?

KHALID: Stop that!

(Terence toasts him, laughing.)

TERENCE: Here's to the last days of the Roman Empire!

SUZIE: We're specifically targeting people with allergies.

JEFF: What's in this dressing? It's really good.

SUZIE: Oh it's so easy. But it's secret. I have to have some secrets, don't I?

JULIA: Virtual gardens. That's depressing. We're all becoming part of an electronic herd of lemmings and rhinoceri.

LYDIA: Rhinoceri? Is that really the plural?

TERENCE: Of course it is.

LYDIA: Oh, you think you know everything.

SUZIE: The British really are better educated than we are, dear. There's no use being defensive about it. Have you ever seen the British version of *The Weakest Link?* It's much harder than the American version.

LYDIA: American television. Ick. No wonder the rest of the world hates us.

KHALID: Yes, yes! You all berate the Arab culture for its impulse to, to to—

TERENCE: Theocratic dictatorship?

KHALID: "Theocratic dictatorship," yes, thank you—

TERENCE: Thank Cambridge.

KHALID: —But you, at the same time you overwhelm the world with cultural dictatorship—

LYDIA: *The Weakest Link* is not culture. God help us. Is that culture?

JEFF: I've never actually seen it.

JULIA: What we have to do is figure out how to support artists. Everywhere.

TERENCE: Oh for god's sake.

ROGER: Funding the arts!

TERENCE: Funding the arts!

ROGER: Grow up!

(They find this hysterical.)

JULIA: Why? Musicians, poets, painters—I need more dressing—

SUZIE: No. No. Try it again!

JULIA: It's the definition of culture, people finding their reflection in art—I really do think, Suzie—

SUZIE: It's swimming, already! I won't let you drown it!

JEFF: Art?

SUZIE: I love poetry!

ROGER: But no one's going to fund it! Please!

SUZIE: "You are the weakest link. Good-bye."

*(They laugh at each other.)*

JULIA: But the way things are going now, pretty soon the only culture left will be in Disney pavilions, or on bad TV.

SUZIE: I love CNN. I couldn't live without it. Reading puts me to sleep.

LYDIA: You just said you loved poetry, how can you love poetry if you don't read?

SUZIE: You're so contentious! Why are you attacking me all the time?

LYDIA: I'm not attacking, I'm asking a question.

SUZIE: Would anyone like more salad?

JULIA: I'd like more dressing.

SUZIE: All right, all right! I surrender under protest!

*(She goes for the salad dressing.)*

JEFF: Oh, great, can I have some too?

SUZIE: *(Outraged.)* Oh!

ROGER: Okay, I'm not going to say culture is superfluous, because that's what you all expect me to say. But, it's kind of superfluous, especially now.

LYDIA: What are you talking about! You write novels!

ROGER: And I make a damn good living at it, too. 'Cause there's a market for what I write about!

SUZIE: Who's seen *Mamma Mia?* I can get you tickets.

JEFF: I wish I could take my wife.

KHALID: Is this spearmint? I'm tasting spearmint.

SUZIE: Thank you for noticing! You subtle, brilliant man.

LYDIA: I think Julia's right. We have to nurture culture as a living reality. It can't just be survival of the richest.

TERENCE: Or the best reviewed.

LYDIA: Oh, not critics. Let's not go there—

JULIA: Well, I have to confess, I'm far more afraid of the *Times* Book Review than I am of Islamic terrorists. They massacred my last book. It took me five years to write that.

SUZIE: What was it about?

JULIA: It was called *Engaging the Moral Eye*. It was basically a series of talks and essays about creativity and community.

*(Roger burps loudly.)*

SUZIE: Roger! Oh, please!

JULIA: The reviewer was really cruel.

TERENCE: Happened to me, once. I was on Zoloft for a year. Now I think I have it in perspective.

*(He drinks a big slug of wine.)*

SUZIE: They usually like my books. You just have to know what they like. They don't want to be touched. They want to be entertained.

JULIA: *(To Suzie.)* You're right. This critic didn't want to be touched. He just didn't want to be touched.

TERENCE: Well, have you seen the people they employ over there? Who would want to touch them?

*(They all laugh.)*

JULIA: Yes, I have to say when I heard someone had sent anthrax to the *Times*, my first thought was, "Isn't that toooo bad."

*(They all roar with laughter, except Roger.)*

TERENCE: How about that fall from grace?

ALL: Aww.

*(They all laugh again, except Roger.)*

ROGER: Sour grapes, sour fucking grapes!

SUZIE: Roger! Language! You know how I feel about that "fucking" word!

ROGER: She uses it! And she wants to bomb *The New York Times*, for Christ's Sake!

JULIA: I'm kidding!

ROGER: *(Takes Suzie in.)* You know, Suzie, when you get stern like that I find you damn attractive.

SUZIE: Really?

TERENCE: What one has to wonder regarding the *Times* is simply, is it the paper of record, or the pacifier of the bourgeoisie? The latter has an equally good ring to it, with the added advantage of being true.

KHALID: Not the bourgeoisie, no no. The rich. The pacifier of the rich.

ROGER: How is money the issue? How did we get here again?

KHALID: You have too much!

TERENCE: Oh it's not just the *Times*. Print news is over. All five sources of television news are now divisions of large conglomerates.

JULIA: Pass the wine, please.

TERENCE: AOL Time Warner, General Electric, Viacom, Rupert Murdoch, and, lest we forget, Disney!

SUZIE: Mickey Mouse?

TERENCE: Yes, Mickey Mouse controls your news, Suzie. The conglomerate vision of America is replacing the democratic ideal and what's emerging is an empire devoted to the bad thinking of a self-protecting elite class. And you know what happens to empires, don't you?

*(Julia reaches for the wine, spills it, scattering one side of the table.)*

JULIA: *(Overlap.)* Oh, I'm sorry, I'm so sorry—

SUZIE: Oh dear, oh dear.

KHALID: Quite all right—

JULIA: Here—

SUZIE: We'll just put this over it.

JULIA: I'm sorry.

SUZIE: Don't worry.

TERENCE: The first wine has been spilt! Which clearly means—we need another bottle!

*(Suzie goes to the sideboard.)*

SUZIE: You're drinking too fast!

TERENCE: No dinner party is any good unless someone is drinking too fast. I'm doing it for you, darling.

KHALID: *(To Julia.)* I like your stockings. They're very smooth.

JULIA: You've had too much to drink, Khalid. I'm not wearing stockings.

KHALID: Oh.

SUZIE: Whooo! We're not supposed to be getting intimate, you two!!

TERENCE: *(A drunken non sequitur.)* But we haven't really looked at globalization yet.

*(People moan in protest.)*

ROGER: I am so sick of that word!

JEFF: I can never figure out what it's supposed to mean.

KHALID: It is at the root of everything—everything—

JEFF: Yeah, but what does it mean?

SUZIE: Oh, dear don't salt that, no no—

TERENCE: How to explain "globalization."

LYDIA: Here we go. He's revving up—

TERENCE: As the world continues to experience the destructive power of the global marketplace, the backlash has produced a whole set of ideologies—

communism, socialism, fascism—all of which originally promised to take the sting out of capitalism. Now that these ideologies have been discredited—there's nothing that can truly soften the cruelty of capitalism and still produce rising standards of living for the working poor. The only thing left standing is modern fundamentalism, which is why we are where we are.

*(A beat.)*

JEFF: I followed that.

SUZIE: I did too.

JEFF: Is he getting clearer because we're getting drunker?

SUZIE: Is drunker a word?

KHALID: So what we have is the very rich—

SUZIE: And, the very drunk—

*(She laughs, so does Jeff.)*

TERENCE: And underneath them, grabbers, criminals, thieves.

LYDIA: You know who predicted this? Marx.

TERENCE: No! God! Don't say Marx!

KHALID: This is true!

TERENCE: I didn't say Marx!

KHALID: Those who can't make the transition to the fast world will create their own counterculture. Which will by necessity be defined as criminal by the ruling money elite.

ROGER: History is turning over. That's what we're looking at here. The last time history turned over, in Europe, the death of monarchy, you know what the consequences were? Two hundred years of war, culminating in the Holocaust, Stalin and the death camps. Eight million dead in Europe, twenty-two million in Russia. That's the possibility we're facing. And you can't dismiss me because I believe in going to war to save ourselves!

KHALID: Oh dear. *(He drinks.)*

JULIA: No one's dismissing you. Hardly.

ROGER: *(Off Lydia.)* She is.

LYDIA: I'm not!

ROGER: You're rolling your eyes, I see you.

LYDIA: Well, now I am.

ROGER: Is there any Ranch?

SUZIE: Ranch!?! Oh no, Roger. Please. This is worse than the profanity.

TERENCE: Or Marx!

SUZIE: I think people are evolving, but the power system isn't.

*(A beat.)*

KHALID: What?

JULIA: What?

TERENCE: What?

SUZIE: Yes. All those guys, the ones on the top are just spinning, see, but a lot of other people aren't. We're ready for a new approach, but they can't relate because they're just stuck.

*(Another beat.)*

JULIA: We're evolving but the power system isn't. That's very good, Suzie.

SUZIE: *Merci.*

LYDIA: Rampant capitalism obviously brings problems everywhere, let's face it, it doesn't serve America, either, we're just drowning in greed and our culture is collapsing—But isn't something else going on in much of the Muslim world? It suppresses, hides and destroys the feminine—the degree to which men try to hurt and annihilate women is the degree to which they have driven themselves insane.

KHALID: Yes, yes, this is very profound, what she is saying.

ROGER: Oh brother.

LYDIA: Oh brother what?

ROGER: Oh brother, I'd like more salad.

LYDIA: *(Curt.)* I realize that because America is still deep in its own misogyny some people will not be able to understand this.

ROGER: I just think that when you reduce something to your own little personal agenda, you're not being very useful.

LYDIA: I'm not taking this on.

ROGER: Take this on. It's their culture. Their culture, and you're trying to impose your idea of culture on everyone.

LYDIA: No, I'm not!

ROGER: You're as big an imperialist capitalist whatever as me or him or any globalization nightmare junkie you're so ready to condemn. You want the whole world to look just the way you like it for you and your little proto-feminist lesbian friends.

TERENCE: And they're off!

SUZIE: No, I worry about that too. Maybe we've just interfered too much already. I see all those men in their robes and their turbans and it's like looking at people living in a different country.

KHALID: Actually, it is still a medieval culture, many Arabs take great pride in that, and feel powerfully that their identity must be protected.

SUZIE: And then all those guns! We gave them all those guns! I saw it on television last week and thought, hasn't anyone ever watched *Star Trek*?

*(There is a short, surprised moment.)*

TERENCE: What a leap! Spectacular! A veritable triple Lutz of a conversational segue!

SUZIE: Thank you, darling. Because the prime directive is you mustn't interfere in more primitive cultures, you just don't go onto someone else's planet and mess around with what they're doing there.

LYDIA: Yes, but then Captain Kirk would just sleep with all the women.

TERENCE: I actually enjoyed that aspect of the original series. The later ones did away with all the sex, it just wasn't as good.

JEFF: You know what that reminds me of? I thought about? That *Star Trek* episode where there were those two guys who were trying to kill each other, and they looked exactly alike, they had faces that were half-black and half-white. Everyone on the *Enterprise* thought they were identical twins or something, but then it turned out that they were really mirror images of each other. One guy was black on the left side of his face, and the other guy was black on the right side of his face. And their whole planet had destroyed itself because of that difference that seemed so big to them, but nobody else could even see it, really. And then at the end of the episode, they killed each other.

*(A moment of silence.)*

ROGER: That was a good episode.

TERENCE: That's touching, really it is. But, honestly, isn't it just one step away from, "Can't we all just get along?" I regret being the one to once again assume the mantle of reality—

ROGER: Ah Christ.

TERENCE: But the fact is that we've never gotten along! Human history is a bloodbath. Killing each other is what we do!

*(Lydia stands.)*

LYDIA: I'm sorry. I'm having a little trouble breathing all of a sudden.

SUZIE: I told you to take the walnuts out!

LYDIA: It's not the walnuts. I'm—The fact is, I have to, well, actually—I'm pregnant. And, the fact is, thinking about bringing a child into this— *(Increasingly upset.)* Bringing a child into all of this—terror, and and—I have to go, I have to go for a moment—

*(She goes to the back of the room, opens the trap. The smoke comes up. She descends.)*

SUZIE: Oh, my. I didn't know. She's pregnant. And I didn't make anything that she could eat. I feel terrible! No, you can't have any more of the salad, Roger—you can eat the meat, but the rest of the salad is for Lydia. Here, somebody pick the walnuts out.

*(She hands Roger's salad to Julia.)*

JULIA: Maybe she could use a few crackers!

SUZIE: Crackers? Yes, crackers! Of course. That's an excellent idea. I'll be right back.

*(She goes, opens the trap. The smoke comes out. She looks back at them before disappearing.)*

SUZIE: *(Continuing.)* "Saltines" will be just the thing.

*(She goes into the smoke.)*

ROGER: Okay. I don't want anybody expecting me to be nicer because she's pregnant. I hate that.

JULIA: I'm trying not to be reactive, but, you know, you make it hard.

*(The trap opens. Lydia comes out, followed by Suzie. She carries a box of Saltines.)*

SUZIE: Everything's fine! She's had a little throw up, and feels much better.

JULIA: Here here, maybe you should have some water?

LYDIA: Yes, thank you.

SUZIE: We saved the salad, I'm so sorry that I didn't—I just didn't realize—oh and even the sight of all this meat and all that salmon!

LYDIA: No no, I'm fine—these Saltines are a big help—

*(She eats them hungrily.)*

KHALID: How far along are you?

LYDIA: Uh, three months.

ROGER: *(Dry.)* Who's the lucky guy?

LYDIA: I, um—I don't know, actually.

SUZIE: Oh, how refreshing! And we can just talk about it now, at the dinner table. When I was young, this would not have been possible. Was it a petri dish sort of thing, all anonymous? So many lesbians are having babies this way now, and it's so funny, because you know, it means that we really don't need men anymore! We can just go ahead and have babies without them!

LYDIA: It wasn't that.

ROGER: But you don't know who the father is? How'd that happen?

LYDIA: Okay, it's not a petri dish sort of thing but it's also not an I'm a slut sort of thing. It's more like a sleazy, I can't believe I got myself into the biggest mess imaginable sort of thing. You don't want to hear it.

*(All voraciously agree that they should hear it.)*

ALL: Oh yes we do!

TERENCE: Absolutely.

JULIA: I want to hear it.

LYDIA: Okay. There was this guy I was involved with in college. And he was, it was one of those relationships that are completely maddening and inexplicable but passionate and deeply truthful, we were—but we were also you know, twenty, twenty-one, and he was completely insane.

TERENCE: Thus, your dynamic attraction to him.

LYDIA: I swear to god, talking to this guy was like diving to the bottom of a lake. And sex was unbelievable.

SUZIE: I like this story already.

LYDIA: He was also a cheater, cheating on me, and then lying about it—

SUZIE: Good sex and cheating. I love this dinner party!

LYDIA: —and I would find out and try to get out of the relationship, and he would become desperate, but not desperate enough to actually stop sleeping with other women—

SUZIE: Of course not.

TERENCE: And the sex?

LYDIA: Unbelievable!

KHALID: What did you do?

LYDIA: I finally, I tried honestly for over a year to get myself out of this thing, but he would, and then I would—oh god. I do think he loved me, I know he did—

TERENCE: In that particular way that cheaters love.

LYDIA: Yes, yes, so one day I finally said to him, I never want to see you again. I don't want you to ever speak my name again. You are not allowed to even think about me. We do not inhabit the same planet. Stay away from me forever.

JULIA: Good for you!

SUZIE: Then what happened?

LYDIA: That fucking internet. He did a search. I shouldn't have written back! But it was twenty years ago!

ROGER: Cut to the chase. You got back together—

SUZIE: She's doing it, she's telling the story, don't rush her, Roger!

LYDIA: I'm involved with someone! I've been in a wonderful relationship for five years! I love this man deeply.

TERENCE: But the sex, with the other guy—

KHALID: I want to hear about the man she's with.

JEFF: Yeah.

SUZIE: No, no, we want to hear about the sexy guy from her past—

JULIA/SUZIE: *(Chiming in.)* The sexy guy, the sexy guy—

LYDIA: He lives in London now. I had a conference, just a three-day thing—

ROGER: A conference?

SUZIE: ROG!!

LYDIA: So I called him, at his work, and an Irish man answered the phone.

JULIA: He's Irish?

LYDIA: He didn't used to be! When I knew him, he was from Illinois! But he's been living in Ireland, apparently, for ten years, and now he has an Irish accent.

SUZIE: I love accents.

LYDIA: And then I said, would you still like to meet for a coffee, and he said we should go to someplace very public. The coffee shop at the Barbican Centre.

TERENCE: Ewwww.

LYDIA: He was very clear about this, in his new Irish accent. So I went out there, and it's this huge concrete—thing—

TERENCE: Yes, it's a monstrosity.

LYDIA: Like a maze—giant buildings with windows—

TERENCE: A complete fiasco.

LYDIA: It took me fifteen minutes to find the coffee shop.

TERENCE: You should try to find the bathroom.

LYDIA: So I'm standing in line, wondering if he's going to actually show up, when I hear someone behind me saying my name in an Irish accent— "Lydya, Lydya."

JEFF: Wow!

JULIA: God!

LYDIA: The first thing I thought was thank god, he looks twenty years older. But then we talked for a while, and—

TERENCE: Yes yes and then—

SUZIE: Let her tell it!

LYDIA: I asked him what he did, and he told me he traveled all over the world, doing some sort of health care something—but he couldn't be specific—

TERENCE: Wait wait wait—

SUZIE: Stop interrupting!

TERENCE: Just a minute, darling. Irish? Over-sexed non-specific world traveler who likes to meet at the Barbican Centre?

LYDIA: Yes.

TERENCE: He's in the I.R.A.!

*(Group response.)*

LYDIA: That's what I thought!

JULIA: Did you really think that?

LYDIA: I wasn't thinking. Which is why I spent most of the weekend in bed with him.

*(The whole group cheers.)*

TERENCE: *(Rising.)* Bravo! Well done! You spitfire! You goddess!

SUZIE: It's the mystery. That's so hard to resist.

TERENCE: You slept with a terrorist! I find that fascinating, in light of today's conversation.

JULIA: He wasn't a terrorist. He just couldn't commit.

SUZIE: He was a terrorist of the heart.

LYDIA: I don't know what he was. It was overwhelming, being with him again. But he was never someone you could count on.

ROGER: To say the least.

LYDIA: So I went home and thought that was fun, but not a threat, I didn't want it to be a threat to my—the man I'm with, I love him so deeply, and he is someone you can make a life with—and now I'm pregnant and he's so thrilled, just thrilled—and I—

ROGER: You cheated.

LYDIA: Yes, I did. I did.

TERENCE: Cheated, schmeated. She's a goddess! That's what goddesses do!

JULIA: Don't tell him.

LYDIA: I shouldn't tell him, should I?

ROGER: Here we go.

KHALID: No, she mustn't tell him.

TERENCE: I think she has to. Loose the shackles! Live free!

LYDIA: He's so happy.

JULIA: You can't tell him.

ROGER: This is why men get pissed off at women, you know. It's got nothing to do with the feminine in the culture blah blah blah—

KHALID: She cannot tell him! Why tell him, why make him miserable, when they have love?

SUZIE: I don't know what you should do, dear. Have a cracker.

*(She gives her a cracker. She eats.)*

ROGER: You know—this story is a bit of a surprise. I didn't actually think you liked men.

LYDIA: That's a deep misunderstanding. I want the world to be whole. I want women to be included. That doesn't mean I hate men. "Hating men" is hardly my problem.

JEFF: Don't tell him. *(Beat.)* I agree with *(Points to Khalid.)* that guy. What's the point? Just have your baby and be happy.

SUZIE: There, see! Isn't this nice? We're all agreeing. I knew we could. And as a reward for all of you, being so nice to each other, so nice to dear Lydia— it's time for the surprise!

JULIA: Suzie, please, no more food! You have to just give us a few minutes to rest or we'll explode!

TERENCE: Yes, can't eat another bite. Maybe one. And a little more wine. I'm keeping track now.

SUZIE: No no, not food. Tonight's special guest.

TERENCE: Oh, I thought I was the special guest.

ROGER: I thought I was.

*(They both laugh.)*

SUZIE: Of course you're all special, you know I think that or you wouldn't be here. *(Pleased with herself.)* But in addition to all my favorite people, I did manage to tempt a rather interesting young man to stop by for just a few minutes. To answer some of the many questions we've all been discussing tonight in such a lively fashion. I have a terrorist! *(She throws a chador over her head.)* Mohammed, darling, we're ready for you! Come on in!

*(Mohammed comes out. Jeff stands, backs away from the table.)*

SUZIE: *(Continuing.)* Did you have any trouble parking? Or did one of your friends drive you in his taxi?

*(Mohammed approaches the table, sullen.)*

MOHAMMED: These are the people you spoke of? The ones who are interested in our story? You say you want to know us. Is that what you want?

SUZIE: Yes, darling—

MOHAMMED: The world does not want to know the Arab. You only want to erase the Arab. You want to take our land, and steal our oil, to corrupt our women, demean our culture, and degrade our god. That is what you want.

SUZIE: Oh, now don't be negative! It's a party! This is Julia, and Roger, Lydia, Terence, Jeff, he's a fireman, and Khalid, he's an Arab, like you.

KHALID: *(Speaking first.) Salam Aleichem.*

MOHAMMED: You greet me with the words of our people. But you are no true Arab.

KHALID: I am a true Arab, my friend.

*(Mohammed immediately starts to insult Khalid. Khalid starts to shout back at him.)*

MOHAMMED: *Anta mush aarabee, kafir, tarak't Allah, tarak't Allah wa ah'lak, aarr, anta fadeeheh al aarab, anta as'wa min yahudi—* [Translation: You are no Arab, infidel, you have abandoned your god, you have abandoned your god and your people, shame, you are a disgrace to all Arabs!]

KHALID: *(Overlap.) Mujrim, ma hada ra'yeh lil jan'nah, shou aal'mak min al'lah, tarak't Allah, yashtanizz min'nak al'all—* [Translation: Murderer! No one is going to paradise for these acts, what do you know of god? Monster! You have abandoned your god! You disgust god!]

TERENCE: Whoa whoa—

ROGER: Back off, asshole—

JEFF: Get him out of here!

SUZIE: Oh, dear—

JULIA: *(Shouting them all down.)* Please! Stop it, please!

*(There is a moment of silence.)*

JULIA: *(Continuing.)* Perhaps we should, as Suzie suggests, take the opportunity to, um, try to have a more lively understanding of each other.

ROGER: Has anybody frisked this guy? Check his shoes!

SUZIE: Oh, no, he's promised me not to do anything like that here, haven't you? Everyone sit. And let's get him a seat, there's an extra chair somewhere… Here, catch up, have some wine.

*(She grabs some wine bottles.)*

JULIA: Muslims don't drink, Suzie.

SUZIE: But Khalid has been a complete fish, all night!

JULIA: Strict Muslims don't drink. Fundamentalists.

SUZIE: Oh.

ROGER: Not that it stopped them from getting tanked the night before they blew up the World Trade Center.

MOHAMMED: Here is one of your famous American firemen. He is no hero. We are heroes, we do what we do for Allah, we know we are dying. They die without knowing. They are no hero. We die for paradise.

KHALID: No one is going to paradise for these acts!

MOHAMMED: You dine with the infidels!

TERENCE: He dines exquisitely with the infidels.

KHALID: You are the infidel, sir! These people, all of them, are the people of god!

MOHAMMED: You dine with them, you are God's enemy—

KHALID: You murder innocents, women and children—

MOHAMMED: U.S.A., the first terrorist in the history of mankind. You drop an atomic bomb which killed hundreds of thousands of women and children, kill them by burning them to death. You dropped the atomic bomb! Nobody else. In every single war you go to, you kill civilians and innocent people, not soldiers. And you go to wars more than any other country in history. Including the massacre of your own Native Peoples. I'm a terrorist? I only support terrorism so long as it's against the United States government, and against Israel, because you are more than terrorists, you are butchers and liars and hypocrites.

(There is a terrible pause at this. Khalid speaks.)

KHALID: Of all the people killed or harmed in some way by this attack, you cannot name one who was against you or your cause. You didn't care. Just so long as you left dead bodies, and people hurt. You are not fit to represent Islam. Your god is death. You say you act in the name of Allah, but that is a dark lie. You are a barbarian, a scourge, part of a group of rejects of the Noble Muslim civilization.

(The terrorist starts to yell at Khalid in Arabic. Khalid yells over him.)

MOHAMMED: *Ana baa'raf alle aa'malou wa laysh aa'malou, shou aal'mak min al'lah, kafir, khan't asss'lak, anta fatheehat all aarab*— [Translation: I know what I do and why I do it, what do you know of God? Infidel! You betrayed your race! You are a disgrace to all Arabs!]

KHALID: *(Overriding him.)* You adore not Allah but the evil that you yourself have become!

(Mohammed jumps on the table, grabbing a dinner fork or breaking a bottle of wine. He is about to attack Khalid. The whole table starts to yell. Roger and Terence and Jeff finally tackle him.)

SUZIE: Oh dear. No, no, no. Please! Mohammed you promised. Don't. Roger!

TERENCE: *(Overlap.)* Good heavens! Everyone stay calm. This situation is under control—

JULIA: *(Overlap.)* Please, stop. Please. Don't hit him, don't hit him!

KHALID: *(Overlap.)* Dear God. This is a nightmare. Please, I beg you, don't harm each other.

LYDIA: *(Overlap.)* Whoa. Somebody call the cops. Suzie call the cops.

SUZIE: *(Overlap.)* Oh, no, no.

*(Jeff slugs him, hard. Mohammed falls to the floor, still. They all are silenced for a moment.)*

TERENCE: Completely under control.

SUZIE: Okay, that was not as much fun as I thought it would be.

LYDIA: Well, what are we going to do with him now? You can't just leave him lie there.

JULIA: He's hurt.

JEFF: Good.

JULIA: Good?

ROGER: Those crazy Muslims.

LYDIA: Not all—

TERENCE: No no, not all Muslims—

JULIA: Not all, don't do that—

ROGER: *(Brushing them off.)* Ahhh!

*(Mohammed stirs, weakly tries to sit up. Everybody except Jeff backs away for a moment, afraid.)*

ROGER: *(Continuing.)* We're going to have to tie him up, Suze!

SUZIE: I have just the thing! Something from nothing, you take the napkin, fold it on the diagonal, a twist and a twirl and there you are. More linens, will that help?

*(She grabs a napkin, folds it quickly and ties it to another one, gives it to Jeff, who ties Mohammed's hands together and gags him while they continue to debate the situation.)*

TERENCE: *(To Khalid.)* Are you all right?

LYDIA: I don't think this is a good idea.

JULIA: What are you doing?

LYDIA: I don't think this is a good idea.

ROGER: These fundamentalists are crazy.

TERENCE: There are Jewish fundamentalists as well. Who do you think is living in all those settlements?

JULIA: *(Off Jeff.)* That's enough!

ROGER: You're just an anti-Semitic S.O.B., aren't you?

TERENCE: I'm half-Jewish, Fucko!

ROGER: A self-hating half-Jewish anti-Semitic S.O.B., then.

JULIA: Please!

TERENCE: Whenever I listen to people like you, I have to confess I feel that freedom of speech is overrated.

JULIA: Please!

LYDIA: She's right, stop!

ROGER: *(Overlap.)* You just get us to question ourselves to the point of stupefaction. We got caught off guard. And that's never going to happen again, I can tell you that.

TERENCE: Yet another moment of sophisticated American analysis.

ROGER: Fuck you, asshole.

JULIA: You've already subdued him.

TERENCE: Fuck you, you fucking Nazi moron!

ROGER: Fuck you, faggot!

SUZIE: Roger—

LYDIA: *(To Jeff.)* He's hurt!

JEFF: Am I supposed to care about that?

KHALID: Stop it, stop it! In my moment of shame can you not see, can you not learn—my world is disintegrating, my people cannot speak to each other, we are descending into utter hell and this is all you can do for us, for yourselves—For the earth, think of the earth!

*(Khalid weeps. The others stop, silenced for a moment.)*

JULIA: Well, I'm going to take that gag out of his mouth. I concede he might need to be restrained. But I will not see him gagged.

*(She pushes by Jeff, leans over Mohammed, and takes the gag out of his mouth. Immediately:)*

MOHAMMED: Everything you do to silence the Arab community. America's corrupt global policy. Silence the Arabs! You take our oil, you take our wealth, but you will not listen!

LYDIA: Listen, Mohammed—you should probably try not to provoke people right now.

MOHAMMED: American women are whores.

LYDIA: Okay. My mistake. Carry on.

MOHAMMED: Three thousands of your people die in the World Trade Center, do you know how many you've killed in Afghanistan and Iraq, how many you abandoned to die under your trade embargoes in Pakistan?

ROGER: You tested nuclear weapons!

MOHAMMED: You *invented* nuclear weapons! You come into our lands only to murder us, how many Iraqi children murdered in their homes, so you can have your oil—

ROGER: Listen to me. Your leaders are conning you.

MOHAMMED: *(Overlap.)* You are the bully of the world—

ROGER: Listen to me, will you just—

JULIA: Stop, it's going nowhere—

MOHAMMED: *(Overlap.)* —We suffer and die under your war machine everywhere, you only export war to our peoples in Palestine, in Afghanistan, in Iraq, everywhere, everywhere you kill us—

ROGER: By making America the perpetual target of your troubles, you allow your leaders to deceive you and steal from you… ahh forget it!

MOHAMMED: *(Overlap.)* —And your media distorts and lies about our world, and makes us look like simpleminded masses, so you can continue to murder us without feeling—

ROGER: My blood pressure is soaring— I'm not listening!!

MOHAMMED: You know this to be true!!!!

JEFF: *(Yelling, sudden.)* But that doesn't give you the right to come into our country and kill us—

MOHAMMED: Nor you! Nor you!

JEFF: You fucking—You fucking—

*(Jeff hauls off, about to slug the helpless Mohammed in the face. After a moment, Jeff shakes his head.)*

JEFF: *(Continuing; vulnerable.)* I'm sorry. I can't… It's too… I can't, Suzie…

SUZIE: It's all right, dear.

KHALID: *(To Mohammed.)* Who are you speaking to? Do you think you are speaking to me? To these people, you have already said you have nothing but contempt for them, you want to destroy them. So I ask you, are you speaking to me?

MOHAMMED: I speak for the Arabs.

KHALID: You are alienating the group you are fighting for. This is what I want to ask you. If you get to the place that you want, the land of milk and honey, how will you be able to forget how you got there? Can you kill and slaughter your way into heaven? And if you get in, then, that way, do you really belong there?

MOHAMMED: I do what is asked of me.

KHALID: I ask you something. I ask you to answer me, as a fellow Arab. I ask you to explain. Because I tell you, we can find peace through negotiation, with the other peoples of the world, our neighbors, or we can find peace by killing off all our enemies. Both will bring peace. *(Beat.)* But which is peace?

MOHAMMED: They will give us nothing if we give them peace! The only power we have is to deny them peace, to be the destroyers of the universe. It is the only power they have left us.

JULIA: Oh my god—

MOHAMMED: You know this to be true!

KHALID: No, my friend. I do not accept that. *Anta jooan?* [Are you hungry?]

MOHAMMED: *Kul shaebna jooan.* [All of our people are hungry.]

KHALID: *Lehake lazim takul.* [Then you must eat.]

*(He goes to him and brings him to the table, finds a seat for him.)*

JULIA: What, what did you say to him?

KHALID: I asked him if he is hungry. He says yes. We must feed him, Suzie.

SUZIE: *Une place à la table maintenant!*

TERENCE: Quite right. Can't have him critiquing our manners, on top of everything else he has to complain about.

ROGER: Hey. Call me crazy, but I don't actually want to have dinner with a destroyer of the universe!

JULIA: Is there an extra plate?

SUZIE: Of course. *Mais oui!!*

*(She clears a place for him.)*

JULIA: We'll have to untie his hands.

ROGER: No.

JULIA: How else will he be able to eat?

ROGER: I don't give a shit if he eats or not.

MOHAMMED: Yes, this is American policy toward the Arab world. Let them starve.

SUZIE: It's not American policy, sweetie, it's just old RogPog being a sourpussy again. Don't forget the relish, and Lydia, dear, could you give Mr. Mohammed a half-dollop of salad, just so there's something dynamic on the plate?

LYDIA: Fine, but I'm not giving up my crackers.

*(Plates are passed.)*

JULIA: I'm going to untie your hands now.

ROGER: I don't think that's a good idea.

*(Mohammed looks at her. She unties his hands. All are watching, alert. He reaches over and picks up a fork. For a moment, it looks like a weapon in his*

*hand, then he starts to eat with it. All visibly relax, watch him eat for a moment.)*

MOHAMMED: This is very good.

SUZIE: And, it's been blessed by a Rabbi, I mean, Oh God, I mean, not the Rabbi, it's whatsitcalled, the the the Muslim version of of of Kosher—

MOHAMMED: Halel.

SUZIE: Halel! Halel! Of course, Halel!

TERENCE: Wine?

SUZIE: I'll have some.

TERENCE: Wine? *(Offers it to Mohammed, who declines.)* Quite right, here's to moral integrity.

*(Terence drinks.)*

MOHAMMED: So much food. This would be enough to feed my children for a week.

JEFF: You have children?

MOHAMMED: Two little girls. Beautiful. Like their mother.

ROGER: What a liar.

LYDIA: Why would he lie about that?

ROGER: They're pathological liars!

JEFF: I have three myself. Two boys and a little girl. They're all great, but she's, she's … my heart. I sure wish I could see them grow up.

JULIA: *(Cautious, confused.)* You're not going to watch them grow up?

JEFF: No.

JULIA: Why, what happened?

SUZIE: I'm sorry. Didn't I tell you? He's dead, dear.

JULIA: He's dead?

JEFF: Yeah.

JULIA: You died?

JEFF: Uh-huh.

JULIA: In the—I had no idea!

TERENCE: I'm sorry, I'm a tad fuzzy. Did you just say—

SUZIE: Yes, yes, he's dead! I told you—

TERENCE: Suzie, I think I'd remember *that.*

ROGER: I didn't know.

SUZIE: I told someone, didn't I?

*(They all stare at her in shock.)*

SUZIE: *(Continuing.)* Oh dear. I'm sorry. There's so much to remember, putting together the perfect dinner party, the details all start to run together—

TERENCE: Details?

SUZIE: I'm sorry, I said I'm sorry!

JEFF: Look, it's okay. Could I have more of the lamb, even though we already had salad?

SUZIE: Of course dear. Absolutely.

*(She finds it for him.)*

TERENCE: Is anyone else here dead?

SUZIE: I don't think so.

TERENCE: Suzie, your reliability has already been shot on this matter.

MOHAMMED: I'm dead.

*(All except Jeff and Mohammed in a panic.)*

KHALID: Are we all dead? Is that what that pit's all about?

JULIA: Oh, dear.

LYDIA: Come on!

ROGER: No no, come on. There was no tunnel, no light!

MOHAMMED: No virgins.

KHALID: The pit, the air, the fire—are we in hell?

SUZIE: Let's just say we're in a hellish situation. But we're not dead! We're too lively to be dead! Mohammed, would you like more?

MOHAMMED: Yes of course.

KHALID: I feel myself…heartbroken.

SUZIE: No, no darling really, everything is fine! We're all fine!

KHALID: Nothing is fine! Is this the end? Is this all we have made of ourselves? Look at the world! We have created a world in which only the most amoral behavior, whatever makes a dollar, whatever sells, whatever tastes good, whatever feels good, that is what is promoted! And that, that is the logic of the pornographer! It is the logic of the child pornographer, who abandons all human feeling, who corrupts the world for his own emptiness! Who destroys the children—

MOHAMMED: Yes, yes, that's what we've been saying!

KHALID: No! Look at what *you* do to the children! What *you* teach them! The innocence you destroy! You know it is true! And why, why is it when anyone speaks about the *power* of love it's suddenly an esoteric conversation!?

TERENCE: Well, Khalid—

KHALID: No! No! You who talk so well must learn to listen! We haven't got a lot of time to evolve here! This will be a compassionate universe or it will cease becoming altogether! Let America strive to become the, the size of a true hero, like our friend the firefighter! Let her assistance be brave and supernatural!

TERENCE: And how would you go about doing this?

KHALID: By feeding everyone!

LYDIA: With what?

KHALID: With food! The fear we feel is because we do not see where or how or if a new world will be born!

ROGER: Look, you're not providing us with any viable plan of action, man!

KHALID: *(Hitting table.)* The action of love, my silly friend, the action of love. Forgive me, you're not silly. Not entirely. You're just hungry too, aren't you? Aren't we all? Oh, I'm so depressed. I wish I had no brain, just a heart the size of a giant fruit, then I would feed us all. I would. I would feed us all.

*(Pause.)*

JEFF: I'll toast to that.

KHALID: *(To Jeff.)* You are a very kind man. A brave man, truly. I like you very much. Here's to Jeff.

*(They all clink glasses.)*

ROGER: Here. Here.

LYDIA: Will you tell us what happened?

JEFF: What, you mean when it happened?

LYDIA: Yes. When it happened.

*(There is a short pause while he figures out what to say.)*

JEFF: It was strange. Going down there? We knew it was bad. You could see, we're in the engine shooting down Flatbush, watching the smoke pouring out of the tower, someone says Jesus God, there's another one. Watching the second plane hit. Running into the buildings. People, falling, raining from the sky. I never saw that before. None of us did. We thought they would hold, the towers, they were like beings, huge old men holding themselves up as long as they could, so that we could save as many, so many pouring down, while we rushed up and up, to the clouds and the wind and the fire. People ask me about life and death, I don't know what to say, they're the same thing to me now. Harm was… I don't know. I have children. But what else is my life for? We went up and up until the old men couldn't hold anymore, and death came down on all of us. The living and the dead. *(Beat, embarrassed.)* Is there dessert?

SUZIE: Why yes! Of course! *Où est ma tête? Où est ma tête?*

ROGER: Let me give you a hand, doll.

*(They go off, to get the desserts.)*

TERENCE: Anybody hear the one about the Buddhist Monk, the Rabbi and the Catholic Priest?

JULIA: Oh dear god.

TERENCE: *(Undaunted.)* Well, there was this Buddhist Monk, a Rabbi and a Catholic Priest on the *Titanic*. The *Titanic*, I tell you! And it hits—an iceberg. The ship is tossing, it's about to go down! People are falling into the sea as they scramble for the lifeboats. The life preservers are nowhere to be found! And then the Monk, the Rabbi and the Priest find—three! Three life preservers! But just as they're about to put them on, the Monk says, "Wait—what about the children?" The Rabbi, who is in a total panic now, says, "Fuck the children!" And the Catholic Priest says, "Is there time?"

*(Terence laughs, uproariously amused.)*

KHALID: That is a terrible joke, my friend.

TERENCE: My father was a Catholic priest, I can say whatever I want. Don't look at me like that. I'm not an alcoholic!

*(Roger and Suzie return, with desserts. They serve them, all round.)*

SUZIE: Ta ta ta ta ta ta! Sweets for the sweet!

JULIA: That looks amazing!

SUZIE: A cavalcade of citrus tartlets, fresh fruit jellies, caramel truffles, sweet and smoky Earl Grey chocolates and, finally, a tri-star strawberry and mascarpone mill-foo-ee-ay. All for you!! All for you!!

*(Everyone screams with delight and applauds as she passes the desserts around.)*

LYDIA: What is it?

SUZIE: *(To Lydia.)* Napoleon! But it's just named after him. It hasn't got a face. Unless dairy's a problem?

LYDIA: Oh god I want this!

*(She eats voraciously.)*

TERENCE: Dessert. My favorite course. Once, at a small delecteria at the heel of the boot of Italy I had the most exquisite crème brûlée—

SUZIE: It must've been Panna Cotta. They don't do crème brûlée over there.

TERENCE: It was sexual, it was sensual, it was mother's milk reconceived, a creamy dream, an addictive consistency with an eighth of an inch of crusty crispy tempered caramel which fractured into shards of naughtiness with the mere "tap tap" of my cool spoon. All senses alert, culled, dedicated and foresworn. This dish quelled all desire, all anxiety, all the world fell to a generous hush all about me.

*(They all fall into hush, just like the one he describes. After a moment, there is a sound of helicopters, which grows very loud very quickly. The sound grows and grows, the chandelier shakes, people look around, frightened; this is far more serious than any interruption so far. There is the sudden sound of a loud explosion, right next door. Everyone reaches out and grabs onto their neighbor for a long moment, as the sound of the helicopters finally fades. They all look at each other, frightened.)*

ROGER: *(To Lydia.)* Sorry. Sorry, dear.

LYDIA: No, it's all right.

KHALID: *(To Julia.)* Are you all right?

JULIA: Yes, yes—

JEFF: Anyone hurt?

SUZIE: Oh, please, I hope not—

TERENCE: I think everyone's fine, Suzie. Really.

*(People laugh, relieved, for a moment.)*

LYDIA: *(Subdued.)* This is a good dinner party.

SUZIE: A dinner party is only as good as the guests.

KHALID: Thank you.

TERENCE: Omnium Gatherum. A collection of peculiar souls.

ROGER: Speak for yourself.

LYDIA: Can I have another?

JULIA: You can have mine. I'm watching my weight.

KHALID: But why? You are the most beautiful woman I've ever seen.

JULIA: Why thank you—Khalid—

*(He suddenly pulls her into a passionate kiss. Everyone applauds.)*

SUZIE: Oh, this really is a perfect dinner party. It's what I yearn for. The way I yearn for wisdom, or grace.

*(There is a short beat, and she suddenly tears up.)*

SUZIE: I'm sorry. Oh. It's just, you are all so important to me. And even though it hurts to be so scared, I don't want to forget. I don't want to feel safe anymore. I want to feel just like this. Oh dear, what kind of a host am I, all of a sudden? Carry on! Giddy-up! *Sils vous plait*, please, please! *La Jour de Fête est arrivez!!*

*(Music comes up; Frank Sinatra singing, "I've Got the World on a String…" Paper confetti begins to waft from the ceiling.)*

ROGER: Come on, Suzie…

*(He takes her hand. They start to dance. Terence lights up. Lydia takes a moment to reflect on her stomach. Khalid and Julia look into each other's eyes*

*and kiss. Mohammed eats, hungry. The music continues. In the distance, the rumble of faint explosions can be heard. The explosions get closer and closer until one loud, terrifying explosion bathes the room in a sudden white light.)*
*(Blackout.)*

END OF PLAY

# Trepidation Nation
A phobic anthology by
Keith Josef Adkins, Stephen Belber,
Hilary Bell, Glen Berger, Sheila Callaghan,
Bridget Carpenter, Cusi Cram, Richard Dresser,
Erik Ehn, Gina Gionfriddo, Kirsten Greenidge,
Michael Hollinger, Warren Leight,
Julie Marie Myatt, Victoria Stewart
and James Still

# Trepidation Nation
## A phobic anthology

We've all experienced the touch of fear. From those vague apprehensions about turning the lights out at night to ordinary human worries about the world and our place in it, dread comes in all shapes and sizes. But what about the phobia—that particular species of fear that holds a special fascination because of its extreme, illogical nature? Actors Theatre of Louisville asked sixteen playwrights to conquer their own cold feet and contribute short pieces to *Trepidation Nation: A phobic anthology*, a diverse collection of scenes and monologues inspired by these irrational, all-consuming, and disturbingly specific fears.

We chose to focus this project on phobias because they offer unlimited potential for creativity. More than 500 phobias have been named and documented, and the variety is stunning—from A (*alektorophobia*, a fear of chickens) to Z (*zemmiphobia*, fear of the great mole rat), the list seems endless. These obsessions center around the idiosyncratic and the universal alike, at times appearing in clusters of neuroses, some strangely comic and others strikingly poignant.

This anthology, premiered by the twenty-two members of Actors Theatre's 2002–2003 Apprentice Company, marks the fourth consecutive year that the Humana Festival included a piece commissioned from myriad writers around a central question. Beginning with *Back Story*, a family narrative approached from multiple perspectives, up to last year's *Snapshot*, inspired by a single photograph, a collection of playwrights has annually plumbed the depths of a provocative idea. For this year's festival, we asked them to look into the psyche, examining our fear and trembling and expounding on this oldest of human emotions.

*Steve Moulds*

# BIOGRAPHIES

Keith Josef Adkins' plays include *Salt on Sugar Hill* (Mark Taper Forum's New Work Festival), *Sweet Home* (Bay Area Playwrights Festival, NYSF New Work Now!), *The Yucca Man* (Alabama Shakespeare Festival's Southern Writers' Project), *Farewell Miss Cotton* (Underwood Theater Company, Playwrights Horizons' Black Ink series), *Hollis Mugley's Only Wish + 2* (National Black Theatre Festival, Cleveland Public Theatre, Intersection for the Arts, HERE), *Wilberforce* (Cleveland Public Theatre New Plays Festival, Southern Writers' Project, Playwrights Horizons' Black Ink series, Carnegie Mellon's New Plays Project, Hartford Stage New Voices), *On the Hills of Black America* (Imua Theatre Company/HERE, Intersection for the Arts, Stanford University, Crossroad's Genesis Festival). Awards include: *Wilberforce* (Best Play Award—Cleveland Public Theatre New Plays Festival), *On the Hills of Black America* (Best Play Award—Cleveland Public Theatre New Plays Festival). Recent commissions include: ASF and EST/Sloan Foundation (*The Yucca Man*) and the Mark Taper Forum. Mr. Adkins currently writes for the UPN show *Girlfriends*.

Stephen Belber's play, *Tape*, has been produced in numerous theatres in the U.S. (including runs in New York and L.A. produced by Naked Angels), as well as in London, Germany, Canada, Australia, Greece and Japan (upcoming). The play was also made into a film by Richard Linklater. Mr. Belber is a member of Tectonic Theater Project and was one of the three Associate Writers for *The Laramie Project*, which has been performed around the world and was made into an HBO movie (nominated for four Emmy awards including screenwriting). His plays, including *One Million Butterflies, Finally, The Transparency of Val, Drifting Elegant, The Wake, Psychotic Busboy Blues* and *The Broken Fall*, have been produced at theatres such as Primary Stages, the Magic Theatre and New Repertory/Boston. A graduate of the Juilliard Playwriting program, he is currently working on commissions for Playwrights Horizons, Philadelphia Theatre Company and the Huntington Theatre.

Hilary Bell's plays include *Wolf Lullaby* (Steppenwolf, Atlantic); *Shot While Dancing* ('99 Susan Smith Blackburn finalist); *The Anatomy Lesson of Doctor Ruysch* (Australian Writers Guild Award); *Eye of the Storm* and *The Falls*, both workshopped at the National Playwrights' Conference, the former traveling to the Russian Playwrights' Festival. She has written libretti for musicals, song cycles, the opera *Mrs. Satan*, and most recently Phillip Johnston's score to

Murnau's silent film *Faust*, premiering at the New York Film Festival. For her plays, she is a recipient of the Philip Parsons, Jill Blewitt, Bug'n'Bub and Eric Kocher awards, and the Aurealis for a novel. A graduate of the Juilliard Playwrights' Studio and the Australian Film, Television and Radio School, Ms. Bell has taught playwriting and screenwriting at Wesleyan and NYU, respectively. She is currently writing a feature film, and is the Tennessee Williams Fellow in Creative Writing at the University of the South.

Glen Berger was a member of Annex Theatre in Seattle before spending the last seven years in New York with his wife and new son. His plays include: *Underneath the Lintel* (2001 L.A. Ovation Award for Best Play, and one of *Time Out New York*'s Ten Best Plays of 2001), *Great Men of Science, Nos. 21 & 22* (1998 Ovation Award and 1998 L.A. Weekly Award for Best Play), *I Will Go...I Will Go* (published in Applause Books' *Best Short Plays of 2001* Anthology), *Bessemer's Spectacles* (1993 King County Emerging Artist's Grant), and *The Birdwatcher* (1990 New City Playwrights Festival Winner). Mr. Berger was a recipient of a Manhattan Theatre Club Sloan Foundation fellowship and is a member of New Dramatists. He has also written several episodes for the PBS children's series *Arthur*.

Sheila Callaghan's plays have been produced and developed with A.S.K. Theater Projects, Playwrights Horizons, South Coast Repertory, New Georges, Annex Theatre, Printer's Devil, Moving Arts and LAByrinth, among others. Ms. Callaghan is the recipient of a 2000 Princess Grace Award for emerging artists, a 2001 *L.A. Weekly* Award for Best One-act, a 2001-02 Jerome Fellowship from the Playwrights' Center in Minneapolis, a 2002 Chesley Prize for Lesbian Playwriting, and a 2003 MacDowell Residency. She is currently working on commissions from Playwrights Horizons, South Coast Repertory, and EST/Sloan. Her other full-length plays include *Kate Crackernuts, Scab, The Hunger Waltz, We Are Not These Hands, Dead City,* and her opera *Elemental* with music by Sophocles Papavasilopoulos. She is a member of the Dramatists Guild.

Bridget Carpenter is a 2002 Guggenheim Fellow as well as the NEA/TCG Playwright in Residence at Alaska's Perseverance Theatre. Her plays have been produced and developed at Berkeley Repertory Company, Center Stage, Trinity Repertory, the Public Theater's New Work Now! Festival, Shakespeare & Company, and many other venues. Awards include a 1997 Princess Grace

Playwriting Award, two Jerome Fellowships, a McKnight Advancement Grant, and a 1999 NEA/TCG Playwriting Residency at the Guthrie Theater. Ms. Carpenter's play *Fall* is the recipient of the Susan Smith Blackburn Award and is currently under option for a New York production. Her play *Up (The Man In the Flying Lawn Chair)* will premiere this spring at Perseverance Theatre. Bridget, a member of New Dramatists, lives in Los Angeles.

Cusi Cram's plays include *Landlocked, The End of It All, Lucy and the Conquest* and *Fuente.* Her work has been performed at South Coast Repertory, The O'Neill Playwrights Conference, MCC Theater, The Cherry Lane Alternative, The Williamstown Theatre Festival, Naked Angels, Joe's Pub, The Women's Project, HERE, New Georges, The Lark Theatre, P.S. 122 and The Dag Hammarskjold Theater at the United Nations. She is a recipient of a fellowship from the Lila Acheson American Playwrights Program at Juilliard, the Le Comte du Nouy Prize and a Daytime Emmy nomination for her work on the children's animated program *Arthur.* She has been commissioned by South Coast Repertory, New Georges and Theatreworks USA. Her plays are published by Applause, Smith & Kraus and Broadway Play Publishing.

Richard Dresser's Actors Theatre of Louisville plays include *Below The Belt* and *Gun-Shy,* both of which moved off-Broadway and on to regional productions. Other Actors Theatre plays include *What Are You Afraid Of?,* set in the front seat of a car, *Alone At The Beach* and *Wonderful World.* A new play, *Rounding Third,* is opening off-Broadway. His most recent play, *Greetings From The Home Office,* opens at Capital Repertory in Albany, NY, and has no actors.

Erik Ehn is married to scenic artist Patricia Chanteloube-Ehn. Mr. Ehn's work includes *The Saint Plays, Heavenly Shades of Night Are Falling, Maria Kizito, No Time Like the Present, Wolf at the Door, Tailings, Beginner, Ideas of Good and Evil,* and an adaptation of Faulkner's *The Sound and the Fury.* He is an artistic associate at San Francisco's Theatre of Yugen, most recently writing *Crazy Horse* for them, which combined Noh forms with Native American music and dance. His plays have been produced in San Francisco (Intersection, Thick Description, Yugen), Seattle (Annex, Empty Space), Austin (Frontera), New York (BACA, Whitney Museum), San Diego (Sledgehammer), Chicago (Red Moon), and elsewhere; he has a longstanding collaborative relationship with the Undermain Theatre in Dallas. He is co-founder of the Tenderloin Opera

Company, San Francisco (with Lisa Bielawa). He is a graduate of New Dramatists. He teaches playwriting at Cal Arts, Valencia.

Gina Gionfriddo has been the recipient of the 2001-2002 Susan Smith Blackburn Prize, the 2002 Helen Merrill Award for Emerging Playwrights, a Lucille Lortel Fellowship, and a Rhode Island State Council on the Arts Fellowship. Her work includes *After Ashley* (Eugene O'Neill Playwrights Conference), *U.S. Drag* (Clubbed Thumb, New York; published by Smith and Kraus in *Women Playwrights: The Best Plays of 2002*), *Guinevere* (Eugene O'Neill Playwrights Conference, A Contemporary Theatre's Women Playwrights Festival), and *Briar Rose* (Providence New Plays Festival; published in *NuMuse: An Anthology of Plays from Brown University*). Her plays have received developmental support from Denver Center Theatre Company, Trinity Repertory Company, Atlantic Theater Company, Connecticut Repertory Theatre, The Cherry Lane Alternative, Perseverance Theatre, Philadelphia Theatre Company, Basic Grammar, and Chicago Films.

Kirsten Greenidge has enjoyed development experiences at New Dramatists, the Mark Taper Forum, The Bay Area Playwrights Festival, Hourglass Theatre, A.S.K. Theater Projects, the Eugene O'Neill Theater Center and the Boston Women On Top Festival. Her work has been read at Playwrights Horizons, New Georges Performathon 2002, Flirting With the Edge Festival of New Work and the Boston Playwrights Theatre. Recent awards include The Cherry Lane Alternative, The American College Theatre Festival, the University of Iowa (IRAM Award 2000 and Richard Maibaum Award 2001), and the Sundance Theatre Laboratory (Residency at Ucross Ranch, Ucross, Wyoming). Ms. Greenidge earned her M.F.A. at the Playwrights Workshop at the University of Iowa, where she was a Barry Kemp Fellow, and her B.A. at Wesleyan University. She is a member of the Dramatists Guild.

Michael Hollinger is the author of *Red Herring, Incorruptible, An Empty Plate in the Café Du Grand Boeuf,* and *Tiny Island,* all of which premiered at Philadelphia's Arden Theatre Company and have together enjoyed productions around the country, in New York City and abroad. For PBS, he has written three short films and co-authored the feature-length *Philadelphia Diary.* Awards include the Roger L. Stevens Award from the Kennedy Center's Fund for New American Plays, a Barrymore Award for Outstanding New Play, the F. Otto Haas Award for an Emerging Theatre Artist, a Mid-Atlantic

Emmy Award, a commission from The Ensemble Studio Theatre/Alfred P. Sloan Foundation Science and Technology Project, and fellowships from the Independence Foundation, Mid-Atlantic Arts Foundation and Pennsylvania Council on the Arts. Mr. Hollinger is a resident playwright of New Dramatists and Assistant Professor of Theatre at Villanova University.

Warren Leight's *Side Man* won the 1999 Tony Award for Best Play. He premieres two new plays this year: *No Foreigners Beyond This Point* (Baltimore's Center Stage) and *James and Annie* (Ensemble Theatre of Cincinnati). Other theatre: *Glimmer, Glimmer and Shine* (American Theatre Critics Association Nomination); *Mayor, the Musical* (Drama Desk Nomination); *Fame Takes a Holiday* (co-written); *Stray Cats*; and *The Loop*. Recent publications: *Leading Women: Plays for Actresses II*; Dramatists Play Service's *Outstanding Men's Monologues 2001-2002*; *Ensemble Studio Theatre's Marathon 2000* collection; and *Dramatics* magazine. Screenplays include *The Night We Never Met* (starring Matthew Broderick and Annabella Sciorra), which he also directed. He is a writer/co-executive producer on *Law & Order: Criminal Intent*; Vice-President of the Writers Guild of America, East Council; and a member of the Dramatists Guild Council.

Julie Marie Myatt has had plays produced in New York, Los Angeles, Ohio, Washington, and at Actors Theatre of Louisville. Recently, her play *Cowbird* was produced by Eye of the Storm Theatre in Minneapolis, as well as *The Joy of Having a Body* at the Guthrie Lab. Her ten-minute play *Lift and Bang* is published in *30 Ten-Minute Plays for Two Actors from Actors Theatre of Louisville* by Smith & Kraus, and *What He Sent* is published in *The Best American Short Plays, 2000-2001* by Applause Books. She received a Walt Disney Studios Screenwriting Fellowship in 1992-93, a Jerome Fellowship at the Playwrights' Center in 1999-2000, and a McKnight Advancement Grant for 2001-2002. Her other plays include *August is a thin girl, The Pink Factor, The Sex Habits of American Women, Alice in the Badlands*, and *49 Days to the Sun*.

Victoria Stewart graduated from the University of Iowa Playwrights Workshop in 2001, where her three plays *Nightwatches, The Last Scene* and *800 Words: The Transmigration of Philip K. Dick* were produced as part of the Iowa New Play Festival. She is the winner of the Helen Merrill Award, the Richard Maibaum Award, the IRAM Award, a Jerome Fellowship at the Playwrights' Center, and a Norman Felton Fellowship. Her play *Live GIRLS* was produced at Wellfleet Harbor Actors Theater in 2003. Her plays have been workshopped by The Hourglass Group in New York, Bread Loaf in Vermont, and the Market Theater in Boston. Before concentrating on her writing, Ms. Stewart worked as a stage manager for Peter Sellars, Anne Bogart and David Rabe, among others.

James Still's award-winning plays have been produced throughout the U.S., Canada, Europe, and Australia. They include *He Held Me Grand, Looking Over the President's Shoulder, Amber Waves, The Velocity of Gary* and *And Then They Came For Me.* He is the recent winner of the William Inge Theatre Festival's "New Voices in American Theatre" Award and is a two-time recipient of the TCG/Pew National Artist Residency Artist grant with the Indiana Repertory Theatre, where he is the Playwright in Residence. New theatre projects include commissioned plays with Indiana Repertory and Cornerstone Theatre Company in Los Angeles. Mr. Still is also a two-time Emmy nominee, Humanitas Prize Finalist, and Television Critics Association Award nominee for his work in television. He grew up in Kansas and lives in Venice, California.

## HUMANA FESTIVAL PRODUCTION

*Trepidation Nation* was commissioned by Actors Theatre of Louisville and premiered at the Humana Festival of New American Plays in March 2003. It was directed by Wendy McClellan  with the following cast:

> *The Gallows Monologue from*
> *Sidney Ryan's* Gunpowder and Blood . . Michael Rosenbaum (Morris)
> by Glen Berger
>
> *The Message* . . . . . . . . . . . . . . . . . . . . . . . Beth Collins (Juliet) and
> by Hilary Bell                        Robert Lee Simmons (Max)
>
> *Down to Sleep* . . . . . . . . . . . . . . . . . . . . . . Kate Bailey (Ellen) and
> by Victoria Stewart                      Natalie Sander (Anne)
>
> *Cobra Neck* . . . . . . . . . . . . . . . . . . . . . . . . . Bobbi Lynne Scott
> by Keith Josef Adkins
>
> *Seal Skin*  . . . . . . . . . . . . . . . . . . . . . . . . . Eleni Papaleonardos
> by Erik Ehn
>
> *I Am Not Alone* . . . . . . . . . . . . . . . . . . . . . Brad Smith (Brad) and
> by Richard Dresser                        Justin Tolley (Justin)

*The Joys of Childhood* . . . . . . . . . . . . . Jamie Askew (Claudette Cox)
by Kirsten Greenidge

*Octophobia* . . . . . . . . . . . . . . . . . . . . . . . Lori McNally (Skater)
by James Still

*Hold This* . . . . . . . . . . . . . . . . . . . . . . . . . . . . John Catron
by Sheila Callaghan

*Naked Lunch* . . . . . . . . . . . . . . . . Dimitri Meskouris (Vernon) and
by Michael Hollinger                                   Jenna Close (Lucy)

*Normal* . . . . . . . . . . . . . . . . . . . . . . . Daniel Evans (Lewis) and
by Cusi Cram                                   Jason Kaminsky (Chase)

*Euxious* . . . . . . . . . . . . . . . . . . . . . . . . . . Megan Ofsowitz
by Bridget Carpenter

*I'm Here for You* . . . . . . . . . . . . . . . . . . . Brian Nemiroff (Jules) and
by Warren Leight                                   Valerie Chandler (Amy)

*Safe* . . . . . . . . . . . . . . . . . . . . . . . . . . . . . . . . Jen Grigg
by Gina Gionfriddo

*Phobophobia* . . . . . . . . . . . . . . . . . . . . . Richard Furlong (Paul)
by Julie Marie Myatt

*Yes* . . . . . . . . . . . . . . . . . . . . . . . . . . . . Chris Ashworth
by Stephen Belber

and the following production staff:

Scenic Designer . . . . . . . . . . . . . . . . . . . . . . . . . . . Paul Owen
Costume Designer . . . . . . . . . . . . . . . . . . . . . . . . John P. White
Lighting Designer . . . . . . . . . . . . . . . . . . . . . . . . . Paul Werner
Sound Designer . . . . . . . . . . . . . . . . . . . . Colbert S. Davis IV
Properties Designer . . . . . . . . . . . . . . . . . . . . . . April Hartsook
Stage Manager . . . . . . . . . . . . . . . . . . . . . . . . Justin McDaniel
Dramaturg . . . . . . . . . . . . . . . . . . . . . . . . . . . Steve Moulds
Directing Assistant . . . . . . . . . . . . . . . . . . . . Tiffany Noelle Taylor

Chris Ashworth and Eleni Papaleonardos
in *Trepidation Nation*

27th Annual Humana Festival of New American Plays
Actors Theatre of Louisville, 2003
photo by Harlan Taylor

# Trepidation Nation
## A Phobic Anthology

## The Gallows Monologue from Sidney Ryan's *Gunpowder and Blood*
### by Glen Berger

*In the darkness, we hear an announcement:*

"Due to the unfortunate fencing mishap in the scene previous, the part of Robert Keyes will be played the remainder of this evening by the assistant stage manager, Morris White."

*Lights up sharply (a tight spot) on Morris White in an ill-fitting early seventeenth-century costume (either Morris is far too large or fat, or too small or thin for the costume), and ill-applied red vandyke beard, standing on a platform attempting to get a period shoe on his foot. A tennis shoe is on his other foot. A noose dangles next to him, suspended from above. Upon noticing that the light is on him, he gives up on the shoe (leaving him with one stockinged foot and one sneaker) and stares straight out. He appears nervous to the point of fainting. He swallows, puts the noose around his neck, and croaks out:*

MORRIS AS ROBERT KEYES: I am not.... *(Heavy breathing, more swallowing, then whispers:)* ...afraid... *(More breathing and swallowing.)* ....to die....

*(He feels about his person until he finds a folded piece of paper. With trembling hand, and clearly sick to stomach, he unfolds it, and reads:)*

'Tis the last day of January, 'tis the last day of Robert Keyes. This year of our Lord 1606. I say "our Lord," aye, I say it, though our goodly King would have otherwise. He would have that one Lord is reserved for the Protestants and another for the Catholics. And thus I stand before you.

*(The paper is quite evidently shaking, for indeed, Morris is in the throes of a monstrous stage fright.)*

I am Calm, Trembling Not, Assurèd in my faith, though I wear this adornment about my neck. Yea, at Ease, even as I know that after I am hanged but not killed, my privates are to be torn asunder and burnt to cinders in front of me. Aye, there shall be a different fire in my privates than the fire they have previously known, but I am not afraid. Indeed, I see there the Fire already burning in yonder brazier that shall char my privates, my privates, which by decree shall henceforth be made public, and that organ I hold most dear, and have held most dear for all my days, henceforth shall no longer be my privates, but my publics! And I say it is most unbefitting a so-called Christian nation to publicize a Christian's privates and then cook them down to a black powdery ash.

Yea and verily, I stand here with mien serene, even though I know that those flames, which shall soon be licking at my privates with most indecorousness, are also reserved for my bowels, which I understand are to be indelicately ripped from the inside of my body, and transplanted to the outside of my body, where I daresay they shall not function as smoothly as they do now, and ye shall all witness the last movement of my bowels, as they are transferred to that brazier beyont, where they too, my bowels, shall be roasted in front of my eyes. But would that I had a thousand bowels for my Catholic faith! But, alas, God has granted me but one bowels, and one bowels I will gladly proffer to the goodly King James and his most rabblous parliament that narrowly escaped just retribution—hold out your hands sirs, I give to you—my bowels. And though my bowels shall crackle and moan in the flames, they are quiet now, I assure you. And though my privates shall spurt, sputter and curl in the unforgiving fire, know that they are most tight-lipped now—no stream of sparkling fear yellows the insides of my trunk hose. Nay!

*(Morris's attempt to gesture dramatically has made him lose his place on the page and he panics as he searches:)*

…but…but…where was I…what…Privates severed……fear…disembowelment…quartered…displayed on pikes…dipped in pitch…crooves and…what the…what is…I can't read this!…croons?……Crowns!…and were all the Crowns and Kingdoms of this World laid at my feet…were I given the chance to remove this noose and slink away to freedom, I….I…

(These words prompt Morris to hatch an idea, and he looks to wings desperately, and feigns:)

…ah…but thither I see I am being summoned…

(He exits into the wings. Beat. Then evidently shoved violently back onto the stage. He runs back into the wings, and still more violently shoved back onto the stage. He slowly puts the noose back around his neck, looks once imploringly at the wings, then resumes, near tears from his predicament:)

"Where am I going?"…"Fret Not," my Faith assures me. "Must I leave this Earth so soon? My wife….My children…" "Worry Not," my Faith assures me…

…the End comes for us all…We blithely turn away from this most Incontrovertible of Facts…that the end comes for thee, and thee, and thee…On your own day, in your own way, you will be standing on the veritable gibbet, your veritable privates primed for gross molestation by the veritable fires beyont, but how many of us can embrace our most appalling and unsatisfactory Fate, how many of us will say…as I can say on this day…how many of us can say with placid affect and unjaundiced eye…how many of us can be taken by the hand of Black Death Himself, and say…I am not afraid…..I am not afraid………I am not afraid…….I am not….afraid….

(A moment, as we see Morris's face, frozen in mortal terror. Then, lights out.)

# The Message
## by Hilary Bell

*Juliet and Max are both in their twenties.*

*Wherever the symbol (-) appears in Max's lines, it's to indicate a word that he can't say. He should signal this somehow—a grunt, a facial expression—not just sail smoothly over it. But it should also be clear that they are both used to this form of communication.*

*Juliet, wearing the costume of an Elizabethan gentlewoman, is breast-feeding a baby. She rocks with anxiety.*

*She glances at a note clasped in her hand and then away, further distressed.*

*Max runs in. He too is in the period costume of a soldier. He is wild-eyed and pale.*

JULIET: Was it her?

MAX: *(Nods.)* She's at the bar.

JULIET: Oh God oh God.

But it's too early, she said midnight. Why is she here?

MAX: I don't know! Why does a (-) do anything? She gave me a message for you, and said by the end of our scene she'd be gone.

JULIET: It must be about where to leave him.

MAX: Well, (-) her! We won't do it!

JULIET: If we don't she'll kill him with a wasting disease, remember?

...Then we have five minutes. What's the message?

MAX: It's going to be hard—you know when I get upset—

JULIET: You do it on stage though, you know you're able to do it. *(Embracing him.)* Come on, take a deep breath, it's important. Tell me.

MAX: *(Caressing her.)* I've missed you.

*(She carefully withdraws.)*

JULIET: Darling? We don't have long.

*(Max touches the baby's face.)*

MAX: How did this happen to us?

JULIET: Don't, I want to get him to sleep: I couldn't bear to walk away while he's looking at me. Where must we leave him?

MAX: She said the message is for you as the (-) was caused by your appetite.

JULIET: *You* got caught in her garden, if you'd been more careful we wouldn't be losing our child to a witch!

MAX: You were craving silverbeet! You said get it any way I could!

JULIET: I didn't say give up our baby to save your skin.

*(Max is stung.)*

MAX: I wasn't thinking, it was my only way out. Harry wasn't born yet, I didn't know how much we'd love him.

JULIET: *(Pause.)* Let's not waste time.

MAX: She said it was no coincidence we were doing *(-)*.

JULIET: *Macbeth.*

MAX: Shh!

JULIET: We can't be any more cursed than we are!

MAX: And it's not by chance that there's a (-) in the play.

JULIET: A what?

MAX: A (-)!

*(He indicates someone short.)*

JULIET: A child! A child's ghost! *(She gasps.)* What else?

MAX: She said to beware of (-).

*(Juliet shakes her head: "What?")*

Of (-). That we should never make a (-) again.

JULIET: Pact?

MAX: And if we're going to (-) from a (-), then we have to (-) the (-).

JULIET: Pay the price. If we're going to…

MAX: To (-) from a—

JULIET: I know, you just said that! Oh Max, please, please don't do this now.

MAX: I can't (-) it. I'm trying—

*(A voice comes over the P.A.:)*

STAGE MANAGER: *(Off.)* All Courtiers, three minutes. Three minutes, Courtiers.

MAX: If we're going to…to *(Whispers.)* steal…

JULIET: Steal from a witch!

MAX: Yes, then—

JULIET: Pay the price.

*(The baby cries.)*

Jesus, oh Jesus. *(To baby.)* Shush, Harry, I'm here, go to sleep sweetheart. This is the last time I'll ever hold him.

MAX: Juliet—

JULIET: Finish the message.

MAX: My life's threatened, I'm given one chance— ...What would've happened to *you* if she'd killed me?

JULIET: You didn't seem to have any trouble getting that sentence out.

MAX: None of the words were in it.

JULIET: Can we talk hypotheticals later? I'd like to save his life.

*(Pause.)*

MAX: She said next time you want...

JULIET: Silverbeet! For Christ's sake, silverbeet!

MAX: I can say "silverbeet." Next time you want it, keep out of her (-).

JULIET: Will "garden" make you spontaneously combust? Is the world going to end?

MAX: She said: "Because your (-) would've (-) with his (-) rather than save his unborn (-), I pity you."

*(Beat.)*

JULIET: You're doing it on purpose, aren't you?

*(Max is speechless.)*

You'd rather he died.

MAX: He's my (-) too! You don't have the sole rights to grief!

| JULIET: | STAGE MANAGER: *(Off.)* |
|---|---|
| Better he died than have to say what really happened, that you used him to spare yourself. Convenient to have this affliction, isn't it? | Courtiers, please take your places for the final scene. |

MAX: You've changed.

JULIET: Yes! I tolerated this for years, five years, even found it charming, respected it, covered for you, did everything in my power to help you. I could do all that because I loved you more than life. But now it's killing me! And once we lose our child I'll never forgive you. Never.

MAX: ...Loved?

*(Juliet is silent.)*

You would have rather I let her (-) me?

JULIET: Than take our baby? Well wouldn't you rather she'd killed me?

MAX: No. You're my wife. Harry we've only known six months.

*(They stare at each other, neither one knowing whose revelation is more appalling. Then Juliet hands him the sleeping child and turns away, packing the baby's few belongings.)*

STAGE MANAGER: *(Off.)* Ladies and gentlemen, this is your last call. Please take your places for the final scene.

JULIET: You haven't told me where to leave him.

MAX: That's when she started mocking me.

JULIET: She left out the words?

MAX: *(He nods.)* She pitied you for being—

JULIET: *(Without sarcasm.)* Your wife.

MAX: Being greedy!—Yes, and that. Then she said, "Be w- next time, but go h-." She said they're in Malcolm's final speech. I've never listened to his speech, we're done by then.

JULIET: Watchful. Home.

> *(Silence. Then:)*

She's passed us over.

"Be watchful but go home." She's not going to take him.

> *(A moment.)*

> *(She takes the baby and puts him in his makeshift bed.)*

MAX: You're not going to *leave* him back here?!

JULIET: He's safe.

> *(They stare at each other for a beat.)*

We're on.

> *(Blackout.)*

# Down to Sleep
## by Victoria Stewart

*Dimly lit, a girl's room with twin beds. Anne is breathing deeply, lying in bed. Ellen sits up in bed, awake.*

ELLEN: What was that? Anne? Don't be asleep.

Anne? What was that?

ANNE: What?

ELLEN: That noise. A creak. Outside the door.

ANNE: Probably Mom.

ELLEN: What is she doing up?

ANNE: Big day tomorrow.

Do you want me to check?

ELLEN: No. It's better to let her be.

*(Anne sits up, lights a cigarette.)*

ANNE: I'm not partial to wakes. Funerals, that's fine. They have some value. Wakes—they're just maudlin.

ELLEN: Or the opposite.

ANNE: Sure. Everyone's happy to see each other. It's a fucking reunion. "Did you have some of the ham? She gets it precut like that, in spirals. It's so clever."

ELLEN: We never see you anymore.

*(Ellen coughs a little.)*

ANNE: *(Stubbing out her cigarette.)* Suddenly everyone's allergic.

ELLEN: Do you think it was Mom?

ANNE: Who else would it be?

*(She looks at the door.)*

I hope I'm allowed to smoke tomorrow. It's bad enough to be back in the old room with you.

ELLEN: Do you think a lot of people will come?

ANNE: I could never sleep in this room.

ELLEN: It's snowing. Bad weather.

ANNE: And it was sudden.

ELLEN: Yeah. Probably not.

ANNE: Why would they?

ELLEN: We should get some rest.

ANNE: I don't sleep much.

ELLEN: You should try some relaxation, you know, techniques. You breathe in for three seconds, hold for three seconds and breathe out for three seconds. I learned that from somewhere.

ANNE: Why'd you need it?

ELLEN: I don't know. Just having trouble.

ANNE: I sleep three hours a night.

ELLEN: Is that true? I don't believe that.

ANNE: Yeah. There's something—it's this drift. That slow lapse. You know? Like a boat easing into the water but you don't know how deep the water is. You don't know what's underneath the surface.

ELLEN: But three hours—

ANNE: Anything could be there. When you close your eyes.

ELLEN: I mean, I would sleep for fourteen hours, all day if I could. When I can.

ANNE: "If I die before I wake."

ELLEN: Who taught us that? Grandma? Did Grandma teach us that?

ANNE: Dad.

ELLEN: Just some nursery rhyme. Some kid's prayer. When did we learn that?

ANNE: It's always been like this.

ELLEN: I remember you sleeping. I've seen you sleep.

ANNE: I simulate sleep. Close my eyes. Breathe deeply.

I stay awake as long as I can. But my body has to sleep sometime.

ELLEN: How come I never noticed? We slept in the same room for 15 years.

ANNE: You were *sleeping*.

ELLEN: Ah.

ANNE: Mom knew.

ELLEN: What?

ANNE: That I didn't sleep. She asked me once. "Don't you ever sleep?"

ELLEN: What did you tell her?

ANNE: I lied.

ELLEN: So she didn't know. Because you lied.

ANNE: She knew anyway.

ELLEN: Go to sleep, Anne. Or don't. You don't have to "simulate sleep" if you don't want to. Now that I know.

(*Pause.*)

ANNE: El. Did Dad—

ELLEN: What?

ANNE: Touch you—I don't know. You know.

ELLEN: No. I don't know.

ANNE: Mess with you. You know.

ELLEN: Why would you ask that? No. How could you ask that?

ANNE: He liked you.

ELLEN: He loved both of us.

ANNE: You were his—He didn't like me. The way he liked you.

ELLEN: That's—I mean—that's a leap. He was, you know, difficult. You
know, with you.

You're accusing someone who's dead. Someone who can't defend himself.
I mean, you weren't the perfect daughter.

ANNE: And you were.

ELLEN: *(In disbelief.)* You're accusing *me*. You're not even accusing him. You're
accusing me. I don't believe this.

ANNE: So it never happened.

ELLEN: You tell *me*. To hear you talk you've been lying awake for 20 years. Or
you're just lying, you know, now, in some last ditch effort to—sully—
to—get back at some perceived slight—

ANNE: It was a question.

ELLEN: Did you see this in some Lifetime TV movie? Something to explain
why I'm fine and you're not? Yet another of Anne's stories, another reason to feel sorry for yourself—

ANNE: I don't feel sorry for myself—

ELLEN: *(Overlapping.)* Some fiction, a created memory of someone in the doorway. A dark shape framed by the light in the hall, saying, "There's nothing to be scared of—"
*(Ellen stops. Pause.)*

ANNE: *(Softly.)* I don't know why I asked. I don't remember anything. Let's
just leave it. *(Silence.)* Go to sleep, El.

ELLEN: Don't you think I would? If I could?

ANNE: I'm sorry, El. I don't know what I was—His dying has fucked me up
more than I thought. Just sleep. Sleep, El. Do that breathing thing.
*(Anne lies down.)*
In two three. Hold two three, out two three. Lie down, Ellen.
*(Ellen lies down.)*
In two three. Hold two three, out two three.
*(Then Anne just breathes in the sequence for awhile. SILENCE.)*

ELLEN: *(Whispered.)* Anne? Where *were* you? If it's true? Where were *you*?
*(There's a creak outside the door. Ellen sits up with a start. She stares at the
door.)*

# Cobra Neck
## by Keith Josef Adkins

*Allodoxaphobia: fear of opinions.*

*Lights up on a young African-American woman entering a bathroom. She slams the door behind her, and locks it.*

WOMAN: *(Yelling at someone on opposite side of door.)* I do not have a neck like my momma!!!
*(She begins pacing the room.)*
I can't believe Freddie Jean Renfroe sat right out there, in the middle of margaritas, and said that my neck is shaped like a cobra, like my momma's. And that if I took my tail over to India somewhere, the people would follow me down the road with a pipe, and expect me to snake my way out of a basket. Ha-ha! *(To Freddie Jean on the other side of door.)* Well, that's just ignorant.
*(Goes to the medicine cabinet, and begins searching it, frantically.)*
*(Yelling at door.)* Besides, you can't talk, Freddie Jean. Not only do you have an extra nipple on your left breast, you have one growing on your nose. So there!
*(Back into the medicine cabinet and sink cabinet.)*
*(Mocking Freddie Jean.)* "It's not a nipple. It's an extraordinary mole dillybub, and my momma has them too." Well, I took a peep at you once in tenth grade gym class. I sure did. And the only thing extraordinary was that you *had three damn nipples!*
*(Finding cotton swabs, and getting calm.)*
Anyway… who cares what she and her momma share.
*(Looking at cotton swabs with a keen, seductive eye, and then she looks up at the mirror. A beat, then a sad yet surrendered recognition.)*
Freddie Jean is right. It is a cobra neck. Just like my momma's.
*(She slowly and tenderly caresses her neck. The front, the right and left side.)*
Why did I have to be her daughter?
*(She then finds a bottle of rubbing alcohol and sits on toilet. And during speech, she applies alcohol to her neck.)*
The one woman in town who goes to a Tupperware party and opinionates that we're living on a toxic dump in this town, which is doubling our

risk for cancer, get out or die, she pleaded. Watches as their jaws drop to the floor, and then checks for extra appendanges before laughing. Then she ditches this death-trap to live on a tanker with a musician from Belize. And what about the backlash those opinionated opinions would have on small-minded folks in a small-minded town who wouldn't believe the sky was falling if it dropped over their heads. They laugh at you, Momma. They put your picture up at the Pic-n-Sav, and somebody drew a mustache over your lips. They don't like know-it-alls and opinion-ators. Only truth-telling somebody they want is the one nailed to a cross.

*(She puts the rubbing alcohol and cotton balls to her side.)*

*(Calmly.)* So they just keep pointing out my arms, feet, and say they're just like yours, praying some truth will come bubbling up from my inside, through my long snake neck, and spill on their shoes. I say, no, I'm you all, not her. But they don't care. They just want a reason to post my picture up at the Pic-n-Sav, and draw a mustache over my lips. *(Then:)* And, oh, how I wish.

*(Crosses to door, with her face into it.)*

I do try. To opinionate. *(Takes a breath, then:)* Your weaved hair is aiding in the rise of self-hatred. But it won't leave the brain, Momma, connect to the voice and fall from my mouth. I try to telepathy it to 'em.

*(She takes a second to "telepathy" the opinion to the partygoers.)*

See. Nothing.

*(Crosses back to toilet and sits. Pulling up sleeves to display scarrings.)*

It's because I wasn't born to speak something great, and educate a town strutting around with extra nipples. And even if I did say something great, it would fall flat, and not-a one jaw would drop to the floor. At least what you said made them think for one split second.

That's why I gotta keep making it harder for them to recognize me in you. 'Cause I don't have the gumption for that honor. Yet.

*(She pulls a pair of scissors from her sock, then takes the scissors to her neck. And as she begins scarring, lights go down.)*

# Seal Skin
## by Erik Ehn

WOMAN: Her body is between herself and herself and whenever she is about to fall into her body she swims.

She works fast food fest feat fear and skinnies herself so she can fit through a door ajar should one appear. To skinny herself she swims.

First year college, chose by water, Mica Cavin thinks he can dance but she's a mile gone and Pacific, as thin as water in water. What does she study? She studies unbegun. Water in water in water in water in water.

Girl in wetsuit
Teenage girl
Ocean swimmer
Shell of the sea
Interiority

Spiral girl
Off from work
Midnight shift
The curl

Study work-study and supplement
Long,
Longmuscle crawl
Snotness gray
Shell at your quiet pulse and
Can almost hear the girl;
You can abstract

Fire and wave
Stare and swim
Fire and wave are third person worlds
She works and crawls
The midnight 3rd

The pool has no dynamic, the river is low in the winter and all year long she wants to throw her body out from under teeming; arm over 1 2 3 4 5 6 7 8 9 10 11 12 20 21 22 23, knocked against the pier, rolled under, sawed at until there is nothing left between herself and herself and the door closes behind her, dark until she wakes like kelp at the washout grade of blatant day.

She will not be teened no not ready yet third third third; the question that hopefully in her twenties more moot and on from there until she is the unanswer prior to the question, sub-curiosity under the No one, No one See.

12 plus 6 at two A.M. swimming shell crushed by wave's finger the ocean has her celibacy. Red wisp, she follows, blent. You do not take her, you relocate her, the celibate celiba-sea. Otters are nuns and as long as she is in the water she is where her younger was, spiraling, capturing means; she is able to spend days in the flux of exceptions, over lapsing/massing parabolae, collapsing nattering captions to image beyond capture, the ocean.

Water tumbles, thumb-knuckle blunt

Seal
Skin

She slid a herd of cattle across that madman griddle and raked her nails down the Lava soap; still she smells 18 and 18 smells her so she blues her body in agitation of tides.

How her body appears and how bodies appear to her: cracked, subject and subjecting, trying to fold a fan out of a dinner plate. The/his alkali, tang of failed baking powder Play-Doh volcano.

For two years she never sets foot on land and wishes that all seven. Either unbegun or done, out from where unformed gets inside your unformed and messes you all up, so better be same as sameless.

She says sea says shell is where you are. She makes her breaker relocate her, her sex is ocean wide. Then seal skin, you can't come in, her particularity is moon secant.

For two years I stopped counting until suddenly I was old. Kiss my neck and taste salt my skin is historical young man I am coincident with myself.

Longmuscle crawl
Snotness gray
Shell at pulse
Almost hear;
You can abstract
The sea

# I Am Not Alone
## by Richard Dresser

*Lights up on Justin, who is sipping wine and rapidly skimming his suicide note.*

JUSTIN: Darling... sorry it had to end this way... don't understand why you are condemning me to eternal nothingness... you *know* I cannot be alone... most men would hold it against you but I'm not most men... fondly, Justin.
*(Justin puts the note and his wine glass on the table. He steps up on a chair and puts a noose around his neck. He hesitates, takes a deep breath, gets down from the chair, and goes back to finish his wine. Then he gets back on the chair and puts the noose around his neck again. Knocking at the door.)*

JUSTIN: Damn damn damn. It's always something.
*(Justin opens the door on Brad, all in white, carrying a large pizza.)*

BRAD: Bobby Bobby Bobby! Got your pizza, Bobby! Pretty fast, huh?

JUSTIN: Oh... yes. Come in, come in.
*(Brad enters and puts the pizza on the table.)*

BRAD: Twenty-two buckeroos. Tipping optional but highly highly appreciated, bud.

JUSTIN: Excellent! Let me find my wallet.

BRAD: You're one hungry bastard, huh? You order our Maximum Pizza and it's just you?

JUSTIN: That's right. I'm all alone.

BRAD: This was an easy gig. If it takes more than fifteen minutes it's a free pizza, and I just did it in, what, nine?

JUSTIN: Something like that.

BRAD: Most customers time it. Sit there staring at the clock, praying for disaster, one minute late and BANG! Free pizza for them and a kick in the ass for us. That's life, huh?

JUSTIN: *(Trying to make conversation.)* So... is fifteen minutes usually a problem?

BRAD: Let's just say there have been incidents. Some dawdling in front of the van, some failure to cross the street fast enough by certain citizens, mainly in the "senior" category. But the good news is I never miss on the fifteen minutes.

JUSTIN: Congratulations. Would you like a beverage?

BRAD: What I'd like is my money, Bobby-Boy. I'm on a schedule here, and I'm only as good as my last delivery.

JUSTIN: Oh, right.

*(Justin gets the money as Brad reads the suicide note on the table.)*

BRAD: Hey, wait, you're not Bobby.

JUSTIN: Of course I am! Look at me!

BRAD: Then who's this Justin crybaby?

JUSTIN: Previous tenant?

BRAD: Look me in the eye, pal. If this isn't your pie then I'm in a world of trouble.

JUSTIN: *(Picks up the pizza.)* Relax. It's my pie.

BRAD: Then what kind is it? And no peeking!

JUSTIN: I don't recall... it was a while ago—

BRAD: It was eleven minutes and twenty seconds ago! *(Gets out a pizza cutter.)* Tell me the pie you ordered! I could cut off your digits and sleep like a baby.

JUSTIN: *(Freaked.)* Pep-pep-pep-peroni?

BRAD: *(Bites a towel so he won't scream.)* Jesus Christ. You are so not Bobby!

JUSTIN: I'm Bobby, I'm Bobby!

BRAD: Give me the pie... *Justin!*

JUSTIN: No! I've paid for it and now it's mine.

BRAD: Oh, really? Well what about Bobby, the real Bobby, counting the minutes, no pie, dialing his phone, and all of a sudden I'm one more poor bastard with no job.

JUSTIN: Oh, please, I'm sure you won't lose your job over one infraction.

BRAD: And I'm sure you don't know dick. I can't play loosey-goosey with the rules. My boss, George, has a one strike policy—

*(Brad's radio suddenly emits loud static.)*

BRAD: See? Did you think I was kidding? Huh? *(Obsequiously into radio.)* Hi, George. Righto. I'm on the stairs, taking'em three at a time! Almost there. Still got a few minutes. Over. *(Looks at order, then, to Justin.)* Is this 391 26th?

JUSTIN: That's right.

BRAD: Then I'm in the right place. Except you aren't Bobby.

JUSTIN: This is 26th *Street*. There's also a 26th *Avenue*. And a 26th *Place*.

BRAD: That's insane.

JUSTIN: That's Queens.

BRAD: Dear God. I have to go.

JUSTIN: Please stay. Please. I have this condition. I can't be alone. The world closes in and swallows me up and I try to scream but no sound comes out so I flop on the floor gasping for breath while my life slips away because there's no one else anywhere. Just me, all alone in a dark and endless void and it's just too much to bear, too much without someone, anyone, even a stranger, even you, so I'm not alone and can maybe get through one more day...

BRAD: You're kind of needy, Justin.

JUSTIN: I get that a lot. You have to stay.

BRAD: Or what?

JUSTIN: *(Going to the window.)* Or the pizza takes a dive.

BRAD: *(Bites towel so he won't scream.)* Calm down. I can't deliver a wounded pizza.

JUSTIN: I am trying to save my life!

BRAD: Yeah? I'm trying to save my job!

JUSTIN: My life is more important than your job!

BRAD: You don't know the first thing about my job. I have seniority on half the staff. Things fall right in six months I'll be answering the phone. But right now I'm almost out of time! So give me the pizza!

*(A stand-off. Justin holds the pizza hostage. Brad wields the pizza cutter. Brad fakes one move and suddenly has Justin from behind.)*

BRAD: If you won't surrender the pizza I'll cut your throat.

JUSTIN: I can live with that.

*(As Brad puts the pizza cutter to Justin's throat, the radio emits static.)*

BRAD: *(Obsequiously to radio.)* Hi, George. *(Pleading.)* I know I'm out of time... it just said 26th, how could I have known? *(Static.)* Good point. My bad. I'll cover the cost of the pizza. *(Static.)* I'm sorry, George. You believed in me when no one else did. Please give me another chance. These have been the happiest months of my life. *(Static.)* I understand. My best to your family. *(Beat.)* I can't believe I'll never hear that voice again.

*(Brad stands forlornly with his radio. Justin goes to the table with the pizza.)*

JUSTIN: No reason to leave now, is there? What have we got here? Mushroom and sausage! What a treat!

*(Brad numbly cuts the pizza with the pizza cutter. They sit at the table and eat.)*

BRAD: When we're done eating, I'm going to leave. And you'll be all alone again, gasping for breath. So this is at best a temporary solution.

JUSTIN: Hey, life is temporary. And right now it's pretty good.

BRAD: Maybe for you.

*(Brad, dejected, stares appraisingly at the noose while Justin happily eats the pizza as lights fade.)*

# The Joys of Childhood
## by Kirsten Greenidge

CLAUDETTE COX: *(Sits cross-legged with pen and clipboard.)* So. *(Smiles.)* Let's see here. *(Regards clipboard.)* Vassar: wonderful. I'm a Yalie, myself. Study abroad: fan*tas*tic. Although I see here you spent your time in Paris and the children study Spanish—personally I'm with you: *viva* la *France*—so maybe you could take a class? Or listen to one of those tapes, one of those language tapes. Yes? Now, the position isn't terribly difficult. School ends at three, violin on Mondays, ballet Tuesdays and Thursdays, pottery every other Wednesday, calligraphy every other *other* Wednesday and riding every Friday. *(Pause.)* No. No, no it's not too much activity: they're *bright*; they're *exceptionally* bright. Now where was…oh, yes, Riding-on-Fridays. Except every third Friday when Sequoia—my oldest and the one with the *(Motions around her eyes with her pinky finger, then whispers:)* …patch: yes. We don't talk about that. *(Zips her mouth shut.)* Every third Friday Sequoia visits Woody. Woody is our code name for Dr. Green. Dr. Green-the-therapist. Even though Sequoia's down to once a month we don't talk about Woody, either. *(She motions around her eyes, and then her ear in a circle with her pinky finger, then makes a slicing motion with her hand in the air.)* Which brings me to my next point: we have several rules we follow for Sequoia. Woody/Dr. Green-the-therapist suggested them and they seem to, um, keep her calm. *(Smiles uneasily and consults her clipboard.)* First, when preparing food: use spices that are white. Nothing green, nothing black and under no circumstances *ever*: red. She says spices look like eyes staring at her and Dr. Woody, I mean, Woody/Dr. Green-the-therapist explained we should treat her fears with understanding. Eyes: what a robust imagination: we may have an artist on our hands, I'm telling you. Now: two: when the girls are home we… *(Smiles.)* …we cover the floors—well, anywhere Sequoia needs to walk—with towels. I keep the linen closet stocked so you shouldn't run out: Sequoia has developed an aversion to our wall-to-wall. She says the bristles are like spears. Little spears piercing the soles of her feet. As you can understand we can't let her feel like that so—….No, she can*not* "*just* wear *shoes*": no, no, no, no, no. Woody explained that would be insensitive, monstrous even. Imagine clipping a bird's wings or chopping a gazelle's legs off at the knees so it's forced to leap around with bloody stumps instead of legs.

Woody says Sequoia's preferences are part of her nature, her very being. So we lay down towels and she gets around the house perfectly fine that way. But make sure you line each hallway: we don't want her stuck in a room somewhere. Third, when serving snacks and dinner *don't* use the cobalt blue plates. Or the glasses, or the bowls: any of the dishware, really. Apparently she can taste the glass; she says it rubs off onto her food. One night one of the nannies forced her to eat off those glass plates and she began choking. Shards of glass were tearing her throat, she said, the blue from the cobalt glasses was staining her teeth and tongue, poisoning her, she said. She got so upset we let her have dessert without finishing first. I scraped the foil off those Hershey's Kisses myself—she hates the foil-feel, you'll want to remember. She calmed right down which is... *(Touches her nose with her pinky:)* exactly what Woody thinks is best: yes, *yes*. I *like* you. I'm confident you'll fit in beautifully. Not like that other nanny; that glass-wielding nazi-nanny. The night she tried to kill my Sequoia, she said that she thinks Sequoia is making all this up, that she's pulling our legs, that while I was removing the wrapping off of Sequoia's prematurely presented sweet snack Sequoia winked at her. Winked? How preposterous. Sequoia is a *gazelle*. We are to help her *Leap*, Woody explained. Winked: can you believe that? Honestly: I'm glad we got rid of *her*. Now, when can *you* start?

# Octophobia
## by James Still

*In darkness, hushed voices:*

MAN'S VOICE: *(V.O.)* This young woman has the whole world holding its breath, Peggy.

WOMAN'S VOICE: *(V.O.)* That's right, Dick. She's lovely, the picture of concentration.

MAN'S VOICE: *(V.O.)* You've been there, Peggy. You've been in her shoes. What is going through her mind?

WOMAN'S VOICE: *(V.O.)* You're thinking about one move at a time, trying not to get ahead of yourself. All of the practice, all of the sacrifice, all of that is gone—and all you're thinking about—is this one moment.

*(The lights come up on a young woman wearing a glittery-spangled skater's costume. And ice skates.)*

SKATER: I'm skating. I FEEL myself, SEE myself, I HEAR myself skating. I hear my past, I hear my heartbeat, I hear God—laughing. I think that he's laughing because skating around and around on frozen water is something he never imagined we would invent. I just don't think he thought it through far enough. Maybe we've been around too long if it's come down to ice skating. God made roses. Man made ice skating.
*(Beat.)*
My dad says that roses have been growing on this planet for over 35 million years. That sounds like a long time. I was skating when I thought about THIS for the first time: that dinosaurs couldn't survive, but roses did. I bet God just shakes his head about that one.

I'm skating. I'm thinking about a moment when I was eight years old... It's snowing, it's Los Angeles. I'm in the backyard, wearing a one-piece bathing suit surrounded by my father's roses which he loves more than he loves my mom. When he calls his roses "Hybrid Perpetuals"—it sounds like he's making a wish. I hold a rose against each ear like—ear muffs... Like hearing the sounds of the ocean in seashells, the roses turn the sounds of my parents fighting into... Romance.

I'm skating. The other little girls would cry when they fell on the ice. I would just lie there, listening to the frozen water moving under my weight. It sounded like God—singing. And I started to sing along. This coach watched me skate and fall and sing with God—and she thought it was poetry. I thought it was heaven. Skating early in the mornings, when it's still dark, with no one sitting in the stands but your dreams and fears—THAT'S poetry. I don't dream when I sleep. I dream when I skate. This one dream that I have is about me, I'm running from something—a dinosaur, a judge, a TV camera—and I'll realize I'm running—not in circles. I'm running in figure-eights. It's the only shape I know by instinct… I stop running from the dinosaur and start running from the figure-eight. But I'm running in a figure-eight AWAY from the figure-eight and so I never get away. Pushing off one foot to another, making these big sweeping turns, tracing a giant "eight" in the ice—I feel like I'm crawling along the outside of my grandmother's hips. Or I'm stuck to the lips of that man who always stares at me. An oval-shaped table—family dinners where the food kind of all mushes together and makes this quilt of smells that makes me want to throw up. When I get that look in my eyes, my coach calls it nerves, that I'm nervous, that it's just butterflies. And when she says this, I open my mouth to deny it and all of these butterflies spill out of my mouth and fly around my head in little figure-eights. And then I spend the next four-and-a-half minutes chasing butterflies across the ice… Running away from butterflies, jumping/turning/leaping/spinning—turning my fear of figure-eights into something beautiful, heartbeat by heartbeat, like a rose in the snow, like a wish, like romance. I'm skating— *(Gasping for breath, whispers.)* I can hardly breathe.

# Hold This
## by Sheila Callaghan

*Based on the phobia Alektorophobia: fear of chickens.*

YOUNG MAN: Hold this. Here. Take it. Hold it. Take it. Hold it.

No, he says.

Take it. Put it with the other ones.

No, he says. They aren't alive, he says.

Don't think about that. They're sleeping.

They are not sleeping, he says. Their chests flutter when they sleep.

Listen. I can't pay someone to do it. Do it. Take it. Hold it.

So he holds it. In his right hand. Cream-yellow puff of fuzz. Orange pencil-point beak. Its chest does not flutter.

Voices are banging behind him. Commercial people making their commercial. His mother's voice the loudest among them. "We only have nine more. Try not to give them *all* heart attacks."

But most of them do not die from heart attacks. Only two. Most of them die from the heat of the commercial lamps. Baby chicks can thrive in sunlight, in moonlight, in infrared light that does not exceed temperatures of 70 degrees. They cannot survive 800 watts of stage lighting.

So he holds it. In his right hand. He thinks of. An infrared light bulb. The black X's he drew on all the eggs that were about to hatch. The pickle jar lid filled with marbles and drinking water, marbles to keep the chicks from drowning. The new velour sofa his mother ordered after she was told how much the agency would be paying her.

He hears a man's laugh behind him; a pointy, pickaxe laugh. "It got cooked. This must be how they make chicken nuggets."

His mother does not laugh. She contemplates her son over the frames of her Ray-Bans. This is the first time it occurs to her that he might be gay.

He lays the dead chick into a cardboard box lined with newspaper. He makes sure its head is aligned with the heads of all the other dead chicks, so they might dream of one another. He lifts the box and walks towards the house. Something twitches inside. Still alive! Startled, he trips on a lighting cable. Newspaper lifts, twelve yellow puffs soar through the air in fuzzy arcs. Hit the concrete almost noiselessly. But not. Pat. Pat pat-pat. Pat. They bounce lightly.

Twelve yellow puffs on the concrete. None of them twitching.

He steps away from the dead chicks. He walks over to the water spigot. Retrieves a metal bucket. Fills it with water and bleach. Thrusts his right hand into it. Scrubs the hand with an iron brush.

His mother shouts his name.

He scrubs. Metal in his throat, the taste of fear. He scrubs.

His mother shouts.

He scrubs.

He scrubs.

# Naked Lunch
## by Michael Hollinger

*Lights up on Vernon and Lucy sitting at a small dining-room table, eating. There's a small vase with too many flowers in it, or a large vase with too few. A bottle of wine has been opened. Vernon regales Lucy as he vigorously devours a steak. Lucy discreetly nibbles on her corn-on-the-cob.*

VERNON: Larry thinks the whole show's a fake. He says the guy's just an actor and all the crocs are trained. I said, you can't train a crocodile! It's not like some poodle you can teach to ride a bike. It's got this reptile brain, a million years old. All it knows, or wants to know, is whether or not you're juicy. Anyway, this one show the guy's sneaking up on a mother protecting her nest. And she's huge—I mean, this thing could swallow a Buick. And the guy's really playing it up: *(Australian accent.)* "Amazing—look at the size of those teeth!" But just—
*(He stops, looking at Lucy. Pause. She looks up from her corn.)*

LUCY: What.

VERNON: What's the matter?

LUCY: I'm listening.

VERNON: You're not eating your steak.

LUCY: Oh. No.

VERNON: How come?

LUCY: I'll just eat the corn.
*(She returns to nibbling.)*

VERNON: What's wrong with the steak?

LUCY: Nothing.

VERNON: Then eat it. It's good.

LUCY: I'd…rather not.

VERNON: Why not?
*(Pause.)*

LUCY: I'm vegetarian.
*(Beat.)*

VERNON: What?

LUCY: I don't eat meat anymore.

VERNON: Since when?

LUCY: Since we, you know. Broke up.

*(Pause.)*

VERNON: Just like that?

LUCY: Well—

VERNON: You break up with me and boom next day you start eating tofu?

LUCY: I'd been thinking about it for a while.

VERNON: First I ever heard of it.

LUCY: Well, I'd been thinking. *(Pause. Lucy picks up her corn again, guiding him back to the story:)* So anyway, the guy's sneaking up on the mother...

VERNON: Was it because of me?

LUCY: *No...*

VERNON: Something I said, or did...

LUCY: It's nothing like that.

VERNON: You were always fond of cataloguing the careless things I said and did...

LUCY: I just did some soul-searching, that's all.

*(Beat.)*

VERNON: Soul-searching.

LUCY: About a lot of things.

VERNON: And your soul said to you "no more meat."

LUCY: You make it sound silly when you say it like that.

VERNON: Then what, what did your soul tell you?

*(Beat. Lucy exhales heavily and sets down her corn.)*

LUCY: I decided I didn't want to eat anything with a face.

*(Beat.)*

VERNON: A *face?*

*(He gets up, stands behind her and looks at her plate.)*

LUCY: Vern...

VERNON: I don't see any face...

LUCY: This doesn't have to be a big deal...

VERNON: I don't see a face. Do you see a face?

*(He lifts the plate toward her face.)*

LUCY: There's other reasons.

VERNON: No face.

*(He sets the plate down again.)*

LUCY: I've been reading things.

VERNON: What things?

LUCY: You know, health reports...

VERNON: You can't believe that stuff.

LUCY: What do you mean?

VERNON: You can't! One day they say bran's good for you—"Want to live forever? Eat more bran."—the next day they find out bran can kill you.

LUCY: Whatever.

VERNON: Too much bran boom you're dead.

LUCY: There are diseases you can get from meat.

VERNON: Like what?

LUCY: Well, listeria…

VERNON: That's chicken. Chicken and turkey.

LUCY: Or Mad Cow.

VERNON: *Mad Cow?* Did you—That's not even…that's *English*, they have that in *England*. This isn't English meat, this is from, I don't know, Kansas, or… *Wyoming.*

LUCY: Even so,—

VERNON: No. Now you're making stuff up.

LUCY: I'm not; I saw an article—

VERNON: You're just being paranoid, this whole… You know what this is? Do you?

LUCY: What.

VERNON: Carnophobia.

LUCY: "Carnophobia"?

VERNON: It's a word, look it up.

LUCY: It's not like I'm scared of meat…

VERNON: How do you think this makes me feel?

LUCY: Look, let's just drop it.

VERNON: Huh?

LUCY: We were doing so well…

VERNON: I invite you over, cook a nice steak, set out flowers, napkins, the whole nine yards…

LUCY: I appreciate the napkins.

VERNON: …figure I'll open a bottle of wine, apologize…maybe we'll get naked, be like old times.

LUCY: So let's start over.

VERNON: Then you get *carnophobic* on me.

LUCY: Can we?

VERNON: Throw it in my face.

LUCY: Please?

VERNON: Start *cataloguing* what's wrong with everything…

LUCY: I never meant this to be a big deal. *(Beat. She puts her hand on his. He looks at her.)* I really didn't.

*(Long pause.)*

VERNON: Then eat it.

*(Beat.)*

LUCY: Vern… *(He picks up her fork, jams it into her steak, and cuts off a bite with his knife.)* Why do you always have to—

*(He extends the piece of meat towards Lucy's mouth.)*

VERNON: Eat the meat.

LUCY: I don't want to.

VERNON: *Eat the meat.*

LUCY: Vernon…

VERNON: I SAID EAT THE MEAT! *(They are locked in a struggle, he menacing, she terrified. Long pause. Finally, Lucy opens her mouth and takes the bite into it. Pause.)* Chew. *(She chews for fifteen or twenty seconds.)* Swallow. *(She swallows. Cheerfully, without malice:)* Good, isn't it. *(Lucy nods obediently.)* Nice and juicy. *(He stabs his fork into his own steak, cuts off a bite and lifts it.)* See, nothing to be afraid of.

*(He pops it into his mouth and begins cutting another. After a moment, Lucy goes back to her corn. They eat in absolute silence. Lights fade.)*


"Naked Lunch—*a frozen moment when everyone sees what is on the end of every fork.*"—William S. Burroughs

# Normal
## by Cusi Cram

CHARACTERS:
CHASE: male, 28.
LEWIS: male, 30.

*New York. The waiting room of an ICU. Chase sits and stares out. Lewis enters with two deli cups of coffee.*

LEWIS: I tried…

CHASE: Tried what?

LEWIS: To figure out how to make coffee in your apartment. There were just so many instruments and so many different kinds of coffee. I think you said what you really needed was Arabic something…but…there were two bags that had Arabic on them and I thought what if it's the wrong Arabic, what if the one I choose is totally inappropriate.

CHASE: It's fine, Lewis.

*(Lewis hands Chase the coffee.)*

LEWIS: I'm no good with choice. I'm a Folgers and a Mr. Coffee kind of guy.

CHASE: Don't sweat it, man. I'm fine with deli coffee. It's an adventure.

LEWIS: Like Janine got it into her head to paint the den a color, you know she's sort of gotten into decorating. And she brought this little book of colors home and it stumped me, totally stumped me. Every room I've ever lived in has been white.

CHASE: *(Sipping his coffee.)* In France, they call this kind of coffee *pipi du chat.*

LEWIS: And what does that mean?

CHASE: Cat piss.

LEWIS: Aren't you involved in some coffee thing?

CHASE: A buddy and me do some importing of top of the line beans from Brazil and Morocco, mostly. You can't go back after you've had Marrakesh Mud.

LEWIS: That's where you were last Christmas, right? Morocco?

CHASE: We had a run-in with customs. It got complicated…

LEWIS: Mom said. I mean, she was just so thrilled that you were spending Christmas in Casablanca. She talked and talked about it. Janine got a little…I dunno. I mean Christmas in Baltimore, just doesn't have the same ring to it.

CHASE: It was an interesting Christmas.

LEWIS: Ours was pretty interesting too. Everyone but me got strep throat. I thought, I have two weeks off from school, I'm just going to sit in my very berry den, that's the color we decided on, sort of raspberry/strawberry blend, it's a little loud but warm, as Janine likes to say. I didn't do much sitting.

CHASE: I was stuck in Casablanca for two months! It was a customs nightmare. *(Beat.)* There was an upside, I had the exclusive company of a half-Moroccan, half-Swedish ballerina, named Tamir.

LEWIS: And where is Tamir ballerina now?

CHASE: Probably somewhere with her husband.

LEWIS: You talk to any doctors?

CHASE: I was thrown out of the ICU.

LEWIS: And, I thought you would have bedded the entire nursing staff by now and all the female interns, at least the pretty exotic ones. Mom's been in the ICU for what two days and you haven't scored a uniform yet?

CHASE: Lay off, Lewis.

LEWIS: It's just you can charm every last good coffee bean out of North Africa but you can't get the lowdown from a doctor.

CHASE: I got the lowdown.

LEWIS: And what? It's like top secret information? What did the fucking doctor say, Chase?

CHASE: Seems that I was interrupting rounds, interrupting his teaching. None of those interns asked a single question about Mom. She was just a bunch of numbers and tubes to them.

LEWIS: She's not *their* mother.

CHASE: I got the Peruvian doctor to talk to me.

LEWIS: The one that smells like vanilla?

CHASE: He smells of bay rum. Good bay rum, I might add.

LEWIS: Who cares what he smells like. What did he say?

CHASE: He wasn't going to say anything. But then I started mentioning some people that I know in Lima, and he came 'round.

LEWIS: Peru has coffee too?

CHASE: It does but it's not very good. I manage some bands there. It's part of this world music company I started with a Paris-based conglomerate. I appealed to him as a son.

LEWIS: To who?

CHASE: The doctor.

LEWIS: The world music thing. I didn't know about it.

CHASE: I'm involved in a lot of businesses, Lewis.

LEWIS: I know, I know, music was just never one of your things. I'm the musical one.

CHASE: I told him how Mom had raised us alone and put us both through college on a nurse's salary and how I had sold my first company for three million dollars by the time I was twenty-five.

LEWIS: And what did you tell the Peruvian doctor about me?

CHASE: That you were the principal of a huge high school in Baltimore.

LEWIS: I'm the assistant principal of a junior high, it's not that big. Never mind. What did he say about Mom?

CHASE: They've managed to stabilize her and control the clotting. She'll probably be moved out of the ICU tonight. They want to keep her under observation for a few days.

LEWIS: Well that's better than I thought.

CHASE: It would be so weird without her. I can't even imagine it.

LEWIS: You know Mom, she always pulls through.

CHASE: Yeah.

LEWIS: I'm sorry…for whatever I said. I just…I guess I'm tense.

CHASE: It's OK. I mean I get it. I mean who has this life but me, right?

LEWIS: But…I mean…that's the point, right?

CHASE: Of what?

LEWIS: Your life. The point is that it's not like anybody else's. I mean…right?

CHASE: The point is…the point is…that it is exciting, my life is exciting.

LEWIS: And everyone else's is, therefore, boring?

CHASE: I didn't say that. I have a life that is exciting to me. I hope your life is exciting to you. I really do, Lewis.

LEWIS: No you don't. Look, I'm fine with my suburban life with my wife who's just plain Irish-American on both sides and my two kids and my big mortgage and my ever growing mountain of debt that precludes me from ever traveling. But you judge me. I mean admit it, since college you wanted to get as far away from Mom and our growing up as possible.

CHASE: Let's go and see Mom.

LEWIS: I'm not finished. I just want you to admit…

CHASE: *(Interrupting.)* Admit what? Admit that I'm afraid of every single thing that constitutes everyday American life. That I am terrified of big houses you can't afford filled with children whose orthodonture you can't afford and a wife who the more money you make somehow figures out ways to spend more. Alright Lewis, I'm afraid of fidelity, matrimony, fatherhood, and lawn maintenance. I made as much money as I could as soon as I could, so I could leave whenever I felt afraid. *(Beat.)* And I don't judge you. I envy you.

LEWIS: What?

CHASE: I'm a postcard, blank on the back, waiting to be filled in. You live life, Lewis. I avoid it.

LEWIS: Come on, Chase. I didn't mean…

CHASE: You always apologize when you're not really sorry.

LEWIS: I'm sorry that you feel that way about your life.

CHASE: Wanna help me?

LEWIS: Of course I do.

CHASE: The doctor said there was no way Mom was going to be able to live alone, maybe ever.

LEWIS: We're already renovating a room above the garage for her. I was planning for it, before all this.

CHASE: Let me take Mom.

LEWIS: What? To fucking Casablanca and Peru by way of your Paris conglomerate. No way.

CHASE: Give me a reason to stay, Lewis.

LEWIS: Fuck you. *(Long beat.)* I'm renovating the room, anyway, just in case.

CHASE: Thanks.

LEWIS: And…Chase…you know…I'm scared of…of all of that stuff too. I mean…who really aspires to be normal, right? *(Taking a sip.)* This coffee is sub-cat piss. It's like hog sweat. When we get back to your place you're making me some of that Marrakesh Mud. You're going to teach me to use all those contraptions too. Deal?

CHASE: Deal.

*(Lights fade on the brothers.)*

# Euxious
## by Bridget Carpenter

*A woman sits at a metal table, bright light. She has a cut over one eye and her hand is bandaged.*

WOMAN: I'd like a glass of water please. —I suppose most of the people ask for the one phone call, right?

Oh…the bag…

*(She shrugs, dumps the bag out. Stuff. A cell phone. It rings. She twitches. Doesn't answer.)*

No that's… I'll just…

*(Phone stops ringing.)*

I mean it's not like it's a good time to talk.

You've just started to ask questions. So.

*(The phone rings again. She jumps.)*

Usually I answer first ring.

*(She stares at the phone; it stops ringing.)*

I know I know it's a dreadful cliché, I have a cell phone and I drive an SUV, *mea culpa*. My son Ian continually says, "You're getting cancer of the ear, mom." Very precocious. I know, everyone says, "You're too *young* to have a second grader *and* a production company." *(Laughs.)* I say, *(Serious.)* deal with it. Ian just drew a cartoon for the school paper, it's a picture of God's throne in heaven, and next to it there's a telephone answering machine. And in a bubble over the answering machine it says, "Hello, this is God, I'm everywhere right now, and I can't get to the phone." *(Laughs.)* He has a little Unitarian friend named Kevin.

*(The phone rings again. She jumps.)*

No I'd rather not.

*(Phone stops ringing.)*

Everyone in that minivan was all right, weren't they? The people in my ambulance didn't know. Of course I'm concerned, I'm concerned and troubled. *(To herself:)* "Croubled." …I drive an Escalade. My husband calls me the demigod of Wilshire Boulevard. Yes yes yes emissions, the environment, global warming blah blah blah—please, I've heard it, and I'm sorry but I spend a *lot* of time in my car and I *need* to be *comfortable*. Bob *Redford* is an environmentalist and *he* drives an SUV and nobody gives him an attitude. I drive best when I'm above things. There should be a word for that.

Is there *any* word on the condition of the people in the minivan?

*(The unheard answer is "No." She starts to touch phone, then stops.)*

I wear a headset in the car, it's *not* a hazard. Well considering the current situation you could say that it was *momentarily* hazardous but I wasn't the car running the red light. —My *job* depends upon my availability. If you could see our slate right now…the number of projects we are juggling… Insane. The point is, I don't miss a call, because *every* call is significant and important. My husband would say, "Sigportant." He has this thing…if I say that I feel, oh, *weary* and *strange*, he'll say, "Wange." He thinks it's very funny… He always says, "There should be a word for that." Instead of my using two words.

*(The phone rings again. She trembles slightly. Phone stops ringing.)*

What do I remember before the impact.

It's a little difficult. Well because you're going to think I'm crazy. I was driving, the phone rang—no caller ID number, so I assumed it was my husband, and I clicked on and said, "Tell me you didn't forget about soccer practice," because he always forgets, only…it wasn't him. There wasn't any voice. There was just a, a sound, a hum, I don't know. *Not* a dial tone. More like a song. But not music. There was a feeling, if you could *listen* to a feeling, it would *sound* like what I heard. And—this is the crazy part—I knew it was God. Calling. On the phone. I knew it. This was God. I just listened. I felt so, so…wonderful and sad…euphoric and anxious… *(Pause.)* It was like feeling every emotion you could possibly feel all at once no I am not on medication. I *do* understand what this sounds like, there should be a word for how idiotic I feel telling you that I heard GOD through my headset driving on fucking Santa Monica Boulevard! I DON'T *KNOW* WHY HE WOULD CALL! WHY HAS NO ONE CALLED YOU PEOPLE ABOUT THE FAMILY IN THE MINIVAN!

*(The phone rings. She picks it up and hits it against the table several times until it breaks and stops ringing.)*

The thing is. The thing is. If it was God…why did that minivan run that red light at that exact moment? Why was there so much blood? Why did I get scratched and everyone, they… Why would God call and do that?

*(The phone rings. Even though it's broken.)*

You answer it. I can't. I'm afraid. And alone. There should be a word for that.

*(The phone keeps ringing.)*

# I'm Here for You
## by Warren Leight

*A hotel room, New York. Small. Cramped. Jules sits on the bed, channel surfing. A decent mild-mannered guy, mid-twenties. A bit naive for his wife Amy, mid-twenties who now bursts into the room. She is, at the moment, OUT OF HER MIND.*

AMY: Fuck me.

JULES: What?

AMY: Fuck me Jules. Take off your clothes and fuck me.
  *(She gets on top of him.)*

JULES: What's going on?

AMY: I think it's pretty clear. She's using him.

JULES: What?

AMY: Fuck me. *(Looks down at him.)* Is something wrong?

JULES: Um...um. It's just, what about, you know. The mood. The setting? I thought you and the couples therapist said that I should—
  *(She takes the clicker. Turns the TV off. Still, Jules isn't aroused.)*

AMY: OK? Fine. There's my mood. Let's go.

JULES: What about...protection?

AMY: Screw it. If she can have a baby, I goddamn well can have a baby. C'mon.

JULES: *(Sits up.)* What is going on?
  *(She pushes him back down. Tries to force the issue. No go.)*

AMY: *(Looks down at him.)* Not much—
  *(She gets off of him. Angry.)*

JULES: Amy, I can't just flick a switch and—

AMY: He can.

JULES: Who?

AMY: JOSH. "Dad." He just can't flick it off.

JULES: Look I can try again. I just wasn't—

AMY: It was a setup. This whole trip. "Why don't you kids come join me in New York. Jules and I can get a few meetings in, and"—this part kills me—"it would be nice for the whole family to be together again." Bullshit. He...he—

JULES: I thought it was nice of him.

AMY: He's...he's ridiculous. He's fifty-eight years old. He's dating a woman who says she's younger than me, and now he's going to be a father. A father! Is he completely over the deep fucking end or what.

JULES: I don't know.

AMY: You don't know? You don't know! He's already a fucking father. Not that he has any idea what that means. So now, it's like, he botched it the first time, so he wipes the slate clean and gets to go again.

*(She starts to pack. Slamming drawers and closets. Stuffing a bag and a suitcase.)*

JULES: Where are you going?

AMY: Well fuck him.

JULES: You know, maybe...maybe it will be a good thing—

AMY: WHOSE SIDE ARE YOU ON?

JULES: I'm not on any—

AMY: And don't say you're not on anybody's side. Whenever people say that it means they're not on your side.

JULES: Amy, calm down. OK. Take a breath here.

*(She keeps packing.)*

JULES: Where are you going?

AMY: I mean he is going out right now to buy the right crib, the right stroller. The right this the right that. He didn't even know our names until we were nineteen.

JULES: That's not—

AMY: We were just, "the girls," as in, Do the girls really need back-to-school wardrobes? Do the girls really need to come with us? Can't the girls leave one toilet seat up in one bathroom in the whole goddamn house?

JULES: Look, it's upsetting.

AMY: FUCK YOU.

JULES: You have every right to be—

AMY: Don't patronize me Jules. I hate when men do that.

JULES: AMY—I am not men. I am not all men. I am not your father.

AMY: You're all the same.

JULES: Thank you.

AMY: You are all ruled by your dicks. Completely incapable of honesty or decency or even simple basic common sense. I mean, do we think this woman—

JULES: I never liked her.

AMY: —really got pregnant by accident? Accidents don't happen. He's probably not even the father.

JULES: You don't know that.

AMY: Wake up. She's out for him for his money. She's playing him like a fool. It's all your fault.

JULES: Me?

AMY: You introduced them.

JULES: She asked me to. She's an actress, he's a—

AMY: See? Mom thinks she set him up. From the beginning.

JULES: He told your mom?

AMY: He has to. Not that he did. He had me tell her. Which is why he flew us in.

JULES: Am I missing something here?

AMY: Look—he has to get Mom's…permission, because she handles his money.

JULES: What?

AMY: She always has.

JULES: They've been divorced for—

AMY: They're not divorced.

JULES: I thought you said—

AMY: Not technically. She walked out on him when she walked in on him. When he and John Huston picked up some Brearley girls.

JULES: Your dad knows John Hughes?

AMY: Huston, you idiot. Not Hughes. John Huston. *The African Queen* not *Pretty in Pink*. I knew I shouldn't date someone dumber than me. Mom thought it might give me some control, but—

JULES: Date? We're married.

AMY: Well, so are Mom and Dad.

JULES: Wasn't he married to Sheila?

AMY: SHELLY.

JULES: The tall one?

AMY: Sidney. No they weren't married. I mean, he went through some ceremony in Barbados once on their honeymoon but technically he and Mom never split. She still handles his finances and he says it's good because this way no gold digger will try to get his money, or they can try but they can't because he's married so it's not his to give away and it gives him a way out.

*(She starts packing again. Closes suitcase, goes to door.)*

AMY: Until now.

JULES: Amy...Amy... *(Sees she's leaving.)* Where are you going?

AMY: I have to get out.

JULES: We just got here.

AMY: I need some air.

JULES: *(Goes to her.)* I'm really sorry.

AMY: Don't touch me. OK. I need...some...air. That's all.

JULES: Then you don't need this. Do you?

  *(He gently takes the suitcase from her. Puts it in the closet.)*

JULES: I want you to know I'll be here for you, Amy.

AMY: I know that.

JULES: I mean it. Go get some air. Go walk. Do whatever you have to do. I'll wait here for you.

AMY: OK.

JULES: Call me if you want me to come get you.

AMY: Jules—

JULES: Will you call me?

AMY: I'll probably just walk around the block and come right back up.

JULES: I'll be here.

  *(He puts his arm to hold her. She lets him hold her for a few seconds. Then she leaves.)*

# Safe
## by Gina Gionfriddo

WOMAN: I went to a cancer group. I went for a while, actually. *(Pause.)*

The cancer group was full of those women you avoid at parties, you know, the sort of righteously clean-living people who bring their own mugs to Starbucks. Not that that's a bad thing in and of itself. I mean, save the trees. Good for them. They're just not people you want to know. Each of these women had her *thing*, some natural, spiritual, nutritional *thing* that was going to keep her from getting sick again. I heard about macrobiotics, directed visualization, the yeast connection, the sugar blues… Rolfing, Reiki, chelation…

We had this young man come one night. He'd had two brain surgeries in the last five years and his odds, I gather, were less than fifty-fifty. He also had a lot of substance abuse issues which don't go over real well with people who think refined sugar is a drug. But they listened to his story and they thanked him for sharing. Then this woman gave a presentation about essential oils. Aromatherapy. She got about midway through when the boy just stood up and said, "Fuck this." Then he stormed out. And I went after him.

He was a mess this kid. Twenty-three years old. Doing a lot of cocaine which… I've never done it, but it struck me as something a person with two brain tumors probably shouldn't do. We had a cup of coffee and he was just… he was furious. He'd been sick his whole adult life. What I went through, he went through twice and that I can't imagine. It's one thing to go through it when you don't know what to expect but to go through it once you do know… *(Pause.)* Anyway. I gave him my number, but I didn't really think he'd call.

I went back to the group the next week. I couldn't help it. There was a woman in there who was fourteen years out. She was annoying as hell—her thing was raw foods—but she was fourteen years out and it made me hopeful just to know that she existed.

The week after that, he called me. He said he'd met a woman who walked down forty floors to get out of the World Trade Center. She was still pretty messed up but she was going to a group in Brooklyn and it was helping her. He had gone to the group with her and he said it made him feel better and he thought I would like it, too. So I went.

The Trade Center thing sort of put me off. I mean, I'm sorry for what they went through and I don't doubt that it was terrible, but as far as their ongoing struggle... The odds of them having to flee a burning building again are negligible. The odds of my cancer coming back are considerably more sobering. But I went.

The best I can describe it... it's like nap time at preschool. Big loft in Brooklyn. No furniture. Lots of candles, some kind of spices burning. You walk in and take a blanket and then you just... lie on the floor. And the man... the leader... plays a CD of bells and he talks over it. He says stuff like, "Here and now, in this room, you are safe. You are fine." On and on like that. Repetitive, present-tense reassurance like you do with a hysterical child. Often I don't even listen. I like the bells and the spices. I like being on the floor with all these people.

It works. I feel better. And maybe the reason it works is nothing more sophisticated than nap time at preschool. Time out for comfort.

It's the one place I have where I'm allowed to not be over it. All the groups, the therapy... is all about coping. Aggressive positivity. Even professional people—therapists—when you say how scared you are they want you to make a list of things to do instead. Go jogging! Take a bath! Get a cat! All the time I was sick, people expressed their concern in the form of constructive questions: "What can you do?" "What can we do?" How many treatments... what kind of foods... And that's all very nice, but what I really wanted was for someone to stop—just for a minute—being solution-oriented and proactive and positive and to just say, "This sucks. This is very, very bad." Because it was. It is. And buying a puppy and eating raw foods and breathing clary sage is not going to change that.

Being "over" cancer, it's like... The best I can describe it is it's like the end of that movie *Halloween*. You know that movie? The bogeyman is so bad, they can't kill him. They stick a knitting needle through his brain and he keeps coming. Finally Donald Pleasance shows up and shoots him a bunch of times until he crashes through the window into the front yard. At the end of the movie, he is lying in the front yard looking very, very dead. And the heroine breathes this sigh of relief because it's over. It's finally over. But Donald Pleasance can't quite believe it. He has to look again, just to be sure, and when the camera pans out the window... the bogeyman isn't lying on the lawn anymore. He's gone. And that's what the fear is, for me. I'm afraid that we didn't kill it. I'm afraid there's going to be a sequel.

# Phobophobia
## by Julie Marie Myatt

*n.: a morbid fear of developing a phobia; fear of fear.*

*Paul stands dressing in front of his girlfriend, Lisa. It is his first day on the job as a traffic cop. He's nervous. His uniform is brand new. This is his big "start" on the "force." Shoes are polished. Uniform starched to cardboard. Impeccably shined badge waits in Lisa's hands. (She is careful not to actually touch it…she lets it rest in her hands. Hence, Paul's constant asking for various articles of clothing and help in his getting ready pose a terrible problem in not smudging, dropping, or "ruining" the badge, or this big moment, in any way, shape or form. Also, Lisa has one if not all of the possible phobias/fears that Paul mentions.)*

PAUL: Do, do I look scared—Hand me those socks—Please. I've been through all the training. I proved myself—Belt…right there by your feet, honey…Though this has been no easy road…no sir; I don't need to tell you that. You've heard what I've been through. You saw me through it—watch the badge—fingers, Lisa, fingers, more grease than a bucket of Kentucky Fried Chicken on a simple set of ten human fingers, and I'm not going to even start with that…Lord knows they put me through every godforsaken thing to test my courage. Shoved me in, in, those tiny boxes with no air, crammed me in elevators full of people, most of them with a serious case of B.O., I might add…dangled me from high buildings on nothing but dental tape, floss really is stronger, you know, covered me in spiders, then snakes, then dolls of every shape and size, none of which, I soon discovered, could even close their stupid eyes…my shoes are right behind you, sweetheart…thanks…not to mention, being left alone in a dark room, with no chance of light, without a soul to speak to for a month, sent me to a Yankees game on the most crowded day of the year, without a seat, and made me sing the national anthem, a cappella, without even a toot to set me in key…sent me out on a raft in the middle of the Atlantic with nothing but a teaspoon to push my way back to shore, I got rickets en route,… *(Sighs…thinks.)* …made me get a root canal I didn't even need, dropped me out of an airplane with a faulty parachute, made me eat raw eggs, then beef tartar from England, only to be topped off by that unprotected sex with those really fun flight attendants—you knew about that, of course it meant nothing, Lisa—but, they really were great at their job—gin does taste better out of those tiny bottles—put me in a straightjacket, then brought a mime troupe in, and some laid-off Barnum and Bailey clowns who kept sticking their big fat cold red noses in my ear...they covered me in dachshund poop and rat droppings, mentioned a rabies and plague epidemic in the area—oops, shit, forgot my pants, where are my pants?...you're sitting on them, Lisa...Jesus Christ ...wrinkles—I'm not going to start with that—you know I don't have time for—the badge, fingers, fingers—if that's not bad enough, to top it all off, they bring my parents in, both of them, at the same time, you've heard their voices, and tell them to berate me in front of the entire squadron. Loud and clear. Told them to tell everyone about my bedwetting, my cross-dressing, my Dungeons and Dragons phase, my tour with the Jim Jones—it wasn't a cult, I swear—and my brief—it really was brief—love affair with our goat, Roderick—that had the squad room shaking for 3 days with laughter. How many cases of chèvre did I have coming to my place? I gave you a case remember...oh, you made a real nice salad with it and those sun-dried tomatoes... delicious... Did I break then? No. Not even a glint of panic crossed my face, did it?—Do these pants look tight?...Hell...maybe...I'm just bloated, ... *(He buttons his shirt.)* I hope I'm not putting on weight...that's all I need at a time like this, that kind of fear will break a man, Lisa. *(He does a few traffic movements.)* ...Nope. Of course I'm solid. Of course. Nothing to be afraid of—hand me that—don't touch it!—Jesus!—fingers!—I'm not going to even start with that—Badge?

# Yes
## by Stephen Belber

*A man stands alone before a large crowd, his arms stiffly at his side. He is not a man of whom it would be said he is comfortable in his body. Silence. Eventually, he speaks, but when he does it is in a small, somewhat over-whelmed voice.*

MAN: You may be wondering. *(Beat.)* What I'm doing. *(Beat.)* Why I'm here. *(Beat…)* At first my doctor said….he thought….he said he thought, that I don't like being stared at. *(Beat.)* Which is true. *(Beat.)* I don't.
*(Silence, as he boldly attempts eye contact with the large number of people now staring at him.)*
I don't like crowds.
I don't like public speaking.
I don't like thinking about having an erect penis.
*(Beats; and then, re: his penis.)*
It's not. *(Beat.)* Although the idea scares me. Especially in public. *(Pause.)* When people are staring at me.
*(Beat; he takes off a layer of clothing, most likely his shirt.)*
Eventually we thought it was nudity. *(Pause.)* *Fear* of nudity. Which may not be far off. But not really on either. *(Beat.)* I mean…I guess…to a certain extent.
*(Beat; he takes off another layer, perhaps his undershirt.)*
For awhile I went to a specialist who treats people who have a disorder in which they fear…rectum….or *recti*. *(Pause.)* Rec*tums*. *(Beat.)* But then it turned out that someone was trying to set us up together; romantically. Me and the specialist. *(Pause.)* Like some sort of trick rectal blind date. *(Pause.)* It didn't work out.
*(During the following he takes off his shoes and socks.)*
My mother thinks I'm afraid of flowers. She thinks that they represent, for me, beauty, and that beauty is a concept, a notion, a reality that I'm simply unprepared to accept; or embrace; or be bowled over by. *(Beat; he speaks to a somewhat elderly woman in the front row.)* And maybe you're right, Ma. But I *do* love your Cherokee rose.

*(The man takes off his pants; he is wearing boxers or perhaps briefs—either way, his crotch is rather extremely large; to audience, after letting them take this in.)*

The fact is—I'm just scared. *(Pause.)* I'm scared. *(Pause; honest.)* I'm scared. *(Pause.)* Which is why I'm here.

*(He reaches into his underwear and takes out a Cherokee rose.)* Every day I'm working to overcome my fears. *(He gently tosses the rose into the audience.)* Working to love.

*(He produces another flower and tosses it to the audience.)*

And maybe to *be* loved; *(Tosses another flower.)* And to show you that I no longer *want* to be scared. *(Tosses another flower.)* Because I don't. *(Another flower.)* I'm tired of it. *(Another flower.)* I want to be *here*— *(Another flower.)* —in public— *(Another flower.)* —with flowers— *(Another flower.)* —Beautiful. *(Pause; he is out of flowers; simple:)* Even if it scares me. *(He adjusts his underwear; beat.)* Don't worry, Ma, I won't take 'em off. *(To audience.)* I just want there to be love instead of fear. I just want to be *here*, for one moment, *this* moment— *(He spreads his arms out wide.)* Just be here before you; alone; scared; not scared…..and say *Yes*.

END OF PLAY

# Rhythmicity

## A convergence of poetry, theatre and hip-hop

Curated by Mildred Ruiz and Steven Sapp
Created by Regie Cabico, Gamal A. Chasten,
reg.e.gaines, Rha Goddess, Willie Perdomo,
Mildred Ruiz and Steven Sapp

# About *Rhythmicity*

A ground-breaking form is taking shape in the arts, one that has been evolving for years. Young artists, unwilling to remain within the conventional bounds of music, literature and theatre, are experimenting with vastly diverse influences, producing acts of performance that defy traditional categorization. Poet merges with actor, storytelling melds with music, and speech comes alive through dance and movement—all subject to the truth of the word. At the 2003 Humana Festival, *Rhythmicity* brought to Actors Theatre of Louisville the eclectic and inventive performances of seven spoken word artists. Both individually and in conversation with one another, these acclaimed innovators invaded the lobbies and public spaces of the theatre with thrilling rants and rhythms, ranging from the personal to the political and everything in-between.

Curating this collective of artists were Steven Sapp and Mildred Ruiz of New York's Universes, an ensemble company of multi-disciplined writers and performers responsible for the genre-bending hit *Slanguage* at New York Theatre Workshop several seasons ago. Universes describes *Slanguage* as "a full work where traditional theatre synthesizes with poetry, storytelling, rhythm, music, song and dance." Indeed, they list their numerous influences with pride: gospel singer Mahalia Jackson, poet Amiri Baraka, the films of Bruce Lee and the one-man monologues of Eric Bogosian all inform their work. Their performance style fuses poetry and theatre with jazz, hip-hop, politics, down home blues and Spanish boleros to bring together the unique mix of language and culture that is life on the American streets. The work of Universes can be placed in a larger context that many critics have taken to calling "hip-hop theatre," but it's a label Sapp and Ruiz resist. "Why classify us as one thing when we address so many other things?" Ruiz has said. "Once hip-hop is listed alone, it becomes difficult to give an equally potent light to our other influences and backgrounds."

This diversity was also reflected in the performers who joined them. The list of names reads like a who's-who of spoken word artists in America today: Gamal A. Chasten, a poet, playwright and verbal DJ (and one of Sapp and Ruiz's compatriots from Universes); independent recording artist and social activist Rha Goddess, with her trademark style called Flowetry; Regie Cabico, National Slam champion and comedic wordsmith; Willie Perdomo, considered by many to be the "Nuyorican Poet Laureate"; and reg. e. gaines, accomplished poet/playwright and the writer of the musical *Bring in 'da Noise, Bring in 'da Funk*.

This group of diverse talents performed over the final two weekends of the Humana Festival, filling the lobbies with the sounds of poetry, song, speech and rhythm. They performed individually and together, at all times of the day and night. Signs bearing snippets of verse hung on the walls around the theatre's public spaces. Finally, they presented *Flipping the Script,* which was billed as a performance/panel in one of Actors Theatre's mainstage spaces. The performance that followed both spoofed and exploded the traditional panel discussion format, but it also provided another showcase for the dynamic work of these seven poets. The text in this volume is a transcript of that performance.

*Steve Moulds*

# BIOGRAPHIES

Regie Cabico's television credits include HBO's *Def Poetry Jam*, PBS' *In the Life*, and MTV's *Free Your Mind*. Solo shows include *Faith, Hope & Regie*, *RegieSpective* and *onomatopoeia and a quarter-life crisis*. His work appears in over thirty anthologies, including *Aloud: Voices from the Nuyorican Poets Café* and *Spoken Word Revolution*. His most recent theatrical work is *Exposures* at Baruch College's Nagelberg Theatre. He is literary curator of Dixon Place's Writers on the Ledge Series, and resides in Williamsburg, Brooklyn.

Gamal A. Chasten has been a professional writer and performance poet for the past seven years. The last five years he has spent co-writing and co-creating pieces as a member of Universes. As an actor, he has performed in the shows *In Case You Forget, You Can Clap Now*, and reg. e. gaines' *Tiers*. He is also the author of the one-man show *God Took Away His Poem*. Chasten's directing credits include *Stakes Is High* and *All I Have Left*. He is a New York Theatre Workshop Usual Suspect.

reg. e. gaines has written three books of poetry, *24-7-365*, *Head Rhyme Lines* and *The Original Buckwheat*. He wrote the text for the musical *Bring in 'da Noise, Bring in 'da Funk*, which garnered him a Grammy Award and two Tony nominations. He has released the poetry CDs *Please Don't Take My Air Jordans* and *Sweeper Don't Clean My Street*, and has since created an independent label, Countee Jail Records. He recently co-founded Scratch DJ Academy, a school for which he runs the theatrical division. gaines lives and writes in Jersey City, New Jersey.

Willie Perdomo is the author of *Where a Nickel Costs a Dime* and a bilingual collection entitled *Postcards of El Barrio*. His work has been included in several anthologies, including *Metropolis Found*, *The Harlem Reader*, *Poems of New York*, and *Bum Rush the Page: A Def Poetry Jam*. His work has also appeared in the *New York Times Magazine*, *Bomb*, *Russell Simons' One World Magazine*, and *Pen America: A Journal for Writers and Readers*. He is the author of *Visiting Langston*, a Coretta Scott King Honor Book for Children, illustrated by Bryan Collier, and has been featured on several PBS documentaries including *Words in Your Face* and *The United States of Poetry* as well as HBO's *Def Poetry Jam* and *B.E.T.'s Hughes' Dream Harlem*. Poetry by Willie Perdomo originally appeared in *Where a Nickel Costs a Dime* (W. W. Norton, 1996) and *Smoking Lovely* (Rattapallax Press, 2003). Copyright 1996, 2003 by Willie Perdomo.

Rha Goddess is a world-renowned performance/recording artist and activist. She has been featured in multiple international festivals and on numerous international music compilations, including *A Rose that Grew from Concrete*, a musical tribute to the poetry of Tupac Shakur, and the critically acclaimed *Eargasms*. Her solo debut, *Soulah Vibe*, received phenomenal industry reviews. She is currently working on her sophomore release, *Eucalyptus*, and her debut theatrical project, *Meditations with the Goddess*.

Mildred Ruiz is a member of Universes and the Founding Director of the UniverseCity Theater Network. She co-founded The Point Community Development Corporation, and is an Artistic Associate at New World Theater. She has worked as a song consultant for shows such as *Soular Power'd* and Alfred Jarry's *UBU: Enchained*. With Steven Sapp, she co-wrote *Eyewitness Blues*, and she has co-created *Slanguage* and *The Ride* with Universes. Ruiz has performed at the Nuyorican Poets Café, Joe's Pub at the Public Theater, and Sing Sing Prison, to name a few.

Steven Sapp is a member of Universes and a Director of the UniverseCity Theater Network. In addition to work with Live From the Edge and El Grito Dance Studio at The Point, he has been recognized by the Bronx Council on the Arts and New Dramatists. His directing credits include *Soular Power'd*, *Tiers*, and *UBU: Enchained*, an international exchange with Teatre Polski in Poland. He is the recipient of the 2002 TCG National Directors Award. With Mildred Ruiz, he co-wrote *Eyewitness Blues*, and he has co-created *Slanguage* and *The Ride* with Universes.

## HUMANA FESTIVAL PRODUCTION

*Rhythmicity* premiered at the Humana Festival of New American Plays in March 2003. It featured the following performers:

Regie Cabico

Gamal A. Chasten

reg. e. gaines

Willie Perdomo

Rha Goddess

Mildred Ruiz

Steven Sapp

and the following production staff:

Production Supervisor . . . . . . . . . . . . . . . . . . . . . Frazier W. Marsh

Lighting Supervisor . . . . . . . . . . . . . . . . . . . . . . . Hillery Makatura

Sound Supervisor . . . . . . . . . . . . . . . . . . . . . . . . . . Jason Czaja

"Moderator" . . . . . . . . . . . . . . . . . . . . Jen Grigg and Steve Moulds

Gamal A. Chasten, Steven Sapp, Rha Goddess (performing, center),
Mildred Ruiz, and reg. e. gaines
in *Rhythmicity*

27th Annual Humana Festival of New American Plays
Actors Theatre of Louisville, 2003
photo by Harlan Taylor

# Flipping the Script
## A Performance/Panel

*Lights come up. Moderator is seen at the table alone; all chairs, mics, water glasses and nameplates in place. Moderator begins a cacophony of questions, not necessarily in this order.*

MODERATOR: How would you compare your work with the epic poets...such as Milton and Homer?

Are you a rapper?

How do you memorize your work?

You guys are so musical, how do you do that?

Did you guys write that?

How does it feel to be a woman in an ensemble of so many men?

What do you think of Lil' Kim?

You are so articulate—how do you do that?

I hear the iambic pentameter in your work, you must be a fan of Shakespeare?

You have such an amazing voice, do you have Black in your background?

Is English your first language?

What is it like for you coming from poetry to work on Theatre?

What is your favorite color?

MILDRED: *(Singing.)*
SOMETIMES I WANNA
   ASK YOU QUESTIONS
DON'T WANT THE ANSWERS TO...
DON'T WANT THE ANSWERS TO...
LEARN

MODERATOR:
Favorite curse word?
Do you consider yourself a
   black writer or a writer?
I love your hair, how do
   you get it to do that?
How do you wash it?

STEVE: This is a show tune
But the show hasn't been written for it yet

RHA: I'm getting diesel for the revolution
On black-eyed peas, hog mog and collard greens

REG: Blacks and Jews can get along;
We just need some kosher spare ribs

REGIE: Together they got a nine octave range
 Keeping the whole world humming
ALL: M-m-m
GAMAL: It was 1971 when Bruce Lee came to the projects
 Brought an alternative form of ass-whoopin'
 Now we have black eyed please,
 Pasteles and shrimp lo mein
WILLIE: Title for a jazz riff
 A catwalk
 Stroll Fifth Avenue
 Strut black
 Boot leather
 Bass fashion
 Mama look good
 As hell
MILDRED: *(Song.)* OH YEA
STEVE: Love, spelled backwards is Evil
RHA: Evil eyes
 Evilyne
 Evil land
 Evil seas
 Love lost
 Be flippin' in the breeze
REG: Love
 Compassion
 Serenity
 Joy
 Africa brass
 Afro blues
REGIE: I gotta write how beautiful it must be
 To leave apparition on tile
 And crack a sky at night
GAMAL: Wishing I could place my hand on your smile
WILLIE: But I had to catch myself
 Before I slipped and broke something
 So I flipped it one time
 If you can be with the one you love
 Don't love the one you're with

MILDRED: But little girls grow
    And grow
    And grow
    And grew
    And grew
    And grew
    Straight up
    And learned
    To clear their throats
    And bite the man that feeds them
STEVE: So she huffs and puffs
    And blows down her walls
    A torn-a-do
    Turning her white slippers ruby red
RHA: Infinity sucks her nipple
    The ripple nectar
    Like new hope
THE GUYS: Now watch her sling the dope shit
REG: A dash of Salt & Pepper
    A bite of MC Lite
    And you know that dissin' women
    To Latifah wasn't right
REGIE: Breathe in
    Breathe out
    Money runs out like a cab ride to nowhere
GAMAL: Shit, if you could catch one.
    So come tie a black ribbon
    Round my fuck finger
    Why?
    'Cause
    Because
WILLIE: I called you "mami" by mistake
    Even after you told me
    That you ain't into that papi thing
    You know that ay papi
    Si papi, cojelo papi
    Que es tuyo papi thing
    and I told you yes mami

WILLIE: *(Cont'd.)* it's okay, sugar
    I can call you honey, baby
    Don't you know you my
    sweetheart, boo?
MILDRED: That bitch
    Up there at her window
    She don't quite like how I think
    She just sits her ass there watchin'
    Like a motherfuckin' sphinx
STEVE: So come and See this schizophrenic side show
    See Sekou Sundiata
    Scratch Sketches of Spain on an SP 1200
    See Nina Simone sing her signature secular spirituals
    See Sonia Sanchez speak in syncopated style to the socialist
RHA: We are cards shuffled in the deck
    Passed around like spliffs at a gangster party
    Landing in the hand of villains and heroes
    Who will play us nonetheless
    Rules made to be broken
    Pecking order established
    Nothing beats a Joker
    Unless that Joker's better dressed
REG: Same ol same ol
    Flashes a Leon Sphinx gap
    Boom box blazing
    Armani staining
    Scratching out an introspective mud club rap
REGIE: Did a sacred tablet crumble in the choir loft of Amen?
GAMAL: *(Chant.)* Bismiallah Rahman ni Raheem
    El Hamduli Alah Rabiel Amen…
WILLIE: Coke-n-dope
    Dope-n-coke
    Yellow top cracks
    Black is out
    Purple! Purple!
    Deuces!
    How many?
    Got plenty!

fifty, sixty, ninety, milligrams
What's up papa?
What you need?
Sets and points
Loose joints
Got it good money
Walk me by and you won't get high
If I'm lying I'm dying
But don't come back crying

MILDRED: Rhythm, Rhythm, Rhythm ah Rhythm
    *(Rhythm begins and is continuous.)*
    *(Each player joins the chant as they deliver their lineage line.)*
STEVE: Beckett / Baldwin / Bogosian
RHA: Angela / Amiri / Asada
REG: Ain't supposed to die another death
REGIE: Audre Lorde and Essex Hemp Hill
GAMAL: Nikki, Ali, Coltrane and Lee
WILLIE: Manteca / Barretto and Cuney
MILDRED: Mahalia Jackson, Odilio Gonzales, Nina Simone, and my Momma
ALL: Rhythm, Rhythm... *(The piece speeds up.)*
    *(The beat drops [foot work] into the* Slanguage *"Don't Front" piece.)*

MILDRED: *(Singing.)*                    MODERATOR:

SOMETIMES I WANNA              Did you guys write that?
    ASK YOU QUESTIONS          How do you feel about all
DON'T WANT THE ANSWERS TO          the violence in hip-hop?
DON'T WANT THE ANSWERS        Is English your first language?
DON'T WANT THE ANSWERS TO


SOMETIMES I WANNA ASK YOU QUESTIONS
*(Steve begins his lines; Mildred continues the song.)*
DON'T WANT THE ANSWERS TO
LEARN THE WALK AND WALK IT RIGHT
LEARN THE WALK AND WALK IT RIGHT
STEVE: Sometimes I wanna ask you questions
    That I don't know if I want the answers to
GAMAL: Sometimes I wanna ask you what the
    Hell you lookin' at
STEVE: Do I walk, the walk, like the others walked...

GAMAL: You got to walk just like you know where you at,

> Your bop has got to represent that time and place you in…

STEVE: That ditty bop walk,

> That kinda walk that lets us know
>
> That no matter where you was from
>
> What job you didn't have
>
> Or what bills you couldn't pay
>
> You was gonna walk that
>
> Walk with some style…

GAMAL: Like if you're lost walking by some projects

> In a neighborhood you ain't never ever been in,

STEVE: Cool…

> Just maintain your space

GAMAL: And if brothers are standin' on the corner

> Then you gotta show some character

STEVE: Remember when you was the kid

> Who was just learning how to bop.
>
> And there were so many different flavors…

GAMAL: Different stares, glares and glances…

STEVE: There was that one brother who'd, just bop too hard

GAMAL: There's that stare from across the room…

STEVE: Overdoing the bop…

GAMAL: when the population didn't resemble you

STEVE: And that sad junkie

> Who ain't got nothing but the bop,
>
> But just holding on, just a little too long.

GAMAL: Looking for that other brother,

> Sister,
>
> Bus boy,
>
> It don't matter,
>
> 'Cause when you spot 'em
>
> *(Rhythm pause.)*
>
> Eye contact,
>
> And then…
>
> You nod…
>
> *(Rhythm starts again.)*

STEVE: I don't even know where I learned it…

> But word has it that the walk was born

Way down in the jungle deep,
Before that signifying monkey stepped on that elephant's feet.
*(Rhythm shifts.)*
It got tangled up by some brothers who was working on the chain gang
And was steppin' and fetching that cake walk
Way before them black and white movies discovered us.
But the walk stayed

MILDRED: *(Sings.)* LIKE THE BEAT BEAT BEAT AND THE MILES
  MILES
WHEN YOU'RE TRYIN' TO CATCH THAT TRAIN

STEVE: Walkin', Walkin' Walkin' Walkin'

| Walkin' miles and miles | MILDRED: GOES FOR MILES MILES |
| | MILES MILES |
| and miles and miles | MILES MILES MILES MILES |
| Trying to catch that train | MILES MILES MILES MILES MILES |
| With them jazz cats | WITH A BEAT BEAT BEAT BEAT |
| Even when it was marching | BEAT BEAT BEAT BEAT |
| For somebody's rights | BEAT BEAT BEAT BEAT BEAT |
|    shuffling with Ali, | |
| Walking like a panther, | |

*(All rhythm and song stops abruptly after "a panther.")*

STEVE: Always on the one,
  *(Continue Rhythm and Mildred singing, "Learn the walk and walk it right"*
  *throughout.)*

STEVE: Now be it, Gators or timbs or shell toe Adidas with the fat laces.
  That walk left footprints on your back
  If you didn't get off your ass and learn the rules

GAMAL: That nod that says it's you and me against the world.
  That stare, that glance, that look that goes way back.
  That primitive look,
  The same kinda look that animals give one another…

STEVE: Now if you gonna give some dap,
  Or give 'em five, on the black hand side,
  Or just simply shake their hand, let it be firm

GAMAL: But that ain't what I'm talkin' 'bout,
  See what I'm talkin' 'bout is
  When you take a man's heart through his eyes
  Watch his soul wither,
  'Cause at that moment you willin' to die

STEVE AND GAMAL: And most-men-ain't.

GAMAL: That look that challenges him to a duel
    To the death
    Through his eyes
    Then they just drop their heads    MILDRED: *(Sings.)* DROP YOUR HEAD
        and walk away,
    They just turn and walk away        TURN AWAY
    And walk away.        WALK AWAY

    See That's the look I'm talkin' about
    When I'm in that moment and I'm there,    STEVE: Where
    When I'm in that moment and I'm right there,    STEVE: Where
    You see,
    Some brothers look back 'cause they willin' to die too,
    At least they act like they are.
    But if you're not,

STEVE AND GAMAL: Don't:

GAMAL: 'Cause we can sense it just like dogs…

STEVE: And hold your ground and never ever give the left 'cause that's disre-
    spect…

GAMAL: That's right.

STEVE: And if you gonna give somebody a pound
    And they got some extra flavor,
    Like a shake that starts at the thumb
    With a hug out of respect
    And with a finger pop at the end
    Then you need to know it

GAMAL: Don't front

STEVE: Or the block did not have a lot of respect for you

GAMAL: So when you see me smile,
    Smile and shake my hand,    MILDRED: *(Sings.)* SHAKE MY HAND
    Say what's up,        SAY WASSUP
    Walk away        WALK AWAY
    'Cause I ain't trying to feel no confrontation

MILDRED: *(Sings.)* SOMETIMES I WANNA ASK YOU QUESTIONS
    *(All harmonize.)*

ALL: DON'T WANT THE ANSWERS TO
    LEARN THE WALK AND WALK IT RIGHT
    LEARN THE WALK AND WALK IT RIGHT

STEVE: All that to learn at a neighborhood near you
REGIE: The government asks me to check one
    If I want money
    I say how can you ask me to be one race

    I stand proudly before you a fierce Filipino
    Who knows how to belt hard gospel songs
    Played to African drums at a Catholic mass
    And loving the music to suffering beats
    And lashes from men's eyes on the Capital streets

    Southeast D.C. with its sleepy crime
    My mother nursed patients from seven to nine
    Patients gray from the railroad riding past civil rights

    I walked their tracks when they entertained them at the chapel
    And made their canes pillars of percussion to my heavy gospel
    My comedy out loud
    Laughing about
    Our shared stolen experiences of the South

    Would it surprise you if I told you
    That my blood was delivered from North
    Off Portuguese vessels who gave me spiritual stones
    And the turn in my eyes?
    My father's name when they conquered the Pacific Isles
    My hair is black and thick as negrito
    Growing abundant as sampaguita—
    Flowers defying civilization
    Like Pilipino pygmies that dance in the mountains

    I could give you an epic about my ways of life or my look
    And you want me to fill it in one square box?
    How could you tell me to fill Gilgamesh
    With all of its waters
    In one square box?
    From what integer or shape do you count existing identities?
    Grants loans for the mind

REGIE: *(Cont'd.)* Or crayola white census sheets
There's no one kind to fill for anyone
You tell me who I am!
What gets the most money!
And I'll sing that song like a one-man caravan
I know arias from Naples
Tunis and Accra
Lullabies from welfare
Food stamps and nature
And you want me to sing one song?
I have danced jigs with Jim Crow
And shuffled my hips to the sonic guitar of Clapton and Hendrix
Waltzed with dead lovers
Skipped to bamboo sticks
Balleted kabuki and mimed cathacali
Arrivedercied da rhumba
And tapped tin pan alley
And you want me to dance the Bhagavad-Gita
On a box too small for a thumbelina thin diva?

I'll Check Other
RHA: Drop me inside the phattest beat
And I'll tell you a story
I'll paint the backdrop of Planet Rock
Up against subway car
Careening Past a Cipher
Fully equip with a handstand
Drop into a helicopter
Cuttin' good times with Beethoven's 5th at a basement party

Throw me up against the wall
And I will speak to you through
An aerosol haze, touting the memoirs
To the fallen soldiers of street life
This shit ain't nothin' new even though
I left my tag on it.
Ghetto po-pos already knew who to chase

Beat me down and I'll uprock with the
Shuffle of hard times to better days
Swinging low on a sweet chariot called
The number 2 train
I rock steady on the foundation of nothing.

Scratch me back and forth
Then break me fresh from the crate home made
Spinning on my back, spinning on my head
Spinning on my mother's kitchen table I'm stable
As I blend fantasy and reality in time
And intoxicate the world
With what I'm feeling that day.

I got grass in my roots from being underground
Pushed down, forced to make do with myself
I'm rockin broken pieces like they whole and
Running a bargain basement sale on the future

My culture be the reality of hard times
With not enough in my brain
But way too much on my mind
Not to be brilliant resilient
And shine!

Hip hop be the elements of
Unfinished business
Recycled to complete the legacy
Of creative expression that began
Way before the charting of time
I can't help but be the X factor

Earth, Fire, Water, Air
The elements I don't just do
But AM!

MODERATOR: I love your hair?
How do you get it like that?

MILDRED: *(Sings.)* DON'T WANT THE ANSWERS TO...

MODERATOR: Do you wash it?

MILDRED: *(Sings.)* DON'T WANT THE ANSWERS TO...

REG: I don't feel like writing today
    But I'll write anyway because how else could I get good
    Sitting around, waiting for a poem to slap me upside my head
    Shit don't work,
    Least not for me
    Guess it's like a car
    You don't jump in, jet sixty miles an hour
    Got to warm it up, let it breathe, I mean...
    If you wanna make love to your woman
    Who you haven't seen for three weeks
    'Cause you was in Los Angeles
    Doing rewrites on this script you never should have done in the first place
    But you overextended yourself
    Putting on a show
    Loanin' niggas money, you ain't even know
    Can't pay the IRS fifty grand you owe
    So you whore yourself out
    Writing coon show number seventy-five
    For some big corporation
    Then you step to the door
    Smell the rice and beans
    And that coco butter shit she puts in her dread
    And you grab her
    Start rippin off her clothes
    She says, "Easy Baby, Take it slow"
    But you go berserk because of the frustration
    All the ass kissin' and booty lickin'
    Which you should have been doing for her
    And it pisses you off
    And you want her so bad
    As the pants legs of the pajamas you bought her for Christmas
    Are down round her ankles
    Then you bend her
    Flex her
    And finally thrust
    And she's not wet

And you're not hard
And it hurts
And she screams
And suddenly
You realize
You're nothing more than a rapist who writes
Which is why I write
When I don't feel like writing
Because I might find out shit about myself
I never ever knew

MODERATOR: So, what color were those pajamas?

MILDRED: Oh hell no! Hell no! Hold up!
We're about to have to break shit down right here
I can't Remember where the begin began
So let's begin at the Beginning.
Yo Wils,

WILLIE: Yo

MILDRED: Where were you?

WILLIE: Finally fixed
I get to the café
in time for my spotlight.
I ask Julio the Bouncer
If he's gonna stay inside to hear me read tonight.
He says, only if I read something happy,
none of that dark ghetto shit
Because tonight's crowd got him pissed.
He is the best random judge in the house
As he soothes a low scoring slam poet.
"C'mon man, you know you can't
take this shit too seriously."
Julio strengthens my aesthetic
As I walk through the door
And spot the spoken word racketeers
Who get close enough to dig into my pockets
When I fall asleep.
I just spent my last ten dollars
and they look at me stupid
When I ask if they can spare some real change.

WILLIE: *(Cont'd.)* I was just a poet
      wanting to read a poem
      the first night I came here.
      Since then
      I have become a street poet
      then somebody's favorite urban poet
      a new jack hip-hop rap poet
      a spoken word artist
      a born-again Langston Hughes
      a downtown performance poet
      but you won't catch me rehearsing,
      my spit is ready made real.

      I walk up to the cherubic man with white hair
      whose smile will not close until the
      poetry café is demolished;
      Who will allow himself to die
      only when love fails to create.
      He starts telling me stories about his soul brother
      Mikey the Junkie Christ
      Creator of the ghetto Genesis
      Where shit begat fucked up.
      Saint Miguelito who saw God and said,
      "Vayaaa! Papa Dio! Wassup yo,
      I heard you got the good shit."
      The cherubic man with white hair
      Stays alive by sniffing Mikey's ashes
      in the Avenue B air.

      I go to the back of the bar
      and sit next to the blind man
      Who's waiting for me to light his cigarette.
      "Where you been you jive nigga you? I'm glad you here
      cuz these motherfuckers wanna cop pleas
      and sell Cliff notes before they
      read a goddamn thing."
      A guest poet from the academy
      is invited to the stage.

He begs the audience to please be gentle
Because his work is really built for the page.
The blind man tells him to
shut up
and read the goddamn poem.

I kiss the lady with the sunglasses.
Sometimes used to deflect rays,
always to look where I can't see.
She's been taking notes on the scene,
watching poets exchange business cards,
as they tap dance toward the stage.
She takes a moment to hug me tight
And begs me to take care of myself
Because the bigger picture needs me.

The impresario leaps onto the stage,
grabs the mic and tells the DJ to give him a
hippiddy hop and a hippiddy ho, for the hype
"Is Word Perfect in the house?"
The flame on a white prayer candle
Above the bar is doing the Cucaracha.
In the photo portrait behind it,
Mikey is looking dead into the camera.
Before I reach the mic
the good Reverend Pedro hands me
a condom and says, here, man.
Practice safe poetry tonight.
You never know what you might
Catch up there.

MILDRED: Yo Regie, where were you?
    (Slanguage, *Uptown # 2 train beat begins.*)
REGIE: 1993 was a bad year to be a Filipino actor,
    So I left acting to go into something more lucrative
MILDRED: Like what?
REGIE: Like poetry
MILDRED: Oh, God.

REGIE: It was 1993 at the Nuyorican poets café
Grand Slam Championship
And I was the winner
MILDRED: Work it
REGIE: Honey, I just got tired of playing Chino from *West Side Story.*
(*West Side Story snapping. Regie begins the sharks' dance.*)
MILDRED: (*In Spanish.*) …No me digas…Que carajo es eso?
Chino did that in *West Side Story?*
STEVE: Everybody did that in *West Side Story.* (*Mildred walks off mumbling.*)
(*West Side Story snapping. reg.e.gaines counts down 1-7 repeat.*)
MILDRED: You Motherfuckers, are crazy.
REG: I need a poem
Which tells the tale of a slave in the hull of a slave ship,
But it must sound like a love poem.
Yo nigga, I could do that

*Majestic vessels break*
*Against a rippling white capped foe,*
*Magnificent wood weeps silently*
*Round royal undertow*
*Lush clouds tear*
*Silver eyelids muddle shadows*
*Blue echo shaded pain*
*Rhythmic sway of crows*
*Spy crushed against a grease slide board*
*Through IL gurney's door*
*Can't go back no more*
STEVE: Was I dreaming while the others suffered?
Am I dreaming now?
Tomorrow, when I awake, or think I do
What shall I say of today?
I learned this shit
Sitting on a project roof
Of 965 Tinton Ave in the South Bronx
Waiting for Gódot in the Ghetto.
MODERATOR: Isn't it pronounced Godót?
REG: No motherfucker,
I got Peter Hall on video

Saying
"It's Gódot"

GAMAL: Not I,
My father read me Nikki Giovanni in the living room,
While I watched Muhammad Ali
Talk shit on eyewitness news.

MODERATOR: I hear the iambic pentameter in your work; you must be a fan of
Shakespeare?

WILLIE: Yea, Johnny Shakespeare from New York City.
He works his Jones like a natural birth control cycle:
Every two days he comes to shoot tar and watch snow
On Ron's second-hand TV.
I wave him in from my cage
Where I sell rough toilet paper and give out old towels.
One day Johnny Shakespeare was late for his flight back home.
"They can wait," he said.
He checked for his wallet as he watched an Aztec chief
Spray paint a self-portrait on a brick wall near a chop suey joint.
He had faith that love could still work when he got back East.
On the BART back to Oakland he went through his file of excuses.
The police put him in jail for talking to the ghost of Huey Newton
On the top step of the Alameda County Courthouse.
He was trying to restore the face of the Virgen de Guadalupe.
He was kidnapped by a department store security squad
Who thought that he was a member of Al Qaeda.
He was mugged and had to read poems for train fare.
He met two girls who had a tweed blazer fetish.
He went to Fisherman's Wharf and recreated a romantic weekend he
once had.
He needed to get his thoughts together
So he walked up and down The Crookedest Street in the World.
He had a meeting with the local community board
To let them know that Lake Merrit was filled with blood.

He turned into a penthouse panther
And went prowling through the streets
Looking for someone to finance the revolution.

MILDRED: *(Singing.)* YOU'VE GOT TO BELIEVE IN SOMETHING

WILLIE: Something

MILDRED: SO WHY NOT BELIEVE IN ME… *(Company starts talking shit.)*
YOU'VE GOT TO BELIEVE IN SOMETHING *(Harmony.)*

WILLIE: Something

MILDRED: SO WHY NOT BELIEVE IN ME…

*(Train beat drops.)*
YOU'VE GOT TO BELIEVE…

RHA: *(Sings.)* …SEE SEE SEE SEE
SEA LINE WOMAN,
SHE DRINKS COFFEE,
SHE DRINKS TEA,
AND THEN COMES BACK HOME
SEA LINE WOMAN,
SEA LINE WOMAN,
SEA LINE WOMAN…

MILDRED: I heard Nina Simone sing that song and I was hooked….

STEVE: one day we Was in rehearsal right
And we're doin' this shit right
We're vibin' off the beat
And our director was like
Y'all singin' too much in the show
You need to take the words out
So we took the word out of the song beat ride
So as we're sitting there
It sounded like…a train and shit
So we did this

MILDRED: Battery one dollar *(Heavy Spanish accent throughout.)*
Battery one dollar
Battery
Battery

STEVE: May I have your attention please?
May I have your attention please?

MILDRED: Bring
Bring
Bring
Bring
Bring

Bring
Bring
Bring
Yo Yo
Yo Yo
Yo Yo
Yo Yo
Incense Sticks and Scented Wicks
And Yo Yo
Yo Yo
Wind-up puppy dog with pens
Tamales,
Sorullos,
And Bean Pies
And Pee-Pee,
Little Pee Pee,
Pee-Pee doll—toy,
Little plastic—boy
Drops jeans
To knees
And slowly pees
With his tiny
Ding ding
A ring ring
A Bring, Bring, Bring
Toy cellular phones,
And socks
Wallets
Keychains
Gold chains
No change,
No change
Yo Yo
Yo Yo
Bring Bring
Bring Bring
Yo Yo
Yo Yo

STEVE: Pleeeeease.

Can somebody help me?
Can somebody help me?
You see I'm kinda having a bad life
So I think, I mean, I wish, I mean, I hope
I mean, I wish, I mean, I hope, I wish
You got a little love in your heart tonight
'Cause I'm the hardest working man in this business
But I've watched my tears,
Stolen from me
Bottled and sold
As after-shave lotion
So could you, would you, can you pleeeeease
Give a brother some change.
Give a brother some change.
Give a brother some change.
Give a brother some change.

MILDRED: Battery one dollar.......

STEVE: changing, changing, changing

REGIE: I have this infatuation with a poet
And he didn't want me to write about him
And I said I wouldn't
But screw it, he's not here
So this poem is called
"I want to make out with Mark Bibbins"
Leave behind your Sexton books,
Your kitten
And your Saturday night solitude
Mark Bibbins
I'll kidnap you and save you
From your East Village dungeon on Avenue C
For I am a lonely Chelsea Queen
With only the time spent counting on
Open prophylactics from 1988
Let's go up state to Albany
Your birth place
Where golden rubbers shoot like mushrooms

Nibbling your nipples
I'll blow your house down
Till you shiver and quake the way Jack shook his beanstalk
Past the cloisters
Through a forest of fairies
We'll skip
Like Hansel and Hansel
Leaving trails of used condoms like magical breadcrumbs
So let us partake of this Trojan as our heavenly host
I'll tear the foil in half
And we'll make Holy Communion
Forever cumming
Hosanna, Hosanna, Hosanna

Then, I dated this older guy named Don
And he said, "You're not writing about us, are you?"
'Cause he heard about the Mark Bibbins poem
And I said, "No Don, I'm not…uh…but I am writing
A fiction piece about dating an older guy…The chapter is called 'Donn'…
But I spell it with two n's."
And he says, "Regie, you're crazy, I can't go out with you"
And I said, "I can't help it Don,
You bring out the writer in me….
Your breasts are couplets
Your body is a sonnet
Your thoughts share my soliloquy
Your kiss is imagery
Your eyes are iambic
Your tongue is tropic
Your touch is stream of consciousness
Your complexity is Eliot
Your neck is Steinbeck
Your stubble is cacophony
Your presence is from fantasy
Your brilliance is Asbury
Your ass is assonance
Your penis is epic"
*(Pause.)* guess you had to see it

REGIE: *(Cont'd.)* "Your torso is a Tanka
Your rambling a renga
Your fucking is foreshadowing
Your size for the climax
Your orgasms are onomatopoeia
Onomatopoeia
Onomatopoeia
Onomatopoeia
Your clinging is Sexton
Your ejaculation is sprung rhythm
Your testicles are testaments
Your backbones are stanzas
Your viewpoint omnipotent
I see you in epilogue…
Going…
RHA: It is like
REGIE: Going
RHA: The Plague,
REGIE: Gone"
RHA: Highly contagious and rapidly moving to an individual near you.
What used to be precipitated by blue moons
And "not supposed to be kissing cousins"
Dysfunctional family inbreeding has become more common than place.
Has the whole world gone mad?
The modern culture has declared that there is no such thing as a down day,
And certainly not more than two in a row…
So if your ass is feeling blue, look out!

Prozac's gettin' popped like tic tacs
And chiclets have had to give it up to Ritalin…
"Johnny's got to curb his enthusiasm"
And my sister has just laid 5 chapters of "Driven to Distraction" in my lap.
As I flip through the pages I am told I will find her there.
When she is very clearly standing right in front of me.
"You don't understand," she says…but maybe this will help you.

Help me understand, how to show compassion,
Without being sucked into the abyss,

That deep dark roller coaster ride affectionately called "an episode"
Coming fully equip with my niece roaming at the eyes,
Foaming at the mouth, and restraints.
How do I stare those that I love in the face
As they contort into locations of the psyche
That I would never want to visit
No, not even with the biggest nigga from the projects…

Help me understand how to love you and remain sane.
What a funny ass word,
I still ain't clear about the definition…
As I thumb through the pages…
I begin asking myself these questions…
Not to belittle her pain, but to really understand…
I need to understand, because I am surrounded by diagnoses
That were attached to people I love and once knew…
Do I have ADD too?

In more innocent times,
I'd just say they was "buggin'" you know…
"Buggin' out"
"trippin'"
"Actin' ill"
Whatever, "whiling"
Now they are "bi-polar,"
"Manic depressive,"
"Anorexic,"
"Psychotic,"
"Schizophrenic,"
Attention Deficit with Pathological features,
Delusional w/ dimensional features,
Borderline,
Pre, Post
And Currently
Traumatically Stressed,
I am in constant conversation with psychiatrists,
Therapists
And mental health practitioners,

RHA: *(Cont'd.)* tryin' to get a broken down system to understand
Highly functioning and intelligent people
Who do not fuckin' feel like taking their medicine
In a tweety bird Dixie cup!
While chanting "today is a good day."

We are so ill equipped to deal with this.
We the community,
We the society,
We the nation,
We the world,
And especially we Black folk,
That's right I said it.
I got peeps slipping through my fingers
Chasing alternative forms of medication
Like alternate forms of transportation,
Ridin' round the outside,
Round the outside,
Round the outside…
Just to come back…
"Yo, right that other shit kills my sexual drive" they say
TMI,
"I don't wanna do shit when I'm on it" they say
TMI
"I can't sleep when I take it," they say
TMI,
My body has become accustomed to it,
And I've started hearing voices again…
My doctor took me off my meds
To switch me to something new
And my psychiatrist,
Therapist,
And caseworker, are all on vacation
Too much information to do absolutely nothing with…

No longer the dusty trench coated
Piss smelling man on the train
That continues to shout hallelujah
To no Motherfucking body in particular…

My phone rings with the urgency and desperation of your situation
And it is all I can do not to freak…
You just need to talk it out you say
It is 3 a.m. in the morning….
Has the whole world gone mad?

Although I am generally distrustful,
There are days I want you to take your medicine.
And there are days when I can tell when you have not…
'Cause those be the days when I want to die,
So that I do not have to watch you…. Run from yourself.

I am in the grit and grime of mine
Rendered powerless because your prescription costs $87.95
And neither you nor I got it.
You been cuttin' the pills in half,
Taking them every other day to make um last
You didn't wanna tell me because you were ashamed

Help me understand, why Donny is gone,
Help me understand why I don't recognize Chavon,
Help me understand why Nita can call, and call, and call, and call…
Why Shay Shay's so sad,
And Beverly's so mad and don't trust a goddamn thing I say…
I don't wanna go to a CODA group.

I just want my people back from this modern day slave
This spook who's been sitting by the door of societal protocol
Waiting to be served…
How dare we ignore the signs,
You know,
The writing on the wall,
The words spelled in the blood of victims
Unfortunate enough to be in the proximity
Of tightly wound rubber bands that have snapped…
Carrying postal bags,
Carrying executive pink slips,
Carrying jam sport back packs,

RHA: *(Cont'd.)* Fresh new babies,
  Freshly worn heartbreaks and I don't love you anymores…
  Pretty soon the random is no longer the random
  But the pattern of a patchwork society
  That would rather drug
  And confine
  Than love

  Far worse than small pox, Tuberculosis or scarlet fever
  It is the mental HIV of the new millennium,
  And we are surrounded,
  Nobody move,
  Nobody drink the water….
  Until they can assure any of us…
  At least one of us…
  Is sane.

MODERATOR: So now, I'm confused, is this theatre?

REG: Villain
  Be sure thou prove my love a whore
  Be sure of it
  Bring me the ocular proof—
  Had I only paid closer attention in freshman's honors English…
  I would not have been so confused about
  OJ…

GAMAL: Somebody said,
  Somebody said,
  Somebody said

  Let's have a town hall meeting 'bout the slave trade
  And I said Niggers been done left Africa,
  What's the point?
  Then let's have a meeting about the Indian situation,
  I said what situation
  The Indians been wiped out,
  Kicked off land,
  Kicked out teepees
  Geronimo been done jumped
  And Pocahontas been done got poked

That's a shame,
That's a shame,
That's a crying shame
But ain't you been evicted your damn self
You ain't got a pot to piss in
So he said let's march then
Let's march down the boulevard
March of dimes,
Million man march,
Million youth march,
March of the wooden soldiers
For the kids,
For the kids
Let's do it for the kids
Jerry's kids,
Lou Rawls' kids,
Bebe's kids
I said I-didn't-feel-like-marchin'
My feet hurt
He said I could riiiiiiiiiiide
Ride longsiiiiiiiiiide
Richard Pryor and Christopher Reeve
While I was shaking hands with Muhammad Ali
Said do it for the publicity
You gonna be on TV
Broadcast all over the world
You could talk about whatever you want
Whatever I liked
World peace,
Teenage pregnancy
Na
Fuck that.
Tiananmen Square,
Murdered Monks
Don't know shit about that
Farm aid,
Band aid,
Right aid

GAMAL: *(Cont'd.)* Right!

    Human rights and right now
    Right!
    Beat down,
    Lowdown,
    Held down
    Right On!
    Can you dig it?
    Right On!
    Can you dig it?
    Right On!
    Can—you—dig it?

    But I ain't looking for inclusion or exclusion
    'Cause the Ozone
    Oh no
    Ozone
    Uh oh
    Got a hole,
    And the sky might open up
    Clouds may come tumbling down
    But I don't give a
    I done gave
    I don't gotta
    Give two spaces and a semicolon
    For them, theirs, mine, ours or yours

    Then that brother said
    That brother said
    I'm searching for a Cause
    'Cause
    Why,
    'Cause
    Be-cause
    'Cause I like to swim
    Got to save the Sea
    And I like Tuna fish
    So you gotta to save the dolphins

And I read *Moby Dick*
So you gotta save the whales
Save the flag
Burn that shit
Raise the flag
Burn that shit
I don't give a shiiit,
'Bout your moral obligation,
Shiiit
For your family values
Your cultural heritage
Spear chucker,
Redneck,
Grease ball,
WASP,
Chink
Swatza
What's a
Swatza
Sticker on my bumper
Eleanor Bumper,
Bumped off
Dead,
Still dead
Like beating a dead horse
Gone,
Like gone with the wind
Wind done gone
Past
Like passst due
So what color ribbon you gonna pin on my chest today
How 'bout yellow?
Who got yellow?
How 'bout red, white or blue?
Going once for pink,
Purple,
Green
Got a rainbow one too

GAMAL: *(Cont'd.)* What color for a teenage car Crash!
Intoxicated car Crash!
DWI CRASH!
He was so young
That was my baby!
He was so young
That was my baby!
Shouldn't have been drinking and driving
Should've read the black label
Motherfuckers fighting for a cause
'Cause
You hitting the sauce
Mothers against drunk driving
Sisters against drunk driving
Gays and Lesbians against drunk driving
Same fight
Just might
As well
Call selves
Mothers and fathers and sisters and cousins
Who fuck each other
Against drunk driving
So come tie a black ribbon round my fuck finger
'Cause I don't give a fuck
About none of the above
Why,
'Cause
Be-cause
Global cause
Put my ass on the line for minimum wage benefits
While activist act like Mumia must be free
But who-really-gives-a
Who-really-gives-a
Who-really-gives
From the heart
Without taking from the soul
Black on black crime
Black on black crime

Black on black crime happened while
Tupac and Biggie were killing a track
So I don't give a damn
If them Negroes ever come back
Why,
'Cause
Be-cause
'Cause
At the end of the day
When it's all said and done
If your house ain't in order
If the 2 ends don't meet
If you can't feed your children
If you can't stand the mirror looking back at
Cryin' back at you
If you're trying to save the world
And you can't save you
What good does all that other shit do?!
*(reg.e.gaines begins musical riff, Mildred sings in and out of it.)*
WILLIE: This is definitely for the brothers who ain't here
who woulda said,
I had to write a poem
about this get together
like a list of names on a
memorial that celebrated
our own Old-Timer's Day

For those of us
who age in hood years
where one night can equal
the rest of your life
And surviving the trade off
Was worth writing on the wall
and telling the world
that we were here
forever

WILLIE: *(Cont'd.)* The barbecue started with a
snap session
Jerry had the best snap of the day
when he said that my family
was so poor
And the fellas said, "how poor?"
And he said, "so poor that
on Thanksgiving they had to buy
turkey-flavored JuJu Beads"
The laughter needed no help
When we exposed the stretch marks
Of our growing pains

Phil had barbecue on the grill
He slapped my hand
When I tried to brush extra sauce on a chicken leg

Yo, go find something to do
write a poem
write something
do something
I got this
I'm the chef
you the poet
talk about how you glad to be here
look at that little boy on the baseball diamond
look at him run circles around second-base
today is his birthday
write about how the wind
Is trying to take his red balloon

it use to take a few shots of
something strong
Before we could cry and say I love you
we have always known how
to curse and bless the dead
now we let the silence say it
and like the little boy's sneakers

disappearing in a cloud of dirt
we walk home in the sun
grown up and full

This is definitely for
the brothers who ain't here
who woulda said
I had to write a poem
about this get together
like a list of names on a memorial
That celebrated our own Old-Timer's Day

For those of us
who age in hood years
where one night can equal
the rest of your life
And surviving the trade off
Was worth writing on the wall
and telling the world
that we were here
forever

MILDRED: *(Spanish Song—Bravo, into poem.)*
It don't come with no instructions
No how-to manuals,
No learn while you sleep audiotapes.
'Cause it's gonna take more than common sense
To make sense, out of this non-sense
How to see it, before it sees you, see?

STEVE: And it goes a little something like this.
This is another autobiography from at-risk agitators,
Assaulting and assembling articulation and alliteration,
From Allah to Amos and Andy.
And there ain't no artistic affirmative action here,

Just an autopsy on those asphalt archives,

Brick by Brick by Brick by Brick by Brick by Brick by Brick by Brick
Big head bowlegged B-boy brothers

STEVE: *(Cont'd.)* Build in front of Boogie Down Bronx Bodegas,
    Braggin' 'bout Bambaataa's blessings
    And the beats of Bobbito the Barber
    While Brooklyn bohemians break bread at breakfast
    Rebirthing boilerplate blues.

    Coons under concrete constellations
    Croon classics at the crossroads,
    With no copyright or compensation
    From constipated conquistadors
    With their Christ complex
    Who can't even conceive the concept of coolness

    So here it is,
    Our dramatic debut of a discourse on dueling dialogues,
    Deconstructed by the drum, the DJ and the dramaturg
    We dare to decipher Dante's descent,
    Drinking and dancing 'til we are drunk with dreams.

    And our epitaph will read:
    This ensemble echoed the exodus from exaggerated Ebonics
    To an eclectic experiment examining the everyday expression

    So I flashback to those funky fables,
    The foundation for these flamboyant
    Freelance,
    Free verse,
    Freestyle,
    Figures of speech.

    A gathering of the geechies,
    Grateful for this ghetto gift of gab.
    Gazing at the Hieroglyphics of the homeboy,
    Looking for his honor like a hip-hop headless horseman.
    Singing Hallelujah for the holy hymns of Hector the jibaro

    So I Improvise

Just like them juke joint jigaboos jump from jamboree to jamboree
Flipping Jedi jive in their special jazz jargon

'Cause Kipling and Keats
Be kicking it with KRS-One and Kool Keith,
Recreating the King's English.

Long live the linoleum for the breakers
And the loose limbed lockers,
The literature of Langston and Lorca
And the liberation of linguistics

Now maybe there is too much Ado
About this microphone minstrel movement
But like Miles, Milton and Melle Mel
We are motivated by our Muse.

To create a natural no-nonsense
Bilingual nigger novella

Ohhhhhhhhh, Tay

This is not a persona put on by pathetic parasites
Performing for high percentages

We, question equality and the quid-pro-quo,
Will kick that ass with the quickness on the Q.T.
Remember, There is no redemption
Without the rhyme, reason and rhythm of our rituals

So step right up and
See the schizophrenic sideshow
See Sekou Sundiata scratch Sketches of
Spain on an SL 1200
See Nina Simone sing her signature secular spirituals
See Sonia Sanchez speak similes
In syncopated style to the socialists

STEVE: *(Cont'd.)* But the tragedy in the trials and tribulations
　　　Of this Tale of Two Tongues,
　　　Is the tendency to lose this talented talk
　　　Without proper translation.

　　　Enter the underground university,

　　　Where a variety of verbal vandals'
　　　Voices evolve the vernacular verbatim.

　　　Wielding words like weapons, whenever wherever.

　　　And an X will mark this spot.

　　　So we yell for the local yokels of yesteryear
　　　And the yes yes yallers of yesterday

　　　Cause it is zero hour for the zeitgeist,
　　　And we're in the zone
　　　Resisting that do nothing disease
　　　And that government cheese
　　　Would rather die on our feet than live on our knees
　　　Catching zzz's

　　　ZZZZZ ZZZ ZZZZZZZ
　　　ZZZZZ ZZ ZZZZZZZZ
　　　*(Company picks up the ZZZZ and travel offstage as Moderator fires questions.)*
MODERATOR: What's your favorite curse word?
　　　I've never heard of you—what have you done?
　　　Do you consider yourself a black writer or a writer?
　　　Do you invite your family to your performances? What do your parents
　　　　think?
　　　I love your hair, how do you get it like that?
　　　How do you wash it?
　　　Rha as in Hurrah? Or as in Rah Rah sis boom ba?
　　　How did you feel when Ben Brantley coined your Poetry labored lyricism?
　　　Your work is rooted in such an urban experience—do you think others
　　　　will understand it?

Isn't slam prison poetry, used to stop a fight?

How do you feel about all the violence in hip-hop?

Do you consider Langston Hughes to be the Grandfather of Rap?

How would we classify you: Hip-Hop Theatre, Latino Theatre, Black Theatre?

ALL: *(Turning to the moderator for the first time.)* Shut the fuck up!

*(Turning to the audience.)* Are there any questions?

*(Talk-back begins.)*

END OF PLAY